Globalization and Austerity Politics in Latin America

In an age of financial globalization, are markets and democracy compatible? For developing countries, the dramatic internationalization of financial markets over the last two decades deepens long-standing tensions between politics and markets. Notwithstanding the rise of left-leaning governments in regions like Latin America, macroeconomic policies often have a neoliberal appearance. When is such austerity imposed externally and when is it a domestic political choice?

Employing a multi-method research strategy that includes statistical tests and extensive field research from across Latin America, Stephen B. Kaplan builds and tests a theory that explains the effect of financial globalization on economic policy making. Focusing on both the structural and individual influences on policy making, he argues that a country's composition of international borrowing and its technocratic understanding of past economic crises combine to produce dramatically different outcomes in national policy choices. Incorporating these factors into an electoral politics framework, Kaplan's book then challenges the conventional wisdom that political business cycles are most likely in newly democratizing regions. Inflation-spurring expansions may occur when countries are unhindered by bond market indebtedness and inflation crisis legacies, but otherwise a political austerity cycle emerges characterized by macroeconomic discipline. This book is targeted toward a broad audience within political science, economics, and Latin American politics, but is especially relevant for scholars of political economy of global finance, development and democracy, and the politics of economic policy making.

Stephen B. Kaplan is an Assistant Professor of Political Science and International Affairs at George Washington University. He received his Ph.D. in political science from Yale University in 2009. For the 2009 to 2010 academic year, Stephen was awarded a postdoctoral research fellowship at Princeton University's Niehaus Globalization and Governance Center at the Woodrow Wilson School of Public and International Affairs. The dissertation on which this book is based won the Mancur Olson Award from the Political Economy Section of the American Political Science Association (2010) for the best dissertation in the field of political economy completed in the previous two years. Prior to his doctoral studies, Kaplan worked as a senior economic analyst at the Federal Reserve Bank of New York, writing extensively on developing country economics, global financial market developments, and emerging market crises from 1998 to 2003. His current work focuses on the political economy of global development, the politics of international finance, macroeconomic policy making, and Latin American politics.

D0036285

Cambridge Studies in Comparative Politics

General Editor

Margaret Levi   *University of Washington, Seattle*

Assistant General Editors

Kathleen Thelen   *Massachusetts Institute of Technology*
Erik Wibbels   *Duke University*

Associate Editors

Robert H. Bates   *Harvard University*
Stephen Hanson   *The College of William and Mary*
Torben Iversen   *Harvard University*
Stathis Kalyvas   *Yale University*
Peter Lange   *Duke University*
Helen Milner   *Princeton University*
Frances Rosenbluth   *Yale University*
Susan Stokes   *Yale University*

Other Books in the Series

Ben W. Ansell, *From the Ballot to the Blackboard: The Redistributive
    Political Economy of Education*
David Austen-Smith, Jeffry A. Frieden, Miriam A. Golden, Karl Ove Moene,
    and Adam Przeworski, eds., *Selected Works of Michael Wallerstein: The
    Political Economy of Inequality, Unions, and Social Democracy*
Andy Baker, *The Market and the Masses in Latin America: Policy Reform
    and Consumption in Liberalizing Economies*
Lisa Baldez, *Why Women Protest: Women's Movements in Chile*
Stefano Bartolini, *The Political Mobilization of the European Left,
    1860–1980: The Class Cleavage*
Robert Bates, *When Things Fell Apart: State Failure in Late-Century Africa*
Mark Beissinger, *Nationalist Mobilization and the Collapse of the Soviet State*
Pablo Beramendi, *The Political Geography of Inequality: Regions and
    Redistribution*
Nancy Bermeo, ed., *Unemployment in the New Europe*

Series list continues following the Index.

Globalization and Austerity Politics in Latin America

STEPHEN B. KAPLAN

George Washington University

CAMBRIDGE
UNIVERSITY PRESS

CAMBRIDGE UNIVERSITY PRESS
Cambridge, New York, Melbourne, Madrid, Cape Town,
Singapore, São Paulo, Delhi, Mexico City

Cambridge University Press
32 Avenue of the Americas, New York, NY 10013-2473, USA

www.cambridge.org
Information on this title: www.cambridge.org/9781107670761

© Stephen B. Kaplan 2013

First published 2013

Printed in the United States of America

A catalog record for this publication is available from the British Library.

Library of Congress Cataloging in Publication Data

Kaplan, Stephen B., 1973–
Globalization and austerity politics in Latin America / Stephen B. Kaplan.
    p.   cm. – (Cambridge studies in comparative politics)
Includes bibliographical references and index.
ISBN 978-1-107-01797-9 (hardback) – ISBN 978-1-107-67076-1 (paperback)
1. Latin America – Economic policy.   2. Latin America – Politics and
government.   3. Globalization – Latin America.   I. Title.
HC125.K334   2012
330.98–dc23   2012019692

ISBN 978-1-107-01797-9 Hardback
ISBN 978-1-107-67076-1 Paperback

For Kaplans everywhere, both North and South.

Contents

List of Figures   *page* xi
List of Tables   xv
Acknowledgments   xvii

1   Introduction   1
    1.1   Globalization and Economic Policy   6
    1.2   From Political Business Cycles to Political Austerity Cycles   15
    1.3   Method and Plan of the Book   20
2   Globalization and Austerity Politics   25
    2.1   The Inflation-Unemployment Trade-Off   27
    2.2   Political Austerity Theory   30
    2.3   It's a Wonderful Market: The Politics of Bond Finance   36
    2.4   Economic Risk-Aversion: The Politics of Inflation Control   49
    2.5   Summary and Conclusions   68
    2.A   Appendix   71
3   The Political Economy of Elections   72
    3.1   Dial M for Manipulation? The Evidence   73
    3.2   Statistical Models: Key Concepts and Measures   77
    3.3   Statistical Tests on Elections and the Economy   86
    3.4   Statistical Tests on Partisanship and the Economy   95
    3.5   Discussion: From Macro to Micro Policy Tools   102
    3.A   Appendix   103
4   The Electoral Boom-Bust Cycle   123
    4.1   Case Study Design: The Latin American Experience   125
    4.2   The Classic Case of Electoral Opportunism   131
    4.3   Comparative Case Study Evidence   136
    4.4   Summary   161

5   From Gunboat to Trading-Floor Diplomacy   163
    5.1   *The Case of the Market-Constrained Politician*   164
    5.2   *Comparative Case Study Evidence*   174
    5.3   *Summary*   186

6   When Latin American Grasshoppers Become Ants   188
    6.1   *The Case of the Inflation-Averse Politician*   190
    6.2   *Comparative Case Study Evidence*   200
    6.3   *Summary*   248

7   The Political Austerity Cycle   250
    7.1   *The Case of the Cash-Strapped, Inflation-Scarred Politician*   251
    7.2   *Comparative Case Study Evidence*   254
    7.3   *Summary*   276

8   Conclusion   277
    8.1   *The Political Roots of Austerity*   278
    8.2   *Implications: Quality of Democracy and Growth*   280
    8.3   *Implications: Partisan Politics and Economic Policy*   286
    8.4   *Implications: Austerity in the Developed World*   288

Appendix: Field Research Interviews   291

Bibliography   293

Index   315

List of Figures

1.1 Fiscal Policy Stance in Presidential Elections (Argentina and Venezuela: 2002–2007)   *page* 4
1.2 Fiscal Policy Stance in Presidential Elections (Selected Latin American Countries: 2002–2007)   6
2.1 The Phillips Curve Trade-Off   29
2.2 Bond Issuance Supplants Bank Lending (16 Latin American Countries, Aggregate)   38
2.3 Creditor Relations under Centralized Commercial Bank Lending   40
2.4 Creditor Relations under Decentralized Bond Financing   42
2.5 Political Austerity Boosts Brazilian Incomes and Cardoso's Presidential Candidacy   48
2.6 Decision Making with High Inflation Aversion   56
2.7 Decision Making with Low Inflation Aversion   58
2.8 Latin American Inflation Troubles Begin in Mid-1970s (CPI, Annual %)   59
2.9 Support for Fighting Latin American Inflation (Survey of 16 Latin American Countries, 1995–2008)   63
3.1 Decentralized Bond Financing Improves Latin American Government Budget Balances (16 Latin American Countries, 1990–2009)   75
3.2 Past Inflation Crisis Spurs Greater Fiscal Conservatism in Latin America (16 Latin American Countries, 1990–2009)   76
3.3 Latin American Presidential Elections (16 Latin American Countries, 1961–2009)   80
3.4 Marginal Effect of Elections on Inflation Rates   91
3.5 Marginal Effect of Elections on Growth Rates   92
4.1 Policy Makers Just as Likely to Slam Brakes Before Elections   129
4.2 Policy Makers Slam on Brakes During Final Years of Team   129

4.3   Policy Makers Are Cautious with Monetary Policy   130
4.4   Monetary Policy Caution Prevails in Final Term Years   130
4.5   The Traditional Political Business Cycle (H1)   133
4.6   The Traditional Political Business Cycle (H1)   136
4.7   Frei Confronts Surging Strike Activity (Number of Strikes,
      1964–1970)   139
4.8   President Frei Swells Chile's Budget Deficit During the 1970
      Elections   140
4.9   Venezuela's Petro Rollercoaster (Brent Crude Oil Prices in US$)   145
4.10 Punto Fijo's Crude Electoral Expansions (Change in Average
      Deficit/GDP in Final Two Years Before Elections)   146
4.11 Venezuela's Petro–PBC (% of GDP)   147
4.12 A Traditional Electoral Expansion (2006 Venezuelan
      Elections)   157
5.1   Bank Claims on Latin America (US$ billion, 1982–1988)   165
5.2   Bond Issuance Supplants Bank Lending (17 Latin American
      Countries, Aggregate)   168
5.3   The Market-Induced Austerity Cycle (H2)   172
5.4   The Market-Induced Political Austerity Cycle (H2)   174
5.5   IMF and Banks Lend Despite Ecuador's Reform Drift
      (US$ million, 1980–1990)   175
5.6   Ecuador's Credit Plummets Before 1998 Presidential Elections
      (Bond Yield Differential Between Ecuadorean and U.S.
      Treasury Debt)   178
5.7   Venezuelan Credit Sinks Before 1998 Presidential Elections
      (Bond Yield Differential Between Venezuelan and U.S. Treasury
      Debt)   185
6.1   Latin America's Inflationary Crises Spur Economic Ministry
      Professionalization (1960–2009)   192
6.2   The Inflation-Averse Austerity Cycle (H3)   197
6.3   The Inflation-Averse Political Austerity Cycle (H3)   200
6.4   Taming Chile's Inflationary Beast (Average Annual Inflation,
      % Change)   213
6.5   Global Copper Prices, 1932–2009 (Higher Grade Copper
      Prices, 5-Year Moving Average)   214
6.6   Falling Inflation Allows for Mild Stimulus Before Chile's 1999
      Elections (Average Annual Inflation, % Change)   217
6.7   Lagos's Approval Soars in Chile, Approval Ratings (%)   223
6.8   A Political Austerity Cycle (2005 Chilean Elections)   225
6.9   Argentina Taps Market Despite Tight Credit Before 1999
      Elections   234
6.10 Argentina's Spending Steady in 1990s (Primary Expenditures,
      % GDP)   237
6.11 A Provincial Political Business Cycle (1999 Argentine Elections) 240

6.12 President Collor's Popularity Plummets Amid Inflationary
      Chaos   243
6.13 Real Plan Red Lights Inflation, But Green Lights Cardoso's
      Candidacy   245
7.1   The Political Austerity Cycle (H4)   253
7.2   The Political Austerity Cycle (H4)   254
7.3   Menem's Political Dilemma: Inflation Stabilization vs.
      Unemployment   257
7.4   Bonds Supplant Bank Lending (Argentina's External Financing)   258
7.5   Tequila Crisis Forestalls Spending (Argentina's 1995 Elections)   260
7.6   A Political Austerity Cycle (Argentina's 2003 Elections)   266
7.7   Bonds Supplant Bank Lending (Brazil's External Financing)   267
7.8   Brazil's Sovereign Spread Spikes Before 1998 Presidential
      Elections (Bond Yield Differential Between Brazilian and U.S.
      Treasury Debt)   270
7.9   Brazil's Market Turbulence Boosts Cardoso's 1998 Reelection
      Bid   271
7.10 Lula's Impending Presidential Victory Sparks Financial Market
      Fears   274
8.1   Latin America's Financial Insurance (US$ billion, 1975–2010)   285

List of Tables

2.1 Macroecomonic Policy Expectations: The Spendthrift or the Miser?   *page* 33
3.1 List of 16 Latin American Countries   79
3.2 Marginal Effects of Elections and Decentralized Finance on Fiscal Indicators   87
3.3 Marginal Effects of Elections and Inflationary Crisis History on the Economy   99
3.4 Marginal Effects of Partisanship and Past Inflationary Crisis on the Economy   100
3A.1 Variable Definitions and Sources (16 Latin American Countries, 1961–2009)   106
3A.2 Descriptive Statistics for Regression Variables (16 Latin American Countries, 1961–2009)   109
3A.3 Effect of Elections on Government Budget Balance (OLS Regressions with Fixed Effects)   110
3A.4 The Relationship Between Government Budget Composition and Elections (OLS Regressions with Fixed Effects)   111
3A.5 Effect of Elections on the Economy (Basic OLS Regressions with Fixed Effects)   112
3A.6 Effect of Elections and Decentralized Finance on the Economy (OLS Regressions with Interactive Terms)   113
3A.7 Effect of Elections and Decentralized Finance on the Economy (Sensitivity Analysis for OLS Regressions with Interactive Terms) 115
3A.8 Effect of Elections and Past Inflationary Crisis on the Economy (OLS Regressions with Interactive Terms)   117
3A.9 Effect of Partisanship on Government Budgetary Balance (OLS Regressions with Fixed Effects)   119

3A.10 Effect of Partisanship on the Economy (OLS Regressions with
       Fixed Effects)   121
4.1   Macroecomonic Policy Expectations: The Spendthrift or the
       Miser?   131
4.2   Case Study Overview (H1 and H2)   134
5.1   Macroeconomic Policy Expectations: The Spendthrift or the
       Miser?   171
5.2   Case Study Overview (H1 and H2)   172
6.1   Macroeconomic Policy Expectations: The Spendthrift or the
       Miser?   196
6.2   Case Study Overview (H3 and H4)   197
6.3   Chile's Economic Ministry Professionalization under
       Democracy (1960–1973; 1990–2010)   212
6.4   Argentina's Economic Ministry Professionalization under
       Democracy (1983–2005)   231
6.5   Brazil's Central Bank Professionalization under Democracy
       (1985–2010)   242
7.1   Macroecomonic Policy Expectations: The Spendthrift or the
       Miser?   252
7.2   Case Study Overview (H3 and H4)   254

Acknowledgments

With the Thai currency and asset markets in a free fall during July 1997, I printed a raft of Bloomberg charts and charged into the office of Chase Manhattan's Global Head of Emerging Markets. When I signed up for this summer internship, little did I know that Thailand's economy would incur such devastation. Throughout the previous decade, Thailand had been the star performer among the group of market reformers known as the Asian tigers. Confronted with a massive speculative attack, however, a currency devaluation and abrupt capital outflows soon left the economy in shambles. How does a country's economy transform from a tiger to a turkey seemingly overnight? How do politicians govern in such an environment? Can they concurrently appease flighty foreign investors fretting about default and domestic constituents worried about jobs? Is there a political middle ground? I found myself repeatedly asking these questions not only as the crisis spread throughout East Asia but also as it rippled around the globe to my area of expertise, Latin America. Over the next fifteen years of following global economics and markets, I worked to answer these questions as I moved from a Chase summer research associate to a senior economic analyst at the Federal Reserve Bank of New York, and then from a Yale doctoral student to eventually a professor at George Washington University.

As this book goes to press, the crisis wave has settled on developed country shores, upsetting years of economic stability and threatening a eurozone split. Amid this financial volatility, this book is an effort to think through the compatibility of markets and democracy. I study this question through the lens of economic policy in the developing region of Latin America, but the research findings offer governance lessons for highly indebted countries everywhere, including developed countries. From Greece, Portugal, and Spain to the United Kingdom and the United States, the recent global financial crisis has underscored that even developed countries are not insulated from default risk, capital flight, and credit downgrades. When facing these bond market pressures, Latin American leaders have often governed with more macroeconomic discipline than conventional wisdom would have anticipated in a newly democratized region. In navigating this delicate terrain, politicians have often sought to reconcile two seemingly opposing forces: economic austerity and social responsiveness. In the wake of the 2008 global financial crisis, this governance challenge is likely to persist well into the future for countries around the world. Against this backdrop, this book develops a framework for thinking systematically about the political effects of global bond market indebtedness.

In researching the politics of sovereign debt, I became highly indebted to a rich, scholarly world. It is a pleasure to acknowledge the many professional and personal debts that helped me advance this book project. I extend my deepest gratitude to my dissertation committee; they exemplify superlative scholarship and mentoring. Their unparalleled commitment to teaching, advising, and the intellectual community is an inspiration. Their wisdom was essential to the development of this book. I am grateful to Susan Rose-Ackerman, who has been a source of steadfast professional support and extraordinary scholarly guidance. From early in my graduate career, her intellectual openness was crucial to fostering an independent voice. My deepest gratitude to Susan Stokes for her exceptional mentoring, her finely tuned balance of intellectual criticism and encouragement, and her dedication to my development as a writer. Susan Rose-Ackerman and Susan Stokes also kindly gave me considerable guidance on the book's publication. I also enthusiastically thank Frances Rosenbluth for her mentoring throughout the publication of my first article and her valuable scholarly and career counsel over the years. My debt to James Vreeland is also large. I appreciate his tremendous support for my intellectual and professional development, sharing my passion for the political economy of global finance. I also greatly benefited from the advice and support of Eduardo Engel, who has served as a valuable consultant on Latin American macroeconomics.

I gratefully acknowledge financial support from the Elliott School of International Affairs at George Washington University (GWU), Princeton University's Niehaus Globalization and Governance Center, the Yale University Leitner Program on Comparative and International Political Economy, and the Whitney and Betty MacMillan Center for International and Area Studies at Yale University. I am also thankful for the opportunity to present this project at numerous forums, including George Washington University's Institute for Global and International Studies; Princeton's International Relations Colloquium; Yale's Comparative Politics and Political Economy Workshops; Columbia University's Initiative for Policy Dialogue; The New School; the Society for Comparative Research; the University College Dublin's Financialization Workshop; the University of Manchester's World Policy Institute; Argentina's Universidad Torcuato Di Tella and Universidad de Buenos Aires; the American Political Science Association; the International Political Economy Society; the International Studies Association; the Latin

American Studies Association; the Midwest Political Science Association; the Society for Advancement of Socio-Economics; the Workshop for Comparative Political Economy; the Institute on Qualitative and Multi-Method Research (IQMR) at Arizona State University; the Institute for International Studies at the University of California, Berkeley; the political science departments of George Washington University, New York University, and Penn State University; the research department at the Inter-American Development Bank; the Office of the Western Hemisphere at the U.S. Department of the Treasury; and the department of economics at the University of Maryland. By presenting earlier versions of the manuscript at these institutions and conferences, I received excellent comments and critiques that enhanced this book project.

During a spring 2010 book workshop at the GWU Institute for Global and International Studies, Javier Corrales, Bruce Dickson, Thad Dunning, Henry Farrell, Cynthia McClintock, Kate McNamara, Kimberly Morgan, and Susan Sell provided valuable advice and suggestions; a special thanks to Varun Paplani for his excellent note-taking. I greatly appreciate Susan Sell's efforts to coordinate this forum, which has fostered an ongoing exchange of ideas. The workshop also served as a terrific introduction to the GWU faculty, who provided a fun, intelligent, and thoughtful environment to finish my book project. I would also like to extend my gratitude to Helen Milner, Andrew Moravcsik, and Pat Trinity at the Niehaus Center for Globalization and Governance for providing a wonderfully rich and stimulating setting to revise the manuscript.

Many other people also read portions of the manuscript and/or helpfully discussed its development with me. I would like to thank Ana Arjona, Andy Baker, Laia Balcells, Nathaniel Beck, Alejandro Bonvecchi, Lawrence Broz, Daniela Campello, Brandice Canes-Wrone, Terrence Chapman, Jose Cheibub, Robert Dahl, Ana De la O, Allan Drazen, Martha Finnemore, Amaney Jamal, William Keech, Robert Keohane, Yong Kyun Kim, Dominika Koter, Basak Kus, Noam Lupu, David Mayhew, Helen Milner, Layna Mosley, Jose Antonio Ocampo, Seán Ó'Riain, Robert Person, Ken Scheve, Beth Simmons, Abbey Steele, Joseph Stiglitz, Dawn Teele, and Matt Winters. Eric Kaplan and Manny Teitelbaum kindly read the entire manuscript, while Heather Walsh perpetually provided an important litmus test for appealing to readers beyond the social sciences. Don Green, Eric Lawrence, and Paul Wahlbeck gave many helpful suggestions on the data analysis in Chapter 3. I am also grateful to Helen Harris, who provided valuable research assistance regarding the educational and professional backgrounds of presidential cabinet officials in Chapter 6. Kaj Thomsson was the source of many enriching discussions on global economics, international finance, and other topics. I was also lucky to have Christina Davis as a colleague for a year during my Princeton postdoc, as she gave me both detailed comments on the manuscript and guidance on the publication process. It was also fortuitous timing to have my close friend, Stephen Engel, publish a book one year ago. In addition to moral support, he offered me a wealth of advice about the book's publication. I also had the good fortune to share a hall-way and neighborhood with three GWU scholars, Harris Mylonas, Elizabeth Saunders, and John Sides, who greatly eased my transition to faculty life by answering my countless questions about the profession. Surrounded by senior faculty with open doors, I also benefited from numerous discussions about the publishing world with Bruce Dickson, Henry Farrell, Martha Finnemore, Charles Glaser, Henry Hale, Forrest Maltzman, Cynthia McClintock, Susan Sell, and Paul Wahlbeck.

I am forever thankful for the outstanding six-year professional education in applied macroeconomics I received at the Federal Reserve Bank of New York, before returning to academia. While at Yale, I also learned a tremendous amount about economics and politics serving as a research assistant to Professor Emeritus Robert Dahl and former Mexican President and Director of Yale's Study for the Center of Globalization, Ernesto Zedillo.

At Cambridge University Press, the anonymous reviewers made many excel-lent suggestions that greatly enriched the manuscript. I am also grateful to my editor Scott Parris for his unbridled enthusiasm for the project, and Margaret Levi for accepting the manuscript for publication in the Cambridge Studies in Comparative Politics series. Thanks also to my Project Manager Adrian Pereira and Marielle Poss for her skilled production management.

My field research profited immensely from the kindness of Latin American scholars and the resources of Latin American universities. I was fortunate to have research affiliations at the Universidad Torcuato De Tella in Buenos Aires, Argentina; the Universidad Diego Portales in Santiago, Chile; and the Instituto de Estudios Superiores de Administración (IESA) in Caracas, Venezuela. I par-ticularly appreciate the generosity of Rossana Castiglioni, Francisco Monaldi, and Catalina Smulovitz, who served as my local university contacts and helped facilitate my field research. I am also indebted to Javier Alvaredo, Alejandro Bonvecchi, Haley Cohen, Thad Dunning, Eduardo Engel, Mathew Haarsager, Tricia Kissinger, Martín Rapetti, Franciso Rodríguez, and Dan Rosenheck for sharing their knowledge of Latin American political economy and helping build my Latin American Rolodex. I also would like to thank Jazmin Sierra Adeff and Luis Schiumerini for their assistance in arranging interviews with Latin American dignitaries. A salute to my many friends and colleagues who eased my adjustment to life in Argentina, Chile, and Venezuela: Magdalena Arata, Felipe Coddou, Maria Costa, Lisandro Kahan, Blai Mesa, Anita Pantin, Luis Paragi, and Oriana Piffre. A special thanks to Ramon J. Serrano, who served as my social entrepreneur throughout South America; Eudald Lerga, who intro-duced me to the wonders of Compensar; and Stephen Engel for co-founding the Van der Woodsen Institute for the Study of Omphaloskepsis.

Finally, I am eternally grateful for the support of a dense network of colleagues and friends from my Yale graduate studies, Princeton's postdoc-toral fellowship, and George Washington University faculty that supported me throughout this challenging process. Within these rich, intellectual communities, a truly impressive group of smart and humorous colleagues deepened my thinking about the topic and sustained my spirit and energy. A special thanks to Ana Arjona, Laia Balcells, Kush Choudhury, Stephen Engel, Ryan Garcia, Arunabha Ghosh, Jennifer Green, Sandy Henderson, Nicole Kazee, Dominika Koter, Joseph Lampert, Harris Mylonas, Tom Pepinsky, Robert Person, Juan Rebolledo, Ryan Sheely, Abbey Steele, and Drew Volmert.

I am also thankful for the unwavering support of my friends outside of academic circles, including Robert Becker, Eudald Lerga, Eric Padua, Bruce Pierce, and Eric Poolman. I cannot imagine a more fruitful and fun livelihood than being a professor. Earlier in my life, I had many competing aspirations, including playing centerfield for the New York Yankees, skiing the World Cup alpine downhill, or rocking out in front of a sold-out Madison Square Garden. I am indebted to my Swedish ski buddies in the Alps; my comedy improv cadre, *Phabricated Data*; my fellow Yale co-ed intramural softball champions; and my mock rock band, *Sephardic Bonobos*, who all helped me keep the dream alive these last several years. I also thank my Adams-Morgan Saturday soccer mates, my Wyoming circle of friends, and my fellow South American trekkers, who also ensured that I had fun, creative, and carefree social outlets while enduring the rigors of research and writing.

I dedicate this book to my wife, Heather, my son, Jasper, and our families. When beginning work on this project, my wife and I were intrepidly pursuing both my doctorate and her medical degree. As the years passed, we increasingly complicated the work-life juggling act by starting a family, buying a home, and beginning new jobs in Washington, DC. During this process, I have learned that it takes a village to write a book. This project could not have been accomplished without the emotional support of two terrifically caring families. My heartfelt thanks to our parents, Mark and Cynthia Kaplan and Michael and Beverly Walsh; our siblings Eric and Amanda Kaplan and Michael Walsh and Karen Batt; and our nephew and nieces Benjamin, Lauren, and Bridget Kaplan.

With such all-consuming undertakings, we risk living for the future; I applaud my son, Jasper, for always ensuring that I live in the present. The love of my traveling companion, Heather, was vital to my intellectual and spiritual journey.

Stephen B. Kaplan
Washington, DC
July 18, 2012

1

Introduction

In Greek mythology, the Gods condemned Sisyphus to the absurd task of repeatedly rolling a boulder to a mountaintop only to have the rock fall back to the ground. Sisyphus has freedom, but it is limited by divine circumstances. He can brace the boulder with his shoulder, thrusting the rock with all of his body's momentum arduously up to the peak. But the rock's fate is beyond his control, rushing back down the mountain with boundless fury.

In a financially globalized world, politicians in developing countries suffer a similar fate. Hoping to lift their countries to development's pinnacle, they toil against the fierce force of globalization. They repeatedly roll the policy boulder up the mountain. Hoping to please mercurial markets, governments cut spending, hike interest rates, and balance budgets. With each economic crisis, however, the rock repeatedly tumbles back down the mountain. In this manner, financial volatility has wreaked havoc on the economies of developing countries over the last two decades.

Why are some countries able to surmount the gravity of globalization, whereas others suffer from Sisyphus-like misfortune? Let us begin by taking a brief South American sojourn to Argentina and Venezuela. With the rise of the Latin American left[1] over the last decade, many scholars and the popular press have often placed these two countries under a similar radical or populist banner. They share other political and economic characteristics too. They are both presidential, upper-middle-income countries that feature comparatively sized economies and populations.[2]

In terms of their macroeconomic approaches, however, their policy stances have often diverged. For instance, throughout the last decade, Venezuela

---

[1] A burgeoning scholarly literature offers a variety of classification schemes to explain the rise of the left and its consequences for Latin America (Panizza 2005; Castañeda 2006; Lynch 2007; Weyland 2009; Weyland, Madrid, and Hunter 2010; Levitsky and Roberts 2011).

[2] World Development Indicators.

has consistently intervened heavily in the economy to meet Hugo Chávez's redistributive goals. By contrast, Argentina's left was first characterized by a rigid commitment to fiscal discipline under President Néstor Kirchner before his wife Cristina Fernández steadily drifted from the economic center. What accounts for these varied approaches to economic policy making? Why, for example, would Néstor Kirchner surprisingly keep an eagle eye on the government's budget, ensuring a fiscal surplus?

This governance strategy was partly a remnant of the country's international borrowing. The government's heavy reliance on global bond markets throughout the 1990s created a creditor coordination problem that at first merely narrowed its policy freedoms, but ultimately left Argentine authorities without international financing. In fact, its 2001 debt default shut the country out from global credit markets, leaving it with few options beyond austerity.

Budget discipline also reflected the importance of inflation control in Argentina, a country where the 1980's hyperinflation destroyed middle- and lower-class incomes. In the wake of the 2001–2002 debt crisis, Argentines feared that the collapse of its currency board system, which had anchored inflation expectations throughout the 1990s, would unleash a new bout of runaway inflation. Kirchner's economic team initially embraced budget austerity, hoping to deliver an important baseline for the economic vote: low and stable inflation. To keep inflation at bay, they built primary budget surpluses[3] to signal that they were committed to living within their means. According to Roberto Lavagna, Argentina's Minister of the Economy, earlier this decade:

Maybe the most important reason why [Argentina] was able to have a quite relevant fiscal surplus was the decision, in the middle of a deep crisis, to say no to all the special interests.[4]

Ironically, however, a hefty budget surplus also endowed Kirchner with another political asset. It created a stockpile of pesos that the Argentine president could spend freely on politically important provinces. In fact, in the years following Lavagna's November 2005 departure from Kirchner's government, the president managed a clever political feat. He signaled economic discipline to the public, businesses, and investors with budgetary surpluses, but increased the executive branch's ability to funnel discretionary spending to special interests. During the 2007 Argentine elections, for instance, the Kirchner government forecasted a 4 percent increase in real GDP growth, well below consensus estimates of 6 to 7 percent in its budget.[5] Notably, this low estimation yielded higher-than-expected tax revenues and a 2007 budget surplus. Benefiting from

---

[3] Throughout the book, when examining governments' budget policies, I use primary fiscal balances (net of interest payments on public debt) rather than the general government balances (inclusive of interest payments), because it is the more appropriate measure of fiscal policy stances in highly indebted countries.

[4] Comments by Roberto Lavagna at the Council on Foreign Relations in New York City on April 21, 2004.

[5] *Financial Times*, 2006.

the 2005 law known as *superpoderes*, Argentina's chief executive could reallocate extrabudgetary revenues without congressional approval. Facing minimal oversight, this law enabled Kirchner to discreetly funnel personalized line-item spending to key supporters and sectors during elections. For example, line-item budgetary spending on public transfers to the provinces increased by about 1.4 percentage points of GDP during the 2007 election year, equivalent to almost one-tenth of total government expenditures.[6] Notably, Kirchner's macroeconomic discipline, consisting of steady primary budget surpluses (Figure 1.1) and rising interest rates throughout the electoral campaign, did not quash his political impulses.[7]

Since taking the baton from her husband in 2007, economic discipline has relaxed under the presidency of Cristina Fernández de Kirchner. Argentina's microeconomic distortions have increasingly become macroeconomic distortions. She has sustained politically popular microeconomic measures, such as price controls in the energy and transportation sectors. Benefiting from a commodity boom, however, Cristina Fernández also raised government expenditures by 4 percentage points of GDP in her first two years in office.[8] Banned from international capital markets,[9] she had to finance part of this new spending domestically through the printing press. In fact, the Argentine president tweaked domestic laws and institutions to redirect central bank reserves and national pension savings toward preserving a dwindling primary budget surplus. A similar pattern is reflected in Argentina's trade policy, where Cristina Fernández maintained a trade surplus while using import licensing to protect vulnerable toy, fabric, leather, and farm machinery manufacturers.

In the prelude to Cristina's 2011 reelection bid, the president accelerated these expansionary policies, until she finally eliminated Argentina's primary budget surplus and firmly entrenched national accounts in deficit. Compared to her husband's electoral fiscal austerity, Cristina Fernández had greater latitude to engineer the macroeconomy before elections. By building new sources of non-market financing, her administration helped free Argentina from the scrutiny of global bond markets. Surfing a commodity tide, the Argentine president decided to test the bounds of the public's inflation aversion. Fueled by increased energy and transportation subsidies, a 25 percent hike in the minimum wage, higher social spending and public employment, and a cheap currency, the political business cycle returned to Argentina for the first time in

[6] CEPAL's Estadísticas de Finanzas Públicas.

[7] My analysis has benefited from more than forty primary interviews I conducted during my field research in Argentina in 2007. In these open-ended elite interviews, I discussed economic policy in the context of the approaching elections with politicians, government ministers, and technocratic advisers.

[8] CEPAL.

[9] In an effort to re-open the spigot of global market financing, Cristina Kirchner negotiated a settlement with two-thirds of the outstanding holdouts from Argentina's 2005 debt restructuring (see Chapter 2). However, legal disputes involving the remaining original bondholders, the recent YPF nationalization, and the United States' opposition to new multilateral lending would likely place a high premium on any new sovereign bond issuance.

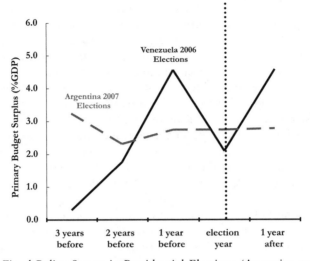

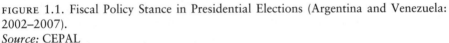

FIGURE 1.1. Fiscal Policy Stance in Presidential Elections (Argentina and Venezuela: 2002–2007).
Source: CEPAL

two decades. Ironically, however, the government has attempted to contain the fallout by artificially suppressing government inflation statistics.[10] Moreover, it has used heavy-handed foreign exchange rate controls to avoid a potentially inflation-spurring devaluation. Notwithstanding its departure from macroeconomic discipline, these actions demonstrate that the Kirchner administration remains concerned about a public backlash against rising inflation that threatens to undercut popular wages.

In Venezuela, by comparison, inflation has little political importance. Without hyperinflation's political scars, Venezuelan presidents are typically not concerned about the potential inflationary costs of aggressive state intervention. Rather, it is quite common for politicians to overheat the economy during election periods. In fact, former Central Bank President Ruth De Krivoy discusses the lack of inflation saliency in Venezuela:

Unless Venezuelan society goes through an inflationary process that is painful like Argentina, Chile, Peru, and Mexico... it's not enough to make people realize that inflation is a problem.[11]

Compared to Argentina's debt market woes throughout the 1990s and early 2000s, Venezuela's access to steady proceeds from non-market financing sources – mainly oil revenues from state-owned companies – often allows

[10] The Argentine statistical agency, Instituto Nacional de Estadística y Censos (INDEC), has been accused of tampering with national inflation statistics for several years. In fact, private sector Argentine economists project inflation is two to three times higher than INDEC's official rate.

[11] Author's interview with Central Bank President Ruth De Krivoy in Caracas, Venezuela, on March 9, 2007. She was president from 1992 to 1994.

the country to escape the scrutiny of global financial markets, and thus, intervene in the economy more readily and openly. For example, over the past decade, nearly half of all revenues flowing into Venezuelan government coffers were non-tax commodity revenues compared to a paltry 8 percent of non-tax revenues in Argentina.

For example, if we return to Figure 1.1, we observe that the recent 2006 Venezuelan elections also featured a very different pattern from Argentina's political austerity during the 2007 elections.[12] Against the backdrop of an already-booming economy, President Hugo Chávez aggressively stimulated the economy by slashing both interest rates and Venezuela's lofty budget surplus. If a budgetary expansion were not sufficient, Chávez also swelled off-budget discretionary spending by another 2 percentage points of GDP. Perhaps, former President Ramón José Velásquez most aptly summarizes Venezuelan politics:

In the end, all that matters is a politician's ability to distribute benefits and carry out development projects.[13]

Not surprisingly, the pace of average annual inflation in Venezuela tripled in two short years following the elections, reaching 30 percent by the end of 2008.[14]

In summary, notwithstanding the rise of the left in Latin America, we have observed considerable variation in macroeconomic policy choices among two of the countries that are often widely labeled as populist. Their leaders sometimes revert to the electoral tendencies of past Latin American decades, but at other times, are surprisingly austere. These three election cases of the politics of macroeconomic policy are but a brief preview of the patterns observed in twenty different election cases employed in this book's comparative case study section. Indeed, the policy pendulum has swung widely from economic austerity to economic stimulus across time and space in the region.

The roots of this variation reflect both structural and individual factors. When governments have access to bountiful domestic resources – whether it is commodity income or the printing press – they have the budgetary capacity to overtly engage in macroeconomic populism. Political leaders, from Hugo Chávez to Cristina Kirchner, leverage these resources to redistribute through heavy government stimulus. By contrast, when governments must tap external

---

[12] These policy differences are consistent, when comparing structural rather than primary government balances. The structural balance excludes cyclical sensitive taxes and expenditures commonly referred to as "automatic stabilizers." For example, tax receipts typically increase during an economic boom, which would improve budget balances even if the government did not attempt to improve its underlying structural or non-cyclical component. Notwithstanding the commodity boom, Argentina's structural deficit increased by a tepid 0.5 percentage points of GDP during the final two years of the Néstor Kirchner's presidency, compared to Venezuela's whopping 4 percentage point structural balance deterioration during the comparable period of Hugo Chávez's presidency (IMF World Economic Outlook Database).

[13] Author's interview with President Velásquez in his Caracas house on March 23, 2007.

[14] CEPAL.

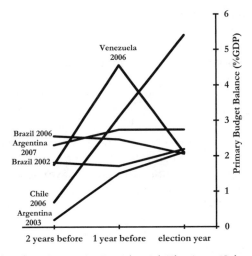

FIGURE 1.2. Fiscal Policy Stance in Presidential Elections (Selected Latin American Countries: 2002–2007).
Source: CEPAL.

borrowing through global capital markets, they are susceptible to credit disruptions that roil such political plans. Facing a treasury left barren from sagging oil prices, even a young Hugo Chávez governed like a thrifty neoliberal in hopes of appeasing foreign creditors. Notwithstanding their financing structures, individual influences on policy making are also important. Politicians like Néstor Kirchner might have left-leaning proclivities but govern more conservatively to avoid a repeat of past inflationary shocks. Behind this veil of austerity, they often raise executive discretion to find new, creative ways of targeting their support base. Alternatively, leftist presidents from inflation-scarred countries may instead choose to build state capacity more transparently by introducing new taxes and streamlining expenditures. In recent years, for example, Brazilian and Chilean governments have both opted for electoral austerity (Figure 1.2) but leveraged greater state capacity to funnel a higher share of budgetary funds toward social spending. Before elaborating on this book's cases[15] or methodology, however, let us first review its theoretical framework.

1.1. GLOBALIZATION AND ECONOMIC POLICY

Financial integration has posed a catch-22 for political elites. Cash-strapped governments have tapped international markets to increase their spending

---

[15] This book deals with developing countries in Latin America, which include both advanced emerging market countries such as Brazil and Chile and small developing countries such as Nicaragua and Honduras. These cases vary considerably based on both the structural and individual factors previously discussed. While the latter countries typically depend more on foreign aid, this variation in bond market exposure is essential to examining the relationship between financial market dependence and economic policy.

possibilities, only to subject their budget decisions to financial market scrutiny. Austerity, or a commitment to budgetary discipline, has become a key governance credential for developing countries that have integrated into the global economy. Facing redistributive pressures from vulnerable economic sectors, however, how do governments manage globalization's gains against domestic political costs? How do they strike a balance between market and society? When is austerity imposed externally and when is it a domestic political choice?

1.1.1. The Convergence-Divergence Debate

During the last two decades, international and comparative political economy scholars have wrestled with this question of how countries can maintain economic autonomy in an era of global capital. They have offered two competing perspectives about the impact of financial globalization on government choices. Convergence thinkers argue that financial globalization curtails domestic policy autonomy, placing new competitive challenges on national governments.[16] In the race for global capital, governments adopt laissez-faire market policies to appease mobile capital owners.[17]

Beyond global competition for capital, the diffusion literature presents an alternative explanation for economic convergence: a global paradigmatic shift away from interventionist economic policies.[18] Indeed, a social construction of laissez-faire capitalism that originated with Thatcher and Reagan scattered throughout the globe via Western diplomacy, multilateral institutions, and an Americanized global economics profession.[19]

By contrast, other scholars anticipate greater economic divergence or cross-national diversity in economic policy choices. Building on the notion of embedded liberalism,[20] they expect governments to intervene in the economy to offset globalization's dislocations.[21] Political leaders hope to strike a balance between economic and social stability.

Most recently, political economy scholars have sought to advance the convergence-divergence debate by identifying the causal mechanisms underlying policy choices.[22] These approaches explore both the nature of the external constraint and the ability of governments to insulate their populace from international market pressures.

Scholars examining financial globalization's constraints have found that market pressures are strongest in developing countries where investors are

[16] Andrews 1994; Helleiner 1994; Cerny 1995; Rodrik 1997.
[17] Cardoso 1973; Lindblom 1977; Bates and Lien 1985; Frieden 1991; Kurzer 1993; Keohane and Milner 1996; Strange 1996; Pauly 1997; Rodrik 2000; Boix 2003.
[18] Hall 1993; Babb 2001.
[19] Hall 1993; Babb 2001; Babb and Fourcade-Gourinchas 2002.
[20] Ruggie 1982; Katzenstein 1985.
[21] Cameron 1978; Katzenstein 1985; Garrett 1998a, 1998b; Garrett and Mitchell 2000.
[22] Cohen (1996) challenged political economy scholars to move beyond a general discussion of globalization as a policy constraint and instead to examine when and how the market disciplining effect works.

most concerned about default risk.[23] Why are these governments willing to comply with creditor demands? Political regimes frequently appease creditors because a reliable reputation is necessary to maintain access to foreign capital.[24] By contrast, when political regimes depend on the support of domestic fixed capital owners, they are more likely to turn inward, placing restrictions on capital mobility.[25]

In developed countries, however, international capital mobility alone is not sufficient to explain economic policy choices. Rather, scholars have found that ideational and partisan factors also explain government choices. In the aftermath of the 1973 oil crisis, for instance, policy makers became more accepting of a monetarist approach to economic policy.[26] Notwithstanding this new baseline, however, policy choices still often reflected differences in partisan preferences.[27]

Other scholars examining domestic institutions' impact on globalization have found a similar dichotomy between developed and developing countries. In developed countries with strong welfare-state institutions, pro-labor forces have the institutional clout to dampen pressures for neoliberal reforms.[28] By contrast, labor groups in developing countries have considerably less political power, leaving them ill-equipped to defend social spending.[29] In fact, global income shocks often magnify social retrenchment by closing the spigot of developing country finance.[30] Diminished labor power under globalization also translates to the other side of the government's balance sheet, where labor often incurs a higher tax burden relative to capital in Latin America.[31]

Accordingly, we should observe a high prevalence of economic orthodoxy in developing countries because they are plagued by institutional weaknesses and capital market dependence. However, I argue that the financial means and the political motivation to pursue such an economic agenda vary considerably in the developing world. Indeed, "capital's veto is not absolute."[32] Why do some countries enjoy more policy autonomy than others?

1.1.2. The Market Enforcement Mechanism

To explain this variation in economic policy choices across both time and space, I developed a new framework dubbed *political austerity cycle theory*.

---

[23] Mosley 2000, 2003.
[24] Tomz 2007.
[25] Pepinsky 2008.
[26] McNamara 1998.
[27] Bearce 2003.
[28] Swank 2002.
[29] Rudra 2002, 2008.
[30] Wibbels 2006.
[31] Wibbels and Arce 2003.
[32] Cohen 1996.

This framework offers a dual-level explanation for the rise of laissez-faire economic policies in developing countries: one rooted in the structure of government's international borrowing and one featuring the role of economic crises in shaping domestic ideational views.[33]

Chapter 2 discusses the first part of political austerity theory and argues that a key structural shift in the global financial architecture – or the method by which developing countries finance their debt – narrowed governments' policy space. I claim that the shift to decentralized bond market financing in the 1990s curtailed politicians' budgetary capacities to spend on their domestic agendas. In constructing this theory, I offer a new insight about global capital's constraints on domestic politics that goes beyond the conventional globalization straitjacket argument. I argue that what reduces policy autonomy is not the amount of financial integration, but rather the nature of creditor-debtor relations.

I claim that creditor behavior is often conditional on governments' foreign debt structures, creating enormous differences in policy climates for sovereign borrowers. My reasoning is premised on a counterintuitive collective action logic in finance-strapped states. When governments use foreign financing to cover their budgetary expenditures, they typically tap one of two sources: bank loans or bond issuance. For both types of creditors, borrowers' financial viability is a collective good. Notwithstanding the size of their debt share, all creditors benefit from steady, uninterrupted repayments. For this reason, lenders typically encourage sovereign borrowers to pursue austere policies that maximize the likelihood of debt remuneration. When borrowers encounter financial difficulties, however, these two types of creditors create very different strategic environments for their debtors.

When a government's foreign debt is comprised mostly of international bank loans, the small number of lenders facilitates creditor coordination. Each lender has a high personal stake in the debtor's financial future. Oddly, they do not use their collective action advantage to withhold new funds from the borrower during hard economic times. If they were to concertedly cut financing, it would only accelerate the debtor's road to default and eliminate any hope of recovering their investment. Instead, the difficult-to-dissolve links that ties lender profitability to borrower's loan repayment fosters a common good of borrower solvency. To keep the borrower afloat, bankers extend fresh funds. Notwithstanding IMF conditionality clauses embedded in loan agreements, however, the promise of new funds creates a moral hazard problem.[34] The mere presence of an IMF agreement is not a sufficient condition for austerity. Rather, the influx of new money enables sovereign borrowers to drift from

---

[33] I follow in the tradition of other scholars who have combined the roles of both economic structure and human agency in explaining the evolution of economic policy decisions (Woods 1995; McNamara 1998).

[34] Moral hazard occurs when an individual or institution does not bear the full consequences of its actions, and therefore, does not change its behavior.

budgetary discipline. Ironically, solving their collective action problem leaves bankers with less sway over debtor government policies.

By contrast, when global bond issuance constitutes the majority of foreign debt, creditors have little incentive to coordinate to secure the common good of borrower solvency. The ownership dispersion that is characteristic of bond markets leaves creditors with a low personal stake in a borrower's future business. If a country does not demonstrate its commitment to restrictive economic policies that ensure debt repayment, bondholders can cut their financial ties without incurring a severe profitability shock. Rather, their livelihood in an investment management industry based on short-term, relative returns often depends on minimizing even the most minor losses from bad investments. They would rather sell bonds for a marginal loss in secondary markets than risk underperforming industry benchmarks. Such actions yield a higher-risk premium quickly that translates into rising funding costs for sovereign borrowers. Hoping to avoid such interest rate shocks that impair their capacity to finance large expansions, governments comply with market conditionality. Therefore, compared to vested bankers, bondholders' credible exit threat allows them to more crudely impose their austerity demands. Surprisingly, creditors benefit from their coordination problem. Normally, collective action failures should hinder societal groups from pressuring governments. In the world of bond finance, however, it enhances their influence over debtor governments.

1.1.3. The Latin American Experience

Latin America – a region noted for its hefty foreign borrowing during the most recent wave of globalization – is ideally suited for examining creditor-debtor relations. Moreover, the region endured a key structural financing shock, the 1980s debt crisis, which catalyzed the market securitization of much of the region's debt. By the early 1990s, the composition of its debt stock had swiftly transformed from bank loans to bond issuance, creating considerable variation in the structure of Latin American borrowing.

Before this debt securitization, a few large international banks accounted for most of the loans made to Latin America. They had a vested interest in the financial viability of their borrowers, even during the debt crisis. As majority owners of Latin American debt, bank profitability was directly tied to the health of their lending portfolios.[35]

However, recall that international bankers faced a credible commitment problem with their borrowers. In exchange for new loans today, borrowers pledged to implement restrictive economic policies that raised the likelihood

---

[35] For example, 46 percent of the top ten banks' total profits flowed from their global lending portfolios, which had a sizeable Latin American exposure. At the time of the 1982 debt crisis, the eight largest U.S. banks (such as Citibank, Chase Manhattan, and Bank of America) had claims on Latin American countries that totaled 10 percent of their assets and 217 percent of their total capital and reserves (FDIC 1997). Citibank's South American exposure alone accounted for 25 percent of its total 1980 profits.

of debt repayment tomorrow. However, these conditionality promises were plagued by the time-inconsistency problem.[36] Governments often defected from their commitments to economic orthodoxy, preferring to cater to domestic supporters with big spending politics. They missed their conditionality targets and waived out of bank and IMF-supported programs.[37] For example, in Argentina, President Raúl Alfonsín's free-spending government was out of compliance with almost all of its IMF agreement's requirements, yet it secured new funding from its creditors in July 1987.

In the aftermath of the crisis, the U.S.-led Brady Restructurings swapped Latin America's defaulted bank loans for global bonds. Debt holders surged from a handful of large banks to gaggles of small, globally decentralized bond market investors. In a new world of round-the-clock trading, portfolio investors – who had a low personal stake in borrowers' financial futures – could readily withdraw their financing.

When debtors veered from policies that raised the likelihood of debt repayment (such as low inflation and fiscal discipline), investors unloaded their bond holdings in secondary markets. These capital reversals, dubbed by the finance literature as sudden stops,[38] unleashed precipitous falls in bond prices and interest rates spikes that sparked emerging market crises and constrained politicians' ability to fund expansions. The shift from long-term banking to short-term speculative investment altered Latin America's political economy. When countries became more indebted to global markets, they also became more vulnerable to severe credit shocks that stifled their economic autonomy.

1.1.4. The Market As Prison, Or Commodity As Freedom?

I used to think if there was reincarnation, I wanted to come back as the president or the pope or a .400 baseball hitter. But now, I want to come back as the bond market. You can intimidate everybody.

– James Carville, U.S. President Clinton's political strategist

Are markets truly this powerful that they can awe a U.S. presidential advisor at the height of the country's hegemonic power? Or, might there be an escape from globalization's straitjacket?

---

[36] Barro and Gordon 1983.

[37] Haggard (1985) finds extremely low rates of compliance with the IMF's Extended Fund Facility (EFF) between 1974 and 1984. Of the thirty cases studied, sixteen were cancelled and eight more were not implemented in their original form. Compliance with fiscal targets was especially poor. In a study of 1983's IMF programs, Edwards (1989) found that conditions on the government's deficit were achieved in only 30 percent of the thirty-four programs in place during that year. In 1984, compliance was even worse; conditions were met for only 19 percent of these programs (Edwards 1989). Notably, in a later study, Edwards (2001) finds that IMF program interruptions were particularly frequent between 1988 and 1991, the period before Latin America's shift to debt securitization.

[38] See footnote 60.

To the extent countries borrow from centralized bank creditors, they can avoid market discipline. As we have observed in Latin America, for instance, bank lending often induces moral hazard, allowing governments to avoid conditionality.

In such an interdependent world, how else might countries escape the market's grip? Their room to maneuver depends on governments' fiscal space,[39] or the availability of resources to fund budget shortfalls. To finance new spending, developing country governments typically borrow externally to a much greater extent than rich countries.[40] However, when governments possess alternative sources of income that are independent of global bond markets (such as proceeds from state-owned enterprises, foreign aid, and privatizations), they often bypass market calls for austerity. For instance, from copper mines to oil rigs, many developing countries are blessed with bountiful natural resources that provide them with policy flexibility. During commodity booms, windfall profits from state-owned enterprises and export taxes boost government revenues and decrease their reliance on external financing.

1.1.5. Rise of Austerity Politics

Is austerity solely an international economic phenomenon? Or, does it also have domestic roots? When might austerity be a political choice?[41] Perhaps, there are developing country parallels to President Bill Clinton's political third way in the 1990s. The U.S. President broke with Democratic party ideals by accepting many conservative market assertions about government and declaring that "the era of big government [was] over."[42]

Do we observe a similar phenomenon in developing countries? Not unlike the emergence of Bill Clinton and Tony Blair's third-way politics in the 1990s, economic centrism has become en vogue in many parts of the developing world. Seeking the middle ground between left and right, Lech Walesa, Fernando Henrique Cardoso, and Boris Yeltsin all embraced free market orthodoxy. Even the iconoclast Hugo Chávez resembled a third-way candidate during the 1998 Venezuelan presidential campaign. Perhaps, austerity politics is more

---

[39] Fiscal space can be defined as the availability of budget room that allows governments to provide resources for a desired purpose without any prejudice to the sustainability of a government's financial position (IMF, 2005).

[40] With limited tax bases and shallow capital markets domestically, developing country governments often have fewer internal financing options than developed countries (Gavin and Perotti, 1997).

[41] For example, Vreeland (2003) demonstrates that political leaders and economic reformers often use IMF conditionality as a tool to achieve their own domestic agenda priorities, including implementing laisez-faire economic policies. In fact, Pop-Eleches (2009) finds that Right governments are more likely than Left governments to turn to the IMF during crises, causing policy to diverge along partisan lines.

[42] President Clinton's 1996 State of the Union address.

surprising in these regions, however, where widespread inequality and poverty typically translate into strong popular pressures for government spending.

The second part of political austerity theory developed in Chapter 2 seeks to explain this phenomenon by examining domestic politics. I argue that economic austerity does not simply reflect "competition for capital" or a "race to the bottom," but rather the policy choices of political elites. When might domestic politicians proactively opt for orthodoxy?

Conservative macroeconomic policies are typically associated with right-leaning parties. In fact, the political economy literature traditionally divides domestic politics in the developed world into two camps.[43] Right-leaning politicians, hoping to appease private sector supporters, tend to value inflation control even if it translates to fewer jobs and lower growth. By contrast, left-leaning politicians aim to create jobs and growth to win favor with middle-class and working families, even if such expansion breeds higher inflation. Do we find a similar ideological divide in the developing world?

In Latin America, a seminal scholarship finds that the traditional left initially helped facilitate the adoption of the 1990s neoliberal reforms,[44] before financial and economic volatility opened the door to a resurgence of statist and nationalist parties.[45] In light of this pattern, might partisan economic cycles ebb and flow with the rise and fall of neoliberalism? Or, alternatively, is macroeconomic policy making, a policy space often reserved for the musing of technocrats, more insulated from these ideological swings?

Notwithstanding the return of a visible government hand in certain economic sectors from Argentine oil to Bolivian natural gas, I claim that the invisible hand continues to guide macroeconomic policy throughout much of the region. For instance, the Bolivian economy minister, Luis Alberto Arce, today touts "recurring budget surpluses, a prudent fiscal attitude.... responsible fiscal management" and "defeating inflation" as hallmarks of the country's current economic model.[46] Why do such left-leaning governments adhere to conservative macroeconomic principles, notwithstanding an ostensible departure from their neoliberal past?

I contend that macroeconomic policy choices are typically a reflection of the region's volatile economic histories. In the aftermath of macroeconomic misgovernance that led to inflationary crises and bred political and social chaos, politicians welcomed alternatives to highly interventionist policies that were blamed for these crises. As a result, macroeconomic orthodoxy prospered in an advantageous environment where Latin American leaders gained political credibility through inflation control. These transformative experiences blurred

---

[43] Hibbs 1977; Alesina 1987; Alesina and Rosenthal 1995; Bartels 2008.

[44] Roberts 1998; Murillo 2001; Stokes 2001b; Levitsky 2003; Bruhn 2004; Murillo and Martinez-Gallardo 2007.

[45] Roberts 2012.

[46] Luis Arce's remarks to World Bank's 2010 Americas Conference in Miami on September 14, 2010.

partisan lines, helping to forge a new conservative, macroeconomic governing consensus. Notwithstanding ongoing ideological divides on issues ranging
from welfare to privatization, left-leaning politicians pursued balanced budgets
and low inflation in hopes of boosting their credibility as economic managers.
Unlike the traditional partisan divide in developed countries, leftist politicians
prioritized inflation control along with job and growth creation. After past
inflationary shocks had destroyed the incomes of middle-class and poor voters,
they deemed that the low inflation constituency reached well beyond businessmen and financiers.

Why do such past economic lessons cast such a long shadow over policy
making? Why wouldn't they fade with time? Building on the psychology literature[47] about choices under risk and uncertainty, I claim that memory-based
judgments often guide politicians.[48] I assume that politicians are Bayesian
actors, constantly updating their views to reflect new information.[49] In contrast to standard risk preference models that weight all historical information
equally, however, I claim that traumatic experiences often have a disproportionate influence on decision making. In fact, theories of risky choice find that
direct experiences are often more compelling than descriptive, secondhand
information gleaned from books, data, or the Internet.[50]

In the policy world, transformative historical events also leave a strong
impression. I contend that severe economic instability breeds greater risk aversion that often persists even during periods of economic stability.[51] In North
America, for instance, policy makers often evaluate their decisions through the
lens of their crisis past. President Obama's flurry of economic stimulus that followed the 2008 financial calamity was anchored by a powerful anti-depression
discourse. Fearing that a severe credit crunch would unleash a deflationary
spiral not seen since the Great Depression, Obama used massive spending
to avoid an economic collapse. It's not surprising, however, that U.S. politicians place a higher weight on escaping a known economic catastrophe, the
Great Depression, than a trauma they have never experienced like very high or
hyperinflation.[52]

By contrast, devastated by past annual inflation rates in the thousands, Latin
America's defining historical crisis is hyperinflation. Presidents and their economic teams have ingrained low inflation as a priority in their political fabric,

---

[47] I follow in the tradition of Weyland (2002), who was one of the first scholars to employ
psychological explanations of economic policy choices in developing countries.

[48] Weber et al. 1993; Hertwig et al. 2004; Weber et al. 2004.

[49] Bayesian updating uses new evidence to improve a prior probability estimate.

[50] See footnote 48.

[51] By contrast, Weyland (2002) argues that neoliberal reforms reflect the risk-seeking behavior of
politicians struggling to survive economic shocks. They hope to exit their domain of losses by
rapidly rebooting economic growth.

[52] The highest rate recorded in the United States during the twentieth century was 14 percent in
1980, well below the astronomical inflation rates in Latin America during the 1970s and 1980s
(World Development Indicators).

hoping to avoid a repeat of these dire income shocks. In those countries traumatized by runaway inflation, politicians add inflation control to the winning electoral formula of job and growth creation. Undoubtedly, these traditional economic assets offer political gains. However, if the pace of growth is too brisk, inflation threatens to undercut its political benefit by depressing real wages and eliminating jobs. Therefore, politicians prioritize price stability, but within reason. They obviously do not want to unleash a deflationary spiral marked by plummeting growth. Rather, they view that fostering moderate growth and low inflation will draw considerable political support.

Latin American political leaders believe that the traditional low-inflation constituency has widened beyond businesses, financial institutions, and right-wing voters. By providing a baseline of low inflation, politicians enhance their economic governance credentials. A political commitment to fiscal discipline and price stability not only provides businesses and investors with a stable, long-run operational environment, but also protects voters' incomes. Moreover, even years after an inflation crisis, fiscal discipline often generates a positive confidence effect and a fall in interest rates that stimulate the economy.[53]

For example, in our 2010 interview, Chilean President Ricardo Lagos stressed the importance of sound policies that allow for low interest rates and boost the competitiveness of national firms.

In today's world, you have an examination every day according to the country risk that you are going to get from Wall Street. You simply open the *Wall Street Journal*, and you know the country risk of Chile ... From the point of view of domestic firms, from the point of view of investment in Chile, many Chilean firms have been able to get credit in Wall Street; and the big advantage for them is that the rate they pay at Wall Street is much lower.[54]

1.2. FROM POLITICAL BUSINESS CYCLES TO POLITICAL AUSTERITY CYCLES

Soon after they transitioned to democracy, a rich developing country scholarship expects to find evidence of *political business cycle*[55] behavior across Latin American countries. Deeming that voters would reward a booming economy, politicians engineer an election-time boost notwithstanding the extent of the economy's spare capacity; and hence, its potential inflationary costs.[56] Facing strong popular pressures for jobs and growth, presidents hoped to redress high social debts from an authoritarian past with lofty economic expansions. In new democracies characterized by weak legislatures, partly autonomous

---

[53] Alesian and Perotti 1995; Gupta et al. 2003, 2005, 2006; Segura-Ubiero et al. 2010.

[54] Author's interview with Ricardo Lagos, Brown University, April 16, 2010.

[55] Nordhaus 1975; Lindbeck 1976; Tufte 1978; Sachs 1989a; Dornbusch and Edwards 1991; Kaufman and Stallings 1991.

[56] See Chapter 2 for a more extensive discussion about economic policy, output gaps, and inflation.

central banks, and constrained media, politicians should be most likely to use economic policy as an electoral weapon.[57]

While these explanations have uncovered an important facilitating factor to good governance over the long run, such institutional change is often incremental. By comparison, my political austerity theory claims that structural economic changes can quickly undermine historic regularities and reshape domestic political behavior. Indeed, severe crises often constrain economic options and alter political priorities, even in new democracies.

When inflation becomes salient, political survival no longer rests with a traditional interventionist strategy centered on boosting jobs and incomes. Rather, austerity politics becomes an alternative to stimulus politics in democratizing regions such as Latin America. A measured macroeconomic balance between growth and inflation is often more politically rewarding than an aggressive economic expansion that risks igniting inflation.

Nevertheless, the success of either electoral strategy is conditional on a country's indebtedness to financial markets. When countries first tap global bond markets, this new funding often facilitates deficit spending. However, as they build a large stock of outstanding bond debt, they become more vulnerable to credit disruptions and interest rate swings that derail political plans. Even when politicians hope to aggressively stimulate the economy, they are instead compelled to pursue restrictive economic policies that result in a *political austerity cycle* characterized by contained inflation and slow growth.[58]

Why are bond markets able to wield such influence over governments? Why wouldn't politicians simply stray from the market's calls for economic orthodoxy until after elections? Presumably, the political costs of an electoral expansion should appear long after the end of a presidential campaign.

I have argued that when governments develop a dependence on international bond markets for their financing, an incumbent faces an immediate and high-stakes political threat. Bond markets create a short-term financial constraint that competes with the political calendar. Bond investors – fixated on short-term returns in a competitive investment management industry – discourage unsustainable fiscal policies that risk igniting inflation and disrupting debt payments.[59] When countries lack sound policies, investors sell their bonds at a discounted rate that reflects higher inflation expectations and diminished debt service capacity. Recall that in highly-indebted emerging market countries, this capital withdrawal – known as a sudden stop – is often quite abrupt, creating

---

[57] Ames 1987; Schuknecht 1996, 2000; Acosta and Coppedge 2001; Block 2002; Gonzalez 2002; Shi and Svensson 2003, 2006; Brender and Drazen 2005; Barberia and Avelino 2011.

[58] These theoretical claims mark a notable departure from political business cycles that assert an inflationary bias. It also supports Remmer's (1993) political capital hypothesis that elections often catalyze rather than undermine economic reforms. In line with political austerity theory, recent OECD research by Canes-Wrone and Park (2012) finds a similar reverse electoral business cycle trend, however, pertaining specifically to sectors of irreversible investment rather than the total economy.

[59] Mosley 2003; Reinhart et al. 2003; Ahlquist 2006.

a fierce financial shock that jeopardizes the foundation of the economic vote: people's purchasing power.

In fact, a rich economics literature on sudden stops finds that these abrupt capital reversals often quickly translate to severe funding spikes. Surging interest rates pose a direct threat not only to government spending possibilities, but also to the real economy by dampening consumption and investment.[60]

These risks are often more pronounced during election periods, when capital has proven to be most flighty in developing countries.[61] Bond investors often fret that political uncertainty can breed economic uncertainty. An aggressive politically timed expansion can unnerve inflation-wary investors and ignite a currency crisis that undercuts popular living standards.[62] In fact, scholars have found that severe exchange rate depreciation and currency crashes often trigger incumbent job loss.[63] Not surprisingly, in light of these risks, incumbents often tend to follow disciplined macroeconomic policies and avoid devaluations that chance igniting election-year inflation.[64] Politicians might intrinsically prefer to reflate the economy, but deflation is necessary to avoid a shock that calls their governance into question.[65]

1.2.1. Markets and Society

If politicians pursue budget austerity, are they being responsive to their domestic constituents? To the extent that politicians provide a public good of low inflation and economic stability, it benefits many members of society beyond businesses and financiers. In fact, there is extensive scholarship that shows that high inflation has a distributive character, increasing poverty rates and reducing poor and middle class incomes.[66] Budget discipline may also be in the interest of domestic constituents, even years after an inflation crisis, if it helps provide a stable, business environment. Why? Boosting the global competitiveness of national firms can produce domestic jobs and raise workers' salaries. Therefore, markets often create wealth that help stabilize democracies.[67]

Nonetheless, the compatibility of markets and democracy ultimately depends on how politicians allocate budgetary spending within an austerity

---

[60] Calvo 1998; Calvo and Reinhart 2000; Calvo, Izquierdo, and Talvi 2003; Kaminsky, Reinhart, and Vegh 2004.

[61] Leblang and Bernhard 2000; Frieden and Stein 2001; Leblang 2002; Mosley 2003; Block and Vaaler 2004; Vaaler, Schrage, and Block 2006.

[62] This type of stimulus is most problematic when the economy has a small output gap, or little spare capacity, and is at risk of overheating.

[63] Remmer (1991) shows that currency depreciation helps explain incumbent vote loss; Frankel (2005) finds political leaders are twice as likely to lose office in the six months following a currency crash.

[64] Frieden and Stein 2001; Schamis and Way 2003.

[65] In fact, politicians often back their monetary and exchange rate policies with official public declarations to earn greater inflation-fighting credibility (Guisinger and Singer 2010).

[66] Cutler and Katz 1991; Cardoso 1992; Agenor 1998; Rezende 1998; Romer and Romer 1998; Easterly and Fischer 2000.

[67] Przeworksi and Wallerstein 1982, 1988; Przeworski et al. 2000.

framework. Politicians walk a delicate tight rope between budget discipline and social responsiveness. If politicians achieve discipline by shrinking the welfare state, their efforts to stabilize the economy may aggravate social tensions. In fact, slashing social security, education, and pension benefits can quickly diminish popular living standards and fan social instability. For instance, Argentina's former Economy Minister Robert Lavagna discusses the costs involved with this type of budget austerity.

In Argentina, many people tried to get fiscal surplus [by] just reducing the number of public officials or [by] trying to make the universities or the hospitals [inaudible]–things like that, and the reaction was always negative in society.[68]

To mitigate these social costs and avoid pot-banging popular protests, known as *cacerolazos*, many Latin American governments considerably increased their budgetary line-item social expenditures, while maintaining an overall orthodox budgetary framework during the last decade. In fact, scholars find that welfare states have grown in Latin America, consisting of both increases in universal spending (such as education) and progressive measures that target poverty (such as conditional cash transfers).[69] Notably, those Latin American countries with the strongest protectionist histories, or import-substitution industrialization legacies, have been the most likely to emphasize social insurance today.[70]

Within a balanced budget framework, politicians can increase social spending in a few different ways. They can build state capacity by raising revenues through such measures as value-added and export taxes. For example, during the democratic transition in Chile, the new center-left government increased both the corporate and value-added tax to address the Pinochet dictatorship's outstanding social debt.[71] Alternatively, politicians can reallocate resources toward more politically and economically efficient expenditures, such as conditional-cash transfers.[72] These transfer schemes can benefit millions of people for a relatively cheap budgetary cost of 0.5 to 1 percent of GDP. In Brazil, for instance, the federal government, spends about 0.5 percent of Brazil's GDP on the *Bolsa Familia* program, extending cash transfers to more than 10 million poor households, or nearly one-fifth of the nation's total households.[73]

---

[68] Lavagna 2004.
[69] Kaufman and Segura-Ubiergo 2001; Brown and Hunter 2004; Avelino, Brown, and Hunter 2005; Ubiergo-Segura 2007; Haggard and Kaufman 2008; Huber, Mastillo, and Stephens 2008.
[70] Wibbels and Ahlquist 2011.
[71] Social expenditures included pension benefits, low-cost housing, and increased pay for teachers and health workers (Haggard and Kaufman 2008).
[72] Conditional cash transfers (CCTs) provide money directly to poor families via a "social contract" mandating that the beneficiaries send their children to school regularly or bring them to health centers (World Bank 2005).
[73] World Bank 2005; Zucco 2008.

In contrast to such transparent measures, Latin American nations have also developed more furtive ways of spending money on their political priorities. Discretionary budgets and off-balance sheet expenditures are quite appealing tools, for example, because they are subject to less monitoring. Remember for instance that Néstor Kirchner modified domestic laws through *superpoderes*, enabling him to spend lofty surplus budgetary revenues on discretionary political initiatives. Ironically, this crafty political maneuver allowed Kirchner to concurrently use fiscal surpluses for two seemingly divergent political ends. They not only signaled good governance but also boosted the available pot of money for funneling benefits to special political interests.

Some Developed Country Extensions. Moving forward, austerity politics is no longer solely a developing country pattern. In the wake of the global financial crisis, governments spanning North America and Europe are faced with mounting debt burdens and growing financial market constraints.

Greece, for instance, offers an important example of how sovereign debt structure (bank lending vs. bond issuance) may also constrain developed countries' policies, notwithstanding their ostensibly lower likelihood of default. In the wake of Greece's 2009–2010 debt crisis, socialist Prime Minister George Papandreou halved the country's budget deficit in an effort to assuage panicky investors.[74] Vowing to "draw blood" if necessary, Papandreou sought to freeze public sector wages, hike fuel taxes, and infuse frugality into Greece's lavish social security system. After being battered by austerity for two years, the new government coalition, headed by Antonis Samaras, is moving forward with yet another round of budgetary cuts to stem the country's capital outflows. This behavior stands in sharp contrast to Greece's neglect of lending conditionality during the era of bank lending, when its government ignored tighter fiscal policies imposed by the European Commission in 1985.

Notwithstanding Greece's past moral hazard problems, most eurozone nations hope to limit the extent of the market disciplining effect within the new European Stability Mechanism (ESM), a permanent system to deal with the debt crisis, slated to come into effect in 2012. Under this mechanism, new euro area sovereign bond issues would have "collective-action clauses" that facilitate creditor-debtor negotiations during credit downturns.[75] To avoid a similar fallout as Argentina's cessation of financing during its 2001–02 crisis, these clauses would help enable new market financing by allowing a majority of creditors to craft new terms for debt relief.

Compared to the Latin American experience, which featured a massive transformation of global bank loans into bond market debt under the Brady restructurings, Southern Europe's outstanding debt profile today is considerably more

---

[74] The Greece government cut its first-half 2010 budget deficit by 46 percent compared to the previous year (Economist Intelligence Unit database).

[75] Collective action clauses allow a super-majority of bondholders to overrule "holdout" creditors, and hence, ease the pathway to restructuring.

mixed. Speculative bond market contagion has compelled Southern European governments to adopt many rounds of budget austerity, but the concentrated debt exposure of bank creditors has prompted E.U. officials – concerned about systemic bank risk – to orchestrate several bailout packages. Bank creditors also agreed to accept considerable losses on their debt holdings to protect their balance sheets from a more massive profitability shock. Ironically, however, in today's financially integrated world, these bank creditors have been slower to forgive debt or lend defensively because of their shared reliance on decentralized financial markets. Today, global banks also raise new capital via commercial paper and bond markets, subjecting their own balance sheets to the same scrutiny and funding pressures from global markets as sovereign nations.[76]

In summary, even in the developed country cases, the extent of debt ownership dispersion is crucial to understanding the relationship between creditors and debtors, and ultimately government policy. High levels of bond market indebtedness have placed the developed world, from Greece and Ireland to Portugal, Italy, and Spain under the microscope of global capital markets. To contain the economic and financial fallout of capital withdrawal, these countries have adopted a raft of austerity measures. But, how will they protect the losers from austerity politics worried about rising unemployment and dwindling social safeguards?

The relevant lessons from the Latin American experience reflect the importance of building state capacity in a globalized world. Solving the political paradox that pits austerity against social welfare ultimately rest in the technocratic details. Savvy politicians can boost their credit standing by pursuing budgetary discipline, while simultaneously changing the budgetary share that is directed toward social spending. They can also raise new taxes, streamline expenditures, and develop alternative domestic funding sources (such as deepening local currency bond markets) to create the budgetary room to spend on such initiatives. Importantly, for politicians whose countries are highly indebted to global bond markets, the key question is often not *whether* to adopt austerity, but *how* to adopt austerity.

1.3. METHOD AND PLAN OF THE BOOK

This book explores the tensions between markets and democracy in a financially globalized world by examining the Latin American experience. I employ a variety of methods to construct a rich and compelling account of Latin American economic policymaking, combining extensive fieldwork, historical analysis, and cross-national statistical analyses. Between 2006 and 2011, I interviewed more than 100 political leaders and policy makers in Argentina, Chile, and Venezuela (for a list of the interviews, see Appendix). I also complement

---

[76] I am indebted to my brother, Eric T. Kaplan, a compliance lawyer in the U.S. banking industry, for initially drawing the parallel between governments and banks in today's financially integrated world.

my comparative case analysis with evidence from additional Latin American countries, including Brazil and Ecuador. I draw on these resources to examine economic decision making in twenty different election cases. I also use statistical analysis to test for broader patterns in the relationship between elections and economic policy making. Latin America is ideally suited for such statistical tests because the region is inhabited by a preponderance of presidential, middle-income countries with fixed (or constitutionally mandated) election timing and varied exposures to the study's main independent variables of interest:[77] decentralized bond finance and historic inflationary crises.[78]

1.3.1. A Look At What Follows

Chapter 2 offers a new theory to explain the variation in the political business cycle in Latin America. According to the political austerity framework, chief executives make economic policy choices along two key decision-making dimensions: financial means and political motivations. Financial means reflect policy feasibility, or the capacity to deliver an economic boost with monetary and fiscal policies.[79] Political motivations refer to the political incentive to use macroeconomic powers for political gain. Given the long-term costs of engineering an electoral boom – which may include fiscal deficits, inflation, and recession – politicians only stimulate the economy when they expect to be politically rewarded. I argue politicians are most likely to use macroeconomic policy to win votes when they have both the means and motivation to create a political business cycle (H_1). Otherwise, a financially globalized and inflation-scarred world place a premium on political austerity cycles, where leaders demonstrate their managerial competence with budgetary discipline and low inflation (H_2–H_4). Surprisingly, left-leaning governments – hoping to ally private sector concerns about their governance credentials – are often more austere than their right-leaning counterparts.

H_1: **Traditional Political Business Cycle (PBC).** When stimulus-minded politicians face low-funding constraints from global bond markets, they use fiscal and/or monetary policy to boost the economy. Politicians are most likely to create conditions of high growth and low unemployment before elections, but at the cost of inflation and/or recession following elections.

H_2: **Market-Induced Political Austerity Cycle (PAC).** When stimulus-minded politicians face steep funding constraints from global bond markets, they do not use accommodative fiscal and monetary policies to boost the economy. Instead, they use a neutral mix of economic policies or even contractionary policies that yield

---

[77] King, Keohane, and Verba 1994.
[78] See footnote 15.
[79] Expansionary monetary policy lowers interest rates paid by consumers and firms, boosting consumption and investment. Restrictive monetary policy raises interest rates paid by consumers and firms, slowing economic growth. Fiscal policy is considered expansionary when the overall fiscal deficit increases (or the overall fiscal surplus decreases) from one year to the next.

political austerity cycles. Inflation falls before elections, but at the cost of lower economic growth and fewer new jobs.

H_3: **Inflation-Averse Political Austerity Cycle (PAC).** Past inflation crises breed economic risk-aversion; politicians do not use accommodative fiscal and monetary policies to boost the economy before elections. Instead, they use a neutral mix of economic policies or mildly contractionary policies that yield political austerity cycles. Inflation falls during elections, but at the cost of lower economic growth and fewer new jobs. This pattern is more pronounced under left-leaning than right-leaning administrations.

H_4: **Political Austerity Cycle (PAC).** When inflation-averse politicians face steep funding constraints from global financial markets, they strongly contract economic policies in order to stabilize the economy. With this form of political austerity cycles, inflation and growth fall before elections most markedly.

In Chapter 3, I use cross-national economic and electoral data to test for political business cycles across sixteen Latin American countries from 1961–2009 that includes a total of 132 contested elections. In support of political austerity theory, I find that both bond market financing and past inflationary crises have a dampening effect on election-year engineering of the economy. When countries are dependent on global capital markets and/or have suffered from turbulent inflationary episodes, their politicians are more likely to be cautious governors of the economy, settling for lower inflation and growth.

I also test for whether the partisan character of a government influences its policy choices before elections. I find that the 1980's inflationary and debt shocks helped create a third political way, where leftist politicians are just as likely as right-wing politicians to embrace budgetary prudence and economic discipline. Ironically, these statistical tests show that left-oriented governments, hailing from inflation-ridden countries, are often the most ardent followers of budgetary austerity. Moreover, in spite of partisan loyalties, these crisis legacies, along with global bond market headwinds, often create a deflationary bias among parties across the political spectrum.

Notwithstanding these findings, it is difficult to uncover the causes of this empirical trend with statistics alone. My comparative case study work in Chapters 4–7 employs elections as the unit of analysis to test my theory's causal relationships in Argentina, Brazil, Chile, Ecuador, and Venezuela. These Latin American countries provide an ideal setting for evaluating my political austerity theory. They are presidential, middle-income South American countries that are similar along economic development indicators,[80] but also have

---

[80] For example, the World Bank officially classifies four of the five countries as upper-middle-income economies (Argentina, Brazil, Chile, and Venezuela) and one country as a lower middle income economy (Ecuador). Ecuador, however, is a borderline higher middle income economy. Its per capita income, $3,110, places it at the upper end of the lower-middle-income classification ($936–$3,705) using the 2007 Atlas method (US$).

considerable variation in their exposure to global bond markets and historic inflation volatility.[81]

The case study chapters are organized according to my four main hypotheses. In each chapter, I adjudicate between my theory and alternative explanations for the rise in conservative, market-oriented policies from the political economy literature, including central bank independence, IMF conditionality, and neoliberal policy diffusion.

In Chapter 4, I explore when politicians embark on the classic electoral engineering initiative. I find that politicians craft an economic boom when they face few spending constraints from global capital markets and believe that the electorate rewards rapid growth. By tapping alternative funding resources that are independent from bond markets, debtors can avoid being subject to market conditionality. Given the lack of a past inflation crisis, politicians are economically risk-seeking and craft a political business cycle with little concern about a potential overheating of the economy (H_1).

For example, Chilean President Eduardo Frei had both the resources and the political will to "green light" a 1970 electoral expansion. With booming copper prices and a deferential central bank, he conducted a fiscal extravaganza to appease a fervent labor movement's redistributive demands. Indeed, his party, *el Partido Demócrata Cristiano de Chile*, drew important electoral support from a politically mobilized union movement that was concerned about jobs and growth.

Chapter 5 examines the world of a more restricted Latin American politician. Spendthrift behavior is stymied by the conditionality and financial market pressures of global bond financing. Chief executives have the political motivation to craft a political business cycle, but they lack the financial means (they do not have access to non-market financing alternatives such as commodity windfalls and central bank credit). With global bonds accounting for a high share of government financing, politicians restrain their expansionary impulses to forestall the threat of credit shocks (H_2).

For instance, during the 1998 Venezuelan presidential elections, President Rafael Caldera would have liked to spur the economy in the interest of quelling the political rise of Hugo Chávez – a threat to Venezuela's traditional two-party centered political system. To his dismay, 1998's steep fall in oil prices left him with a dearth of available domestic resources to commit to election-year spending. It also sullied the credit of a highly indebted Venezuela, giving policy makers few options beyond austerity. According to Venezuela's planning minister, Teodoro Petkoff, the Caldera administration "had no other choice but to bring down public spending with the second fall of oil prices in 1998. [Their] objective was a strict classic stabilization of the economy."[82]

---

[81] King, Keohane, and Verba 1994.

[82] During my field research, I interviewed Petkoff on March 29, 2007, in his Tal Cual newspaper office in the Altamira section of Caracas, Venezuela.

In Chapter 6, I evaluate economic policy making in countries with histories of inflationary crises. Recall that, according to political austerity theory, chief executives in these nations should be vigilant custodians of economic discipline. Facing an inflation-scarred electorate, they expect to be evaluated on their ability to contain inflation as much as their ability to create economic growth. As a result, these inflation-averse politicians prefer cautious policies that ensure price stability, even when they have alternative non-market funding sources (H_3).

For example, during Chile's 2005 elections, a copper boom padded government coffers, but the governing Socialist Party cut spending and boosted the budget surplus; a drastic policy shift from its massive budgetary expansion under Salvadore Allende that ended in a devastating inflationary spiral.

In Chapter 7, I trace the political consequences of the perfect neoliberal storm: high bond market exposure and a high inflation history. Politicians initially choose stability-oriented policies to appease an inflation-sensitive electorate, but are compelled by financial market pressures to intensify their economic orthodoxy. Their economic agendas are highly restrictive, characterized by contractionary macroeconomic policies. They have neither the financial means nor the political motivation to fashion a political business cycle (H_4).

For instance, Argentine President Carlos Menem cut public salaries during his 1995 election campaign when a regional credit crunch terrorized an already inflation-sensitive electorate. Similarly, when contagion pressures from the East Asian Crisis threatened to shut down financial markets, Brazilian President Fernando Henrique Cardoso announced an economic adjustment package. He raised taxes and reduced spending notwithstanding his 1998 reelection bid. Cardoso also trumpeted his inflation fighting credentials, vowing in a November 1997 radio address, "You can be sure of one thing; we will not let the real lose value and let inflation come back!"[83]

In the concluding chapter, Chapter 8, I explore the future of the political business cycle and partisan politics in developing democracies. If politicians adopted orthodoxy policies during an era characterized by inflation anxiety and financial market dependency, why hasn't mild inflation and booming commodity markets swung the region's economics back to the left? The fate of the Latin American political business cycle ultimately rests with the region's financial means and political motivations. Perhaps, Latin America's memories of its political and inflation trauma might fade with new generations of policy makers. In Argentina, for instance, we have recently witnessed that a severe deflationary shock in the opposite direction – in the prelude to the 2001–2002 debt crisis – opened the political space for greater macroeconomic intervention during the 2011 elections. However, the capacity of Latin American governments to employ such stimulus ultimately depends on their ability to develop alternative forms of financing – from the printing press to commodity proceeds – that are less susceptible to speculative market pressures.

---

[83] *New York Times*, November 5, 1997.

2

Globalization and Austerity Politics

The United States aggressively responded to the 2008–2009 global financial crisis with a flurry of economic stimulus. For the champion of laissez-faire economics, crisis-induced budget spending and interest rate cuts were an about-face from its austerity doctrine exported across the globe. Throughout the post-Cold War era, the U.S. Treasury and International Monetary Fund have tied economic aid to restrictive spending and credit policies. From Latin America to East Asia, the United States has advocated for economic stabilization policies in the face of financial crises. Surprisingly, developing country leaders often have doggedly embraced these free-market principles. Many of these countries are young democracies characterized by fervent popular pressures for growth, redistribution, and jobs, yet their politicians pursue conservative non-interventionist policies. In hard times, the political benefits of a short-term soporific should outweigh the long-term self-healing powers of laissez-faire capitalism. What's the political payoff to being a cautious steward of the economy?

The appeal of non-interventionist economic policies is even more surprising when chief executives are battling for their political survival. Political economy scholars expect politicians to swell the public purse to gain votes, particularly in newly democratized regions that are plagued by chronic unemployment and high poverty.[1] Some politicians abide by this policy making logic, known as the *political business cycle*. According to this logic, politicians are consumed with winning the vote. They create a short-term economic boom designed to curry favor with the electorate that often ends in an inflation-induced economic bust.[2] Their political ambition clouds any concerns about longer-term economic fallout, including higher inflation and slower economic growth.

---

[1] Ames 1987; Schuknecht 1996, 2000; Acosta and Coppedge 2001; Block 2002; Gonzalez 2002; Brender and Drazen 2005; Shi and Svensson 2003, 2006; Barberia and Avelino 2011.

[2] Nordhaus 1975; Lindbeck 1976; Tufte 1978; Ames 1987; Sachs 1989; Dornbusch and Edwards 1991; Kaufman and Stallings 1991.

Scholars have uncovered evidence of political tinkering with the economy across the globe, from Japan and Russia to Turkey, Italy, and Mexico.[3] For example, facing a contentious reelection bid in December 2006, President Hugo Chávez slashed Venezuela's lofty budgetary surplus by half and spent a further whopping US\$7 billion in off-budget discretionary spending to reward his historically marginalized political base.[4] Similarly, Russian president Boris Yeltsin ensured his 1996 reelection with a spending boom that was largely mortgaged by the privatization of Russia's natural resources.[5] For both Chávez and Yeltsin, aggressive government intervention carried a steep inflationary cost, creating serious long-term problems for their economies.[6]

During other elections, however, political behavior does not adhere to this convention. Politicians choose not to stimulate the economy. For example, two months before his May 1995 reelection bid, Argentina President Carlos Menem surprisingly announced US\$1 billion in budget cuts, including a reduction in public salaries. Similarly, during his own reelection campaign, Brazilian President Fernando Henrique Cardoso announced an austerity package featuring tax hikes and spending cuts. Why would Menem and Cardoso slash spending during their most vulnerable hour? What accounts for this odd political choice? During elections, politicians are typically expected to use economic policy to spur growth, create jobs, and boost wages. Why would developing country politicians like Menem and Cardoso swing the political pendulum from heavy government intervention to laissez-faire neutrality? What accounts for this change in political preferences?

To answer these questions, this chapter offers a new framework called *political austerity cycle* theory. Austerity, or a commitment to budgetary discipline and sound monetary policies, has become a key credential of economic governance in a globalized world. Why would politicians value a seemingly long-run asset like economic stability? Politicians operate according to the same incentives, as always. They want to win elections[7] and believe that voters respond to economic conditions.[8]

However, in many cases, their political arsenal has undergone an important transformation. Politicians have swapped large unsustainable fiscal deficits and a high-gear printing press for budget discipline and inflation control. Rather

[3] Kohno and Nishizawa 1990; Krueger and Taran 1993; Limosani and Navarra 2001; Gonzalez 2002.

[4] Venezuelan Finance Minister Cabezas's Inter-American Development Bank presentation, March 2007.

[5] The Yeltsin government grew its budget deficit from 4.9 percent to 7.4 percent of GDP in a single year (IMF).

[6] In a few short years, Yeltsin watched inflation more than double its 1996 levels. For Chávez, inflation had not only doubled within one year of his electoral spending spree, but quickly approached the highest levels of inflation in the world, reaching 31 percent by 2008 (IMF's International Financial Statistics).

[7] Mayhew 1974.

[8] Lewis-Beck 1988.

than using big budget deficits and expansive credit to boost the economy, they prefer to operate within their means. Shrouded by an orthodox budgetary framework, they reward their constituencies with line-item budgetary spending – from poverty programs to public works projects – and distance themselves from aggressive government intervention in the economy. They believe that engineering a high-growth, high-inflation cycle to win votes carries too high a political cost. In lieu of crafting such traditional political business cycles, they instead signal their commitment to sound macroeconomic management during elections.

Why have political business cycles become so costly? What determines when politicians embrace austerity and when they revert to economic stimulus? This chapter offers a theoretical framework for understanding the politics of macroeconomic policy making. The discussion unfolds as follows. The first section places my theoretical approach within the political economy literature on elections and economic outcomes. The next three sections outline the book's theoretical contributions, explaining when and why politicians might surprisingly adhere to economic orthodoxy during election periods. I argue that countries' debt structures and economic histories are key determinants of their policy choices. I frame the analytical structure according to two key decision-making dimensions: a government's financial means and political motivations. When foreign debt is comprised mostly of global bond issues rather than international bank loans, highly indebted governments often do not have the financial means to engineer an electoral boom. At the same time, when countries are plagued by past inflationary shocks, politicians often lack the motivation to create a political business cycle. Rather, a technocratic consensus for macroeconomic discipline and a perceived widening of the low-inflation constituency compels them toward good governance. Finally, I incorporate these mechanisms into a series of hypotheses about elections and economic outcomes. They are evaluated empirically in Chapters 3 to 7. Latin America is an ideal setting for testing these claims given the region's high external indebtedness and inflation volatility during the most recent wave of globalization.

2.1. THE INFLATION-UNEMPLOYMENT TRADE-OFF

Let us begin by reflecting on the political decisions that are central to economic policy making. Most macroeconomic models assume that economic choices reflect politicians' relative sensitivity to unemployment and inflation (Appendix 2.A).[9] In fact, two major strains of intellectual thought have dominated the field of the politics of macroeconomic policy making: Keynesianism and Monetarism. The debate between these two schools centers on the inflation

---

[9] Please see the Appendix as well as Barro and Gordon (1983) and Scheve (2004) for a more detailed description of the theoretical models of macroeconomic policy making.

and unemployment trade-off, popularly known as the Phillips curve trade-off.[10] Both Keynesianism and Monetarism assume that politicians care about inflation and unemployment, but they offer competing accounts of the effectiveness of government intervention.[11]

Keynesianism is more optimistic about policy maker's ability to exploit the Phillips Curve trade-off, using economic policy to permanently create new jobs and growth. When facing an economic slump, Keynesianism holds that the government can use expansionary monetary and fiscal policies to offset the adverse effects of the economic downturn. Creating new capacity and adding new jobs eventually spurs inflation, but only at very low levels of unemployment. Wages and prices are sticky. Workers may ask for higher pay, but these appeals typically occur when there is a booming economy and high demand for labor.[12] During the 2008–2009 global financial crisis, both the Bush and Obama administrations subscribed to a Keynesian view of the economy despite their partisan differences. Indeed, both administrations hoped that low interest rates and high government spending would cushion the economic shock.

By contrast, monetarism contends that inflation is a harmful by-product of expansionary economic policy. In response to economic stimulus, people adjust their inflation expectations higher. Workers demand better wages and firms raise prices. Inflation accelerates, undercutting any initial gains from the stimulus. Indeed, monetarists claim there is a natural rate of unemployment, beyond which any attempts to spur economic activity only yield further inflation.[13] Championed by Milton Friedman, monetarism was first in vogue in the 1960s and 1970s. It offered an explanation for the 1970's puzzling rise of both inflation and unemployment. According to monetarism, the 1973 and 1979 oil shocks not only delivered a serious blow to economic growth, but also jolted inflation expectations considerably higher.[14] Lofty price expectations intensified the original shocks and dampened the benefits of expansionary policy. Hence, monetarists claimed the Phillips Curve was vertical in the long run, rendering the effects of government stimulus ineffective outside of fueling further inflation (Figure 2.1).

Political Business Cycles: Developed versus Developing Countries. Building on these intellectual foundations, scholars have anticipated observing two major types of economic cycles around election periods: *opportunistic*

---

[10] The Phillips curve is named after the British economist A. W. Phillips, who in 1958 observed a negative relationship between inflation and unemployment rates.

[11] The neoclassical synthesis in contemporary macroeconomics has sought to bridge the gap between Keynesian and monetarist schools of thought, advocating for economic governance to be principally conducted through an independent central bank that uses monetary policy to control inflation.

[12] Samuelson and Nordhaus 1995.

[13] Friedman 1968, 1970.

[14] Revisiting the traditional Phillips curve trade-off, Milton Friedman and Edmund Phelps constructed a steeper Phillips Curve that accounted for the growth-diminishing effect of inflation expectations.

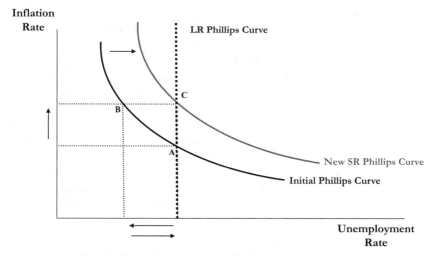

FIGURE 2.1. The Phillips Curve Trade-Off. The figure shows the tensions between Keynesian and Monetarist views. Keynesians suggest that policymakers can readily trade off unemployment and inflation. Monetarist, however, claim that this trade-off is only short-term. Moving from point A to point B, policymakers can reduce the unemployment rate below its natural level with expansionary policy, but only temporarily. Expansionary policies breed higher inflation expectations, shifting the Phillips curve rightward. Moving from point B to point C, the unemployment rate returns to its natural equilibrium, but inflation is permanently higher.

and *rational political business cycles*. The opportunistic view of economic cycles is rooted in a Keynesian view of the world but differs in its policy prescriptions. While strict Keynesians proscribe expansive macroeconomic policies in response to a demand shock, elections serve as the catalyst for political business cycles. Politicians, seeking reelection, deliver an economic boost to win votes notwithstanding the extent of the economy's spare capacity (or size of the output gap).[15] They ambitiously slash interest rates and ramp up spending to create jobs and growth. However, the political choice to exploit the Phillips Curve leads to an electoral boom and bust. The aggressive expansion before elections overheats the economy instead fueling inflation, and ultimately, an economic correction following elections.

By contrast, the "rational" school of thought is rooted in a monetarist view of the world. Politicians attempt to demonstrate their competence by boosting growth and lowering unemployment, but their efforts are only fruitful in a world of incomplete information. When voters are savvy, they are wise to politicians' incentives to inflate the economy. Voters adjust their inflation expectations higher, diminishing the effect of expansionary policy. Political tinkering yields few economic gains for society, but leaves an inflationary nuisance.

---

[15] The output gap is measured as the difference between actual GDP and potential GDP.

When do politicians stimulate the economy and when do they opt not to intervene? Political business cycle theory predicts a schism between developed and developing countries. According to political business cycle theory, reelection-minded politicians should be most likely to prime the economic pump in newly democratized regions, like Latin America, where information is less transparent and presidential power is relatively unchecked. Without independent central banks, strong legislatures, or free media, the political economy literature expects that chief executives engineer an economic bonanza notwithstanding its inflationary cost.[16] Faced with widespread inequality and poverty, developing country politicians rapidly expand the economy, hoping to provide jobs and boost wages. By contrast, in developed countries, scholars have found that politicians often avoid creating political business cycles because they fear that a sophisticated, fiscally conservative electorate will punish them at the polls.[17]

2.2. POLITICAL AUSTERITY THEORY

Do developing country politicians also sometimes choose not to intervene in the economy? If so, what is the trigger for their orthodox economic behavior given that fiscal conservative voters are presumably less likely to be found in countries hampered by poverty and income inequality? Are politicians monetarists who are skeptical of the benefits of stimulus?[18] Or, are they repressed Keynesians? Are they optimistic about the government's ability to create jobs and growth before elections, but nonetheless choose neutrality?

In the following pages, I advance a new theory that explains this variation in elite approaches to economic policy making. Building on the political models of macroeconomic policy making previously outlined, this theory seeks to account for political choices about the unemployment-inflation trade-off.[19] The conventional choice of using economic stimulus to create growth and jobs has its obvious electoral benefits. But, what explains the counterintuitive choice of not tinkering with the economy? Why might politicians come to favor inflation control, even at the cost of creating more jobs and growth?

2.2.1. Financial Means

Political austerity theory argues that politicians approach this economic trade-off based on two critical policy making dimensions: financial means and political motivations. Financial means reflect the policy capacity to deliver an

---

[16] See footnote 1.

[17] See Rogoff and Sibert 1988; Rogoff 1990; Brender and Drazen 2005, 2008.

[18] Monetarists would have claimed that Latin American politicians were confronted with a steeper Phillips Curve in the 1990s. Compared to earlier decades, any government attempts to spur growth and jobs would have instantaneously sparked inflation because of higher inflation expectations stemming from past price shocks.

[19] Political austerity theory only makes a claim about the weights politicians assign to their loss functions for inflation and unemployment; it does not make any predictions regarding the actual shape of the Phillips curve.

economic boost. There are two major ways that governments stimulate the economy. They spend more than they tax from one year to the next, widening a budget deficit that fuels economic growth. Alternatively, the central bank uses open market operations to expand the money supply. It buys government bonds, adding funds to the banking system and spurring lower interest rates. Low rates then boost consumption and investment.

Why might countries not possess such financial means? It is often difficult, for developing countries to use expansionary economic policies. Such policy actions often depend on government's fiscal space,[20] or the availability of budgetary resources to finance budget shortfalls. Unlike most developed countries, narrow tax bases and shallow domestic financial markets leave many developing countries with few funding options domestically.[21] Governments can alleviate such fiscal constraints, however, by borrowing funds externally or compelling the central bank to fund deficits by printing money. When governments use foreign financing to cover their budgetary expenditures, they typically tap one of two sources: bond issuance or bank loans.

For those countries that choose to finance their funding shortfalls in global financial markets, politicians are often at the mercy of investors who are preoccupied with debt repayment.[22] In order to increase the likelihood of repayment, investors demand sound fiscal and monetary policies. With a low tolerance for uncertainty, they often look unfavorable upon large, politically motivated fiscal deficits that might disrupt debt repayment flows. Such policies threaten to spark capital withdrawal and spike funding rates. Therefore, debt-ridden developing country governments frequently do not possess the policy flexibility to create an aggressive electoral expansion. By contrast, when foreign debt is comprised mostly of international bank loans, politicians have more scope for economic stimulus.

Why is international bond financing more constraining than bank lending? Certainly, it is reasonable to conclude that bankers also prefer sound macroeconomic governance. The first part of the theoretical framework, presented later in this chapter, offers an explanation. With orders of magnitude more debt holders in the case of bond markets than international banking, market debt creates a more credible threat of capital withdrawal. This exit threat enhances the power of creditors over debtors, allowing them to impose their austerity demands.

2.2.2. Political Motivations

Political motivations refer to the political incentive to use macroeconomic powers for electoral gain. According to the traditional political business cycle logic,

---

[20] Fiscal space can be defined as the availability of budget room that allows governments to provide resources for a desired purpose without any prejudice to the sustainability of a government's financial position (IMF, 2005).

[21] Gavin and Perotti 1997.

[22] Keohane and Milner 1996; Mosley 2000; Mosley 2003; Wibbels 2006.

election-minded politicians should exploit the Phillips Curve to deliver jobs and growth to their constituents notwithstanding any longer-term costs (such as fiscal deficits, inflation, or recession).[23]

When might governments stray from these traditional political goals? In countries where severe inflationary shocks have scarred the electorate, I argue that politicians often invoke a different electoral calculus. Building on the psychology literature on decision making, the second part of the theoretical framework claims that politicians (and their technocratic communities) often base their economic choices on their own transformative historical experiences. For instance, German political elites today conduct economic policy with a price stability bias even years after the Weimer Republic's extraordinary trillion-fold inflation. Current German Chancellor Angela Merkel, for instance, recently stressed that "protecting people from inflation: that's what really matters."[24] In fact, Germany's strident opposition to looser monetary conditions during the euro crisis partly reflects the country's deep-seated inflation fears.

Like pre-World War II Germany, many crisis-plagued developing countries have suffered from chronic deficits and stubbornly high inflation that eroded living standards. In the worst cases, these severe price shocks dismantled economic and political systems. With the dangers of lofty economic expansions chiseled into their political minds, political and technocratic elites develop a consensus for sound macroeconomic governance. Notwithstanding ideological differences, they place a high weight on inflation control. They may hold a Keynesian view of the economy – maintaining their faith in the government's ability to spur economic activity – but now fear voter retribution for highly accommodative policies that risk inflation. Alternatively, they may subscribe to a monetarist view of the economy, believing that government stimulus in inflation-prone countries will have little economic effect beyond sparking more inflation. Either way, inflationary crises make political and technocratic elites less tolerant of non-orthodox stimulus.

Finally, beyond learning from history personally, politicians also fear that voters have learned from these past shocks. Deeming that a broader constituency favors low inflation – reaching well beyond the private sector – politicians from across the political spectrum gravitate toward the center on macroeconomic issues.

2.2.3. Electoral Economic Strategies: The Spendthrift or the Miser?

Political austerity theory employs these two policy making dimensions to make predictions about elections and economic outcomes in developing countries (Table 2.1). Conditional on these means and motivations, I expect a country's major macroeconomic indicators to vary both intertemporally and cross-nationally. When governments possess both the policy capacity to deliver an

---

[23] Inflation is most likely when there is a small output gap, or little spare capacity, in the economy.
[24] *La Stampa*, July 11, 2007.

TABLE 2.1. *Macroecomonic Policy Expectations: The Spendthrift or the Miser?*

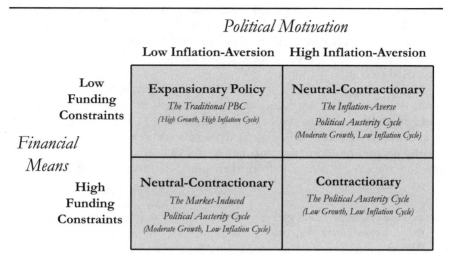

Political Motivation

		Low Inflation-Aversion	High Inflation-Aversion
Financial Means	**Low Funding Constraints**	**Expansionary Policy** *The Traditional PBC* *(High Growth, High Inflation Cycle)*	**Neutral-Contractionary** *The Inflation-Averse* *Political Austerity Cycle* *(Moderate Growth, Low Inflation Cycle)*
	High Funding Constraints	**Neutral-Contractionary** *The Market-Induced* *Political Austerity Cycle* *(Moderate Growth, Low Inflation Cycle)*	**Contractionary** *The Political Austerity Cycle* *(Low Growth, Low Inflation Cycle)*

economic boost and the political incentive to use macroeconomic policy for electoral gains, they are likely to create a political business cycle. Otherwise, we should expect to observe one of three different types of political austerity cycles.

Planning a Politically Timed Boom. In assessing these means and motivations, let us first consider the sequencing of the political business cycle. Recall that the political business cycle logic expects that political strategies for the economy are often crafted several years before the election. Why? Economists have widely documented that the lag between policy decisions and economic outcomes may last as long as nine to eighteen months.[25] Tax cuts and spending initiatives are subject to administrative and bureaucratic delays, whereas interest rate cuts take time to feed through different channels of the economy. Investment decisions, price setting, and wage contracts are typically fairly sticky.

Therefore, chief executives have strong political motivation to lay the foundations of their economic plans several years before elections. For example, evidence from the Nixon tapes – available from the National Archives – shows that during the first year of his presidential term, Richard M. Nixon had already pressured the Federal Reserve to fire up the printing presses and expand the money supply in October 1969. Shortly after the nomination of Federal

---

[25] Long and variable lags associated with macroeconomic policy are well documented by both economists and political scientists. A lag arises when monetary policy does not immediately affect income, employment, and prices (Friedman 1970; see also Bernhard, Broz, and Clark 2002). On average, economists have found that monetary policy changes affect national income with a six- to nine-month lag and prices with a twelve- to eighteen-month lag (Friedman 1970).

Reserve Board Chairman Arthur Burns, Nixon brazenly referred to "the myth of the autonomous Fed," telling his Federal Reserve Chairman, "I'm counting on you Arthur to keep us out of recession."[26] In line with Nixon's expectations, Chairman Burns lowered the key monetary policy target at the time – the discount rate – by 1.5 percentage points in the two years before the 1972 presidential reelection campaign.

Similarly, in my interview with Venezuelan Presidential Secretary Carmelo Lauría, the key advisor to President Jaime Lusinchi boasts that they drafted the blueprint for a political business cycle from day 1. They would carry out a much-needed fiscal retrenchment during their early years, in hopes of surfing an economic upturn in the two years before the 1988 elections.[27] Notably, they ultimately used fresh proceeds from their bank creditors to craft a textbook political business cycle.[28]

Market Indebtedness Roils Political Plans. Even the best laid political plans are dependent on a government's financial means, or its fiscal space to fund new electoral spending. In debt-burdened countries, the structure of creditor-debtor relations often influences the government's capacity to stimulate the economy. A classic electoral engineering of the economy á la Nixon and Lusinchi is most likely when global bond markets account for a relatively low share of government's external debt financing. Tapping alternative external financing resources, including bank lending and bilateral/multilateral aid, allows governments to avoid subjecting their policy decisions to bond market scrutiny. Moreover, governments also become less vulnerable to credit disruptions when they have access to considerable revenues from non-market sources, such as commodity income and central bank credit.

In other words, if we presume that presidents are motivated by the classic electoral calculus – providing growth and jobs to voters – and are unhindered by financial market conditionality, they are most likely to be spendthrifts. The combination of low-funding constraints and low-inflation aversion should yield a tried-and-true political strategy for winning votes: the *traditional political business cycle* (upper left quadrant of Table 2.1).

Otherwise, we should observe one of several types of political austerity cycles, characterized by low inflation and low-to-moderate growth. In the first

---

[26] For further information about Nixon's political influence over Burns, see Tufte (1978), Abrams (2006), and the Nixon Tapes at the National Archives and Records Administration, College Park, Maryland.

[27] Author's interview with Carmelo Lauría, Caracas, Venezuela, March 5, 2007. Carmelo Lauría was the presidential secretary for Jaime Lusinchi (AD) from 1984 to 1988. He later served as Carlos Andrés Perez's Interior Minister following the 1992 coup. An AD party stalwart, Lauría also previously worked as Planning Minister in Perez's first cabinet.

[28] In the prelude to elections, Venezuela's fiscal accounts swung from a 4 percent of GDP budget surplus during 1985–1986 to a 7 percent budget deficit during 1987–1988.

kind of political austerity cycle, politicians maintain the impulse to prime the economic pump. However, when the structure of sovereign debt is comprised mostly of global bond issues rather than international bank lending, market indebtedness acts as an important constraint on political behavior. Although access to international bond markets initially expands economic possibilities, a heavy reliance on bond markets often creates serious vulnerabilities. Major credit disruptions can quickly raise the financial cost of expansionary policies and suddenly foil the best laid political plans in the years, or even months, before new elections. Moreover, elections themselves are often an important source of market unrest; capital flight triggered by political uncertainty can further complicate efforts to fund election-year deficits with global finance.

Fearing capital exit, stimulus-minded politicians strike a macroeconomic compromise, often pursuing neutral (or even contractionary) economic policies that result in a *market-induced austerity cycle*. Indeed, politicians foster a low-inflation environment in hopes of assuaging investor concerns about politically induced debt disruptions, but continue to target moderate levels of growth and job creation (lower left quadrant of Table 2.1). Depending on the severity of the credit shock, however, achieving these growth targets may prove to be quite difficult.

Signaling Macroeconomic Competence. Conversely, chief executives in developing countries may have a different set of political motivations. Rather than preemptively planning an economic boom in the years preceding a national election, they instead opt for a neutral mix of economic policies that yield an *inflation-averse austerity cycle* (upper right quadrant of Table 2.1). These policies are designed to tame the inflationary beast, yet still provide for moderate growth and job creation. Similar to the political business cycle, these economic plans are typically drafted years before an election in light of the lag between economic policy choices and outcomes.

For instance, in the prelude to Chile's 1999 elections, President Eduardo Frei told his budget director, Joaquín Vial, that he was not willing to have "one iota of additional inflation." During budget talks in the summer of 1998, nearly a year-and-a-half before presidential elections, Frei told Vial that he wanted a balanced budget. In Vial's words, politicians like Frei who "had the memories of runaway inflations and massive budget deficits, they know they cannot fool around with economics. They were not willing to take risks with inflation."[29]

In line with this view, I argue that politicians, who arrive in office after devastating inflationary crises, swapped electorally timed fiscal and monetary expansions for balanced budgets and inflation-targeting. Politicians concluded that price stabilization policies could be more effective at signaling their competence in managing the economy than vigorous growth strategies.

---

[29] Author's interview with Joaquín Vial, April 23, 2007.

The extent of the political austerity cycle, however, is conditional on a government's financial means. When governments have ample external financing resources (such as bank lending and multilateral/bilateral aid) or windfall domestic revenues (from commodity income and privatization proceeds) that are independent from global financial markets, they are less vulnerable to market downturns and credit crunches. They can deliver price stability without risking severe deflation. However, when inflation-averse governments possess heavy debt market burdens, an initial effort to control inflation can quickly become a serious drag on the economy. Unexpected credit shocks can catapult interest rates higher, raising the cost of capital for governments and firms. Economic growth often slows considerably more during election years than politicians had initially planned, producing the most severe form of austerity politics (lower right quadrant of Table 2.1). Miserly politicians relentlessly pursue low inflation; first aimed at placating a perceived inflation-sensitive electorate and then their flighty global creditors.

In the following section, I first outline the causal logic of political austerity theory, showing when I expect economics to constrain political choices in developing countries. I then examine when domestic political decisions instead shape economic outcomes. For both of these relationships, I outline how shifts in financial means and political motivations alter not only political behavior generally, but also election-year politics, yielding a political austerity cycle rather than a political business cycle.

2.3. IT'S A WONDERFUL MARKET: THE POLITICS OF BOND FINANCE

In the holiday classic, *It's a Wonderful Life,* Peter Bailey, the manager of *Bailey Building & Loan,* takes a long-term view of his borrowers. When Peter extends a loan to the taxi driver Ernie Bishop to build a house, he does not anticipate an immediate return. Rather, he expects to receive principal and interest payments over the course of many years as Ernie Bishop steadily expands his income. Indeed, *Bailey Building & Loan's* profitability depends on the livelihood of Bishop and other small businessmen and citizens of Bedford Falls.

The same logic holds for international banks that invest in a country's economic growth and development: loan portfolios are built for the long-term horizon. Reminiscent of Peter Bailey, international commercial banks have a vested interest in debtors' economic viability. During hard economic times, this shared financial fate encourages new bank lending. Hoping to forestall a severe profitability shock and protect their future business, bankers extend new funds to beleaguered borrowers. However, the perpetual promise of new funds dampens belt-tightening incentives, creating a moral hazard problem.[30]

---

[30] See footnote 34 in Chapter 1.

Rather than cutting back on household spending, for example, Ernie Bishop might funnel funds to more pressing needs, such as a new taxicab battery or a visit to the family doctor. Similarly, armed with fresh bank loans, sovereign borrowers may choose to spend on politically popular education and health care benefits instead of debt repayment.

When banks become heavily saddled with these bad loans, they too might teeter on the brink of insolvency. Not surprisingly, they eventually search for an exit strategy from this difficult-to-dissolve lending relationship. The cantankerous but thrifty majority shareholder, Mr. Henry F. Potter, for instance, wanted to dissolve the foundering *Bailey Building & Loan* and liquidate its assets.

In the wake of the 1980s' debt crisis, the structure of global finance experienced a transformation worthy of an alternative ending to the holiday classic, where a disenchanted George Bailey opts to follow the path of Potter rather than his father Peter. Initially, heavily exposed commercial banks engaged in Peter Bailey-style lending, offering billions of dollars in fresh funds to debt-ridden developing countries notwithstanding their credit difficulties. By the end of the 1980s, however, many senior global bank executives echoed Henry F. Potter's miserly worldview. Swimming in a wreckage of outstanding developing country debt obligations, they hoped to cut their financial losses before drowning in a sea of red. For example, Jack Clark, Citibank's senior officer for developing country debt, lamented about debtor government's tendencies to ignore conditionality embedded in the loan agreements:

We provided capital for ten years, and they didn't even have to think about turning to their domestic resources to get the very best of them . . . they've really got to think seriously about how to bring in foreign investment, attract capital, and mobilize effectively the resources they have; and they aren't doing it![31]

Following a decade of earnings losses on their Latin American portfolios, the U.S. government and global banking institutions finally advocated a market solution to the debt problem under the banner of the Brady bond restructurings: replacing defaulted bank loans with short-term bond issuance (Figure 2.2). What was the effect of this shift in the method of government financing? International capital, behaving more like Potters than Baileys, demanded an immediate return on its capital. As a result, the global bond market became the enforcement mechanism for the conditionality that was regularly breached under the bank lending system. In Chapter 5, I extend this discussion about the historical importance of the transformation of Latin American debt. In the next section, I advance a new theoretical framework that explains how this structural shift in government debt composition diluted political control of the economy in developing countries.

---

[31] Frieden 1987.

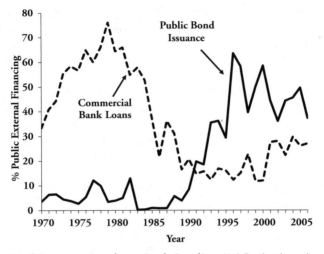

FIGURE 2.2. Bond Issuance Supplants Bank Lending (16 Latin American Countries, Aggregate).
Source: Global Development Finance

2.3.1. Structure of Lending and Creditor-Debtor Relations

International creditors of all shapes and sizes have fairly similar preferences. They want borrowers to repay their debts; therefore, they endorse restrictive economic policies that ensure steady remuneration. If this is the case, why are bondholders more successful than bankers at imposing their austerity demands? Employing a counterintuitive collective action logic, I argue that bondholders operate in a strategic environment that yields a stronger disciplining effect on borrowers.

Informed by Mancur Olson's seminal group theory, we know that members in a small group often prefer to pay for some portion of a collective good than survive without it.[32] In the world of finance, we can think of a country's solvency as a collective good for creditors. When a government's balance sheet is in good health, steady debt repayments benefit all creditors, no matter their size or stake in a borrower's financial affairs. That said, when a borrower encounters financial difficulties, only those creditors with the largest financial stake in the borrower's solvency are likely to commit new funds. Which creditors are most likely to provide this financial backstop? Bondholders, with dispersed ownership and small stakes in the debtor's financial future, are most likely to cut their financial ties. By contrast, I argue that centralized bankers are more apt to overcome their coordination problem and extend new funds to the sovereign borrower. Ironically, however, overcoming the collective action problem leaves bankers with less leverage over debtor government policies than bond markets.

---

[32] Olson 1965.

Centralized Creditors and Sovereign Borrowers. What explains this surprising trend? Commercial bank lending is characterized by a small and centralized pool of creditors. As members of a small group, their size offers them a collective action advantage. They can use this advantage coercively, starving borrowers from future lending until they are repaid. Alternatively, creditors can help borrowers evade default by offering new financing, a phenomenon known as "defensive lending."

Why would creditors extend new fund injections, rather than cut financing completely? Why is borrower solvency a collective good? There is a timeless adage that epitomizes the banker's dilemma.

The old saying holds. Owe your banker one thousand pounds and you are at his mercy; owe him 1 million pounds and the position is reversed.

– John Maynard Keynes

Aiming to recover their money over the long term, creditors often act counterintuitively in the short term. Small creditor groups typically have highly concentrated exposures to their debtors. As a result, the return of their money is directly linked to debtors' financial health. If they were to cut financing fully, it would only accelerate debtors' road to default and eliminate any hope of recovering their investment. By keeping borrowers afloat, creditors are safeguarding their own balance sheets from a severe profitability shock. Therefore, creditors not only lend defensively, but they also often absorb substantial costs along the way, including rescheduling old debts.

Why not take a free ride? Why not refuse to extend new loans to beleaguered borrowers, but enjoy the benefits of other banks' efforts to stave off sovereign bankruptcies? The cost of widespread defection is too high. If all lenders cut their credit lines, they would risk a massive default, a fatal blow to their balance sheets, and a mutually assured destruction to the entire banking consortium.

In the world of global finance, there are numerous examples of small creditor groups injecting new money into their debtors. A small commercial bank cadre with high loan exposure to development country governments renewed their lending throughout the 1980s debt crisis. Similarly, local banks were reluctant to unwind their exposure to Japanese *kereitsu* and Korean *chaebols* during the 1997–98 East Asian crisis, and the U.S. government repeatedly sunk cash into salvaging General Motors in the wake of the 2008 global financial crisis.

In exchange for new funding, creditors often require that borrowers curtail their balance sheet growth to improve their chances of debt repayment. Despite calls for conditionality, however, small creditor groups often suffer from a moral hazard problem. Their large stake in borrowers' solvency – along with the promise of new funds – undermines their capital exit threat and ultimately borrowers' compliance (Figure 2.3).

For example, during the heyday of global bank lending to developing countries in the 1970s and 1980s, bank steering committees were organized to

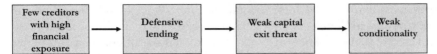

FIGURE 2.3. Creditor Relations under Centralized Commercial Bank Lending.

negotiate with borrowers. In addition to four to five major banks, bank steering committees typically included the International Monetary Fund (IMF), which often offered temporary financial assistance. In return for new loans, countries were expected to follow certain conditions and sacrifice some policy sovereignty. IMF conditionality required a commitment to laissez-faire economic policies – including fiscal austerity and tight monetary policy – that increased the likelihood of debt repayment.[33]

Notwithstanding these calls for economic adjustment, government borrowers frequently missed their conditionality targets and waived out of banker and IMF-supported programs.[34] Ironically, IMF agreements alone were not a sufficient condition to ensure conservative, market-friendly behavior. The high creditor concentration characteristic of global bank lending allowed governments to retain control over their economic decisions.

Decentralized Creditors and Sovereign Borrowers. By contrast, political austerity theory argues that bond markets are plagued by collective action failures, which I claim allows bondholders to more bluntly impose their austerity demands on sovereign governments. Typically, collective action failures should impede societal groups from pressuring governments. Ironically, in this case, the coordination problem increases creditors' influence over debtor governments. Why?

In a world of decentralized finance, collective action failures are quite common because of the ownership dispersion that is characteristic of bond markets. Investors are numerous, anonymous, and scattered internationally. When credit is channeled across such a large pool of financiers, creditors not only reduce their exposure to borrowers, but also their stake in their financial futures. They hold too paltry a share of governments debt exposure to warrant incurring the costs of securing the collective good of borrower solvency. Creditors do not want to provide new funds, or participate in costly, lengthy restructuring negotiations. These predictions are in line with collective action theory,

---

[33] Vreeland 2003.
[34] Haggard (1985) finds extremely low rates of compliance with the IMF's Extended Fund Facility (EFF) from 1974–1984. Of the thirty cases studied, sixteen were cancelled and eight more were never implemented. Compliance with fiscal targets was especially poor. In a study of IMF conditionality programs, Edwards (1989) finds that conditions on the government's deficit were met in only 30 and 19 percent of programs in 1983 and 1984.

which claims that large, heterogeneous groups often experience coordination failures.[35]

Unlike centralized bankers who must lend defensively to avoid a devastating blow to their balance sheets, bondholders can cut their financial ties to borrowers without incurring a severe profitability shock. Rather, they can sell their bonds for marginal losses in secondary markets.

What might prompt bondholders to sell their assets? Wary bondholders want assurances about governments' credit standing; they hope politicians adhere to conditionality pledges of fiscal discipline and low inflation that raise the likelihood of debt repayment. According to Mosley's (2000) mutual fund manager survey, for example, investors rate a stable inflation environment, budget discipline, and debt service capacity as having the greatest effect on their asset allocation.[36]

When governments veer from economic discipline, these actions can create stiff political repercussions for governments known as "sudden stops." When borrowing from decentralized debt markets, governments that rely on bond markets for their funding needs are susceptible to severe reversals of international capital inflows.

According to the economics literature on sudden stops, such capital reversals are often most severe for highly indebted emerging market borrowers.[37] As witnessed by the financial crises in Mexico (1994–1995), Russia (1998), East Asia (1998–1999), and Argentina (2001–2002), investors can literally halt financial flows overnight by dumping their bonds.

How do these capital reversals translate to tighter macroeconomic constraints? The depressed demand for government bonds creates a higher sovereign risk premium in secondary bond markets that reflect investors' expectations about higher deficits and inflation.[38] Not only do higher interest rates pose a direct threat to government spending possibilities through larger interest payments, but also to the real economy by dampening consumption and investment.[39] They also risk inciting a vicious cycle of financial outflows, budget shortfalls, and credit downgrades.

Without access to global capital markets, policy makers cannot spend to offset the downturn. Unlike developed countries that have the capacity to stimulate their economies to protect jobs, even when faced with large-scale capital flight, cash-starved developing countries rarely have the same flexibility.[40] With

---

[35] Group members, with low personal stakes in the collective good, often prefer to survive without the collective good than pay their share (Olson 1965).

[36] Mosley 2003.

[37] Calvo 1998; Calvo and Reinhart 2000; Calvo, Izquierdo, and Talvi 2003; Kaminsky, Reinhart, and Vegh 2004.

[38] Mosley 2003; Reinhart et al. 2003; Ahlquist 2006.

[39] See footnote 37.

[40] Gavin and Perotti 1996; Calvo 1998; Obstfeld 1998; Calvo and Reinhart 2000; Mosley 2003; Kaminsky, Reinhart, and Vegh 2004; Obstfeld and Taylor 2005; Wibbels 2006; Edwards 2007.

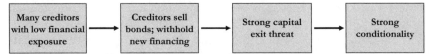

FIGURE 2.4. Creditor Relations under Decentralized Bond Financing.

few alternative domestic funding sources, they are deeply dependent on global financial markets, leaving them at investors' mercy.

In light of these severe costs, decentralized bond markets often act as an enforcement mechanism for conditionality agreements (Figure 2.4). Perhaps, the former Governor of the Central Bank of Argentina, Javier González-Fraga, put it most succinctly jesting that "markets can give you cancer and cost you your life."[41] Hoping to reduce their risk of illness, debt-dependent governments often create a low inflation "market-friendly" environment, even when it detracts from their domestic political agendas.

What Triggers the Market Disciplining Mechanism? When does conditionality gain its teeth? Does issuing an international bond immediately subject governments to these financial pressures? With bond market membership, do countries simply become hostages to the market, living and dying with booms and bust in global liquidity? Alternatively, under what conditions might markets give governments more latitude?

I argue that the market disciplining mechanism does not work instantaneously. Rather, it is a consequence of developing a high dependence on global bond markets for government financing. At low levels of financial market dependence, debt-fueled booms often occur. For example, many countries throughout Latin America initially tapped international markets to finance more government spending in the wake of the 1980s' debt crisis. Beyond Latin America's borders, Greece borrowed for years from global bond markets – boosted by its 2001 euro membership – before eventually encountering funding difficulties.

By comparison, countries are headed for trouble when they become too indebted to global financial markets. Notwithstanding ebbs and flows in global credit, countries are judged by bond investors based on their ability to make debt payments. As bonds account for a greater share of a government's financing needs, the global investment community centers its microscope on government decisions, fretting that rising debt burdens might complicate timely repayments. Countries become more vulnerable to credit shocks, whether they are instigated by external factors (such as global credit downturns) or internal factors (such as domestic economic difficulties).

Conversely, countries that have a low exposure to global bond markets are less vulnerable to changes in global liquidity. They represent a relatively safe

[41] Author's interview with Javier González-Fraga, Buenos Aires, August 16, 2006.

destination for dedicated emerging market bond portfolios that have to invest their resources in sovereign assets. For example, Chile – a country with little exposure to global capital markets – issued US$2.4 billion of new global bonds between 2001 and 2002 despite tight global credit conditions following the September 11 terrorist attacks and neighboring Argentina's debt crisis.[42]

The Strength of Market Conditionality. Does the market mechanism ever fail to enforce conditionality? For instance, what if a group of bondholders account for a considerable amount of a sovereign borrower's outstanding debt? Like bankers, do they act in the interest of the borrower? Might they forgive some debt in hopes of recovering part of their larger investment?

Let us consider Argentina's 2001 debt default, the most acute form of capital exit. The dispersed ownership structure left bond investors with little stake in Argentina's solvency. Their refusal to extend new credit impeded the country from financing not only its outstanding debt payments but also its expenditures. The government's funding difficulties were the catalyst for its austere response to the 2001 crisis and eventually the government's default.

In the aftermath of Argentina's default, a group of creditors representing 24 percent of the original bondholders refused to agree to the terms of Argentina's 2005 debt exchange. Given that these creditors held US$20 billion, or nearly a quarter of Argentina's defaulted debt, why did these "holdouts" opt for litigation? If political austerity theory is correct, shouldn't they lend defensively? Why did they instead obtain court orders banning Argentina from raising funds in international markets?

Notwithstanding the involvement of some peak bondholder associations, I contend that the dispersion of ownership of these "holdouts" across countries and industries was too vast to muster an effective collective action campaign. They spanned the globe in all shapes and sizes, from hundreds of thousands of Japanese, Italian, and German retail bond investors to dozens of foreign corporates and further smatterings of global mutual fund managers, investment banks, and hedge funds. With nearly 100 different lawsuits across both sovereign and international jurisdictions (including the World Bank), litigation strategies differed from improving the terms of the bond exchange to a full recovery of assets.[43] Unlike cross-border bank lending, the financial stake of any individual bondholder's debt was too low to warrant acting in the interest of the sovereign borrower.[44]

---

[42] World Bank's Global Development Finance (GDF) Database.

[43] For further details, see the IMF 2005 Argentina Article IV Consultation and the Congressional Research Service's 2010 report, titled "Argentina's Defaulted Sovereign Debt: Dealing with the Holdouts."

[44] Notably, in order to address this collective action problem with minority holdouts, the new bonds issued during Argentina's 2005 debt exchange include collective action clauses (CAC) that allow a super-majority of holders to overrule holdouts and alter the financial terms of the contract in any future restructuring.

Therefore, creditor defection in the Argentine 2001 case is straightforwardly in line with my theoretical expectations. Ownership dispersion created a coordination problem that left Argentina authorities without international financing, and thus without any options beyond austerity. Alfonso Prat-Gay, Argentina's Central Bank Governor in the wake of the 2001–2002 crisis, recounts this quandary highlighting that "there was no room to maneuver on the fiscal side; the only option was a tighter fiscal stance... There was little fire power!"[45]

In response to these constraints, the Néstor and Cristina Kirchner governments covered their budgetary shortfalls with Venezuelan bilateral financing, the development of local bond markets, and new commodity proceeds.[46] More recently, however, when strapped for cash, Cristina Kirchner reopened global creditor talks in 2010 and reached a settlement with two-thirds of the initial "holdouts." Nevertheless, without any collective-action clauses that force full creditor participation, the remaining "holdouts" threaten to disrupt the government's eventual return to international capital markets.[47] With external funding in short supply, Cristina Kirchner has labeled the creditor ban on government financing as "the most severe restriction on the Argentine economy in recent decades."[48]

In summary, the nature of bond markets is different from bank lending. Both types of creditors hope to recover their investments. However, a long-term view is built into a bank loan portfolio, whether its composition is international or domestic. For example, when a local bank extends a loan financing the expansion of a grocery store, it awaits repayment over the course of years as the store expands its business and revenues. In the short term, it is difficult to recall the loan. Until the store is profitable, the owner is unlikely to have sufficient funds to repay both the principal and interest. Indeed, the financial interests of lenders and borrowers are intertwined.

The same logic holds for international banks that invest in a country's economic growth and development; it's a long-term horizon that allows debtors to have flexibility. By contrast, when credit is channeled through bonds rather than banks, short-term claims are inherently dispersed across a pool of global creditors that can immediately withdraw their financial commitment to borrowers. This capital exit threat narrows the policy space that debtors have to veer from "investor-friendly" balanced budgets and low inflation policies.

---

[45] Author's interview with Alfonso Prat-Gay, Buenos Aires, May 24, 2007. Prat-Gay was central bank governor for both Presidents Duhalde and Kirchner from 2002–2004.

[46] Argentina sold bonds worth US$7.6 billion bilaterally to Venezuela, and US$8.5 billion in the local currency market.

[47] These remaining creditor "holdouts" amount to 8 percent of the original bondholders, and hence, are not subject to the new 2005 collective action clauses that legally bind minority creditors to negotiated restructurings.

[48] *BBC News*, June 24, 2010.

2.3.2. Elections and Decentralized Finance

Decentralized global finance may generally be restraining, but why would politicians choose austerity during elections? Why not instead stimulate the economy before elections and deal with the market fallout later? In this section, I develop the theory's predictions about sovereign debt and elections. I claim that electoral uncertainty intensifies the disciplining effect of decentralized bond markets, making political austerity cycles more likely than political business cycles. Why? Politicians, who fund their debt in a decentralized system, must operate in a world laden with short-term incentives and high uncertainty.

Ironically, short-term political agendas are displaced by bondholder's own myopia. Portfolio bond investors do not hesitate to liquidate their exposure, given their low personal stake in borrower solvency. In fact, their livelihood often depends on minimizing even the most minor losses from bad investments. They are driven by the short-term competition of attracting new clients within the investment management industry. Given that clients evaluate fund managers on their relative quarterly and annual returns, they do not want to hold deteriorating assets that cause them to underperform industry-wide benchmarks.[49] Rather, they are likely to "cut and run" should governments struggle to refinance their obligations.[50]

Bond investors are also a conservative lot that dislike uncertainty, particularly any events that threaten to impair asset values. Not surprisingly, elections in politically less predictable environments raise many concerns. Even if developing country elections do not produce a change in political leadership, investors often fret that they might yield a new set of economic priorities.[51] For example, Mosley's (2000) international fund manager survey reveals upcoming elections are among the five most important factors affecting asset allocation in emerging market countries. Other scholars have also found that speculative behavior increases during election periods.[52] In fact, developing countries typically face a higher cost of capital during election years, when both credit rating downgrades and higher bond premiums are considerably more likely.[53]

How do politicians respond to these mercurial markets? They face a political conundrum. If they ignore these market pressures and engineer a preelection boom, they risk precipitating capital flight, a spike in their sovereign risk premium, and a destabilizing shock that undermines the economic vote. On the other hand, convincing bondholders of their good credit standing often entails adopting deflationary rather than inflationary policies.

---

[49] Calvo and Mendoza 2000; Mosley 2000.
[50] Two characteristics of emerging market bond financing often magnify investors' concerns about short-term default risk. First, when governments have foreign-currency debt, their repayments are subject to foreign exchange losses from devaluation/depreciation. Second, many developing countries issue debt with maturities of one year or less, creating a frequent need for refinancing.
[51] Leblang 2002; Mosley 2003.
[52] Leblang and Bernhard 2000; Frieden and Stein 2001; Leblang 2002; Mosley 2003.
[53] Block and Vaaler 2004; Vaaler, Schrage, and Block 2006.

Fearing the economic pain unleashed by a swift capital exit, politicians of debt-ridden countries often signal austerity to investors notwithstanding upcoming elections. Politicians do not necessarily strive for deflation, but it is often the lesser of two evils. By using fiscal discipline to convince bond investors that they are competent economic managers, politicians hope to generate a positive confidence effect that avoids a destabilizing shock that calls their governance into question.

Does this phenomenon suggest that politicians battling for survival are merely price takers in a world of decentralized finance? When might sovereign borrowers have more policy flexibility? In the following pages, I develop my theory's predictions regarding the conditions that yield both the traditional political business cycle and the globalization-spurred political austerity cycle.

High Growth, High Inflation Electoral Cycle (H1). Notwithstanding their relationships with creditors, governing politicians must first see the political benefit of creating an electoral boom. Not only must they believe that high economic growth translates into votes, they should also place a low weight on inflation control (whether they believe inflation is unlikely or that it simply has a low political cost). Should they possess such political will, their financial means ultimately determines their ability to pursue this political strategy.

Political austerity theory contends that when bond finance accounts for a small share of a country's foreign financing, politicians are likely to possess the financial means to create political business cycles. When governments are less reliant on global bond markets, their policy choices are less subject to the scrutiny of international investors and less vulnerable to capital flight.

How do governments ensure such policy autonomy? I argued earlier that new income from international bank lending can empower governments. Do other types of cross-border flows also create more economic options?

Several types of non-market foreign revenue streams – from natural resources to foreign aid – give politicians the fiscal space to spend more on their domestic agendas. Similar to the moral hazard problem that plagues bank lending, governments can spend without strong external checks on their behavior. More importantly, these proceeds – from copper mines and oil rigs to bilateral government credits – help governments avoid developing an overreliance on global capital markets. Recall that bond issuance often initially facilitates government spending, but a growing reliance on bond financing can lead to higher interest rates that crowd out other government expenditures. When governments can tap financing resources that are independent from global financial markets, it mitigates the likelihood of a market-induced credit crunch, leaving greater scope for economic expansions.

Notably, a new branch of the well-known resource curse literature identifies a similar phenomenon in the study of political regimes. High oil rents and non-tax revenues enhance governments' ability to appease citizens, and thereby increase regime stability.[54] For example, Dunning (2008) claims that resource rents can underwrite democratic stability by reducing redistributive conflict. In the case of elections, commodity booms allow politicians to devote public funds to electoral initiatives like public works and poverty programs, rather than foreign interest payments. Moreover, with a steady stream of new revenues into government coffers, they spend without being subject to external evaluation by international investors.

In summary, my first governing hypothesis is that politicians are likely to create political business cycles when they have the financial means. This capacity is generally associated with a lower dependence on global bond markets. External financing and windfall revenues from non-market sources – including international bank lending, foreign aid, and commodity income – allow countries to avoid the market surveillance (and funding constraints) that comes with bond indebtedness.

> H_1: **Traditional Political Business Cycle (PBC).** When stimulus-minded politicians face low-funding constraints from global bond markets, they use fiscal and/or monetary policy to boost the economy. Politicians are most likely to create conditions of high growth and low unemployment before elections, but at the cost of inflation and/or recession following elections (upper left quadrant in Table 2.1).

Market-Induced Austerity Cycle (H2). By contrast, when global bond markets account for a large share of a country's financing, the economic – and thus, the political cost – of an electoral expansion it too high, making political austerity more attractive. Why is a nation's debt structure constraining even during a president's most desperate political hour?

Let us assume once again that politicians intend to provide their supporters with economic growth and new jobs. Hoping to improve their reelection chances, they plan for an electorally timed economic boost notwithstanding its potential inflationary cost. However, a high reliance on decentralized bond financing leaves the economy vulnerable to severe credit disruptions that are often exacerbated by electoral uncertainty. Ironically, governments' efforts to create an economic boom to coincide with elections can quickly backfire by unnerving wary investors.

Remember that governments pursuing unsustainable fiscal policies not only risk disrupting debt repayment, but also spurring a higher risk premium in global bond markets. Faced with the prospect of plunging asset prices, herds of portfolio investors – without a long-term financial stake in national affairs – would rather liquidate their bonds for a marginal loss in secondary markets than risk subpar benchmark returns.

Hoping to avoid falling bond prices and spiking interest rates, governments are more apt to exhibit economic discipline during elections. Otherwise, they

---

[54] Dunning 2008; Morrison 2009.

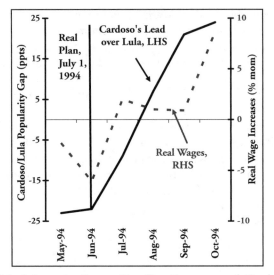

FIGURE 2.5. Political Austerity Boosts Brazilian Incomes and Cardoso's Presidential Candidacy.
Source: Datafolha Opinião Pública and IMF 1997

risk that higher interest rates will translate to other areas of the economy, simultaneously slowing government, business, and consumer spending – or in the worst-case scenario, even precipitating an abrupt income shock that undermines the economic vote. Not surprisingly, the appeal of the high growth-high inflation electoral cycle loses its luster relative to the low inflation political austerity cycle.

Ironically, in countries with a history of economic volatility, providing price stability might even prove more successful at securing the economic vote than electoral expansions. For example, in his 1994 presidential bid, Brazilian Finance Minister Fernando Henrique Cardoso bravely heralded fiscal adjustment under the Real Plan,[55] a mere three months before elections. Notwithstanding a mid-June popularity deficit of more than 20 percentage points against his contender, "Lula" da Silva of Brazil's Worker's Party, inflation stabilization and political austerity helped boost real wages and propel Cardoso to an impressive landslide victory in the October 1994 elections (Figure 2.5).[56]

In summary, my second governing hypothesis is that politicians are unlikely to create political business cycles without having the financial means. Governments with high bond market indebtedness often face steep funding constraints, making electoral expansions both economically and politically expensive. In a globalized world, economic policy decisions are not the sole realm

[55] On July 1, 1994, Cardoso introduced the Real Plan, which called for a balanced budget, tight monetary policy, and a new stable currency anchored to the U.S. dollar.
[56] Cardoso won a first-round victory, taking 54.3 percent of the vote, compared to Lula's 27 percent.

of domestic politicians and central bankers. International investors can place important financial limitations on political behavior. Indeed, the structure of creditor-debtor relations often creates financial market pressures that check traditional political incentives to use macroeconomic policy for electoral gain.

H_2: **Market-Induced Political Austerity Cycle (PAC).** When stimulus-minded politicians face steep funding constraints from global bond markets, they do not use accommodative fiscal and monetary policies to boost the economy. Instead, they use a neutral mix of economic policies or even contractionary policies that yield political austerity cycles. Inflation falls before elections, but at the cost of lower economic growth and fewer new jobs (lower left quadrant in Table 2.1).

2.4. ECONOMIC RISK-AVERSION: THE POLITICS OF INFLATION CONTROL

Imagine life under hyperinflation. Before work on Monday morning, you go to Romeo and Cesare's local convenience store to purchase a loaf of bread. After seeing the clerk type its $5 price tag into the register, you balk. Perhaps, you could buy it more cheaply at the supermarket. You withhold your purchase knowing that you will pass a supermarket during your walk home from work. When you enter the supermarket later that afternoon, you notice that the price of bread has spiked to $7. Dismayed at the gumption of large retail merchants, you deem this price too lofty for a mere loaf of bread. You vow to instead return to your neighborhood store. When you arrive at Romeo and Cesare's store a speedy thirty minutes later, the price is no longer $5 – not even $7 – but rather a shocking $10. You walk out of the store. You decide to wait until tomorrow. Perhaps with a restful night's sleep, Romeo and Cesare will return to their senses. Amazingly, the sun had only risen once by Tuesday morning, but the bread price rose three times to $15. A simple mix of butter, flour, water, sugar and yeast tripled in price within twenty-four hours! In a little more than a week, the price shoots yet another ten times higher.[57]

Unfortunately, during their democratic transitions, many developing countries were inflicted by this once rare scenario. From Argentina and Brazil to Bulgaria and Ukraine, citizens learned about the indelible consequences of hyperinflation. An inflationary spiral not only undermines rational economic behavior, but also basic economic order. Intensifying a country's troubles, economic chaos often quickly spirals into political chaos. The price system's rupture inevitably catalyzes political turnover, and in many cases, even spurs a breakdown of political order, catapulting society into a Hobbesian world where protests, rioting, looting, and deaths became commonplace.[58]

---

[57] This anecdote is based on conversations with Argentine citizens about the rigors of living with hyperinflation.

[58] For example, following the May 1989 Argentine elections, the *New York Times* reported that 15 people died in riots and looting touched off by rising prices.

Many developing countries are haunted by severe inflation crises that have dismantled their political and social stability. Learning from these struggles, political leaders and technocratic policy communities have gravitated toward centrist, conservative policies that are unlikely to repeat past crises. Even when income shocks are characterized by much lower inflation rates than hyperinflation, crisis memories are often politically enduring. In fact, there is a fairly broad consensus that levels above 100 percent per annum inflict severe economic harm.[59] Consequently, these transformative events have changed the political logic in many developing countries.

Austerity politics might be imposed externally during credit shocks or global economic downturns, but it also has domestic roots. Politicians typically retain some discretion over economic choices. Why might they prioritize economic stability and inflation control, even if it means creating less growth and fewer new jobs? In the following pages, I develop the causal argument about the domestic politics of austerity choices.

2.4.1. Economic Decisions in Hard Times

Why would presidents center their economic agenda around such conservative ideas as inflation control? What accounts for this surprising choice? Within Latin America, many scholars have identified a broad emergence of an elite neoliberal consensus in the 1990s,[60] based on a perceived transformation of the traditional left. A new brand of leftist politicians proactively adopted these market-friendly reforms in some countries,[61] whereas the traditional left either acquiesced or mounted little opposition to neoliberal movements in other countries.[62] In a region where the government's budget is often key to addressing redistributive pressures; however, why would the left tolerate economic austerity?[63]

In countries once savaged by inflation, I argue that politicians who experienced severe economic instability are more likely to be risk-averse, and hence, more willing to embrace more conservative, macroeconomic governance. Informed by the psychology literature on risky choices, we know that decisions often reflect both descriptive and experiential information. Both types of information help improve Bayesian reasoning; however, experiential information has a disproportionate influence on people's choices. In other

---

[59] Throughout this study, I employ this 100 percent annum threshold as a cutoff for inflation crises (see Chapters 3 and 6 for further details).

[60] Stokes 2001a; Murillo 2002; Weyland 2002.

[61] Stokes 2001a; Weyland 2002.

[62] Roberts 1998; Murillo 2001; Levitsky 2003; Bruhn 2004; Murillo and Martinez-Gallardo 2007.

[63] Baker (2008) and Baker and Greene (2011) suggest that these actions are a reflection of the region's attitudes, finding that Latin American citizens surprisingly hold centrist economic policy preferences. Similarly, Tomz (2001) finds that the majority of Argentine voters were against debt default in 1999, preferring that the government comply with its international financial commitments. My analysis, by comparison, presents a supply-side explanation for these demand-side phenomena.

words, people place greater weight on personal judgements than secondhand information from newspapers, books, or the Internet.[64] For example, drivers familiar with a town are likely to ignore the electronic bellows of their GPS computer.

Ironically, when people rely on their own experiences, they tend to often miscalculate the variance of the true population. They underestimate the likelihood of experiencing a personal trauma like an automobile accident. Fascinatingly, however, once people experience a crisis, they overestimate its likelihood, fretting about its recurrence.[65] For example, teenagers with collision-free histories often possess a sense of invulnerability. Their driving moves are often reminiscent of Bo and Luke Duke. In the wake of an accident, however, invulnerability can quickly transform into trepidation. Teenagers are more likely to heed the lessons of cautious driving if they crash their car than if they watch an after-school television special.

These findings readily translate to the policy world, where I claim that policy-makers craft economic solutions through the lens of their own macroeconomic histories. Politicians are not necessarily the shrewd operators envisioned by standard risk preference models. Instead, they are often restless, passionate people that are motivated by their "animal spirits." Indeed, economic decision makers do not weigh all experiences and events uniformly. Rather, some historical experiences are more transformative than others, leaving a strong imprint on the worldviews of political and technocratic elites.

Economic crises are often the most salient experiences. Their political, social, and economic trauma typically cast a long shadow over elite decision making. After experiencing severe crises, political and technocratic elites tend to place a high weight on risk-averse policies that promise to avoid repeating past horrors.

The defining historical episode in many new democracies – from Latin America to Eastern Europe – has been hyperinflation. In Chile, for example, politicians have internalized the lessons of President Salvador Allende's failed policies that ended in an inflationary shock and a 1973 coup. Even Socialists Party officials – who had once labored for President Salvador Allende's socialist experiment – have embraced economic discipline and low inflation. For example, Senator Sergio Bitar, who served as both Michelle Bachelet's campaign advisor and as Salvador Allende's mining minister, today stresses the importance of fiscal discipline to the Concertación's governing principles.

In order to understand today's political economy, one has to understand what happened with the Popular Unity government in the 1970s. One of the most important conclusions for the entire Chilean left from this period, was the use of an expansive political economy can have gigantic political costs. Rather, the major electoral and political benefits come from a serious, stable, and responsible political economy. For fifteen years, we have maintained a high level of political discipline, knowing that populism doesn't pay.[66]

---

[64] Weber et al. 1993; Weber et al. 2004; Hertwig et al. 2004.

[65] Ibid.

[66] Author's interview with Senator Sergio Bitar, Santiago, Chile, June 20, 2007. Bitar was President of la Concertación de Partidos Por La Democracia (PPD) on three different occasions:

Beyond developing country frontiers, Germany's technocratic communities have also preserved such governance lessons.[67] For instance, Hanz Tietmeyer, Germany's central bank president between 1993 and 1999, claims that hyper-inflation forever changed national politics.

> The inflation of 1923 left a terrible legacy for the future fate of our country...The objective of stable money was and is deeply rooted in our society. It is based on a wide consensus in broad sections of our population. It is based on a culture of stability. That is why German public opinion – particularly in critical periods – again and again proved a loyal ally of a stability-oriented monetary policy.[68]

Historical lessons are not limited to economics. In foreign policy, for instance, scholars have found that historical analogies are often key elements of military and foreign affairs strategies.[69] For example, many U.S. presidents formulated their post-World War II military interventions, using the historical analogy of Munich appeasement.[70] In 1950, the Truman administration developed its thinking about the Korean peninsula in response to the failures of the Munich agreement.[71] Designed by Great Britain and France (with the United States opting for neutrality), the 1938 Munich Agreement ceded Czechoslovakia's Sudetenland territory to Germany. Aiming to appease Hitler's territorial demands, the strategy opened the door to an eventual Nazi invasion of Czechoslovakia. Rather than repeat this diplomatic mistake, Truman opted to repel North Korea's incursion into its Southern neighbor's territory. Similarly, in the early 1980s, the Reagan administration anchored its Cold War policy in the Americas to the same historical metaphor. In Nicaragua, Reagan supported the contra rebels' efforts to overthrow the leftist Sandinista government, labeling domestic critics of his policy as "appeasers."[72]

Returning to the politics of macroeconomic policy making, the relevant historical analogy in Latin America is hyperinflation and the steep political costs of macroeconomic mismanagement. Inflationary trauma that ended in a near-breakdown of the political economic system prompts politicians to place a disproportionate weight on avoiding another inflationary crisis. Even during periods of economic stability, they are more likely to place a greater relative weight on price stability than growth and job creation. This analysis offers new insights from previous work in the rich literature of economic crises and economic policy making. For example, Weyland (2002) contends that the rise of neoliberal policies reflects short-term political risk-seeking during economic

1992–1994, 1997–2000, and 2006. He was also the director of Michelle Bachelet's 2005–2006 presidential election campaign. Bitar was also a senator from Tarapacá between 1994 and 2002.

[67] Lohmann 1998.
[68] Tietmeyer 2001.
[69] Jervis 1976; Khong 1992; Levy 1994.
[70] Khong 1992.
[71] Truman 1955–1956.
[72] Khong 1992.

crises. Political leaders who face the threat of severe economic losses choose drastic austerity measures to restore stability and growth. However, Weyland's explanation does not account for the persistence of economic austerity over time.

By contrast, I argue that risk-aversion has fueled a steadfast commitment to macroeconomic orthodoxy, grounded in sound governance that does not chance repeating past problems of inflation and debt accumulation.[73] In fact, Chapter 6 finds that inflationary crises tend to increase the professionalization of presidential cabinets.

In the following section, I explore the roots of this inflation sensitivity by examining how this macroeconomic consensus develops among technocratic communities and why politicians would heed their risk-averse advice even years after an inflationary crisis.

2.4.2. Technocratic Communities and Inflation Saliency

How are macroeconomic decisions typically made in developing countries? In regions like Latin America, characterized by a high concentration of executive power, presidential cabinets possess considerable sway over economic choices. In fact, larger-than-life economic ministers like Domingo Cavallo, Alejandro Foxley, and Fernando Henrique Cardoso often gain a powerful voice in their country's economic affairs. How do they amass this power?

Presidents plagued by inflationary spirals appoint economic ministers that promise to contain inflation's political fallout. For instance, Brazilian President Itamar Franco appointed Cardoso to the finance minister post in May 1993, saying, "Hire who you want, and fire who you want. But remember that I need this inflation problem solved." Cardoso knew that his "success as finance minister would be measured by just one thing: whether [he] could beat inflation."[74] Similarly, facing historically unprecedented inflation, Argentine President Raúl Alfonsín appointed Juan Sourrouille to the Minister of the Economy post to stabilize the economy. Invoking the famous Nike slogan before its time, Alfonsín told Sourrouille "no me diga nada, haga!" (don't tell me anything, just do it!).[75]

Given the economic trauma associated with runaway prices, slaying the inflationary beast brought hefty political rewards – as demonstrated by the political popularity of successful reformers such as Brazil's Fernando Henrique Cardoso and Argentina's Carlos Menem in the 1990s. By contrast, politicians

---

[73] Employing prospect theory, Weyland (2002) claims that politicians' value functions are s-shaped; they temporarily adopt risk-seeking orthodox policies to exit their domain of losses and reboot economic growth. By contrast, I anticipate that economic orthodoxy is a reflection of sustained risk-aversion. In line with the traditional utility functions outlined in the appendix, inflation-scarred politicians place a higher premium on price stability relative to growth and jobs.

[74] Cardoso 2006.

[75] Author's interview with Sourrouille, Buenos Aires, May 28, 2007.

who were unable to tame the inflationary beast, such as Raúl Alfonsín, were ousted from office.

Risk-Aversion's Political Rewards. What explains the success and failure of presidents' economic programs in inflation-scarred countries? During their democratic transitions, many governments pursued economic programs that have been collectively dubbed as macroeconomic populism.[76] Aiming to redistribute income and spur industrial development, they heavily intervened in their economies by running large fiscal deficits. They pursued these unsustainable economic policies during periods when they had little or no access to capital markets. Faced with a dearth of funding sources, political leaders turned to their only other financing source – the printing press.

Governments funded huge budget deficits with central bank financing. They "printed money" by ordering the central bank to expand the money supply. Governments oversaw colossal money supply expansions, causing prices to soar without bounds.[77] These policies created rampant inflation, and in some cases, generated hyperinflation.[78] Surging inflation eroded real tax revenues and exacerbated budget shortfalls.[79] Without external financing, governments responded by printing more money, which fueled even further inflation. Therefore, inflation-afflicted countries entered into a vicious cycle of ballooning deficits, booming money supply growth, and unbridled inflation. This inflationary inertia ultimately fueled a moribund period of surging unemployment and plummeting growth and wages.

Governments adopted several different types of economic programs to end this ruthless spiral, but many proved to be ineffective. For example, under heterodox programs in Argentina, Brazil, and Peru, politicians used price and wage controls to tame inflation, while maintaining expansionary policies.[80] These policies were ultimately unsustainable, however, and instead prolonged the crisis.

By contrast, those political leaders that governed according to risk-averse, rather than risk-seeking, economic principles successfully navigated inflationary crises. They adopted fiscal discipline and sound monetary policies that lowered inflation and boosted popular incomes (for instance, Figure 2.5 shows how Cardoso's fiscal adjustment raised Brazilian real wages). Orthodox stabilization measures proved to be a much safer political choice than expansionary

[76] Dornbusch and Edwards 1991.
[77] Sachs 1989a; Dornbusch and Edwards 1991; Kaufman and Stallings 1991; Cardoso and Helwege 1992; Sachs and Larrain 1993; Mankiw 2003.
[78] Hyperinflation popularly refers to monthly price increases exceeding 20 percent, though it has been more strictly classified as monthly inflation over 50 percent (Cagan, 1956). Compounded annually, this yields an inflation rate of almost 13,000 percent!
[79] This phenomenon is known as the Olivera-Tanzi effect. Rising inflation depresses budget revenues and widens the deficit (Mankiw 2003; Sachs and Larrain 1993).
[80] Remmer 1991; Kiguel and Liviatan 1992.

policies that intensified inflationary problems. Their success in curbing inflation raised the appeal of risk-averse stabilization policies throughout technocratic communities whose countries were plagued by runaway prices.

Resilience of Economic Lessons. What keeps the political memory of hyperinflation alive? What explains the saliency of past economic lessons over time? Why fret about past policy blunders? I have argued that inflation-trauma is politically enduring, often having a disproportionate influence on present policy decisions. In the wake of these crises, presidential advisors increasingly developed a governance consensus oriented toward price stability. Ideas grounded in contemporary macroeconomics that promised to control inflation flourished in tight-knit technocratic communities. By contrast, alternative, heterodox policy solutions that could not check inflation became increasingly marginalized. Such highly interventionist policies were instead typically adopted in countries that never experienced inflationary shocks.

Why would political leaders adopt such conservative policies even years after inflation crises? Why not intervene in the economy to address growing concerns about unemployment and income inequality? Repeating past policy mistakes carries prohibitive political costs. Not only do they create grave income shocks that torpedo popular living standards, they also have electoral repercussions. In fact, scholars have found that inflation volatility can create a retrospective voting pattern. High inflation erodes electoral support, discredits political parties, and triggers presidential job loss.[81] The list of crisis-induced political turnover in developing countries is impressive, including Argentina's Raúl Alfonsín's, Peru's Alan García, Bulgaria's Zhan Videnov, and Ukraine's Leonid Kravchuk.

With these inflationary costs chiseled into their minds, politicians and their technocratic advisors learn from the original policy errors that produced these catastrophic shocks. They avoid unsustainable government deficits and instead adopt sound economic policies that promise low inflation. In the most extreme cases, they adopted rigid institutional frameworks, such as Argentina's currency board, to preserve this anti-inflation consensus.[82]

These lessons are surprisingly resilient because of the macroeconomic governance consensus that develops in these inner policy circles. Policy makers gravitate toward economic ideas that promise to prevent new bouts of inflation. In a world of Darwin, genes propagate in advantageous environments. Similarly, in the world of economic ideas, policy prescriptions survive and prosper under favorable conditions.

---

[81] Remmer (1991) finds that high inflation and exchange rate depreciation help explain incumbent vote loss. Stokes (2001) shows that under inflationary conditions candidates favoring growth over inflation stabilization are less likely to be elected.

[82] Galiani, Heymann, and Tommasi 2003.

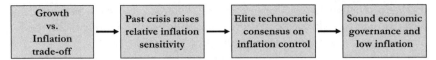

FIGURE 2.6. Decision Making with High Inflation Aversion.

The contemporary macroeconomic notion, favoring control of budget deficits as a pathway to low inflation, gained prominence.[83] Increasingly, presidents' cabinets became more professionalized, with ministers brandishing advanced graduate degrees in modern economics.[84] Whether trained in New Keynesian[85] or monetarist[86] economics, both schools of thought emphasized prudent budgetary management and price stability.[87] Politicians sought out ministers with these credentials in hopes of protecting popular incomes. Beyond controlling inflation, they also thought that macroeconomic discipline would yield a secondary political payoff of promoting long-term growth.[88] Figure 2.6 summarizes the political logic of macroeconomic discipline in countries with a history of high inflation.

For example, in Chile, the center-left coalition that ushered in the return to democracy, known as the Concertación,[89] sought to erase the longstanding memories of roaring inflation and economic devastation associated with the last democratic episode. They governed for two decades according to the economic principles embodied by CIEPLAN,[90] the coalition's main economic think-tank. In fact, since Chile's 1990 democratic transition, four out of six of the country's finance ministers have hailed from CIEPLAN. Flagged by the slogan, "crecimiento con equidad" ("growth with equity"), CIEPLAN's agenda strikes a political and economic balance. It aims to redress the social debt of the military dictatorship without jeopardizing sound economic governance and price stability.

Inflation aversion is not limited to Chile's close-knit policy community. In Brazil, Fernando Henrique Cardoso, the finance minister who tamed hyperinflation, later wore Brazil's president sash for eight years. Gustavo Franco, a key

---

[83] See Agenor and Montiel 1999.

[84] See Chapter 6.

[85] New Keynesian economics is a school of contemporary macroeconomics that advocates for expansionary fiscal and monetary policies to offset the adverse effects of economic downturns.

[86] By comparison, monetarists are more skeptical of the benefits of government intervention fretting that it only fuels inflation expectations.

[87] See footnote 11.

[88] This technocratic belief is in line with a large body of empirical economic research that finds a salutary long-term effect of fiscal adjustment (Easterly et al. 1994).

[89] The Concertación, a coalition of center-left parties, governed Chile from 1990–2010 in the wake of its democratic transition. During this period, there were four different administrations that featured two Socialist Party (PS) presidents and two Christian Democratic Party (PDC) presidents.

[90] The Corporación de Estudios Para Latinoamérica.

member of Cardoso's original ministry advisors, was appointed central bank governor during Cardoso's presidency. Even Cardoso's successor Lula da Silva, the man who had once been his main opponent, upheld Cardoso's economic austerity. In Argentina, José Luis Machinea, Domingo Cavallo, and Roberto Lavagna each served as key members of the economic teams of more than one president, governing with a commitment to budgetary discipline.

Alan García, who returned to the Peruvian presidency sixteen years after a 1990 inflation-spurred ouster, perhaps best illustrates the extent of experiential learning among political elites. After governing through a hyperinflation episode that eroded wages and deepened poverty, García adopted a sound economic policy framework that included fiscal discipline and inflation-targeting during his second presidential life in Peru. To lead his pro-market charge, he appointed Luis Carranza Ugarte, a former banker and one of Peru's most orthodox economists, to the prominent post of Minister of Economy and Finance. He swapped his first-term interventionist policies, once deemed reckless by the International Monetary Fund (IMF), for prudent low-inflation policies that were later praised by the same institution.[91] In a similar pattern to Brazil, García's successor and leftist political rival, Ollanta Humala, also embraced economic austerity. He signaled a commitment to García's low inflation policies by naming his deputy finance minister Louis Miguel Castilla as the Minister of Economy and Finance and leaving Central Bank President Julio Velarde in his post for five more years.

By contrast, when countries lack inflationary scars, cabinet officials favoring aggressive government intervention, such as Venezuelan Finance and Planning Minister Jorge Giordani, are more likely to gain influence in policy circles. Even when reformers happen to take the economic reigns in countries that have never suffered inflationary crises, such about-face policy adjustments are unlikely to be enduring given the lack of elite consensus about macroeconomic policy. For example, Minister of Trade and Industry Moisés Naím helped spearhead Venezuela's early 1990s reforms but lacked this elite consensus and met resistance from both elites and the general public.

I think that the Venezuelan public was inured to arguments about the need to go through a painful experience, or a costly reform process in order to avoid an even costlier stage because Venezuela didn't have that [past inflationary crises]...that was true for the elites too; elites thought that was something that happened to Argentinians but never to us.[92]

When this elite consensus about economic governance is absent, politicians are more likely to give a low weight to inflation control. In fact, where inflation has never reared its ugly head, competing ideologies favoring aggressive government economic intervention are more likely to challenge the orthodox

---

[91] *The Economist*, July 27, 2006.
[92] Author's interview with Moisés Naím, Washington, DC, July 18, 2011.

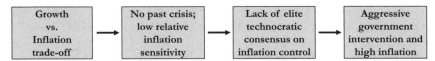

FIGURE 2.7. Decision Making with Low Inflation Aversion.

hegemony. Figure 2.7 outlines the political logic of economic decision making in countries that have never experienced inflation crises.

For example, before the first oil shock in 1973, inflation did not resonate as much of a political issue in the region. Governing in an environment where average inflation fluctuated in a 15 percentage point band around zero (Figure 2.8), the political landscape was lined with a diversity of economic views. In this setting, political elites favoring a structuralist view of the world were more likely to govern the economy believing that government spending was inflation's cure rather than its root.[93]

In the early 1970s, for example, Chile's Unidad Popular (UP) government viewed inflation as a structural phenomenon that could be corrected with a policy mix of state-led demand stimulus and price controls.[94] In Peru, high inflation did not surface until the mid-1980s and did not reach crisis proportions until 1989.[95] Upon assuming power for the first time in 1985, President García's administration questioned the traditional thinking about inflation. The president and his advisors claimed that fiscal deficits and economic expansion were not inflationary. Rather, they were a key part of their redistributive platform aimed at boosting real wages, generating employment, and accelerating growth.[96] In their economic treatise, *El Peru Heterodox: Un Modelo Economico,* they asserted:

It is necessary to spend, even at the cost of a fiscal deficit, because this deficit transfers public resources to increased consumption of the poorest; they demand more goods, and it will bring about a reduction in unit costs, thus the deficit is not inflationary, on the contrary![97]

In both Chile and Peru, these structuralist incumbents not only aggressively intervened in their economies, but their ballooning government deficits led to runaway inflation, and ultimately, their political demise. More recently, outside of Latin America's borders, President Leonid Kravchuk followed a similar path

[93] Structuralists believed that inflation reflected a demand-side shortage that could be alleviated with heavy government spending. This view sharply contrasts with monetarism, which diagnosed inflation as a supply-side excess that could be cured with balanced budgets (Cardoso and Helwege 1992).

[94] Larraín and Meller 1991.

[95] Average annual inflation breached 100 percent for the first time in 1983, but did not reach crisis levels until 1989 when it surged above 3,000 percent (World Bank's World Development Indicators).

[96] For further details, see Dornbusch and Edwards 1991.

[97] See Dornbusch and Edwards 1991.

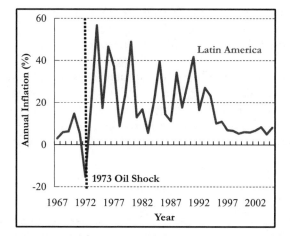

FIGURE 2.8. Latin American Inflation Troubles Begin in Mid-1970s (CPI, Annual %).
Source: World Bank

during Ukraine's democratic transition. Kravchuk believed that budget deficits and cheap industrial credit were a panacea for production shortages. Before the 1994 elections, the Ukraine President lavished huge subsidies on key supporters in the agricultural and industrial sectors. Dashing his hopes for an improved economy, however, his budget deficits and credit expansion also unleashed a whopping bout of price inflation.[98] Ironically, politicians often underweight the likelihood of an inflation crisis, until they experience the economic and political trauma of such severe income shocks.

2.4.3. Inflation Aversion and Elections

I have argued that risk-aversion in the wake of economic crises explains the rise of political austerity. Developing country politicians who like Icarus, once promised to soar their economies to new commanding heights, saw their hopes dashed by inflation's piercing rays. When hyperinflation burned the economy's wax wings, economic and political chaos tore apart the fabric of society. Following these traumatic events, the promise of low inflation and more moderate growth surprisingly carried hefty political rewards.

Notwithstanding these benefits, why would politicians choose austerity during election periods? Why not briefly deviate from economic discipline to aggressively spend on important political constituents? What is the political payoff to low-inflation policies?

Austerity is typically associated with right-leaning parties in developed countries. The political economy literature traditionally divides domestic politics into two camps. Presuming the classic short-run trade-off between inflation and unemployment, it expects right-wing political parties to pursue low inflation

[98] D'Anieri, Kravchuk, and Kuzio 1999.

(at the cost of jobs and growth) and left-wing parties to prioritize high growth and jobs (at the cost of inflation). The right hopes to appeal to its business and financial constituencies, whereas the left attempts to assuage middle-class and working families' concerns.[99]

But, who are the low-inflation constituencies in developing countries? Is there a similar partisan divide? Alternatively, do such partisan cleavages exist in regions such as Latin America, where party systems are less ideological than in Europe and the United States?[100] In this section, I develop hypotheses for two more types of political austerity cycles, each characterized by inflation-aversion.

Low-Inflation Constituency. During his presidential reelection campaign, Brazilian President Fernando Henrique Cardoso vowed to eradicate inflation in the aftermath of the 1997–98 East Asian Crisis. Notwithstanding his leftist roots, Cardoso declared his commitment to preserving Brazil's U.S. dollar peg[101] – the bedrock of Brazilian price stability – in a November 1997 radio address.

You can be sure of one thing; we will not let the real lose value and let inflation come back! We may even have to pay a temporary price for this, but it's better to have higher interest rates for a while than to have salaries lose their value again. The real, and therefore the purchasing power of your salaries, will be protected![102]

Why would a world-renowned sociologist, dependency theorist, and founding member of Brazil's social democratic party (PSDB) talk about the importance of inflation control during a presidential bid? Is this political logic founded? Why not devote your political rhetoric to job and growth creation?

After experiencing severe inflationary shocks, I argue that orthodox macroeconomic policies that ensure low inflation are popular even years after the initial crisis.[103] The traditional low inflation constituency widens beyond businesses and financiers, leading to a blurring of partisan lines in economic policy making. If leftist politicians want to win elections, they believe they not only have to prove their governing credentials to a skeptical business community, but also inflation-wary voters.

Inflation politics trumped traditional partisan politics in Latin America. If a neoliberal consensus emerged among political elites,[104] it was because left-leaning elites perceived that they would be punished for rising prices at the

---

[99] Bartels 2008.
[100] Roberts and Wibbels 1999.
[101] Following the success of the Real Plan in taming inflation, Cardoso's economic team created a crawling peg fixed exchange rate regime designed to allow for a steady, but modest depreciation of the Brazilian real against the U.S. dollar.
[102] *New York Times*, November 5, 1997.
[103] Many scholars find high levels of initial aggregate support for such orthodox reforms at the time of economic crises (Roberts and Arce 1998; Weyland 1998; Stokes 2001b; Weyland 2002).
[104] Stokes 2001; Murillo 2002; Weyland 2002.

polls. By protecting incomes in countries historically plagued by past economic volatility, they hoped to provide an important baseline for the economic vote. Cardoso, for example, believed that "the poor would not tolerate inflation any longer, and the wealthy were tired of seeing business plans and investments distorted by rising prices."[105]

At first, this logic may appear different from developed country politics, where politicians often boost incomes in hopes of gaining votes. However, in countries that have suffered from severe income shocks, the choice to use economic policy to protect voter incomes is as politically sound as boosting voter incomes.[106] Latin American political elites are similar to anesthesiologists. They are unlikely to be credited for stable economic conditions, but are quickly blamed for failing to administer inflation sedation.

Even years after an inflationary crisis, when other issues (such as crime) might be at the forefront of voters' minds, politicians still perceive voters as more instrinsically hawkish than in the past. With a commitment to economic discipline preserved in their technocratic communities, they are more likely to prioritize inflation control even if it means sacrificing potentially higher economic growth. As a result, risk-averse elites often infuse policy with an anti-inflationary bias during election periods to avoid catalyzing inflation that calls their governance into question. For example, more than a decade after inflationary crises in Brazil and Peru, historic leftists such as Presidents Lula da Silva and Alan García did not veer from macroeconomic orthodoxy while they were election-year incumbents. Both of them were committed to fiscal discipline and inflation targeting in the final years of their terms.[107] In a second-term public speech, for example, Lula summarized the left's political approach.

Low inflation is vital ... obviously, we could be growing more ... but distributing income and controlling inflation are just as important. Controlled inflation represents an extraordinary gain for salaried workers.[108]

Middle Income and Poor Voters. Why would politicians believe that voters do not like inflation? Similar to the provision of jobs or growth, inflation also has distributive consequences. Commonly known as an "inflation tax," when governments choose to fund their deficits by printing money, they catalyze inflation and erode real wages. Functionally, policy makers are transferring income

[105] Cardoso 2006.

[106] In fact, the politics of exchange rate literature shows that politicians often avoid election-year devaluation to preserve voters' purchasing power (Frieden and Stein 2001; Schamis and Way 2003). Low inflation offers the same political benefit. The exchange rate is merely one tool that politicians use to protect voters' incomes; interest rates and balanced budgets also provide them with this political commodity.

[107] Lula oversaw a steady, primary budget surplus of more than 2 percent of GDP in the years leading up to the 2006 election. Similarly, notwithstanding the 2011 election year, García brought public finances back into line with Peru's fiscal rule (plus or minus 1 percent of GDP) following some temporary drift in response to the global financial crisis (EIU country reports; CEPAL's Bases de Datos y Publicaciones Estadística).

[108] *Reuters*, June 18, 2007.

away from citizens and to the government. Moreover, economists sometimes dub the inflation tax as the "cruelest tax of all" because inflation hurts the poor relatively more than the rich. Why? Wealthy individuals are generally sophisticated investors that funnel their earnings into financial assets that hedge against inflation. By contrast, the poor typically keep the majority of their earnings in cash holdings that are eroded by inflation. In addition, the poor are often more reliant on state spending, including income transfers and pensions, that are not indexed to inflation.[109]

Many empirical studies support the notion that inflation has a distributive character, showing that high inflation increases poverty rates and lowers the incomes of the poor.[110] In Latin America, scholars have also found that higher inflation is associated with lower real (inflation-adjusted) wages and higher income inequality.[111] For example, spiraling inflation during García's first presidency in Peru caused real wages to decline by more than 60 percent. Real wages also tumbled during Argentina's and Nicaragua's battles with hyperinflation, falling by 30 and 90 percent, respectively.[112]

Notwithstanding the empirical record, are elite perceptions of Latin American voters correct? In his reflections about the Brazilian presidency, for instance, Fernando Henrique Cardoso claims that "inflation acted like a regressive tax that made poor people poorer."[113] Alejandro Foxley, former Chilean finance minister, emphasized a similar point in a 1990 national television address, saying, "in countries with high inflation, the workers lose all of the time."[114] But does this political perception reflect voter concerns?

In fact, politicians' inflation wariness is supported by considerable scholarship showing that middle-class and poor voters fret about inflation. By the 1990s, following severe bouts of inflation across the globe, the poorest voters were ranking inflation as a top national concern in global surveys. Price stability was no longer solely the concern of right-wing constituencies and business elites. Rather, the public, including its poorest citizens, had a vested interest in low and stable inflation.

In a survey conducted by Easterly and Fischer (2000), the poorest citizens in developing countries had a 9 percent higher probability of mentioning inflation as a top national concern than the rich. In its survey of sixteen Latin American countries, the Latinobarómetro demonstrates steady baseline support for inflation control between 1995 and 2008 (Figure 2.9). During this period, 25.7 percent of the Latin American adult population believed that fighting inflation was "the most important issue for their country." The popularity of inflation

---

[109] Easterly and Fischer 2001.
[110] Cutler and Katz, 1991; Agenor 1998; Romer and Romer 1998; Easterly and Fischer 2000.
[111] Cardoso 1992; Rezende 1998.
[112] United Nations' Economic Commission for Latin America.
[113] Cardoso 2006.
[114] Foxley 1993.

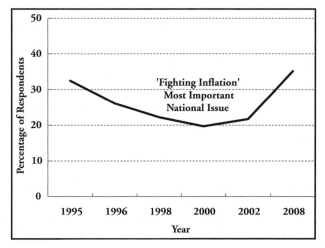

FIGURE 2.9. Support for Fighting Latin American Inflation (Survey of 16 Latin American Countries, 1995–2008.)
Source: Latinóbarometro

control appears to be robust to framing and question wording effects.[115] They are corroborated by a series of World Values Surveys conducted in seven Latin American countries between 1995 and 1997, showing that three-quarters of respondents believed that fighting rising prices was "very important." By comparison, during the same period, only 40 percent responded affirmatively to the identical question in four developed countries.

In general, these surveys about inflation attitudes are broadly in line with recent findings about Latin American public opinion. Baker (2008), for example, uses public opinion data from eighteen Latin American countries to show that most of the region's citizens strongly support free-market reforms with the exception of privatization. Similarly, the Latin American Public Opinion Project's 2008 Americas Barometer finds that Latin Americans rank "inflation and high prices" as one of the five most serious problems facing their countries out of a list of more than thirty-five issues.

Politicians' inflation aversion is also reflected in country-level evidence about voter attitudes. National public opinion polls and presidential approval ratings show that voters from inflation-scarred countries prioritize price stability. For example, Shiller (1997) conducts an extensive survey about global inflation attitudes, finding that the Brazilian public overwhelmingly dislikes inflation because they believe it erodes their living standards. He finds that 88 percent of Brazilian respondents agreed with the statement that "the control of inflation is one of the most important missions of Brazilian economic policy." Moreover, a majority of Brazilians would choose low inflation, even if it meant that millions

[115] See Sniderman and Theriault 2004; Baker 2008.

more people would be unemployed.[116] Similarly in the prelude to Brazil's 1994 elections, national polls showed that 91 percent of respondents rated Brazil's economic situation as "poor or very poor." Most notably, however, these polls showed that more than two-thirds of Brazilians considered economic problems, including inflation, salaries, and cost of living, to be the most important national priorities.[117]

In Argentina, 67 percent of the people interviewed in a 1990 Buenos Aires survey identified inflation as the most important problem facing them and their families.[118] In fact, during Menem's first administration, inflation was inversely correlated with the Argentine president's approval ratings: the lower the inflation rate, the greater Menem's popular appeal.[119] Notably, public opinion polls also showed surprisingly high levels of support for Menem's economic austerity. During the 1995 reelection campaign, 43 percent of respondents supported "controlling the public deficit even if it [meant] reducing personnel and social expenditures."[120] Hyperinflation had bred a societal acceptance of austerity.

By contrast, in countries that have never experienced severe inflationary crises, there is less public support for price stability. For example, a recent 2010 Venezuelan survey finds little evidence of inflation aversion among voters,[121] notwithstanding living with the highest national inflation in Latin America.[122] A mere 8.6 percent of Venezuelan voters flagged inflation as the most important national issue, compared to 41.8 percent of citizens who named their personal safety/crime as the nation's most pressing concern. The same 2010 survey also found that only 3 percent of respondents named reducing prices/controlling inflation as a national priority when asked, "if you were president, what would be the most important issue to improving the situation of you and your family?"

Given such low levels of inflation aversion, perhaps it's not surprising that Venezuelan public officials place less weight on controlling inflation than reducing unemployment. In fact, Finance and Planning Minister Giordani recently commented when asked about the inflation-unemployment trade-off that "the fundamental variable right now is employment . . . we're concerned about inflation, but we have to make every effort to preserve jobs."[123]

---

[116] Shiller 1997.

[117] CESOP 1994; Weyland 2002.

[118] Echegaray and Elordi 2001.

[119] Echegaray and Elordi 2001; Stokes 2001a.

[120] The survey was conducted by Romer and Associates/Roper Center in 1995. Survey participants were asked, "which aspects of the economic model do you agree with, and which do you disagree with?" (Romer and Associates, 1995, as cited in Stokes, 2001a).

[121] A Venezuelan polling company, Consultores 21, surveyed 1,500 voters between May and June 2010, asking them to identify Venezuela's most important national problem.

[122] In May and June 2010, Venezuela's national consumer price index, on average, rose by 30 percent on an annual basis (Venezuelan Central Bank and National Statistics Institute).

[123] El Universal, Caracas, April 2, 2009.

Business Community. Politicians also use sound economic governance and low inflation to convey their managerial credentials to businesses and investors. In contrast to traditional partisan models of the economy that show a political split in policies that favor businesses, politicians from across the political spectrum pander to firms and investors in inflation-ridden countries. This political convergence reflects the enormous power of business and markets.

For example, in a 2003 survey of 231 political elites, 80 percent of respondents said that business exercised "de facto powers" in Latin America. In the words of one former President, "the great de facto power of incipient democracy is private economic power."[124] Businesses may influence government in various ways, from business associations, policy networks, and cabinet appointments to lobbying and campaign contributions.[125] Perhaps in Colombia, private sector influence has been most transparent, with more than half of former President Uribe's cabinet appointees hailing from the business community.[126]

In countries with histories of inflation volatility, politicians often heed private sector opinions given the business community's pivotal role in providing investment, and therefore, growth and employment opportunities. If the private sector does not have confidence in a government's ability to govern the economy, business investment can quickly falter and lead the economy adrift. As a result, left-leaning governments possess a strong incentive to prove their inflation-fighting credentials.

For example, the center-left Concertación in Chile embraced economic orthodoxy in part to demonstrate their managerial competence to a skeptical business community. Edgardo Boeninger, Aylwin's Presidential Secretary during the democratic transition, summarizes the prevailing view among his economic team.

> Convincing the business community of the center-left's ability to govern was very important. Hence, a main economic goal of the transition was to build the trust of the business community. They were suspicious of the center-left coalition; not unreasonably presuming that it would be more statist/interventionist. The product of this skepticism was that the center-left coalition was determined to demonstrate their governability. This led to a higher degree of controls in economic policy; more prudent policy aimed at assuaging the business and investment community. Fiscal policy was orthodox, with the goal of reducing inflation.[127]

A decade after Chile's democratic transition, the Concertación continued to cite the importance of the business community's approval. When Ricardo Lagos prepared for the presidency – the first socialist president since Salvador

---

[124] UNDP 2005; Schneider 2010.
[125] Thacker 2000; Teichman 2001; Schneider 2004; Schneider 2010.
[126] Scheider 2010.
[127] Interview with former Chilean Budget Director Edgardo Boeninger, conducted on June 6, 2007. Boeninger was Budget Director under President Eduardo Frei from 1964–1969. He later became Presidential Secretary under President Patricio Alwyn from 1990–1994 and served as a Senator from 1998–2006.

Allende's catastrophic governance – he knew he had to overcome the business community's distrust for the Chilean left.

> There was something implicit especially when I became President. 'Look what happened with the last Socialist President. This guy does not know how to run the economy.' We were always under suspicion . . . I didn't have to convince the business community. I had to act! It is not a question of talking. You convince them by what you do![128]

Beyond Chile, recent leftist presidents from inflation-crisis countries have followed similar courses of action. In Brazil and Peru, for example, presidential candidates have surprisingly promised austerity and inflation control during their election bids notwithstanding their leftist roots.

In an effort to calm jittery investors' concerns about a return of economic populism, Lula shed his anti-globalization image and vowed to continue Cardoso's macroeconomic policies in his *Carta ao Povo Brasileiro (Letter to the Brazilian People)*. With an eye on turbulent financial markets during the first few days of his presidency, he once again pledged that his "government would not neglect the control of inflation and [would] maintain a posture of fiscal responsibility."[129] In his two terms in office, Lula made good on these orthodoxy promises even during election campaigns, prompting former Brazilian foreign minister Luiz Felipe Lampreia to note that "there is now a national consensus against macroeconomic foolishness."[130] According to Lula's presidential predecessor, "only Nixon could go to China, and only Lula could show the world that the Latin American left could run a stable modern economy."[131]

During his own presidential bid, Peruvian President Ollanta Humala similarly used oaths of orthodoxy to quell private sector concerns. A newly business-clad Humala, who once backed both a 2005 Peruvian military coup and Hugo Chávez's march to socialism, instead portrayed himself as the Peruvian Lula during his 2011 presidential bid.[132] Reminiscent of Lula's "letter to the Brazilian people," Humala pledged economic stability to the national business community in his "commitment with the Peruvian people." Hoping to abate financial market volatility, he also appointed a Wall-Street friendly economist to the finance minister post. In a national radio address, Humala further emphasized that his administration would take its cues from Brazil's economic success. "We recognize there is a successful process underway in Brazil, which has accomplished economic growth that combines social inclusion with respect for macroeconomic equilibrium."[133]

---

[128] Author's interview with President Lagos, Brown University, April 16, 2010.
[129] *New York Times*, October 2002.
[130] *The Economist*, September 30, 2010.
[131] Cardoso 2006.
[132] For example, he emphasized the importance of private investment to economic development in Peru during a September 15, 2010, discussion at the Elliott School of International Affairs at George Washington University.
[133] *BBC News*, April 12, 2011.

Inflation-Averse Austerity Cycle (H3). Before their countries' inflation troubles, politicians were likely to view constituents as straight-forward economic voters.[134] A political business cycle was a viable political strategy for presidents fearing that they might get punished for the economy's poor performance at the polls. Politicians might craft unsusainable economic expansions to win votes, without much fear of a political backlash against inflation.

After experiencing traumatic inflationary episodes, however, politicians from inflation-ridden countries instead wrestle with a thorny economic paradox. Growth and jobs remain a political priority. Fearing retribution from both inflation-scarred voters and businesses, however, politicians realize they must also be vigilant custodians of price stability.

Under these conditions, the traditional electoral logic loses its luster. Presidents may intervene in the economy, but not so aggressively that they ignite inflation. On the other hand, politicians want to avoid making such a staunch commitment to austerity that they sow the seeds for a deflationary downturn. Seeking a macroeconomic balance between low inflation and moderate growth, politicians pursue a neutral mix of economic policies. Politicians operate according to a straightforward political logic: protecting voters' purchasing power.

In summary, my third governing hypothesis is that politicians are unlikely to create political business cycles without having the political will. I contend that policy elites from countries with past inflation crises alter their political strategies. They believe that voters will evaluate them on their ability to contain inflation as much as their ability to create economic growth. Even if the probability of sparking high inflation is low, politicians shy away from unsustainable government deficits. They do not want to risk rekindling inflation's flame, which, like a wildfire, can quickly spread without bounds. Worried about crossing the threshold of price instability, risk-averse politicians choose cautious macroeconomic policies over highly expansionary policies that jeopardize a return of inflation. By selecting policies that guarantee low inflation, politicians demonstrate to inflation-sensitive markets and electorates that they are capable of governing the economy.

H_3: **Inflation-Averse Political Austerity Cycle (PAC).** Past inflation crises breeds economic risk-aversion; politicians do not use accommodative fiscal and monetary policies to boost the economy before elections. Instead, they use a neutral mix of economic policies or mildly contractionary policies that yield political austerity cycles. Inflation falls during elections, but at the cost of lower economic growth and fewer new jobs. This pattern is more pronounced under left-leaning than right-leaning administrations (upper right quadrant in Table 2.1).

---

[134] Economic voters base their voting decision largely on the government's recent economic performance, "assigning credit or blame to the incumbent government" (see Lewis-Beck 1988; Powell and Whitten 1993; Duch and Stevenson 2004).

Low Growth, Low Inflation Austerity Cycle (H4). When high debt constraints and high inflation aversion are simultaneously present, the likely outcome is a deflationary electoral cycle characterized by slowing inflation and growth. Politicians slash spending and raise interest rates to hold inflation at bay, even if these actions curtail the pace of growth and job creation.

What is the political benefit of this most acute form of political austerity cycles? Obviously, politicians do not plan for such a deflationary electoral spiral. Rather, their hopes of balancing price stability with moderate growth are derailed by an unexpected credit shock. Recall that in countries that are heavily indebted to bond markets, politicians intending to prime the economic pump are vulnerable to credit swings and interest rate shocks that quickly foil plans for an electoral expansion.

Similarly, the extent of the political austerity cycle is conditional on a government's financial means. Inflation-averse politicians have budgetary room to maneuver when they have access to windfall revenues (such as commodity income and privatization proceeds) and non-market borrowing resources (such as bank lending) that reduce their vulnerability to global credit disruptions. They can use a neutral mix of economic policies to target moderate growth and low inflation.

However, when these same politicians are highly reliant on bond market financing, it is more difficult to achieve such economic balance. Governments are susceptible to severe credit shocks, particularly during periods of political uncertainty. Capital withdrawal sparked by electoral uneasiness can quickly launch interest rates higher and increase financing costs for both governments and firms. These "sudden stops" cause economic growth to slow more markedly than politicians planned, and yield the most pronounced type of the political austerity cycle.

H_4: **Political Austerity Cycle (PAC).** When inflation-averse politicians face steep funding constraints from global financial markets, they strongly contract economic policies in order to stabilize the economy. With this form of political austerity cycle, inflation and growth fall before elections most markedly (lower right quadrant in Table 2.1).

2.5. SUMMARY AND CONCLUSIONS

In this chapter, I have argued that the classical assumption of short-term policy myopia – embedded in the political macroeconomic literature – should be reexamined to account for the complexities of a globalized world. In regions such as Latin America, many politicians have embraced a long-term technocratic view that emphasizes budgetary discipline and inflation control over aggressive government intervention in the economy. Why have politicians come to value a seemingly long-term asset like economic stability? Why would they even more surprisingly choose election periods to demonstrate their commitment to these austere governance principles? Why not instead aggressively increase the budget deficit in hopes of winning the economic vote?

Political austerity theory offers a dual explanation for this change in political logic. The first part of the theory claims that developing countries' ability to reap the rewards of preelection spending often reflects their capacity to raise external financing. Unlike their developed country counterparts, developing-country governments face significant hurdles to using counter-cyclical,[135] or expansionary policies to stimulate the economy. Shallow domestic financial markets and narrow tax bases leave many developing countries dependent upon international capital markets for financing budget expenditures.[136]

Beginning in the 1990s, structural changes in the global economy – in this case, the international financial architecture – transformed the relationship between debtor countries and their international creditors. Following the 1980s debt crisis, developing country governments increasingly financed their debt with capital markets rather than cross-border bank lending. This financing shift altered the classic electoral trade-off that pitted jobs and growth against price stability.

Regardless of ideological proclivities, I contend that as these highly indebted governments developed a greater reliance on global bond markets for budget financing, they sacrificed the policy freedom to aggressively target domestic constituents with jobs and growth. This is the financial catch-22 of developing country politics. Governments tapped international markets to increase their spending options, only to subject their budget decisions to financial market discipline. This disciplining effect is often most constraining during elections, when investor uncertainty is high, and governments hope to avoid "sudden stops" of international credit that lead to higher borrowing costs and slower growth.

Notwithstanding a government's debt structure, incumbents may instead voluntarily choose the path of economic orthodoxy. The second part of political austerity theory examines when developing-country governments lack the electoral motivation to induce an economic expansion. Rather than responding to external pressures, this part of the theory contends that the low-inflation impetus is the product of a country's own economic experiences. Grounded in psychological theories of risky choice, it claims that the saliency of past inflationary trauma transforms political thinking in developing countries. Political and technocratic elites learn from the policy errors that produced these catastrophic shocks and develop a macroeconomic consensus against unsustainable government deficits. Moreover, they adopt risk-averse orthodox policies that promise to provide low inflation, an important baseline for the economic vote.

In Chapters 3 to 7, I test my theory, using a multi-method approach involving both statistical and case study evidence. I intend to show that when politicians

---

[135] Gavin and Perotti 1997; Kaminsky, Reinhart, and Végh 2004; Lupu 2006; Pinto 2010.
[136] Kaufman and Stallings 1991; Gavin and Perotti 1997.

operate in a globalized world, they are more likely to prioritize inflation control, even if it means potentially providing their constituents with fewer jobs and slower growth. The statistical analysis in Chapter 3 tests these two mechanisms and finds broad support for the constraining effect of bond finance and crisis history on budgetary and economic outcomes during elections.

Despite this evidence, how do we disentangle the effects of these two explanations, given the importance of both inflationary and debt shocks to the region's credit history? After buoyant credit-driven expansions produced hyperinflation, Latin American governments financed their political agendas with international bond issuance rather than the inflation tax. Not surprisingly, bond creditors initially incorporated this inflation history into their country risk assessments. In fact, the international finance literature claims that baseline borrowing rates often reflect historic economic performance.[137] That said, it also finds that interest rates account for investors' expectations about more dynamic factors, including current economic, budgetary, and credit conditions.[138] Consequently, it's plausible that a country's bond market exposure and inflation history might be related to one another, but also affect government policy and the economy through independent channels.

In the book's comparative case study chapters, I assess whether the effects of these two mechanisms are conditioned on each other. Employing elections as my unit of analysis, I examine how variation in debt structure and inflation aversion interact to yield different electoral policy and economic outcomes according to the four hypotheses outlined earlier in the chapter. Exploiting this variation across twenty different elections allows me to evaluate both the independent and interactive effects of the two main explanatory variables of bond market dependence and inflation crisis history.[139] For example, political business cycles were quite common in Chile's early democratic period before the country's inflationary shocks and bond market entry, but fail to materialize in the post-inflation crisis return to democracy, notwithstanding a lack of bond market indebtedness.

The case study chapters are also instrumental in identifying when politicians develop alternative tools to political business cycles. If politicians are more likely to live within their means today, how do they reward key political constituencies? They have several options. Governments can take a cue from Chile and Brazil and bolster state capacity by introducing new taxes, allowing them to raise social spending within a balanced budget framework. Alternatively, they can signal fiscal responsibility to investors, while increasingly employing discretionary tools – including administrative controls, subsidies, off-balance sheet spending, and clientelistic transfers – to target key domestic supporters. For example, Argentina's Kirchners modified domestic laws to boost

[137] Obstfeld and Rogoff 1996.
[138] Mosley 2003; Reinhart and Rogoff 2004.
[139] See Chapter 4 for the complete case study design.

discretionary spending, implement price controls in the energy and transportation sectors, and redirect central bank foreign reserves toward political initiatives. Ironically, financial globalization may give politicians not only an incentive to reach macroeconomic balance, but also the incentive to develop alternative policy tools subject to less global scrutiny.

2.A. APPENDIX

The literature on the political economy of macroeconomic policy making provides a theoretical structure for economic policy choices. In these models, government preferences are captured through loss functions. The Barro-Gordon loss-function is one of the most commonly employed theoretical models. It shows politicians' relative sensitivity to unemployment and inflation. Their utility varies directly with employment (or growth), yet indirectly with inflation.[140]

$$L = a(U_t - kU_{t^n})^2 + b(\pi_t)^2$$

where U_t = employment rate; U_{t^n} = natural rate of unemployment; π_t = inflation rate; a = relative weight of unemployment in the loss function ($a > 0$); b = relative weight of inflation term in loss function ($b > 0$); k = extent of distortions (such as unemployment compensation and income taxation) that make U_{t^n} exceed the efficient or socially optimal rate ($0 < k < 1$).

This loss function shows how policy makers value full employment and price stability. More specifically, the ratio of its parameters a and b captures the benefit of employment (and growth) relative to the cost of higher inflation. In other words, these parameters indicate policy makers' level of inflation aversion. A government favoring a Keynesian view is likely to tolerate some inflation in exchange for higher growth and lower unemployment. They assign a lower weight to inflation relative to unemployment in their loss functions. By contrast, a government favoring a monetarist approach to policy making does not sanction a government-induced expansion, deeming that it only yields higher inflation. To prevent inflationary pressures, they choose price stability over jobs and growth creation. They assign a higher weight to inflation relative to unemployment in their loss functions.

Building from the intuition of these models, my theory seeks to explain when inflation aversion occurs in developing countries.

---

[140] The functional form of these loss function varies across the literature, but their main intuition is that policy makers and voters dislike inflation and unemployment, but support economic growth. For a more detailed description of loss functions and macroeconomic policy making, see Barro and Gordon (1983) and Scheve (2004).

3

The Political Economy of Elections

When my grandchildren ask me: 'Daddy, what did you do for the New Frontier?,' I shall
sadly reply: 'I kept telling them down at the office, in December, January, and April
that what this country needs is an across the board rise in disposable income to lower
the level of unemployment, speed up the recovery and the return to healthy growth,
promote capital formation and the general welfare, insure domestic tranquility and the
triumph of the democratic party at the polls.'
                                        – Paul Samuelson, economic adviser to President Kennedy.

More than thirty years ago, political scientist Edward Tufte and economist
William Nordhaus of Yale University put forth a seminal new theory, known
as the political business cycle. While a business cycle typically refers to the
economy's regular booms and busts, their central insight was that politics
also influences the business cycle. In line with Paul Samuelson's blunt quip to
President Kennedy about the economy, they expected incumbent presidents to
maximize the economy's growth performance in the prelude to new elections
today, even at the cost of an economic bust tomorrow.

In mapping out his research design, Tufte employs the metaphor of a detec-
tive solving a murder mystery. After establishing a motive of inflating the
economy before elections, he searches for clues (such as changes in economic
policy and outcomes) that prove his suspicions that there is a political business
cycle. Tufte's study of developed country politics finds electoral cycles in fiscal
transfers, growth, and unemployment. These patterns are straightforwardly in
line with many popular perceptions today. In the midst of the 2004 U.S. elections, for instance, the *Boston Globe* announced that the "political business
cycle was back with a vengeance" in reference to President George W. Bush's
immense election-year deficits and "the most massive fiscal stimulus program
since World War II." The newspaper editorial further fretted that "the only
question [was] whether the damage will be visible before or after Election Day."

72

Notably, however, political austerity theory expects to unravel a different electoral plot. Rather than finding a culpable Colonel Mustard with a loaded pistol in the billiard room, it instead anticipates an absence of foul play – because the suspect lacks either the motive or the fire power to pull the economic trigger. In other words, a rise in risk-averse macroeconomic politics, along with the financing constraints imposed by international markets, reduces the political payoff to the electoral boom-bust cycle. Before moving forward with the empirical analysis, let us begin by situating this theory within the political business cycle literature.

3.1. DIAL M FOR MANIPULATION? THE EVIDENCE

In developed countries, the evidence for election-year economic manipulation is at best mixed. The original political business cycle literature found considerable support for electoral economic cycles in developed countries ranging from Germany and New Zealand to the United States. Showcased by the famous 1972 Nixon parable of electoral expansion gone awry,[1] they took the expected form – a pre-election growth and jobs boom followed by a post-election inflationary sputtering of the economy.[2]

However, a new generation of political business cycle theorists questioned the persistence of these boom-bust cycles over time, instead anticipating that economically savvy voters punish electoral engineering of the economy.[3] In fact, their large-N developed country panel studies found little empirical support for economic expansions.[4] They did, however, find inflationary evidence, prompting these scholars to conclude that a political budget cycle, market by

---

[1] Tufte (1978) provides not only empirical evidence of hikes in social security and veteran payments before elections, but also Nixon's motivation to prime the economic pump. In fact, the U.S. president delivered a personal note to all retirees notifying them of this boost in social security benefits directly before his 1972 reelection bid.

[2] Nordhaus 1975; Lindbeck 1976; Tufte 1978.

[3] The rational expectations literature casts doubt on the viability of political business cycles. It questions the assumption that incumbents have an incentive to engineer an electoral boom. Replacing a world of naive voters with highly informed voters, these models suggest that voters provide a check on politicians' opportunistic behavior (Lucas 1976; Rogoff and Sibert 1988; Rogoff 1990). Possessing a prospective view of the potential costs of an election-year expansion, voters interpret fiscal deficits and credit creation as electioneering and punish incumbents for their macroeconomic mismanagement. According to these models, incumbents should be less likely to fiddle with macroeconomic policy. Therefore, we should observe smaller and more fleeting political business cycles. If politicians tinker with macroeconomic policy, it is because a world of incomplete information still offers political gains (Rogoff and Sibert 1988).

[4] Alt and Chrystal 1983; Keech and Pak 1989; Alesina and Roubini 1992; Alesina, Roubini, and Cohen 1997; Franzese 1999; Drazen 2000.

an electoral budget expansion, was more common than the political business cycle.[5]

Taking its cue from the democratic governance literature, a third generation of political economists surmised that developing countries are the prime suspects for this budgetary tinkering, offering two institutional explanations. First, developing countries are mired in a transitional state between electoral and liberal democracy.[6] Because many of these countries have a lower level of democracy, chief executives confront fewer institutional constraints on their power. They are less encumbered by strong legislatures, sound legal frameworks, freedom of the press, and autonomous central banks. Therefore, we should observe that elections are a catalyst for budgetary largesse in developing regions such as Latin America.[7]

Second, newer democracies often lack strong institutions that collect and report economic data, leaving voters unable to evaluate government policies. Without a history of electoral experience, competent data reporting, and budget transparency, voters cannot distinguish between competent economic management and electoral engineering.[8] In Latin America, a region where many countries have undergone democratic transitions during the last two to three decades, politicians should be more likely to aggressively intervene in the economy before elections.

3.1.1. Credit and Crises: Explaining Developing Country Variation

Is the choice of electoral stimulus always the most optimal political strategy in newer democracies? When and why might politicians possess a different set of election-year incentives?

Recall from Chapter 2 that political austerity theory claims that aggregate market and individual income volatility can alter these traditional political incentives. First, when governments rely on bond markets for financing, they are more likely to adhere to economic orthodoxy. The ownership dispersion of bondholders creates a capital exit threat during elections that is not present with other types of credit (from bank to multilateral lending), making politicians more likely to comply with their conservative macroeconomic demands. Second, following past traumatic inflationary shocks, politicians are more likely

---

[5] See Drazen 2000 for further details. In addition, Person and Tabellini (2003) find that government revenues contract prior to elections, whereas Clark (2003) shows that politicians tinker with fiscal policy, even when operating in a globalized world.

[6] Liberal democracies generally possess check and balances between government branches, provisions for political and civil freedoms, and a consistent rule of law (O'Donnell, Mainwaring, and Valenzuela 1992; Diamond 1999).

[7] Ames 1987; Edwards 1994; Schuknecht 1996; Schuknecht 2000; Acosta and Coppedge 2001; Block 2002; Gonzalez 2002; Shi and Svensson 2002; Brender and Drazen 2005; Keefer 2005; Keefer and Khemani 2005; Shi and Svensson 2006; Barberia and Avelino 2011.

[8] Alt and Lassan 2006; Brender and Drazen 2005, 2008.

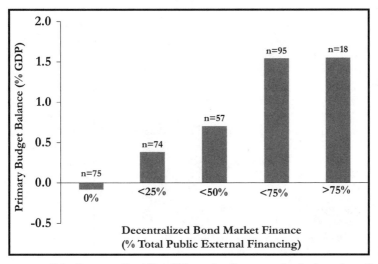

FIGURE 3.1. Decentralized Bond Financing Improves Latin American Government Budget Balances (16 Latin American Countries, 1990–2009).
Source: CEPAL; World Bank.

to be cautious managers of the economy. In effect, they deem that these shocks – after destroying the incomes of middle-class and poor voters – have widened the traditional low-inflation constituency beyond business and financial institutions.

Figures 3.1 and 3.2 illustrate the contractionary effect of global bond market exposure (measured by decentralized bond finance as a share of a government's total external financing) and past inflation crises (measured by the binary variable accounting for whether a country has experienced a past inflation crisis) on government budget balances between 1990 and 2009. Notably, there is considerable variation in both measures over time, making Latin American an ideal region for testing political austerity theory.

In this chapter, I conduct a large-N panel investigation for sixteen Latin American countries from 1961 to 2009, encompassing a total of 132 election periods. In line with the previous predictions, I find that both bond market financing and past inflationary crises have a dampening effect on election-year engineering of the economy. When countries are dependent on global capital markets and/or have suffered from turbulent inflationary episodes, their politicians are more likely to be cautious governors of the economy, settling for lower inflation and growth.

Ironically, the shift in governance incentives rewards miserly macroeconomics and punishes the conventional spendthrift impulse during elections, helping explain *when* and *why* we might observe the exact opposite patterns from those predicted by political business cycle theory. Returning to Tufte's

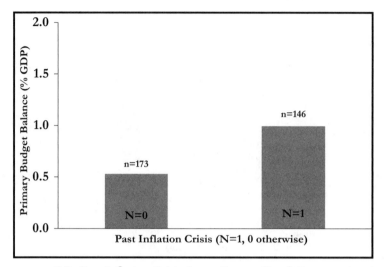

FIGURE 3.2. Past Inflation Crisis Spurs Greater Fiscal Conservatism in Latin America (16 Latin American Countries, 1990–2009).
Source: CEPAL; World Bank.

mystery metaphor, deflationary rather than inflationary weapons may be found at the scene of the electoral caper when conservative motives are rooted in credit and crises.

3.1.2. Has Austerity Politics Replaced Partisan Politics?

Latin America's political shift to centrist economic policies raises a fascinating question. Notwithstanding these inflationary and debt shocks, do ideological and partisan differences persist? Or alternatively, in a region such as Latin America where party systems are less ideological than in Europe and the United States,[9] are such partisan cycles even less likely to exist? Has the 1990s neoliberal convergence[10] forever blurred partisan lines?

In this chapter, I also use a series of large-N statistical tests to examine if partisan behavior instead explains changes in economic policy and outcomes. While pre-electoral economic cycles appear to have fallen out of favor with many Latin American politicians, perhaps they are more popular in the electoral aftermath. Without the political pressure of having to signal their competence as macroeconomic managers, chief executives may have greater scope for policy stimulus following elections.

Indeed, a branch of the political business cycle literature predicts this pattern. Following successful election bids, chief executives and their political parties pursue policies that appeal to their ideological bases, creating *partisan*

[9] Roberts and Wibbels 1999.
[10] Roberts 1998; Murillo 2001; Stokes 2001a; Stokes 2001b; Murillo 2002; Weyland 2002; Levitsky 2003; Bruhn 2004; Murillo and Martinez-Gallardo 2007.

political business cycles.[11] Presuming the classic short-run trade-off between inflation and unemployment,[12] this literature expects right-wing political parties to pursue low inflation (at the cost of jobs and growth) and left-wing parties to prioritize high growth and jobs (at the cost of inflation). The right hopes to appeal to its business and financial constituencies, whereas the left attempts to assuage middle-class and working families' concerns. Most recently, Larry Bartels finds that Democratic incumbents in the United States generally oversee higher growth and lower unemployment (and marginally higher inflation) than their Republican counterparts. Ironically, however, Republicans are much better at timing income gains and economic growth to coincide with elections.[13]

Do we find a similar ideological cleavage in Latin America? Recall that political austerity theory claims that past inflationary crises have helped obscure the ideological divide on macroeconomic governance throughout much of the region. Whereas macroeconomic orthodoxy is historically associated with right-leaning parties, many political elites believe that domestic support for low inflation has widened beyond the business and financial communities.[14] Moreover, politicians prioritize macroeconomic discipline because they believe that inflation control – while not always the most salient political issue – has become an important baseline for the economic vote.

In this chapter, I find that the 1980s' inflationary and debt shocks helped create a third political way, where leftist politicians are just as likely as right-wing politicians to embrace budgetary prudence and economic discipline. Ironically, my statistical tests show that left-oriented governments, hailing from inflation-ridden countries, are often the most ardent followers of budgetary austerity. Moreover, notwithstanding partisan loyalties, these crisis legacies, along with global bond market's headwinds, often create a deflationary bias among parties across the political spectrum.

The rest of this chapter is organized as follows. I begin by presenting several statistical models, along with the study's major empirical concepts and measures: democracy, decentralized debt, inflation crisis legacy, and partisanship. I then turn to the analysis, assessing the extent to which the empirical results are consistent with theoretical predictions. Finally, I conclude with a discussion of the findings and their implications.

3.2. STATISTICAL MODELS: KEY CONCEPTS AND MEASURES

I use multivariate regression analysis to study the effect of presidential elections on economic outcomes in Latin America. Recall that the region's predominance of presidential systems makes it an ideal setting to examine political business cycles. The presence of election-timing that is fixed and

[11] See footnote 43 in Chapter 1.
[12] See footnote 10 in Chapter 2.
[13] Bartels 2008.
[14] See Chapters 6 and 7 for extensive comparative case study evidence regarding the prevalence of inflation aversion among political elites in Latin America.

constitutionally mandated helps avoid endogeneity problems,[15] or the possibility that current economic conditions reflect political tinkering with election dates.

Employing time series cross-sectional data from 1961–2009 for sixteen democratic countries, I perform a series of panel regressions. I present my findings using both fixed effects and a generalized methods of moments (GMM) estimators. The empirical analysis proceeds in two stages. First, I use a series of basic regression models to test for the traditional political business cycle, presenting evidence about the effect of elections on government budgets and countries' core macroeconomic indicators: inflation, economic growth, and unemployment. Second, I test for the partisan business cycle, advancing my findings about the effect of left partisanship on budgetary and economic outcomes. In the crux of both of these analyses, I construct a series of interactive models to test for political austerity cycles. I condition decentralized debt and inflation crisis history on elections (and later partisanship) to observe their effect on fiscal policy and the economy.

All models are estimated with robust standard errors, clustered by country. Fixed year effects were tested and removed since they were not statistically significant and have not affected the main results. In the Appendix, I include a full description of these statistical models (Sections 3A.1 and 3A.2) and the data sources and descriptive statistics (Tables 3A.1 and 3A.2) for the regression variables outlined in the following section.

3.2.1. Independent Variables

Democracy. According to political business cycle theorists, politicians' fear of losing office compels them to aggressively intervene in the economy. In line with this theoretical premise, I limit the unit of analysis to democratically competitive Latin American elections. I classify democratic elections according to Przeworksi et al.'s (2000) criteria. They use a minimalist democracy rule based on Robert Dahl's concept of contestation; democracies are "regimes that allow some, even if limited, regularized competition among conflicting visions and interests."[16]

Notwithstanding historical swings between dictatorship and democracy, the region has enjoyed considerable durability in democratic regimes over the last three decades. Even before the most recent democratization wave (which began in 1978), several Latin American countries had long periods of uninterrupted democracy characterized by consecutive elections, including Chile, Colombia, Costa Rica, and Venezuela.

---

[15] To confirm that the election variable is exogenous (and that the incumbent did not disregard the constitution by changing election timing), I verified that the fixed election dates in my time series (1961–2009) correspond to the constitutionally mandated dates.

[16] Dahl 1971; Przeworksi et al. 2000.

TABLE 3.1. *List of 16 Latin American Countries*

Argentina	Colombia	Guatemala	Panama
Bolivia	Costa Rica	Honduras	Peru
Brazil	Ecuador	Mexico	Uruguay
Chile	El Salvador	Nicaragua	Venezuela

Note: The study employs least square regression estimates with fixed effects.

Using Przeworski's decision rule,[17] I code sixteen Latin American democracies (Table 3.1) between 1961 and 2009, which includes a total of 132 contested presidential elections. Notably, this classification provides us with competitive elections that span the entire data set from 1961 to 2009 (Figure 3.3). I study presidential rather than legislative contests because economic policy in all of the countries studied is much more heavily shaped by executive branches than by legislatures, the courts, or other governmental or societal actors. Additionally, given that immediate re-election is only a recent Latin American phenomenon,[18] I assume that presidential legacies, non-sequential re-election bids, and party continuity also motivate incumbents' policy choices.[19]

In testing the effect of elections on economic outcomes, I construct a binary election variable that accounts for the expected policy lag between economic policy decisions and inflation. Indeed, according to macroeconomic theory, monetary policy does not immediately influence spending, income, and employment. Rather, it affects the economy incrementally, with inflationary pressures slowly building over the course of six to eighteen months.[20]

With this in mind, I employ the binary variable, *election$_{it}$*, as a pre-election dummy for growth and unemployment, but as a post-election dummy for inflation, in hopes of capturing inflation's policy lag.[21] Recall that the *political business cycle* begins with economic growth and ends with high inflation. Therefore, we not only want to track inflation during the election year, but also subsequent years.

I also use this binary variable to test for political budget cycles or fiscal stimulus before elections. Unlike monetary policy, fiscal policy can affect the economy more quickly. For this reason, U.S. politicians included direct income

[17] Przeworski et al. (2000) classify a democracy as a regime where 1) the chief executive must be elected; 2) the legislature also needs to be elected, 3) more than one party exists, and 4) electoral alternation is a possibility.

[18] Only four Latin American countries permitted immediate reelection in the sample, including Argentina, Brazil, Colombia, and Venezuela.

[19] In more than 100 primary field research interviews I conducted with Latin American politicians and their advisors from 2007 to 2011, they cited the following justifications for their electoral policy decisions: presidential legacies, party continuity, and incumbent reelection (whether immediate or non-sequential).

[20] Friedman 1970; Mankiw 1996, 2003; Dornbusch, Fischer, and Startz 2001.

[21] This dummy variable construction is based on standard models that are typically used to test for political business cycles (Alesina and Roubini 1992).

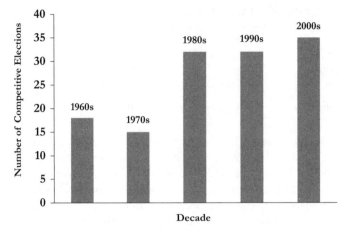

FIGURE 3.3. Latin American Presidential Elections (16 Latin American Countries, 1961–2009).
Source: Political Handbook of the World, Cheibub and Kalandrakis (2004).

and payroll tax cuts in the last few stimulus bills to offset recessionary pressures.[22] Should the pre-election dummy have a positive coefficient, it would point to the existence of a political budget cycle in Latin America.

Finally, I employ this election variable to test for *political austerity cycles*. If such a cycle exists, I would anticipate observing the exact opposite pattern from those expected from political budget and political business cycle theory. Fiscal policy contracts and growth falls in the prelude to elections, yielding lower inflation during both the election and post-election period (see the Appendix for the full statistical models).

$$pre\_election_{it} = \begin{cases} 1 \text{ in the election year, and the preceding } N - 1 \text{ years} \\ 0 \text{ otherwise, where } N = 2 \text{ or } 3 \end{cases}$$

$$post\_election_{it} = \begin{cases} 1 \text{ in the election year, and the subsequent years} \\ 0 \text{ otherwise} \end{cases}$$

Decentralized Debt. To test for the presence of political austerity cycles, I construct a variable, *decentralized_{it}*, to account for the constraining effect of decentralized bond finance. It measures global bond issuance as a percentage of a government's total public external debt.[23] Recall that many cash-strapped

---

[22] However, fiscal policy may still have longer policy lags, depending on how fast new legislative measures are adopted. For example, a change in tax rates may take time before being reflected in paychecks (Mankiw 1997; Dornbusch, Fischer, and Startz 2001).

[23] In a series of robustness checks, I replace the original *decentralized_{it}* variable with a new measure intended to capture the effect of the 1990s Brady Bond restructurings (see Section 3.3 for further details).

developing countries must borrow externally to finance their spending. Political austerity theory emphasizes the importance of this debt structure in determining government spending patterns.[24] If political austerity theory is correct, when global bond markets account for a high share of a government's external financing (relative to bank and multilateral lending), politicians should place more weight on inflation control. In other words, as *decentralized*$_{it}$ increases, global markets should serve as a natural enforcement mechanism for conditionality. In response to the bond market's threat of capital withdrawal, politicians should be more likely to adopt restrictive economic policies that yield lower inflation and growth during election periods.

Inflation Crisis Legacy. Notwithstanding these externally imposed financing constraints, do politicians sometimes choose economic orthodoxy over economic stimulus? Recall that the second part of political austerity theory focuses on the choice of budgetary discipline. In developing countries, it may also pay political dividends to be fiscal hawks. In countries that have experienced devastating inflationary crisis, the political and technocratic elite are more likely to develop a consensus about the merits of conservative macroeconomic governance. After the public has paid for the dizzying cost of fiscal adjustment through a whopping "inflation tax" – that wiped out their purchasing power and pushed many Latin Americans below the poverty line – politicians are often risk-averse. They perceive that the baseline economic vote is not solely about boosting incomes, but also protecting incomes from inflationary shocks.[25]

Seeking to account for the influence of inflationary history on policy making, I design a binary variable, *inflation_crisis*$_{it}$, that measures the effect of past inflationary crises on political and economic priorities. I assign this variable a value of 1 if a country had a previous inflationary crisis and 0 otherwise.[26] Indeed, I anticipate that the political and institutional memory of Latin America's severe hyperinflation episodes alters the traditional political logic of providing jobs and growth during elections. Politicians whose countries were plagued by inflationary crises are more likely to avoid steep budget deficits and target low inflation to appease an inflation-sensitive electorate. What constitutes a past inflationary crisis? I use Sach's definition of "very high inflations," or inflation above 100 percent per annum, as the price threshold that marks a crisis.[27]

$$inflation\_crisis_{it} = \begin{cases} 1 \text{ if country had a past inflation crisis} \\ 0 \text{ otherwise} \end{cases}$$

---

[24] See Chapter 2 for further details.

[25] See Chapter 2 for more details.

[26] In additional robustness checks, I use a second measure of inflationary crisis, *highest past inflation*$_{it}$, that represents a country's highest historic inflation (see Section 3.3 for further details).

[27] See Sachs and Larrain 1993.

Partisanship. Might partisan behavior rather than elections spur political business cycles? Despite the popularity of partisan explanations of policy formation in developed countries, they are difficult to transplant to developing countries. In the developing world, party systems are often less differentiated along ideological and programmatic platforms.[28] In fact, political parties frequently shift their ideological priorities over time. For example, Argentina's Peronists are defined by both Menem's 1990s neoliberalism and Kirchner's twenty-first-century economic heterodoxy. Not only have economic platforms changed in Latin America, parties themselves have often disintegrated and regenerated. For this reason, the political business cycle literature has shied away from using partisan theories to explain economic policy making in developing countries.[29]

Despite these challenges, the World Bank's Database of Political Institutions offers a measure that should help account for partisan behavior in Latin America's complex political spectrum. It codes party orientation specifically with respect to economic policy along a right-left spectrum from 0 to 3.[30] Employing this coding, I designed the binary variable, $partisanship_{it}$,[31] to test for partisan business cycles, or the effect of left-leaning governments (compared to centrist and right-leaning governments) on economic policy and outcomes.[32]

$$partisanship_{it} = \begin{cases} 1 \text{ if government is classified as left-leaning} \\ 0 \text{ otherwise} \end{cases}$$

Notwithstanding partisan preferences, I expect political austerity cycles to persist. In countries with a legacy of inflationary and debt crises, leftist presidential administrations should be just as likely as right administrations to prioritize price stability over aggressive economic stimulus. Indeed, if ideological preferences remain, I anticipate that left partisanship is moderated by structural shifts in global finance and inflation-aversion among politicians.

---

[28] Roberts and Wibbels 1999.

[29] Schuknect 1996.

[30] For example, parties that are defined as conservative, Christian democratic, or right-wing take on a value of 1. Parties defined as centrist take on a value of 2. Parties that are defined as communist, socialist, social democratic, or left-wing take on a value of 3. Otherwise, the variable is 0.

[31] In a series of robustness tests, I replaced the original partisanship variable with a new binary variable constructed from Coppedge's (1997) ideological scores, incorporating updates by Pop-Eleches (2009) and Stokes (2009). The results for these regression models coincided with the initial findings.

[32] Some political economy scholars believe that partisan trends are often stalled by savvy voters that support divided government during mid-term elections (Alesina and Rosenthal 1995). Therefore, in additional robustness checks, I also vary N, or the years that a partisan cycle lasts, to account for this phenomenon (see Section 3.3 for more details).

3.2.2. Control Variables

Fiscal Policy Regressions. In these regressions, many of the major control variables are the same as the following economic regressions; however, there are a few exceptions. These include a measure of the output gap (*Domestic Output Gap*) to control for a country's position in its economic cycle, a demographic variable capturing the fraction of a country's population (*Population*) that is working age (between fifteen and sixty-four),[33] and a country's terms of trade position (*Terms of Trade*), which conditions for commodity booms that are often central to alleviating governments' budgetary constraints in the developing world. In additional robustness checks, I also employ a measure of non-tax revenues (*Non-tax revenues*) in order to control for the effect of foreign aid and natural resource revenue from state-owned enterprises on government deficits.[34] I anticipate that windfall revenues from these non-tax sources reduce governments' reliance on global financial markets, and therefore, make political business cycles more likely. All of these estimations also employ the same inflation and institutional control variables as the following models, and a lagged dependent variable.

Economic Regressions. In testing for changes in inflation, growth, and unemployment, I use a series of control variables to account for other economic and institutional factors that may influence the economy. Given that my sample includes many small open economies, I control for the effect of changes in the world economy (*Global Growth*) on the domestic economic climate. Similarly, because many Latin American countries lack a diversified export base, I also account for any fluctuations stemming from commodity export dependence (*Commodity Price Index*). Finally, I include imports plus exports as a percentage of GDP to control for economic openness (*Trade*). In general, I would expect that global economic and commodity booms would boost economic growth and inflation in Latin America.

When inflation is the dependent variable, I also control for the size of the financial sector (*Domestic Financial Depth*), on the assumption that weaker financial sectors lead to higher inflation.[35] I use M2 as a percentage of GDP, or outstanding banking sector liabilities, as a proxy for financial sector size. I also include annual GDP growth (*Growth*) to control for cyclical movements in the price level.

When economic growth is the dependent variable, I control for the rate of domestic investment as a percentage of GDP (*Domestic Investment*) because

---

[33] These economic control variables are the same to those employed by Brender and Drazen 2005 in their study of political budget cycles.

[34] See Morrison 2009, or Chapter 4 of the IMF's Global Financial Statistics Manual, for further details.

[35] In larger financial markets, individuals are more likely to have large cash holdings, savings, or investments whose real value could be eroded by inflation. Thus, there should be more demand for price stability (Maxfield 1997).

investment is often a key driver of economic growth. I also include the inflation rate (*Inflation*) to control for the effect of price instability on growth.
Indeed, most economic theories predict that high inflation hampers business
and consumer activity.[36]

Finally, for both the inflation and economic growth regressions, I control
for the primary fiscal balance as a percentage of GDP (*Fiscal Balance*) – lagged
by one year to avoid any possible endogeneity – based on the assumption that
fiscal stimulus drives both economic growth and inflation. I use the primary
fiscal balance (net of interest payments on public debt) rather than the general
government balance (inclusive of interest payments) because it is the more
appropriate measure of the government's fiscal policy stance in highly indebted
countries.

How do institutions affect the political trade-off between economic growth
and inflation? Do greater checks and balances on executive power lead to a
demise of the political business cycle, as predicted by the developing country
literature? Alternatively, when countries are under an IMF agreement, does
conditionality prompt economic austerity? Similarly, does the presence of an
autonomous central bank lead to greater emphasis on price stability?[37]

To account for these institutional factors, I add several control variables,
including a measure of constraints on executive power (*Executive Constraints*),[38] an IMF participation dummy (*IMF*),[39] and a central bank independence index[40] that measures the legal autonomy of the central bank (*Central
Bank Independence*).[41] Finally, based on the assumption that past economic
performance influences present economic conditions, I also include a lagged
dependent variable in each specification.[42]

3.2.3. Hypotheses and Expected Effects

Before assessing the statistical results, let us briefly review the main hypotheses
that were developed in Chapter 2. In a region such as Latin America where

[36] Barro 1996.
[37] Independent central banks are generally associated with lower average inflation rates (see
Bernard, Broz, and Clark 2002; Stasavage 2003).
[38] I use the executive constraints (xconst) variable from the Polity IV data set. In additional
robustness checks, I also employ an alternative measure of executive constraints from Henisz's
(2000) Political Constraint Database.
[39] The IMF dummy is coded 1 for the country-years when there was a conditioned IMF agreement
in force and 0 otherwise. I use two different measures of IMF participation from Vreeland (2003)
and Dreher (2006).
[40] Polillo and Guillén (2005) update of the Cukierman, Webb, and Neyapti (1992) index.
[41] I only include the central bank independence index in additional robustness checks since it
assigns numerical values to countries that do not vary over time. The country dummies, which
are already included in the model, incorporate the same effect.
[42] For example, when inflation is the dependent variable, lagged inflation captures any inertial
inflation effect and any unobserved factors that may explain inflation differences over time,
including monetary policy changes.

past inflationary and debt crisis cast a long shadow into the future, when should we observe political business cycles? Recall that I anticipate that political business cycles are conditional on a government's fiscal space. Stimulus-minded politicians (who presumably have low-inflation aversion) are more likely to craft an electoral boom when they have alternative funding resources that are independent from global financial markets. In other words, political business cycles are most likely when decentralized bond finance accounts for a small share of a government's external financing.

H_1: **Traditional Political Business Cycle (PBC).** When stimulus-minded politicians face low-funding constraints from global bond markets, they use fiscal and/or monetary policy to boost the economy. Politicians are most likely to create conditions of high growth and low unemployment before elections, but at the cost of inflation and/or recession following elections.

When are we more likely to observe political austerity than political business cycles? Political austerity cycle theory predicts when countries rely on decentralized bond finance, we should observe that financial market constraints shrink budget deficits (or increase budget surpluses). Though politicians typically slam on the brakes before elections, the lag between economic policy decisions and inflation could last as long as a full year following an election. Should political austerity cycle theory be correct, we should observe low inflation not only during the election year, but also during the subsequent year.

H_2: **Market-Induced Political Austerity Cycle (PAC).** When stimulus-minded politicians face steep funding constraints from global bond markets, they do not use accommodative fiscal and monetary policies to boost the economy. Instead, they use a neutral mix of economic policies or even contractionary policies that yield political austerity cycles. Inflation falls before elections, but at the cost of lower economic growth and fewer new jobs.

Do ideological differences affect macroeconomic policy choices and outcomes in Latin America? Political austerity theory expects that past hyperinflation shocks have blurred the partisan divide on macroeconomic governance. In countries that have experienced these past income shocks, parties from across the political spectrum place a greater emphasis on budgetary discipline. Jobs and growth obviously remain key political objectives, however, politicians place more importance on inflation control (relative to employment) than in a pre-crisis environment, particularly in the prelude to elections. Because of an expanded low-inflation constituency, political austerity theory expects that left-leaning governments – who hope to prove their macroeconomic governance credentials – are surprisingly more austere than right-leaning governments during electoral campaigns.

H_3: **Inflation-Averse Political Austerity Cycle (PAC).** Past inflation crises breeds economic risk-aversion; politicians do not use accommodative fiscal and monetary policies to boost the economy before elections. Instead, they use a neutral mix of economic policies or mildly contractionary policies that yield political austerity cycles. Inflation falls during elections, but at the cost of lower economic growth and fewer new jobs. This pattern is more pronounced under left-leaning than right-leaning administrations.

What happens when governments are constrained by both debt markets and their volatile inflation legacies simultaneously? While this chapter's statistical tests yield broad and consistent patterns demonstrating the deflationary effects of both decentralized bond finance and past hyperinflation episodes during elections, the subsequent (Chapters 4 to 7) are designed to disentangle these two explanations. These chapters find that not only are a nation's debt structure and inflationary experiences independently constraining on economic policy and outcomes, but that when these factors are concurrently present (such as during the 1995 Argentine and 1998 Brazilian elections) they yield the most acute form of the political austerity cycle.[43]

> H_4: **Political Austerity Cycle (PAC).** When inflation-averse politicians face steep funding constraints from global financial markets, they strongly contract economic policies in order to stabilize the economy. With this form of political austerity cycles, inflation and growth fall before elections most markedly.

3.3. STATISTICAL TESTS ON ELECTIONS AND THE ECONOMY

3.3.1. Fiscal Indicators

The first model in Table 3A.3 displays the unconditional effects of the independent variables on Latin American governments' budget balances. These effects are unconditional in that they ignore incumbent governments' financial constraints at the time of the election. As explained earlier, they test for evidence of a political budget cycle in Latin America.

In this basic regression model, I find evidence that, on average, primary budget balances deteriorate more during elections than other periods. Across all four basic statistical models, the coefficient on the election dummy is negative and statistically significant at the 99 percent confidence level (see Model 1 in Table 3A.3 in the Appendix). These results are consistent with empirical studies that have found political budget cycles in developing economies.[44]

By contrast, the unconditional model indicates that decentralized finance strengthens governments' primary budget balances, as indicated by its highly statistically significant and positive coefficient. In light of this pattern, what

---

[43] See Chapter 7 for further details.
[44] Ames 1987; Edwards 1994; Schuknecht 1996; Schuknecht 2000; Acosta and Coppedge 2001; Block 2002; Gonzalez 2002; Shi and Svensson 2002; Brender and Drazen 2005; Keefer 2005; Keefer and Khemani 2005; Shi and Svensson 2006; Barberia and Avelino 2011.

TABLE 3.2. *Marginal Effects of Elections and Decentralized Finance on Fiscal Indicators*

	Marginal effect of elections on budget balance	90% confidence interval
No decentralized finance	−0.669***	−0.914, −0.424
Decentralized finance	0.056	−0.410, 0.552
	Marginal effect of decentralized finance on budget balance	90% confidence interval
Non-election years	2.101*	0.255, 3.947
Election years	2.826***	0.652, 5.001

Inflation is converted to its natural logarithm to minimize influence of extreme values.
Source: Model 1a in Table 3A.3.

happens during elections as bond finance accounts for a larger share of governments' external financing? Do fiscal indicators again worsen, or do bond market constraints instead improve budget balances as predicted by political austerity theory?

The conditional model (1a) in Appendix Table 3A.3 shows that decentralized bond finance has a strong and statistically significant mitigating effect on government budget deficits (or a bolstering effect on budget surpluses), lending support to the market-induced austerity hypothesis (H_2). Conversely, the lower a country's share of debt financing – or the more reliant countries are on government financing that is independent of bond markets – the more likely politicians are to increase budget deficits or decrease budget surpluses (H_1).

Table 3.2 illustrates the marginal effects of these conditional models. During elections where countries have little or no exposure to global bond markets, elections have a negative and statistically significant effect on government budget balances (in other words, elections increase deficits and decrease surpluses). Thus, the political budget cycle is alive and well (H_1). Elections tend to deteriorate government budgets by about seven-tenths of 1 percent of GDP.

Notably, however, when bonds account for a high share of a country's external financing, government balances tend to considerably improve during non-election years. This statistically significant relationship becomes stronger and more precise during election-years, where exposure to bond finance is positively correlated (at the 99 percent confidence interval) with a strengthening of government budget balances. In other words, bond market indebtedness tends to promote fiscal austerity generally, and most intensely during election years (H_2). In fact, these findings suggest that a dependence on global bond markets, on average, improves government budget balances by about 2 percentage points of GDP and adds an additional seven-tenths of a percent of GDP during election years.

Robustness. I subjected these analyses to a battery of robustness checks and found that the correlation between decentralized bond financing and election-year austerity is remarkably robust. First, I constructed an alternative measure to account for bond market funding constraints: non-tax revenues as a percentage of GDP. This variable serves as a proxy for foreign aid and natural resource revenue from state-owned enterprises.[45] According to political austerity theory, windfall commodity and foreign aid revenues should reduce governments' reliance on global bond markets, allowing them to avoid market-induced austerity. The additional room to maneuver should make political deficit cycles more likely.

The evidence supports this pattern. The coefficient on non-tax revenues is positive and statistically significant at the 95 percent confidence level (Appendix Table 3A.4). When governments receive more resources that are independent from global financial markets (such as commodity and foreign aid income), they are more likely to improve their fiscal balances during non-election years, providing them with greater deficit spending flexibility before elections.

Notably, the conditional model finds that during election periods, the coefficient on non-tax revenues changes direction; it instead has the expected negative and statistically significant relationship with fiscal indicators. In other words, whereas governments that see a boost in their non-tax revenues (lagged one year) tend to improve their budget balances during non-election years, their public finances deteriorate during election years – often intensifying the political deficit cycle (H_1).

In further robustness checks, I inserted several additional control variables into the original model (1a) to assess whether electoral budget outcomes are driven by the nature of domestic and international institutions, including institutional constraints on executive power (*Executive Constraints*)[46] and IMF participation (*IMF*).[47] I also added a new control variable, total external public debt as a percentage of GDP (*Total External Public Debt*), to account for any austerity pressures that might stem from a mounting debt burden more generally (rather than the composition of a country's debt). In another series of robustness tests,[48] I controlled for some additional institutional and economic factors, including the age of democracy[49] and the type of exchange rate

---

[45] See footnote 34 for further details.

[46] Recall that I use two different measures of executive constraints: the (xconst) variable from the Polity IV data set and the (polcon) variable from Henisz's (2000) Political Constraint Database.

[47] I also employ two different measures of pariticaption in IMF programs from Vreeland (2003) and Dreher (2006). The results were consistent.

[48] These controls did not have any material effect on the main findings; results are available on request.

[49] I employed a binary variable for *new democracy* that receives the value 1 for the first four elections following a country's democratic transition, and a value of 0 otherwise, representing *old democracies* (Brender and Drazen 2005, 2008).

regime.[50] Finally, I repeated all of the tests just described using the Arellano-Bond first-differenced GMM estimator to control for possible endogeneity in the independent variables. None of these made a significant change to the size, direction, or statistical significance of the key results (see the variants of model 1 and 1a in Appendix Table 3A.3).

Budget Composition and Electoral Spending Patterns. If decentralized bond finance makes political deficit cycles less likely, how do politicians instead target economic favors to their constituents during elections? Recall that political austerity theory argues that when politicians have less means available to pursue deficit-spending during elections, they are more likely to target voters with line-item budgetary spending. In other words, they maintain budget discipline, but reallocate expenditures within an orthodox budget framework to favor particular constituencies. In Latin America, a region historically characterized by many large and politically influential public sectors, government workers represent one potential target of political patronage.

In additional robustness checks, I replaced the government balance variables with a measure of public salaries. If political austerity theory is correct, we should observe greater direct targeting of such constituencies, notwithstanding the higher prevalence of election-induced market austerity. The results of these regressions are straightforwardly in line with these expectations. The coefficient on elections is positive, and statistically significant across several different variants of these models, even when controlling for decentralized bond finance (which has a constraining effect on government spending on public salaries). Indeed, elections, on average, are associated with an increase in government wages (Table 3A.4).

3.3.2. Economic Indicators

Do elections hurt Latin American economies? The first series of basic regression models display the unconditional effects of the independent variables on economic outcomes in Latin America (Table 3A.5 in the Appendix). These effects are unconditional in that they ignore the government's debt structure at the time of the election. They test the classic political business cycle hypothesis that reelection-minded politicians boost the economy before elections to win more votes. If it is correct, we should observe that growth and employment improve before elections, but at the cost of higher inflation following elections.

In these basic models, I find that inflation has the exact opposite pattern than predicted by the political business cycle literature. Elections are deflationary rather than inflationary, lending strong support to the political austerity hypothesis.

---

[50] I used the IMF exchange rate classification to code the exchange rate regime along a four-point spectrum moving from *fixed* to *floating* currency arrangements (Reinhart and Rogoff 2009).

Across the first four models in Table 3A.5, elections have a statistically significant and constraining effect on inflation. Moreover, I find no evidence that elections stimulate Latin American economies. Not only do the election coefficients for the growth regressions have the opposite sign than anticipated by the political business cycle literature, but they are also statistically insignificant. I cannot reject the null hypothesis that elections have no effect on economic growth. Rather, global growth and annual inflation (domestic price stability) appear to be the best predictors of economic growth.

Perhaps, politicians prioritize price stability during election years with the hopes of also boosting business and consumer confidence. But why would politicians in a traditionally left-leaning region believe that inflation control is the pathway to economic prosperity?

I have argued that the 1980's severe debt shocks produced a new international financial structure that shifted economic priorities and reduced the political business cycle's political premium. Following Latin America's 1980s debt restructurings – when bondholders replaced bankers as governments' major creditors – political business cycle should become less common. With the birth of Latin American capital markets, we might still observe political business cycles in countries with low bond market indebtedness. However, we should also observe the emergence of a political austerity cycle in highly indebted countries, where presidents are likely to seek out policies that curb rather than ignite inflation.

Notably, in line with expectations, the basic regression model shows that decentralized bond finance strongly constrains inflation. The coefficient on decentralized finance is negative and highly statistically significant (Table 3A.5 in the Appendix). It supports political austerity theory, finding that policy makers became less tolerant of inflation with the explosion of decentralized capital markets in the wake of the Brady bond restructurings.

Notwithstanding this general pattern, do elections intensify this relationship? Does electoral uncertainty magnify the disciplining effect of decentralized bond markets? Do politicians opt for low inflation to assuage trigger-happy creditors who are worried about short-term default risk? Or, might politicians ignore bond market volatility and aggressively stimulate the economy in hopes of reaping the benefits of an electoral boom?

The conditional models (2a) in Table 3A.6 examine the relationship between decentralized bond finance and the economy during elections. Notably, after conditioning elections on decentralized finance, their effect on the economy is stronger and more precisely measured than the unconditional model. In fact, I find that bond finance has a statistically significant and powerful mitigating effect on both inflation and economic growth during elections (H_2). Conversely, the lower a country's share of debt financing – or the more reliant countries are on government financing that is independent of bond markets – the more likely its politicians are to allow for higher inflation (H_1).

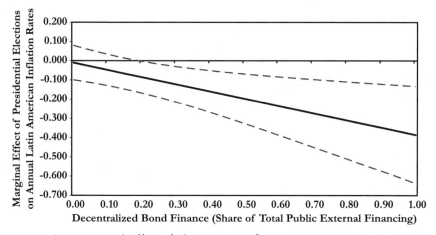

FIGURE 3.4. Marginal Effect of Elections on Inflation Rates.
Source: Model 2a in Table 3A.6.

Finally, the positive and statistically significant relationship between decentralized finance and unemployment during elections suggests that politicians might even be willing to stomach less job creation to preserve price stability.

Results for the control variables, displayed in Tables 3A.5 and 3A.6, generally correspond to expectations. First, when the primary fiscal balance (lagged by one year) is a control variable; its coefficient has a negative and highly statistically significant relationship with inflation. In other words, a decrease in the budget deficit (or alternatively an increase in the budget surplus) is associated with lower average inflation. In addition, the effect of global economic growth is significant across all economic indicators and correlated with higher domestic growth, inflation, and lower unemployment. Not surprisingly, given the region's historic inflation troubles, annual inflation is also statistically significant and inversely related to economic growth. Finally, as expected, domestic investment is associated with higher economic growth and lower unemployment.

Overall, these findings offer strong support for the political austerity hypothesis. The higher a government share of debt financing, the less likely its politicians are to engage in a high-growth, high-inflation election phase (H_2). Instead, politicians are more likely to pursue tempered growth and low inflation in hopes of avoiding capital exit and a destabilizing economic shock.

To provide a meaningful interpretation of this interactive relationship, we can calculate the marginal effects of elections over different values of decentralized bond finance. In Figures 3.4 and 3.5, we observe that election-year austerity becomes more likely as governments become increasingly reliant on debt financing. When countries first tap capital markets, high-growth,

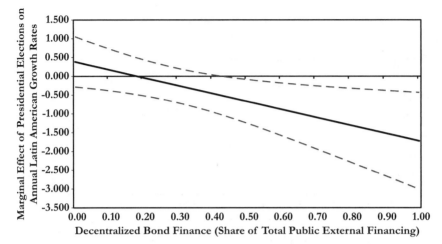

FIGURE 3.5. Marginal Effect of Elections on Growth Rates.
Source: Model 2a in Table 3A.6.

high-inflation electoral cycles remain a possibility.[51] As global bond markets account for a higher share of government financing, however, the effect of elections on inflation and economic growth is not only greater in magnitude but also more highly statistically significant. When governments depend on global bond markets for two-fifths of their external financing needs, for example, election-year inflation and growth rates, on average, are 15 and 45 percent lower than during non-election periods.[52] With greater indebtedness, a country's election-year mix of inflation and growth becomes even stingier. When governments tap three-fifths of their external financing needs with global bonds, average inflation and growth rates in Latin America are 21 and 88 percent lower during election periods than other periods.

Robustness. In a series of robustness checks, I found that the correlation between decentralized bond financing and election-year inflation and growth is markedly resilient. I once again inserted several additional control variables into the original models (2a), including the measures for executive constraints, IMF participation, and size of external debt. In further tests, I also controlled for a range of additional institutional and economic factors, including age of democracy and exchange rate regime.[53] None of these additional controls made

---

[51] The aforementioned marginal effects lose their statistical significance when governments have very little or no exposure to capital markets. Moreover, the interaction term in the economic growth model moves in the opposite direction.

[52] Calculations for the inflation rate are converted from logarithmic regression results in Figure 3.4 and Table 3A.6.

[53] These controls did not have any material effect on the main findings; results are available on request.

a significant change to the size, direction, or statistical significance of the key results (see models 2 and 2a in Tables 3A.5 and 3A.6).

Although the size of external debt alone does not appear to be an important driver of political austerity cycles, might it set an important threshold for debt sustainability? High indebtedness should at least be a basic prerequisite for political austerity cycles. In fact, we should be less likely to observe deflationary cycles when governments have manageable levels of external debt. For this reason, Latin America – a region that features a host of middle-income emerging market countries where external financing has often been the "only financial game in town" – is ideally suited for testing political austerity cycles. In fact, external debt has rarely been manageable, averaging 40 percent of GDP in the region during the last fifty years, a level that is well above the 20 percent threshold that is considered "safe" for many emerging market countries.[54] Latin American governments have often plunged into crises with public debt levels near 40 percent of GDP and far below the developed country standard of 60 percent of GDP.

To ensure countries with sustainable debt levels did not drive the results, however, I reran the statistical tests first dropping any observations below the 20 percent threshold and later omitting those below a more conservative 40 percent threshold. Importantly, the coefficients on the interaction effects do not change sign but are greater in magnitude, confirming the initial negative relationship between bond finance and election-year growth and inflation (Table 3A.7).

In additional robustness checks, I re-estimated the main independent variable – reliance on bond markets – to further establish that the results are driven by debt composition in countries with high rather than low external indebtedness. In these new models, I normalized decentralized bonds outstanding by GDP and foreign reserves instead of total external financing needs. Once again, the re-estimated models confirm the earlier results showing that bond financing has a constraining effect on inflation and growth during election periods (Table 3A.7).

To further probe the robustness of the results, I included an alternative measure of decentralized bond financing. I replaced the original decentralized finance variable with a new binary $brady_{it}$ variable (*Brady*), indicating whether or not a country has undergone a Brady debt restructuring – a proxy for the development of global capital markets. Remember, those countries that participated in these restructurings were the leaders of Latin America's shift from bank loans to bond market financing. I suspect that countries that incurred these restructurings are more reliant on global bond markets for financing, and therefore, more likely to face funding constraints from globally, dispersed financiers. Nations that endured this debt transformation should be more apt

[54] In fact, Reinhart, Rogoff, and Savastano (2003) find that "safe" debt thresholds for emerging market countries are surprisingly as low as 15 percent of GNP.

to pursue market-friendly, low-inflation environments. By contrast, prior to these restructurings or in non-Brady countries – where centralized forms of financing are more common – political business cycles remain a possibility.

For this new $brady_{it}$ variable, those countries with Brady deals receive a 1 beginning in the agreement year, whereas those countries that have never had a Brady deal are assigned a 0.[55]

$$brady_{it} = \begin{cases} 1 \text{ for those countries with Brady restructuring deals in place} \\ 0 \text{ otherwise} \end{cases}$$

The results are consistent with the previous findings that elections in highly-indebted countries are, on average, deflationary. The interactive Brady-election coefficients for the inflation model remain negative and are statistically significant at the 95 percent confidence level (Appendix Table 3A.6). They are also in line with the previous findings that sovereign Brady bond finance leads to fiscal austerity or an improvement in government budget balances (Appendix Table 3A.3).

In additional robustness checks, I repeated all of the tests just described using the Arellano-Bond first-differenced GMM estimator to control for possible endogeneity in the independent variables. For example, inflation can lead to higher interest rates, and ultimately, the accumulation of more bond market debt, creating a problem of reverse causality. Similarly, economic growth may produce higher government revenues and an improved fiscal balance. To ensure that the results are not affected by such inconsistencies, I reformulated the empirical specification in accordance with the first-differenced GMM estimator. The Arellano-Bond GMM estimator allows us to relax the assumption that the independent variables are strictly exogenous and treat these as endogenous variables. The results are also reported in Table 3A.6.

The coefficients confirm our general findings. Elections occurring under decentralized bond financing are negatively correlated with inflation and growth. Overall, the GMM results support my governing hypothesis that the relationship between elections and the economy is contingent on decentralized finance, even if we control for possible endogeneity of the independent variables.

In another robustness check, I modified the structure of the binary election variable to account for policy lags between economic decisions and inflation that are longer/shorter than expected. Political austerity cycle theory predicts that when countries are highly indebted to global bond markets, we should observe a deflationary effect not only in the election year, but also the subsequent year. While cash-strapped politicians might slow the economy to keep inflation at bay, the lag between economic decisions and inflation could last as long as a full year following an election. Varying this initial structure, I

---

[55] From 1990–1991, Mexico, Costa Rica, Uruguay, and Venezuela completed Brady deals. Another five countries followed with Brady agreements between 1992–1996.

added a second year to the binary election variable to account for a potentially even-longer monetary policy lag. I also shifted the election variable to capture the possibility of a shorter policy lag by tracking inflation patterns that predate the electoral campaign. In none of these robustness tests did any of the results change materially.

Finally, one potential alternative explanation for the effect of elections on economic outcomes is that they are conditioned on a country's institutional development. In fact, the developing country literature claims that weakly constrained chief executives are more likely to craft an electoral boom-bust cycle in newer democracies. In other words, fewer institutional constraints place more power in the presidency. With economic policy left to executive discretion, Latin American presidents should prime the economic pump to improve their reelection chances.

In order to examine this alternative explanation, I conducted the same tests replacing the initial interaction term with a new one that conditions elections on institutional constraints on executive power. Nonetheless, the institutional model offers no evidence of a relationship between executive constraints and elections. The coefficients on the institutional interaction term for the inflation and growth models are statistically insignificant and small in magnitude.

Summary. These findings offer strong evidence in favor of political austerity theory's main claim: the rise of decentralized bond finance changes political behavior and economic outcomes around elections. When global bonds account for a low share of government financing (and/or windfall commodity income boosts government coffers), politicians are most likely to widen budget deficits (or shrink surpluses) before elections. Not surprisingly, inflationary cycles are also more likely under these conditions.

By contrast, when governments rely on global bond markets for a large share of their financing, the instantaneous threat of capital exit enforces market conditionality and leads to smaller budget deficits (or higher budget surpluses). Because this exit threat is often most palpable in periods of political uncertainty, politicians are most likely to heed market calls for budget discipline and low inflation during election periods.

With such political austerity cycles becoming more common, how do politicians target their constituents before elections? Within this orthodox framework, I find that politicians instead use micro policy measures, such as public salary increases, to benefit their key supporters.

3.4. STATISTICAL TESTS ON PARTISANSHIP AND THE ECONOMY

3.4.1. Fiscal Indicators

The first set of statistical results demonstrates that the structure of government financing often raises the political and financial costs of expansionary election-year policies, making political business cycle less common. Notwith-standing these international pressures, politicians should retain some policy dis-cretion over their economic choices. It's not surprising if right-leaning admin-istrations willingly implement these policies, given that economic discipline and low inflation often appeals to businessman and financiers. However, what explains the domestic choice of austerity among left-leaning politicians? Do they behave as expected by the political economy literature, targeting working class and poor voters? Are high-growth, high-inflation cycles thus more likely when they take the helm of the economy? Or, do politicians from across the political spectrum embrace macroeconomic orthodoxy?

Recall that political austerity anticipates a blurring of political lines, mak-ing it difficult to discern partisan differences in macroeconomic policy. Hyper-inflation crises promote risk-aversion among politicians and their technocratic communities, making them more likely to adopt conservative governance prin-ciples that protect voter incomes from price instability. Moreover, left-of-center governments – from the Chile's Concertación to Brazil's Worker's Party – are sometimes surprisingly more austere than right governments, hoping to prove their ability to govern the economy to both the business community and inflation-scarred voters.[56]

The first partisan model (3) in Appendix Table 3A.9 displays the uncondi-tional effects of the independent variables on fiscal outcomes in Latin America. These effects are unconditional in that they ignore the political motivations and risk aptitudes of incumbent governments. Rather, they test for any evidence of the traditional partisan business cycles found in the developed world. Notably, the positive and statistically significant coefficient on left partisanship in the unconditional model suggests that left governments, compared to their cen-ter and right counterparts, generally improve the state of budgetary finances (which entails either reducing budget deficits or increasing budget surpluses) by about six-tenths of 1 percent of GDP.

What accounts for the left's surprising turn toward the macroeconomic right? The conditional regression models (3b) in Table 3A.9 test political aus-terity's claim that inflation crisis history explains the left's embrace of macroe-conomic orthodoxy. The positive and highly statistically significant coefficient on the left partisanship-crisis interactive term suggests that left governments that hail from inflation-ridden countries, on average, oversee government bud-get balances that are almost 1 percent of GDP higher than their center and right counterparts. These results lend considerable support to the inflation-averse hypothesis (H3).

Results for the control variables also confirm expected patterns. Decentral-ized finance retains its positive, and highly statistically significant relationship with public finances across the different fiscal policy models in Table 3A.9. In addition to the market disciplining mechanism, IMF agreements, inflation,

---

[56] See Chapter 2 for further details.

improved terms of trade, and a higher external public debt[57] are also associated with improvements in domestic fiscal balances. The coefficients on each of these variables are also statistically significant at the 95 percent confidence interval or higher. Notably, the positive coefficient for terms of trade (a proxy for commodity export earnings) is also quite strong in magnitude, which is in line with the notion that windfall commodity earnings should expand governments' policy flexibility by lining their coffers with additional cash.

Robustness. The developed country scholarship has also found that partisan cycles do not often last the full length of presidential terms. In some cases, partisan shifts are stalled by savvy voters that support divided government during mid-term elections.[58] In other cases, timing accounts for partisan differences, with the economy improving early in Democratic terms and late in Republican terms (right in time for the next campaign!).[59]

In additional robustness checks, I modify the structure of the partisan variable to account for such potential patterns. For example, I shifted the partisan dummy variable to capture any potential temporary effects limited to the first two years (*Early Term*) and final two years (*End term*) of presidential terms. The only material pattern in left partisanship occurs at the end of their administrations and reinforces the previous results (*H3*).

Notably, left-leaning governments that hail from inflation-scarred countries tend to slam on the brakes more heavily than right and center governments before elections (see the positive and statistically significant coefficient on the end-term partisanship-crisis variable in Table 3A.9). This is straightforwardly in line with the notion that left governments are often more apt to use economic orthodoxy to signal their macroeconomic credentials before elections. By contrast, the negative and statistically significant coefficient for left partisanship (end-term) suggests that left governments from countries that have never experienced an inflation crisis are more likely to engage in a public deficit cycle than their right and center counterparts. In fact, their government balances, on average, deteriorate by about 1 percent of GDP more than non-left governments (Table 3A.9).

In these partisan regression tests, I also repeated the same set of earlier robustness checks. I once again added institutional and economic controls for constraints on executive power, IMF participation, and total external debt.[60] I also repeated these tests using the Arellano-Bond first-differenced GMM estimator to control for possible endogeneity in the independent variables.

---

[57] Greater indebtedness may independently lead to higher interest rates, and therefore, more emphasis on austerity.

[58] Alesina and Rosenthal 1995.

[59] Bartels 2008.

[60] Additional controls for age of democracy and exchange rate regimes not only confirmed the main findings, but also strengthened the statistical significance of the partisanship-crisis interaction term in the conditional models.

These robustness checks did not result in any significant changes to the size, direction, or statistical significance of the key findings (see the variants of models 3 and 3b in Appendix Table 3A.9).

3.4.2. Economic Indicators

If inflation-scarred governments tend to have more austere budgets, are they also more deflationary? Moreover, do we observe partisan differences in inflation tolerance? Do left governments muzzle price pressures even more aggressively than right and center governments?

In line with the expectations of the inflation-averse hypothesis ($H3$), the coefficient on past inflation crises has a negative and statistically significant relationship with inflation across the basic partisan regression models (see the variants of model 4 in Appendix Table 3A.10). In other words, controlling for partisanship, governments with a history of inflation problems tend to be more deflationary in the years following a crisis than those where inflation has yet to rear its ugly head. Indeed, political and technocratic elites appear to adjust their inflation tolerance lower following severe inflation crises.

Reflective of the Phillips Curve trade-off, a crisis history also yields a statistically significant, yet opposite pattern for unemployment. Jobless rates tend to be higher in countries characterized by inflation-aversion.[61] Notably, a high share of decentralized finance is also statistically significant across all of the unconditional inflation models, supporting the earlier findings that bond indebtedness is generally deflationary.

Do these deflationary patterns intensify during election periods, as predicted by political austerity theory? In order to examine this possibility, the interactive regression model (2b) conditions elections on countries' inflation crisis histories. During non-election years, past crises are, on average, associated with inflation rates that are about one-half of those of pre-crisis years (see Table 3.3). The magnitude of the effect intensifies during election years, where past crises tend to yield inflation rates that are almost two-thirds lower than pre-crisis years.[62] The coefficients on these variables are statistically significant at the 99 percent confidence interval.

Notably, additional robustness checks do not alter these results. When I employ an alternative measure of inflationary crisis – a country's highest past inflation – the coefficient on the interactive term remains negative and statistically significant at the 99 percent confidence interval. In other words, for every percentage point of highest inflation that a country has experienced in the past, average inflation is about 3.5 percent lower during elections.[63]

---

[61] However, the inflation crisis coefficients for economic growth are statistically insignificant (Table 3A.10). Rather, global growth and domestic investment appear to be the best predictors of economic growth.

[62] Inflation rate calculations are converted from Table 3.3's logarithmic regression results.

[63] Inflation rate calculations are converted from Table 3A.8's logarithmic regression results.

TABLE 3.3. *Marginal Effects of Elections and Inflationary Crisis History on the Economy*

	Marginal effect of elections on inflation	90% confidence interval
No inflationary crisis history	−0.004	−0.163, 0.155
Inflationary crisis history	−0.272***	−0.476, −0.067

	Marginal effect of past crisis on inflation	90% confidence interval
Non-election years	−0.695***	−1.087, −0.304
Election years	−0.963***	−1.528, −0.399

Inflation is converted to its natural logarithm to minimize influence of extreme values.
Source: Model 2b in Table 3A.8.

In light of these findings, the relevant question is not whether there are partisan differences in economic stimulus, but rather whether there are partisan differences in economic stability. We have observed that past inflationary shocks increase the likelihood that Latin American governments preserve price stability, particularly during election periods. Are left-leaning governments as likely to adhere to these patterns as right and center governments?

I explore this phenomenon by once again modifying the structure of the partisan dummy variable to account for the final two years of presidential terms in the conditional regression models (4b). Recall that our previous fiscal findings suggested that left governments from crisis-ridden countries slam on the brakes more heavily than center and right governments before elections. Are they also more faithful guardians of price stability?

In analyzing the marginal effects of these models, we find further support for the inflation-averse hypothesis (*H3*). In general, governments from inflation-scarred countries are more likely to be deflationary during the final few years of their terms. Inflation crisis history has a negative and highly statistically significant relationship (at the 99 percent confidence interval) for both left and non-left administrations (see Table 3.4). Notably, however, left governments from inflation-traumatized countries, on average, are likely to be about 15 percent more deflationary than their political counterparts. In other words, if the baseline pre-crisis inflation rate in a given country were 10 percent, left and right/center governments pursue post-crisis inflation rates during the end of their presidential terms that are closer to 3.2 and 4.7 percent, respectively.[64]

Robustness. Notwithstanding the strong evidence for both the market-induced (*H2*) and inflation-averse austerity hypotheses (*H3*), are these mechanisms independent from one another? Perhaps, the accumulation of bond market

[64] Inflation rate calculations are converted from Table 3.4's logarithmic regression results.

TABLE 3.4. *Marginal Effects of Partisanship and Past Inflationary Crisis on the Economy*

	Marginal effect of left partisanship on inflation (end term)	90% confidence interval
No inflationary crisis history	0.222	−0.279, 0.723
Inflationary crisis history	−0.143***	−0.319, 0.034
	Marginal effect of past crisis on inflation	90% confidence interval
Center/Right partisanship (end term)	−0.751***	−1.253, −0.249
Left partisanship (end term)	−1.116***	−1.926, −0.305

Inflation is converted to its natural logarithm to minimize influence of extreme values.
Source: Model 4b in Table 3A.10.

debt is partly a function of past macroeconomic performance. Following severe hyperinflation crises, for instance, some countries were compelled to swap their defaulted bank loans for new bond market issues. Might sovereign credit evaluations then incorporate past inflation crises? Certainly, the scholarly literature on international economics finds that governments' baseline borrowing rates account for past economic management.[65] However, the cost of capital also reflects dynamic factors that include a nation's current economic and fiscal performance, political risk, and credit environment.[66] Therefore, it is conceivable that a country's bond market exposure and inflation history might be related to one another, but interact with budgetary and economic outcomes through independent pathways.

If this is the case, however, the market-induced and inflation-averse variables cannot be so highly correlated that the statistical model estimates are fragile or imprecise. In order to ensure that the results are stable and reliable, I test for multicollinearity by examining their variance inflation factors (VIF). Across all of the regression models employed in this chapter, the VIF for the predictors of decentralized bond finance and inflation crisis history are slightly above 1, meaning that there is little correlation among the independent variables.[67]

---

[65] Obstfeld and Rogoff 1996.

[66] Mosley 2003; Reinhart and Rogoff 2004.

[67] The general rule of thumb is that VIFs exceeding 4 warrant further investigation, whereas VIFs exceeding 10 are signs of serious multicollinearity requiring correction (University of California, Los Angeles Statistical Consulting Group; Pennsylvania State University Department of Statistics).

A related concern about these two mechanisms might be that they are not completely independent, but rather each variable is conditioned on the other. In the book's ensuing comparative case study chapters (Chapters 4 to 7), I assess whether the effect of the two mechanisms have an interactive relationship, employing elections as my unit of analysis. This level of analysis maximizes the variation in the two main explanatory variables, allowing me to evaluate both the independent and interactive effects of a high reliance on global capital markets and a history of inflationary crises. For example, during Chile's 1993 election, the country had little outstanding bond market debt but a history of severe inflation crises. By comparison, during Venezuela's 1998 elections, the nation had a high reliance on global bond markets yet had never experienced a severe inflationary shock. By exploiting this variation across twenty different election cases, Chapters 4 to 7 find that not only are a nation's debt structure and inflationary experiences independently constraining on economic policy and outcomes, but that when these factors are concurrently present (such as during the 1995 Argentine and 1998 Brazilian elections) they yield the most acute form of the political austerity cycle.[68]

Finally, in the previous partisan regression tests for the economy, I also repeated the same set of earlier robustness checks. For example, I replaced the decentralized finance variable with the alternative dichotomous Brady variable and added institutional controls for constraints on executive power and IMF participation.[69] Once again, I also conducted these tests using the Arellano-Bond GMM estimator to control for possible endogeneity in the independent variables. These robustness checks did not considerably alter the size, direction, or statistical significance of the key findings (see the variants of models 4 and 4b in Appendix Table 3A.10).

Summary. The effect of past inflationary crises on Latin American policy making communities is impressive. In contrast to the typical left-right policy schism in macroeconomic governance observed in developed countries, parties from across the Latin American political spectrum are more likely to value protecting voter incomes through inflation control. Surprisingly, in the prelude to elections, left governments from inflation-ridden countries are often more ardent followers of budget discipline than their right and center counterparts. In fact, left governments tend to allow for more deflation, particularly at the end of their presidential terms. By contrast, however, in countries that remain unscathed by an inflation crises, left-leaning governments – compared to those from the right and center – are more likely to follow traditional partisan lines and craft a public deficit cycle.

---

[68] See Chapter 7 for further details.

[69] In further robustness tests, I also controlled for additional institutional and economic factors, including age of democracy and exchange rate regime, but they did not materially affect the main findings.

3.5. DISCUSSION: FROM MACRO TO MICRO POLICY TOOLS

With their political survival at stake, Latin American politicians often act in surprising ways. During election years, they sometimes cut government spending, reduce wages, eliminate public jobs, and hike interest rates. What explains this puzzling behavior? In a region distinguished by its high levels of poverty, income inequality, and unemployment, are such policy choices akin to political hara-kiri? Or, do these policy decisions instead reflect a deeper, albeit counterintuitive political logic?

Over the last several chapters, I have shown that two key structural shocks altered the traditional priority of creating jobs and growth before elections. Turbulent hyperinflation episodes spurred a new political emphasis on price stability, whereas Latin America's debt securitization placed tighter credit restrictions on cash-strapped governments. Following these structural changes, politicians used economic discipline – often signaled by balanced budgets and low inflation – to curry favor with inflation-sensitive voters and fiscally conservative creditors.

In line with these predictions, my large N-test of 16 Latin American countries, observed between 1961 and 2009, shows that both bond market financing and past inflationary crises have a dampening effect on election-year stimulus. Political drivers might race their economies past their speed limits when they face few market funding constraints. However, as global bonds account for a higher share of national debt, politicians are more likely to be responsible conductors of the economy. Indeed, as the major creditors of government debt become international bondholders rather than bankers, a political austerity cycle replaces the political business cycle.

Similarly, I also find that inflationary shocks helped create a third political way in Latin America, where leftist politicians are just as likely as right and center politicians to embrace budgetary prudence and economic discipline. In fact, my statistical tests show that left-oriented governments, when hailing from inflation-traumatized nations, are often the most ardent followers of budgetary austerity.

The rise of austerity politics has some important implications for developing countries. Greater accountability in managing the macro economy has not precluded politicians from using more targeted tools to gain an electoral advantage. Rather than pursuing policies that risk creating long-run costs (such as inflation, budget deficits, and unemployment) for the majority of people, Latin American incumbents are now more likely to deliver directed benefits to their political supporters within an overall orthodox budget framework.

In the upcoming chapters, the comparative case analysis explores the resilience of electoral economic patterns on a micro- rather than macro-level. For example, while maintaining budgetary balance, politicians are likely to use a range of line-item budgetary expenditures to win votes.[70] Some of these

---

[70] In fact, the political economy literature finds that politicians often change the composition of government spending, rather than overall spending or revenues (Drazen and Eslava 2010).

policy initiatives, such as conditional cash transfers or universal social benefits, are often thought to be welfare-enhancing. Other policy initiatives, such as public sector wage hikes and infrastructure projects, can be plagued by distortionary clientelism or corruption. In any case, such spending is typically timed to coincide with elections, and therefore, maximize political dividends.

Politicians may also employ more discretionary tools – including price controls, subsidies, and clientelistic transfers – to target political constituencies. Not only do these tools create microeconomic distortions, but they are also increasingly implemented through off-balance sheet and less transparent means. Ironically, greater market conditionality may induce politicians to find more elusive methods of freely exercising their executive power.

3.A. APPENDIX

I use a series of basic regression models to test for evidence of political budget and political business cycles. The first two models (1 and 2) assess the basic claim that elections affect government budgets and the economy (such as inflation, economic growth, and unemployment), respectively. By contrast, I developed two alternative models (3 and 4) to test for partisan business cycles in Latin America. Recall that I employ fixed country effects in each of these regressions, along with a host of economic and political control variables (including lagged dependent variables) that are typically employed in models predicting budgetary, inflation, and economic patterns. For a full description of definitions, measurement, and sources for these variables, and their descriptive statistics, please see Tables 3A.1 and 3A.2.

3.A.1. Basic Regression Models

$$f_{it} = \alpha + \beta_1 Elections_{it} + \hat{\beta}_2 X_{it} + \hat{\beta}_3 f_{i,t-1} + n_i + \varepsilon_{it} \tag{1}$$

$$Y_{it^k} = \alpha + \beta_1 Elections_{it} + \hat{\beta}_2 X_{it} + \hat{\beta}_3 Y_{i,t-1} + n_i + \varepsilon_{it} \tag{2}$$

$$f_{it} = \alpha + \beta_1 Partisan_{it} + \hat{\beta}_2 X_{it} + \hat{\beta}_3 f_{i,t-1} + n_i + \varepsilon_{it} \tag{3}$$

$$Y_{it^k} = \alpha + \beta_1 Partisan_{it} + \hat{\beta}_2 X_{it} + \hat{\beta}_3 Y_{i,t-1} + n_i + \varepsilon_{it} \tag{4}$$

where $f_{it} =$ fiscal indicator; where $Y_{it^k} =$ economic indicator; where $k = a, b, c$ with $a =$ inflation, $b =$ GDP growth and $c =$ unemployment; where $Elections_{it} =$ election variable and $Partisan_{it} = partisan\ dummy$. The index $i =$ country and $t =$ year. $X_{it} =$ vector of control variables; $f_{t-1it} =$ fiscal dependent variable (one-year lag); and $Y_{t-1it} =$ economic dependent variable (one-year lag). The term $n_i =$ dummy for each country, intended to capture unobserved country effects, while $\varepsilon_{it} =$ error term.

3.A.2. The Interactive Regression Models

In the conditional models, I test for political austerity cycles. First, I expand the basic specification for the fiscal and economic regressions to include interactive effects. These interactive models examine whether changes in the two key policy making dimensions, financial means and political motivations, lead to a political austerity cycle. Indeed, they test if variation in country's reliance on decentralized global bond markets (1a, 2a) and/or its past inflation history (1b, 2b) produce any noteworthy changes in fiscal and economic indicators during election periods. Second, I also extend the basic model for the partisan regressions to include interactive effects. Models (3a, 4a) examine if financial globalization blurs the lines between right and left, making price stability popular across the political spectrum. Models (3b, 4b) test whether partisan differences persist in countries plagued by inflationary crises, pushing leftist presidents toward the political center.

$$f_{it} = \alpha + \beta_1 Elections_{it} + \beta_2 d_{it} + \beta_3 Elections_{it} * d_{it}$$
$$+ \hat{\beta}_4 X_{it} + \hat{\beta}_5 f_{i,t-1} + n_i + \varepsilon_{it} \tag{1a}$$

$$f_{it} = \alpha + \beta_1 Elections_{it} + \beta_2 \pi_{it} + \beta_3 Elections_{it} * \pi_{it}$$
$$+ \hat{\beta}_4 X_{it} + \hat{\beta}_5 f_{i,t-1} + n_i + \varepsilon_{it} \tag{1b}$$

$$Y_{it^k} = \alpha + \beta_1 Elections_{it} + \beta_2 d_{it} + \beta_3 Elections_{it} * d_{it}$$
$$+ \hat{\beta}_4 X_{it} + \hat{\beta}_5 Y_{i,t-1} + n_i + \varepsilon_{it} \tag{2a}$$

$$Y_{it^k} = \alpha + \beta_1 Elections_{it} + \beta_2 \pi_{it} + \beta_3 Elections_{it} * \pi_{it}$$
$$+ \hat{\beta}_4 X_{it} + \hat{\beta}_5 Y_{i,t-1} + n_i + \varepsilon_{it} \tag{2b}$$

$$f_{it} = \alpha + \beta_1 Partisan_{it} + \beta_2 d_{it} + \beta_3 Partisan_{it} * d_{it}$$
$$+ \hat{\beta}_4 X_{it} + \hat{\beta}_5 f_{i,t-1} + n_i + \varepsilon_{it} \tag{3a}$$

$$f_{it} = \alpha + \beta_1 Partisan_{it} + \beta_2 \pi_{it} + \beta_3 Partisan_{it} * \pi_{it}$$
$$+ \hat{\beta}_4 X_{it} + \hat{\beta}_5 f_{i,t-1} + n_i + \varepsilon_{it} \tag{3b}$$

$$Y_{it^k} = \alpha + \beta_1 Partisan_{it} + \beta_2 d_{it} + \beta_3 Partisan_{it} * d_{it}$$
$$+ \hat{\beta}_4 X_{it} + \hat{\beta}_5 Y_{i,t-1} + n_i + \varepsilon_{it} \tag{4a}$$

$$Y_{it^k} = \alpha + \beta_1 Partisan_{it} + \beta_2 \pi_{it} + \beta_3 Partisan_{it} * \pi_{it}$$
$$+ \hat{\beta}_4 X_{it} + \hat{\beta}_5 Y_{i,t-1} + n_i + \varepsilon_{it} \tag{4b}$$

where f_{it} = fiscal indicator; where Y_{it^k} = economic indicator; where $k = a, b, c$ with a = inflation, b = GDP growth and c = unemployment; where

Elections$_{it}$ = election variable and *Partisan$_{it}$* = *partisan dummy*; where π_{it} = inflation crisis history and *Election$_{it}$* $* \pi_{it}$ = election-inflation crisis interaction and *Partisan$_{it}$* $* \pi_{it}$ = partisan-inflation crisis interaction; where d_{it} = decentralized bond finance/public external financing; and *Election$_{it}$* $* d_{it}$ = election-decentralized finance interaction; and *Partisan$_{it}$* $* d_{it}$ = partisan-decentralized finance interaction. The index i = country and t = year. X_{it} = vector of control variables; f_{t-1it} = fiscal dependent variable (one-year lag); and Y_{t-1it} = economic dependent variable (one-year lag). The term n_i = dummy for each country, intended to capture unobserved country effects; while ε_{it} = error term.

3.A.3. Appendix Tables

TABLE 3A.1. *Variable Definitions and Sources (16 Latin American Countries, 1961–2009)*

	Definition and Measurement	Source(s)
Dependent Variables		
Primary Fiscal Balance	Central government revenues minus expenditures net of interest payments (+/− percentage of GDP).	Comisión Económica para América Latina y El Caribe (CEPAL)
Non-Tax Revenues	Foreign aid and natural resources revenue attained through state-owned enterprises (percentage of GDP).	CEPAL
Government Salaries	Central government expenditures on public salaries (percentage of GDP).	CEPAL
Inflation[1]	Change in log CPI (annual percentage change).	World Development Indicators (WDI).
GDP Growth	Change in real GDP (annual percentage change).	WDI
Unemployment	Change in unemployment (percentage of total labor force).	WDI
Independent Variables		
Election Dummy	For the inflation regressions, the binary variable takes on the value of 1 in election year and subsequent year, and 0 otherwise. For the growth regressions, the binary variable takes on the value of 1 in an election year and the preceding $N - 1$ years, and 0 otherwise, where $N = 2$ or 3.	Political Handbook of the World (2006–2007; 2007–2008; 2008–2009); EIU; Cheibub and Kalandrakis (2004), Global Database of Political Institutions and Economic Performance.
Partisan Dummy	Party orientation with respect to economic policy, coded from 0 to 1. Parties that are defined as communist, socialist, social democratic, or left-wing take on a value of 1. Otherwise, the variable is 0.	World Bank's 2010 Database of Political Institutions.
Decentralized Bond Finance	The government's total bond issuance as a percentage of its public external debt.	Calculated from the World Bank's Global Development Finance Database.

	Definition and Measurement	**Source(s)**
Brady Dummy	Binary variable; takes on a 1 for those countries that have had a Brady restructuring deal beginning in the initial agreement year, and 0 otherwise.	Emerging Market Traders' Association (EMTA) web site: www.emta.org/ emarkets/brady
Inflationary Crisis Dummy	I assign a value of 1 to a country when it has had a past inflationary crisis, and 0 otherwise. I code an inflationary crisis as inflation above 100% per annum. For robustness checks, I use a second measure of inflationary crisis, *highest past inflation*, that represents a country's highest historic inflation.	Sachs and Larrain, 1993; World Bank's World Development Indicators

Economic Control Variables

Global GDP Growth	Average real GDP growth of G-7 economies, weighted by each country's total GDP share.	Calculated from WDI.
Global Commodity Price Index[2]	Percentage change in global commodity (CRB) index; comprised of 17 primary commodities weighted by their importance to global trade.	Global Financial Database; Reuters's Global Commodity Index (CRB)
Trade Openness	Total exports plus total imports as a percentage of GDP.	Calculated from WDI.
Terms of Trade	Export value index (2000 = 100) / import value index (2000 = 100).	Calculated from WDI.
Income	log of GNP per capita, constant US$ (2000).	Calculated from WDI.
Fiscal Balance	Primary budget balance – net of interest payments – $(+/-)$ percentage of GDP (lagged by one year).	CEPAL
Domestic Output Gap	Measure of the output gap, calculated as the log difference between real GDP and its country specific trend.	Country specific trend calculated using the Hodrick-Prescott filter on real GDP change

(*continued*)

TABLE 3A.1 *(continued)*

	Definition and Measurement	Source(s)
Domestic Financial Depth	Broad money (M2), or money in circulation, as a percentage of GDP.	WDI
Domestic Investment	Domestic investment as a percentage of GDP.	WDI
Population	The fraction of a country's population that is age 15 to 64.	WDI
Total Public External Debt	Total public external debt as a percentage of GDP.	Calculated from WDI.

Political Control Variables

Executive Constraints (Henisz)	Measure of political constraints; estimates the feasibility of policy change relative to institutional checks and balances.	Henisz, W.J. (2000). The Institutional Environment for Economic Growth. *Economics and Politics*, 12(1).
Executive Constraints (Polity IV)	Measure of checks and balances on executive power; employs a seven-category scale from unlimited authority to executive parity.	Polity IV Codebook and Database.
Central Bank Independence	Measures the autonomy of central banks as written into countries' laws and legal systems. Updates Cukierman, Webb, and Neyapti (1992) Index.	Polillo, S. and Guillen, M. (2005). Globalization Pressures and the State: The Global Spread of Central Bank Independence. *American Journal of Sociology*, 110(6).
IMF Participation (Vreeland, 2003)	Participation in IMF programs: Dummy variable coded 1 for country-years when there was a conditioned IMF agreement in force, 0 otherwise.	Vreeland, James Raymond (2003). *The IMF and Economic Development*. Cambridge University Press.
IMF Participation (Dreher, 2006)	IMF Participation: Dummy variable coded 1 for country-years when there was IMF standby or EFF agreement for at least five months, 0 otherwise.	Dreher, Axel (2006). IMF and Economic Growth: The Effects of Programs, Loans, and Compliance with Conditionality, *World Development* 34(5).

[1] Average inflation is converted to its natural logarithm to minimize the influence of extreme values resulting from hyperinflation.

[2] Weightings: 17.6% (oil & natural gas), 17.6% (corn, soybeans, wheat), 11.8% (copper, cotton), 11.8% (livestock), 17.6% (gold, platinum, silver), 23.5% (cocoa, coffee, sugar).

TABLE 3A.2. *Descriptive Statistics for Regression Variables*
(16 Latin American Countries, 1961–2009)

	Mean	SD	Min	Max	N
Fiscal Balance (surplus/deficit)	0.74	2.35	−11.50	9.40	319
Government Salaries	4.44	1.83	1.18	11.07	298
Non-Tax Revenues	3.07	2.95	0.01	14.07	299
Inflation[1]	2.78	1.32	−2.30	9.57	792
GDP Growth	3.78	4.38	−26.50	18.30	833
Unemployment	8.64	3.99	1.30	20.50	404
Decentralized Bond Finance	18.29	24.04	0.00	84.00	680
Global Growth	3.55	1.67	−1.9	6.70	833
Global Commodity Price Index	3.13	13.75	−36.00	47.60	833
Trade Openness	42.07	23.38	9.50	145.70	832
Terms of Trade	1.15	0.41	0.40	2.90	509
Income (GDP per capita)	2,924.23	1,911.43	632.52	9,893.81	833
Domestic Financial Depth	28.52	14.24	4.70	88.40	813
Domestic Investment	5.23	16.68	−64.90	152.20	722
Population (15 to 64 years)	56.41	5.16	48.29	68.31	833
Total External Public Debt	40.89	62.62	4.00	824.00	680
Executive Constraints (Henisz)	0.29	0.20	0.00	0.69	769
Executive Constraints (Polity IV)	4.63	2.08	0.00	7.00	784
Central Bank Independence	0.50	0.189	0.21	0.77	163

[1] Average inflation is converted to its natural logarithm to minimize the influence of extreme values resulting from hyperinflation.

TABLE 3A.3. *Effect of Elections on Government Budget Balance (OLS Regressions with Fixed Effects)*

Dependent Variable:	Primary Fiscal Balance								
Independent Variable	(FE) (1)	(FE) (1)	(FE) (1)	(GMM) (1)	(GMM) (1a)	(GMM) (1a)	(GMM) (1a)	(FE) (1)	(FE) (1a)
Elections	−0.593*** (0.174)	−0.450*** (0.141)	−0.441*** (0.147)	−0.414*** (0.123)	−0.844*** (0.212)	−0.686*** (0.155)	−0.669*** (0.149)	−0.456*** (0.153)	−0.392* (0.201)
Decentralized Bond Finance	2.261*** (0.491)	2.364*** (0.792)	1.761** (0.730)	2.259* (1.171)	2.151** (0.906)	2.542*** (1.155)	2.101* (1.122)		
Election*Decentralized Finance					0.850* (0.496)	0.764** (0.352)	0.725** (0.340)		
Brady Restructuring								1.058*** (0.367)	1.080*** (0.341)
Election*Brady									−0.127 (0.302)
Domestic Output Gap	0.104* (0.053)	0.095** (0.043)	0.097** (0.042)	0.130** (0.051)	0.129** (0.059)	0.130*** (0.050)	0.129*** (0.050)	0.105** (0.044)	0.105** (0.044)
Commodity Prices	0.020** (0.007)	−0.006 (0.009)	−0.006 (0.009)	−0.012 (0.008)	0.018** (0.007)	−0.012 (0.008)	−0.012 (0.008)	0.002 (0.008)	0.002 (0.008)
Terms of Trade	1.550*** (0.396)	1.605*** (0.481)	1.482*** (0.500)	2.077** (0.939)	2.184*** (0.802)	2.129*** (0.959)	2.059*** (0.937)	1.781*** (0.545)	1.783*** (0.546)
Annual Inflation[1]	0.531** (0.190)	0.604*** (0.168)	0.568*** (0.141)	0.902*** (0.173)	0.826*** (0.219)	0.926*** (0.186)	0.900*** (0.172)	0.444*** (0.150)	0.445*** (0.150)
Population (15 to 64 years)	−0.073 (0.059)	0.085 (0.073)	0.170* (0.091)	0.188* (0.102)	−0.039 (0.078)	0.141 (0.092)	0.191* (0.100)		
IMF		0.346* (0.177)	0.343* (0.090)	0.283 (0.183)		0.319 (0.198)	0.311* (0.186)	0.131 (0.216)	0.122 (0.218)
Executive Constraints		−0.106 (0.115)	−0.055 (0.114)	0.029 (0.108)		−0.030 (0.103)	0.021 (0.113)	−0.060 (0.085)	−0.059 (0.085)
Total External Public Debt			0.534*** (0.178)	0.288 (0.286)			0.284 (0.273)	0.373** (0.143)	0.376** (0.142)
Primary Budget Balance (1 year lag)	0.374*** (0.094)	0.385*** (0.101)	0.403*** (0.096)	0.369*** (0.079)	0.355*** (0.081)	0.361*** (0.084)	0.369*** (0.080)	0.404*** (0.104)	0.404*** (0.104)
N	303	288	288	272	287	272	272	287	287
Number of Groups	16	16	16	16	16	16	16	16	16
R^2	0.41	0.44	0.47					0.43	0.43

* $p < .1$; ** $p < .05$; *** $p < .01$ (two tailed tests); robust standard errors in parentheses, clustered by country.
[1] Inflation is converted to its natural logarithm to minimize the influence of extreme hyperinflation values.
A constant term is included in each regression, but not reported in the table. FE = fixed effects.

TABLE 3A.4. *The Relationship Between Government Budget Composition and Elections (OLS Regressions with Fixed Effects)*

Dependent Variable: Independent Variable	Primary Fiscal Balance		Government Expenditures on Public Salaries		
	(FE) (1)	(FE) (1)	(FE) (1)	(FE) (1)	(FE) (1)
Elections	−0.422* (0.222)	−0.448* (0.229)	0.147* (0.071)	0.114* (0.062)	0.114* (0.061)
Non-tax revenues (one-year lag)	0.283** (0.101)	0.314** (0.109)			
Elections*Non-tax revenues	−0.078* (0.043)	−0.078* (0.044)			
Decentralized Bond Finance	2.379*** (0.699)	2.097** (0.731)	−0.862*** (0.208)	−0.664*** (0.162)	−0.619*** (0.190)
Domestic Output Gap	0.128** (0.058)	0.131** (0.058)	0.008 (0.008)	−0.003 (0.004)	−0.004 (0.004)
Commodity Prices	0.002 (0.006)	0.002 (0.006)	0.000 (0.001)	−0.002 (0.002)	−0.002 (0.002)
Terms of Trade	1.418*** (0.467)	1.208** (0.496)	−0.210 (0.158)	−0.127 (0.166)	−0.121 (0.173)
Annual Inflation[1]	0.702*** (0.202)	0.690*** (0.207)	0.035 (0.072)	−0.062 (0.080)	0.057 (0.077)
Population (15 to 64 years)	−0.141 (0.089)	−0.120 (0.116)	0.090*** (0.025)	0.055 (0.037)	0.049 (0.042)
Executive Constraints		0.191 (0.129)		−0.043* (0.021)	−0.046* (0.022)
Total External Public Debt		0.234 (0.201)			−0.032 (0.052)
IMF				0.043 (0.057)	0.043 (0.056)
Primary Budget Balance (1-year lag)	0.373*** (0.079)	0.379*** (0.080)			
Government Salaries (1-year lag)	0.794***	0.764***	0.763*** (0.049)	(0.057)	(0.058)
N	284	284	282	267	267
Number of Groups	15	15	16	16	16
R^2	0.37	0.40	0.93	0.95	0.95

*$p < .1$; **$p < .05$; ***$p < .01$ (two-tailed tests); robust standard errors, clustered by country.

[1] Inflation is converted to its natural logarithm to minimize the influence of extreme hyperinflation values.

A constant term is included in each regression, but not reported in the table. FE = fixed effects.

TABLE 3A.5. *Effect of Elections on the Economy (Basic OLS Regressions with Fixed Effects)*

Dependent Variable: Independent Variable	Inflation[1] (FE) (2)	Inflation (GMM) (2)	Inflation (GMM) (2)	Inflation (GMM) (2)	Growth (FE) (2)	Unempl (FE) (2)	Unempl. (GMM) (2)	Unempl. (GMM) (2)
Elections	-0.100* (0.056)	-0.102* (0.053)	-0.093* (0.052)	-0.109** (0.054)	-0.148 (0.330)	-0.019 (0.202)	0.008 (0.189)	-0.009 (0.188)
Decentralized Bond Finance	-0.493* (0.261)	-0.436* (0.251)		-0.833*** (0.338)	-1.153 (2.026)	-0.198 (0.680)	-0.587 (0.652)	-0.527 (0.644)
Brady			-0.211** (0.106)					
Past Inflation Crisis	-0.705*** (0.188)	-0.721*** (0.185)	-0.695*** (0.185)		0.317 (0.581)	1.377** (0.550)	1.831*** (0.682)	
Highest Past Inflation				-0.075** (0.034)				0.860*** (0.159)
Global Growth	0.076** (0.035)	0.073** (0.034)	0.070** (0.033)	0.110*** (0.028)	0.645*** (0.167)	-0.278* (0.115)	-0.266*** (0.095)	-0.252*** (0.088)
Commodity Price Index	0.002 (0.001)	0.001 (0.001)	0.002 (0.001)	0.003** (0.001)	-0.017 (0.010)	0.003 (0.004)	0.005 (0.005)	0.005 (0.004)
Trade Openness	0.007* (0.004)	0.007* (0.004)	0.007** (0.003)	0.007** (0.003)	0.002 (0.011)	0.006 (0.013)	-0.005 (0.016)	-0.010 (0.012)
Fiscal Balance (1 year lag)	-0.032*** (0.009)	-0.033*** (0.008)	0.034*** (0.008)	-0.046*** (0.008)	0.075** (0.034)	-0.080** (0.027)	-0.025 (0.037)	-0.020 (0.037)
Domestic Financial Depth	-0.001 (0.005)	-0.001 (0.005)	-0.003 (0.005)	0.001 (0.005)				
Annual GDP Growth	-0.046*** (0.009)	-0.045*** (0.009)	-0.046*** (0.009)	-0.050*** (0.010)				
Annual Inflation[1]					-0.525** (0.220)	-0.060 (0.144)	-0.172 (0.137)	-0.407*** (0.087)
Domestic Investment					0.156*** (0.021)	-0.041*** (0.007)	-0.043*** (0.007)	-0.042*** (0.007)
IMF	-0.023 (0.093)	-0.018 (0.090)	-0.012 (0.090)	-0.086 (0.087)	0.061 (0.325)	0.343 (0.257)	0.251 (0.226)	0.326 (0.227)
Executive Constraints	0.056* (0.031)	0.056* (0.029)	0.054* (0.028)	0.033* (0.018)	0.078 (0.103)	-0.102* (0.053)	-0.056 (0.072)	-0.104 (0.073)
Dependent Variable (1 year lag)	0.732*** (0.031)	0.732*** (0.029)	0.733*** (0.029)	0.735*** (0.051)	0.169* (0.078)	0.702*** (0.053)	0.705*** (0.047)	0.686*** (0.041)
N	457	440	439	440	428	275	249	249
Number of Groups	16	16	16	16	16	16	16	16
R^2	0.78				0.55	0.79		

$*p < .1$; $**p < .05$; $***p < .01$ (two tailed tests); robust standard errors in parentheses, clustered by country.
[1] Inflation is converted to its natural logarithm to minimize the influence of extreme hyperinflation values.
A constant term is included in each regression, but not reported in the table. FE = fixed effects.

TABLE 3A.6. *Effect of Elections and Decentralized Finance on the Economy (OLS Regressions with Interactive Terms)*

Dependent Variable: Independent Variable	Inflation[1] (FE) (2a)	Inflation (FE) (2a)	Inflation (FE) (2a)	Inflation (GMM) (2a)	Inflation (FE) (2a)	Inflation (GMM) (2a)	Growth (FE) (2a)	Growth (GMM) (2a)	Unempl. (FE) (2a)	Unempl. (GMM) (2a)
Elections	0.017 (0.051)	−0.011 (0.054)	−0.010 (0.054)	−0.012 (0.052)	0.000 (0.048)	−0.001 (0.046)	0.383 (0.405)	0.383 (0.386)	−0.389 (0.224)	−0.478* (0.267)
Decentralized Bond Finance	−0.646** (0.294)	−0.687** (0.332)	−0.656* (0.325)	−0.644** (0.319)			−0.332 (2.053)	−0.332 (1.957)	−0.762 (0.549)	−0.662 (0.725)
Election*Decentralized Finance	−0.380* (0.164)	−0.375** (0.168)	−0.375** (0.168)	−0.372** (0.164)			−2.106* (1.029)	−2.106** (0.981)	0.860* (0.491)	1.057** (0.489)
Brady Restructuring					−0.416** (0.184)	−0.423** (0.175)				
Election*Brady					−0.238** (0.103)	−0.238** (0.099)				
Global Growth	0.103*** (0.017)	0.080*** (0.022)	0.080*** (0.022)	0.079*** (0.021)	0.074*** (0.022)	0.071*** (0.021)	0.637*** (0.164)	0.637*** (0.156)	−0.233** (0.087)	−0.240*** (0.078)
Commodity Price Index	−0.003 (0.002)	−0.001 (0.002)	−0.001 (0.002)	−0.001 (0.002)	−0.001 (0.001)	−0.001 (0.001)	−0.016 (0.011)	−0.016 (0.010)	0.003 (0.005)	0.004 (0.005)
Trade Openness	0.007** (0.003)	0.007** (0.003)	0.007** (0.003)	0.007** (0.003)	0.008** (0.003)	0.008** (0.003)	−0.001 (0.011)	−0.001 (0.010)	−0.004 (0.012)	−0.016 (0.013)
Fiscal Balance (1-year lag)	−0.042*** (0.007)	−0.043*** (0.009)	−0.044*** (0.010)	−0.044*** (0.009)	−0.046*** (0.012)	−0.047*** (0.011)	0.085** (0.033)	0.085*** (0.032)	−0.041 (0.031)	−0.050 (0.041)
Income	0.039 (0.155)	−0.048 (0.153)	−0.105 (0.205)	−0.081 (0.222)	−0.357* (0.192)	−0.259 (0.198)				
Domestic Financial Depth	−0.001 (0.005)	−0.000 (0.005)	−0.000 (0.005)	−0.000 (0.005)	−0.003 (0.005)	−0.003 (0.004)				

(continued)

113

TABLE 3A.6 (continued)

Dependent Variable: Independent Variable	Inflation[1] (FE) (2a)	Inflation (FE) (2a)	Inflation (FE) (2a)	Inflation (GMM) (2a)	Inflation (FE) (2a)	Inflation (GMM) (2a)	Growth (FE) (2a)	Growth (GMM) (2a)	Unempl. (FE) (2a)	Unempl. (GMM) (2a)
Annual GDP Growth	−0.049*** (0.012)	−0.050*** (0.011)	−0.050*** (0.011)	−0.050*** (0.011)	−0.050*** (0.011)	−0.050*** (0.010)				
Annual Inflation[1]							−0.658** (0.236)	−0.658*** (0.225)	−0.431*** (0.086)	−0.426*** (0.152)
Domestic Investment							0.158*** (0.021)	0.158*** (0.020)	−0.041*** (0.007)	−0.043*** (0.008)
IMF		−0.107 (0.095)	−0.105 (0.094)	−0.102 (0.092)	−0.101 (0.090)	−0.091 (0.087)	0.022 (0.307)	0.022 (0.293)	0.370 (0.235)	0.358 (0.244)
Executive Constraints		0.019 (0.018)	0.021 (0.019)	0.021 (0.018)	0.026 (0.018)	0.026 (0.018)	0.049 (0.094)	0.049 (0.090)	−0.085 (0.066)	−0.030 (0.066)
Total External Public Debt			−0.041 (0.050)	−0.040 (0.048)	−0.055 (0.051)	−0.048 (0.051)	0.432 (0.260)	0.432* (0.248)	0.616*** (0.112)	0.596*** (0.185)
Dependent Variable (1 year lag)	0.799*** (0.026)	0.794*** (0.031)	0.802*** (0.030)	0.803*** (0.029)	0.779*** (0.039)	0.779*** (0.036)	0.178** (0.082)	0.178** (0.078)	0.689*** (0.038)	0.682*** (0.079)
N	472	457	457	440	456	439	428	412	275	232
Number of Groups	16	16	16	16	16	16	16	16	16	16
R^2	0.80	0.79	0.78		0.71		0.55		0.83	

* $p < .1$; ** $p < .05$; *** $p < .01$ (two tailed tests); robust standard errors in parentheses, clustered by country.
[1] Inflation is converted to its natural logarithm to minimize the influence of extreme hyperinflation values.
A constant term is included in each regression, but not reported in the table. FE = fixed effects.

TABLE 3A.7. *Effect of Elections and Decentralized Finance on the Economy (Sensitivity Analysis for OLS Regressions with Interactive Terms)*

Dependent Variable: Independent Variable	Inflation[1] (FE) (debt > 20%)	Inflation (GMM) (debt > 20%)	Inflation (GMM) (debt > 40%)	Inflation (FE) (2a)	Inflation (GMM) (2a)	Inflation (FE) (2a)	Inflation (GMM) (2a)	Growth (FE) (debt > 20%)	Growth (GMM) (debt > 20%)	Growth (GMM) (2a)	Growth (GMM) (2a)
Elections	0.033	0.042	−0.014	−0.060	−0.061	−0.059	−0.059	0.423	0.460	0.086	0.204
	(0.087)	(0.075)	(0.079)	(0.059)	(0.057)	(0.048)	(0.046)	(0.471)	(0.418)	(0.299)	(0.278)
Decentralized Finance (Bonds/External Financing)	−0.303	−0.019	0.208					1.293	2.960		
	(0.231)	(0.264)	(0.262)					(2.326)	(2.248)		
Decentralized Finance (Bonds/GDP)				0.191	0.214					−0.057	
				(0.578)	(0.540)					(3.971)	
Decentralized Finance (Bonds/Reserves)						0.064	0.068				0.084
						(0.045)	(0.044)				(0.164)
Election*Decentralized Finance	−0.615**	−0.570***	−0.570***	−1.404*	−1.395**	−0.105***	−0.106***	−2.765**	−2.908**	−3.430***	−0.351**
	(0.281)	(0.199)	(0.189)	(0.683)	(0.654)	(0.035)	(0.033)	(1.280)	(1.124)	(2.031)	(0.153)
Global Growth	0.112***	0.100***	0.125***	0.082**	0.080***	0.086***	0.082***	0.667***	0.665***	0.628***	0.622***
	(0.034)	(0.028)	(0.049)	(0.021)	(0.121)	(0.023)	(0.022)	(0.190)	(0.161)	(0.164)	(0.159)
Commodity Price Index	0.002	0.001	0.002	−0.001	−0.001	−0.002	−0.002	−0.027**	−0.037***	−0.015	−0.016
	(0.002)	(0.002)	(0.003)	(0.001)	(0.001)	(0.001)	(0.001)	(0.010)	(0.009)	(0.011)	(0.011)
Trade Openness	0.006**	0.008**	0.010**	0.006**	0.006**	0.007**	0.007**	−0.004	0.018	−0.004	−0.001
	(0.003)	(0.003)	(0.004)	(0.003)	(0.003)	(0.003)	(0.003)	(0.013)	(0.012)	(0.010)	(0.010)
Fiscal Balance (1-year lag)	−0.055***	−0.063***	−0.081***	−0.043***	−0.044***	−0.045***	−0.048***	0.067**	0.003	0.092***	0.060
	(0.009)	(0.010)	(0.013)	(0.009)	(0.008)	(0.012)	(0.011)	(0.030)	(0.034)	(0.031)	(0.047)
Income	0.218	0.271	0.365	−0.303	−0.231	−0.335	−0.128				
	(0.281)	(0.292)	(0.723)	(0.199)	(0.220)	(0.226)	(0.286)				

(continued)

115

TABLE 3A.7 (continued)

Dependent Variable: Independent Variable	Inflation[1] (FE) (debt > 20%)	Inflation (GMM) (debt > 20%)	Inflation (GMM) (debt > 40%)	Inflation (FE) (2a)	Inflation (GMM) (2a)	Inflation (FE) (2a)	Inflation (GMM) (2a)	Growth (FE) (debt > 20%)	Growth (GMM) (debt > 20%)	Growth (GMM) (2a)	Growth (GMM) (2a)
Domestic Financial Depth	-0.004	-0.006	-0.014	-0.002	-0.002	-0.002	-0.003				
	(0.007)	(0.008)	(0.010)	(0.005)	(0.005)	(0.005)	(0.005)				
Annual GDP Growth	-0.055***	-0.058***	-0.054***	-0.050***	-0.051***	-0.050***	-0.050***				
	(0.012)	(0.011)	(0.012)	(0.010)	(0.010)	(0.010)	(0.010)				
Annual Inflation[1]								-0.740**	-1.168***	-0.601***	-0.596***
								(0.279)	(0.159)	(0.188)	(0.171)
Domestic Investment								0.158***	0.155***	0.158***	0.159***
								(0.020)	(0.018)	(0.020)	(0.019)
IMF	-0.113	-0.149	-0.231	-0.100	-0.093	-0.107	-0.087	-0.299	-0.436	-0.065	-0.103
	(0.101)	(0.113)	(0.151)	(0.090)	(0.089)	(0.095)	(0.093)	(0.422)	(0.357)	(0.295)	(0.304)
Executive Constraints	0.086***	0.080***	0.097**	0.021	0.020	0.017	0.010	0.197	0.271**	0.049	-0.028
	(0.020)	(0.017)	(0.048)	(0.019)	(0.018)	(0.019)	(0.019)	(0.117)	(0.117)	(0.091)	(0.070)
Total External Public Debt	-0.033	0.015	0.065	-0.065	-0.062	-0.112*	-0.122**	0.407	0.622***	0.430	0.062
	(0.048)	(0.054)	(0.060)	(0.045)	(0.044)	(0.056)	(0.051)	(0.274)	(0.141)	(0.302)	(0.372)
Dependent Variable (1 year lag)	0.804***	0.736***	0.641***	0.835***	0.836***	0.844***	0.847***	0.166*	0.145*	0.174**	0.172**
	(0.030)	(0.040)	(0.045)	(0.027)	(0.026)	(0.026)	(0.024)	(0.086)	(0.086)	(0.078)	(0.079)
N	313	302	142	457	440	454	436	303	292	412	408
Number of Groups	16	16	11	16	16	16	16	16	16	16	16
R^2	0.85			0.78		0.78		0.56			

* $p < .1$; ** $p < .05$; *** $p < .01$ (two tailed tests); robust standard errors in parentheses, clustered by country.

[1] Inflation is converted to its natural logarithm to minimize the influence of extreme hyperinflation values.

A constant term is included in each regression, but not reported in the table. FE = fixed effects.

TABLE 3A.8. *Effect of Elections and Past Inflationary Crisis on the Economy (OLS Regressions with Interactive Terms)*

Dependent Variable: Independent Variable	Inflation[1] (FE) (2b)	Inflation (GMM) (2b)	Inflation (FE) (2b)	Inflation (GMM) (2b)	Growth (FE) (2b)	Unempl. (FE) (2b)	Unempl. (GMM) (2b)	Unempl. (FE) (2b)	Unempl. (GMM) (2b)
Elections	−0.004 (0.062)	−0.009 (0.055)	0.046 (0.068)	0.045 (0.065)	−0.202 (0.428)	0.085 (0.416)	−0.050 (0.401)	0.258 (0.436)	0.263 (0.359)
Past Inflation Crisis	−0.695*** (0.152)	−0.651*** (0.142)			0.287 (0.580)	1.347** (0.542)	1.798*** (0.681)		
Election*Inflation Crisis	−0.268** (0.099)	−0.291*** (0.101)			0.155 (0.435)	0.135 (0.521)	0.222 (0.487)		
Highest Past Inflation			−0.024 (0.038)	−0.025 (0.037)				0.491** (0.176)	0.907*** (0.154)
Election*Highest Past Inflation			−0.037*** (0.012)	−0.037*** (0.011)				−0.063 (0.095)	−0.059 (0.076)
Decentralized Finance	−0.477* (0.273)	−0.440* (0.257)	−0.776** (0.344)	−0.745** (0.344)	−1.150 (2.125)	−0.183 (0.729)	−0.565 (0.710)	−0.142 (0.679)	−0.505 (0.645)
Global Growth	0.059** (0.022)	0.051** (0.021)	0.074*** (0.021)	0.072*** (0.021)	0.646*** (0.168)	−0.282** (0.122)	−0.270*** (0.101)	−0.255** (0.101)	−0.242*** (0.080)
Commodity Price Index	−0.001 (0.002)	−0.001 (0.002)	−0.001 (0.002)	−0.001 (0.002)	−0.017 (0.010)	0.003 (0.005)	0.004 (0.005)	0.003 (0.004)	0.005 (0.004)
Trade Openness	0.008* (0.004)	0.007** (0.003)	0.007* (0.003)	0.007** (0.003)	0.002 (0.011)	0.006 (0.012)	−0.005 (0.015)	0.003 (0.012)	−0.010 (0.013)

(*continued*)

TABLE 3A.8 (continued)

Dependent Variable: Independent Variable	Inflation[1] (FE) (2b)	Inflation (GMM) (2b)	Inflation (FE) (2b)	Inflation (GMM) (2b)	Growth (FE) (2b)	Unempl. (FE) (2b)	Unempl. (GMM) (2b)	Unempl. (FE) (2b)	Unempl. (GMM) (2b)
Fiscal Balance (1-year lag)	-0.031***	-0.029***	-0.041***	-0.042***	0.075**	-0.079***	-0.023	-0.078**	-0.021
	(0.008)	(0.008)	(0.008)	(0.008)	(0.033)	(0.026)	(0.035)	(0.027)	(0.036)
Domestic Financial Depth	-0.002	-0.002	-0.001	-0.001					
	(0.005)	(0.005)	(0.005)	(0.005)					
Annual GDP Growth	-0.044***	-0.044***	-0.050***	-0.049***					
	(0.010)	(0.009)	(0.011)	(0.010)					
Annual Inflation[1]					-0.520**	-0.056	-0.165	-0.232	-0.407***
					(0.219)	(0.137)	(0.134)	(0.136)	(0.091)
Domestic Investment					0.157***	-0.041***	-0.043***	-0.041***	-0.043***
					(0.021)	(0.007)	(0.007)	(0.007)	(0.007)
IMF	-0.020	-0.025	-0.085	-0.082	0.062	0.342	0.252	0.399	0.329
	(0.095)	(0.085)	(0.096)	(0.093)	(0.325)	(0.263)	(0.232)	(0.254)	(0.228)
Executive Constraints	0.053*	0.053*	0.042*	0.042*	0.077	-0.111	-0.065	-0.114*	-0.098
	(0.029)	(0.027)	(0.022)	(0.021)	(0.105)	(0.056)	(0.073)	(0.056)	(0.070)
Dependent Variable (1-year lag)	0.715***	0.812***	0.802***	0.803***	0.169**	0.702***	0.706***	0.699***	0.687***
	(0.029)	(0.033)	(0.030)	(0.029)	(0.078)	(0.052)	(0.046)	(0.046)	(0.040)
N	457	440	457	440	428	275	249	275	249
Number of Groups	16	16	16	16	16	16	16	16	16
R^2	0.77		0.80		0.55	0.78		0.75	

* $p < .1$; ** $p < .05$; *** $p < .01$ (two tailed tests); robust standard errors in parentheses, clustered by country.
[1] Inflation is converted to its natural logarithm to minimize the influence of extreme hyperinflation values.
A constant term is included in each regression, but not reported in the table. FE = fixed effects.

TABLE 3A.9. *Effect of Partisanship on Government Budgetary Balance (OLS Regressions with Fixed Effects)*

Dependent Variable: Independent Variable	Primary Fiscal Balance							
	(FE) (3)	(FE) (3)	(FE) (3)	(FE) (3b)	(FE) (3b)	(FE) (3b)	(FE) (3b)	(GMM) (3b)
Left Partisanship	0.589** (0.242)	0.673** (0.251)	0.660** (0.250)	−0.069 (0.289)	0.076 (0.355)	0.018 (0.364)		−1.547*** (0.424)
Left Partisanship (End Term)							−1.051* (0.507)	−0.814 (0.730)
Past Inflation Crisis	0.853 (0.759)	0.335 (0.719)	0.385 (0.729)	0.324 (0.693)	−0.185 (0.633)	−0.091 (0.619)	0.647 (0.738)	
Left Partisanship*Inflation Crisis				0.988** (0.383)	0.936** (0.411)	0.993** (0.410)	1.020* (0.562)	1.145** (0.570)
Decentralized Bond Finance	2.199*** (0.557)	2.308*** (0.865)	1.683** (0.768)	2.041*** (0.481)	2.193** (0.824)	1.562** (0.726)	1.729** (0.729)	2.393** (1.010)
Domestic Output Gap	0.045 (0.032)	0.038* (0.020)	0.043* (0.022)	0.079 (0.053)	0.069* (0.039)	0.070* (0.039)	0.097*** (0.045)	0.133** (0.055)
Commodity Prices	0.023*** (0.007)	−0.003 (0.008)	−0.003 (0.008)	0.023*** (0.007)	−0.004 (0.008)	−0.004 (0.008)	−0.006 (0.009)	−0.012 (0.008)
Terms of Trade	1.314** (0.507)	1.265** (0.513)	1.142** (0.514)	1.447*** (0.428)	1.492*** (0.507)	1.367** (0.524)	1.504** (0.533)	1.965** (0.917)

(continued)

TABLE 3A.9 (continued)

Dependent Variable: Independent Variable	Primary Fiscal Balance							
	(FE) (3)	(FE) (3)	(FE) (3)	(FE) (3b)	(FE) (3b)	(FE) (3b)	(FE) (3b)	(GMM) (3b)
Annual Inflation[1]	0.632***	0.643***	0.617***	0.653***	0.650***	0.626***	0.677***	0.844***
	(0.178)	(0.155)	(0.147)	(0.189)	(0.164)	(0.159)	(0.191)	(0.204)
Population (15 to 64 years)	−0.068	0.094	0.182*	−0.072	0.085	0.174**	0.173*	0.176*
	(0.055)	(0.081)	(0.087)	(0.050)	(0.074)	(0.076)	(0.095)	(0.102)
IMF		0.431**	0.422**		0.377**	0.323*	0.335*	0.306
		(0.166)	(0.179)		(0.168)	(0.181)	(0.191)	(0.191)
Executive Constraints		−0.113	−0.059		−0.126	−0.070	−0.060	−0.013
		(0.114)	(0.109)		(0.094)	(0.086)	(0.117)	(0.105)
Total External Public Debt			0.551***			0.550***	0.335*	0.241
			(0.161)			(0.140)	(0.191)	(0.291)
Primary Budget Balance (1 year lag)	0.316***	0.327***	0.348***	0.332***	0.346***	0.363***	0.406***	0.389***
	(0.084)	(0.094)	(0.090)	(0.087)	(0.095)	(0.090)	(0.099)	(0.080)
N	303	288	288	303	288	288	288	272
Number of Groups	16	16	16	16	16	16	16	16
R^2	0.37	0.42	0.44	0.36	0.41	0.45	0.43	

$*p < .1; **p < .05; ***p < .01$ (two-tailed tests); robust standard errors in parentheses, clustered by country.
[1] Inflation is converted to its natural logarithm to minimize the influence of extreme hyperinflation values.
A constant term is included in each regression, but not reported in the table. FE = fixed effects.

TABLE 3A.10. *Effect of Partisanship on the Economy (OLS Regressions with Fixed Effects)*

Dependent Variable: Independent Variable	Inflation[1] (FE) (4)	Inflation (GMM) (4)	Inflation (GMM) (4)	Inflation (GMM) (4b)	Inflation (GMM) (4b)	Growth (FE) (4)	Unempl. (FE) (4)	Unempl. (GMM) (4)
Left Partisanship	0.208 (0.133)	0.208* (0.127)	0.199 (0.129)			−0.730 (0.462)	−0.164 (0.183)	−0.508* (0.274)
Left Partisanship (End Term)				0.222 (0.194)	0.235 (0.199)			
Past Inflation Crisis	−0.838*** (0.232)	−0.838*** (0.222)	−0.822*** (0.219)	−0.751*** (0.195)	−0.740*** (0.185)	0.696 (0.990)	1.447** (0.565)	1.997*** (0.734)
Left Partisanship*Inflation Crisis				−0.365* (0.220)	−0.400* (0.228)			
Decentralized Bond Finance	−0.519* (0.263)	−0.519** (0.252)		−0.500* (0.262)		−0.849 (2.152)	−0.159 (0.707)	−0.594 (0.635)
Brady			−0.210* (0.124)		−0.235* (0.133)			
Global Growth	0.076* (0.038)	0.076** (0.036)	0.075** (0.036)	0.056** (0.027)	0.054** (0.027)	0.680*** (0.171)	−0.280** (0.116)	−0.271*** (0.100)
Commodity Price Index	0.001 (0.002)	0.001 (0.001)	0.001 (0.001)	0.001 (0.002)	0.001 (0.002)	−0.019* (0.011)	0.003 (0.004)	0.004 (0.005)
Trade Openness	0.005 (0.003)	0.005* (0.003)	0.004 (0.003)	0.005* (0.003)	0.005 (0.003)	0.000 (0.014)	0.007 (0.012)	0.000 (0.014)

(*continued*)

121

TABLE 3A.10 *(continued)*

Dependent Variable: Independent Variable	Inflation[1] (FE) (4)	Inflation (GMM) (4)	Inflation (GMM) (4)	Inflation (GMM) (4b)	Inflation (GMM) (4b)	Growth (FE) (4)	Unempl. (FE) (4)	Unempl. (GMM) (4)
Fiscal Balance (1 year lag)	-0.022***	-0.022***	-0.020***	-0.022***	-0.022***	0.051	-0.081***	-0.021
	(0.007)	(0.007)	(0.007)	(0.007)	(0.007)	(0.039)	(0.027)	(0.032)
Annual GDP Growth	-0.045***	-0.045***	-0.045***	-0.049***	-0.049***			
	(0.010)	(0.010)	(0.010)	(0.011)	(0.011)			
Annual Inflation[1]						-0.423	-0.044	-0.137
						(0.284)	(0.146)	(0.142)
Domestic Investment						0.160***	-0.041***	-0.042***
						(0.022)	(0.007)	(0.007)
IMF	-0.020	-0.020	-0.015	0.076	0.097	-0.124	0.339	0.242
	(0.089)	(0.085)	(0.088)	(0.071)	(0.072)	(0.388)	(0.257)	(0.224)
Executive Constraints	0.051	0.051	0.044			0.117	-0.107*	-0.068
	(0.035)	(0.034)	(0.033)			(0.140)	(0.055)	(0.068)
Dependent Variable (1-year lag)	0.710***	0.710***	0.710***	0.792***	0.789***	0.172**	0.702***	0.706***
	(0.029)	(0.029)	(0.029)	(0.021)	(0.021)	(0.071)	(0.053)	(0.042)
N	425	409	409	342	342	399	275	249
Number of Groups	16	16	16	16	16	16	16	16
R²	0.79					0.57	0.79	

*$p < .1$; **$p < .05$; ***$p < .01$ (two-tailed tests); robust standard errors in parentheses, clustered by country.
[1] Inflation is converted to its natural logarithm to minimize the influence of extreme hyperinflation values.
A constant term is included in each regression, but not reported in the table. FE = fixed effects.

4

The Electoral Boom-Bust Cycle

Ten thousand eyes were on him as he rubbed his hands with dirt. Five thousand tongues applauded when he wiped them on his shirt. Then while the writhing pitcher ground the ball into his hip, defiance flashed in Casey's eye, a sneer curled Casey's lip. And now the leather-covered sphere came hurtling through the air. And Casey stood a-watching it in haughty grandeur there.

– Ernest Lawrence Thayer

Competitive elections share many similarities with national sports contests. When Casey is at the bat, the Mudville slugger must choose the tactic he thinks will produce the most runs: "let drive a single" like his teammate Flynn, or instead "tear the cover of the ball" like his other mate, Blake. When they advance to the bat, presidents like mighty batsmen must choose the political lumber that yield the most votes. But, how do they ensure joy in Mudville? By swinging for the political fences, or by tapping a targeted single?

Let us begin with a brief foray into U.S. politics. In the prelude to the 1960 presidential elections, Dwight D. Eisenhower exposed the virtues of a balanced federal budget and inflation protection, following a disciplined economic strategy throughout the election year.[1] However, this "small-ball" economic strategy never took hold among the Republican establishment. For example, in his political memoirs, Vice President Richard M. Nixon blamed Eisenhower's "inside the park" thinking for his electoral loss to John F. Kennedy.[2] He clearly believed that electorates rewarded economic booms and punished economic dips.

The bottom of the 1960 dip did come in October and the economy started to move up in November – after it was too late to affect the electoral returns... All the speeches, television broadcasts, and precinct work in the world could not counteract that one hard fact.

[1] Tufte 1978.
[2] From Nixon's book, titled *Six Crises*, as quoted in Tufte 1978.

By contrast, during Nixon's 1972 presidential reelection campaign, the Republican president played economic "long-ball." This time, as commander-in-chief of the economy, Nixon aggressively expanded the budget to deliver an electoral boom. Nixon slashed taxes and hiked social security benefits by a whopping 20 percent in the year preceding the election.

The president did not fret about inflation, however, as evidenced by the Nixon tapes at the National Archives.[3] "I've never seen anybody beaten on inflation in the United States. I've seen many people beaten on unemployment." Not surprisingly, since the time of Nixon's successful reelection bid, scholars have found that Republican sluggers aim for an economic blast before elections.[4]

In the developing world, however, presidential approaches to this political game are more varied. Recall that political austerity theory anticipates that the nature of developing countries' political and economic environment reduces the political payoff to the Nixon strategy. In contrast to developed countries, high public spending with little regard for inflation can be a serious political liability in developing countries.

In Latin America, low inflation carries a political premium for two important reasons outlined in Chapter 2. First, governments that have experienced bitter bouts of high- or hyperinflation have internalized the political lessons. Surging inflation can wreak astronomical havoc on middle- and lower-class incomes. Economic growth certainly carries political rewards. However, if growth is too rapid, inflation threatens to undermine its political benefits by destroying wages and eliminating jobs. In developing countries, protecting voter incomes from economic shocks is often as important as boosting voter incomes in developed countries.

Not only might politicians have different motivations in developing countries, their means to create a budgetary expansion may also vary. Indeed, financial globalization's strong winds often prevent politicians from hitting the ball out of the park. As discussed in Chapter 2, Latin America's global bond markets became the enforcement mechanism for low-inflation policies in the 1990s. Notably, the bond market's historical roots were also grounded in the region's crisis past.

Many Latin American governments first stumbled into inflationary crises with policies that featured high budget spending and public credit expansion. Funded by international bank loans and central bank credit, governments searched for new methods to finance their political agendas in the fallout from these violent income shocks. Captivated by the allure of global bond financing, governments tapped international bond markets to fund their spending initiatives. Ironically, however, as their global bond debts quickly mounted in the

---

[3] Tufte 1978; Abrams 2006; Abrams and Butkiewicz 2007.
[4] Bartels 2008.

1990s, politicians confronted a new, external check on their political behavior: market conditionality.

Failure to meet the policy preferences of bondholders (such as low inflation and fiscal discipline) often quickly translated into capital reversals known as sudden stops.[5] Investors, with little tolerance for uncertainty, would demand a higher risk premium to account for a nation's deteriorating debt service capacity. These "sudden stops" of financing not only ballooned the government's funding costs, but also threatened to thwart economic growth, and thus, voter incomes. Like the inflationary menace, Latin American presidents were also keenly aware of these market financing pressures, and both phenomena propelled them toward austerity.

4.1. CASE STUDY DESIGN: THE LATIN AMERICAN EXPERIENCE

From this theoretical framework, I derived four hypotheses in Chapter 2 predicting when we should observe political business and political austerity cycles. I organize my comparative case studies (Chapters 4 to 7) around these four hypotheses that are again listed. This comparative case work uses extensive field research in Latin America to examine the political logic of economic policy making in twenty different election cases that span time and space. It complements my large-N statistical work by uncovering the causes of the broad economic patterns studied in the last chapter. By exploring the reasons for government's policy stances, these cases allow for a more nuanced understanding of the variation in policy making behavior that leads to both political business and political austerity cycles.

H_1: **Traditional Political Business Cycle (PBC).** When stimulus-minded politicians face low funding constraints from global bond markets, they use fiscal and/or monetary policy to boost the economy. Politicians are most likely to create conditions of high growth and low unemployment before elections, but at the cost of inflation and/or recession following elections.

H_2: **Market-Induced Political Austerity Cycle (PAC).** When stimulus-minded politicians face steep funding constraints from global bond markets, they do not use accommodative fiscal and monetary policies to boost the economy. Instead, they use a neutral mix of economic policies or even contractionary policies that yield political austerity cycles. Inflation falls before elections, but at the cost of lower economic growth and fewer new jobs.

H_3: **Inflation-Averse Political Austerity Cycle (PAC).** Past inflation crises breeds economic risk-aversion; politicians do not use accommodative fiscal and monetary policies to boost the economy before elections. Instead, they use a neutral mix of economic policies or mildly contractionary policies that yield political austerity

---

[5] See Chapters 1 and 2 for a more extensive discussion of the economic literature on sudden stops.

cycles. Inflation falls during elections, but at the cost of lower economic growth and fewer new jobs. This pattern is more pronounced under left-leaning than right-leaning administrations.

H_4: **Political Austerity Cycle (PAC).** When inflation-averse politicians face steep funding constraints from global financial markets, they strongly contract economic policies in order to stabilize the economy. With this form of political austerity cycles, inflation and growth fall before elections most markedly.

For each hypothesis, I test its claims against alternative political economy explanations using evidence from extensive field research in Argentina, Chile, and Venezuela. My comparative case study work traces the process of domestic macroeconomic policy formation through an extensive series of in-depth interviews with national finance ministers, budget directors, central bank, legislators, and top political party officials. I also support these primary sources with a variety of secondary sources, including a more detailed analysis of high-frequency data from local government resources (such as ministries of finance and central banks) and archival evidence from local universities, public institutions, and consultancies.

I originally conducted these case studies in Latin America from 2006 to 2008, using a combination of primary interviews, primary documents, and secondary sources. I have since added several additional interviews between 2009 and 2011. In aggregate, I interviewed more than 100 Latin American economic policy makers in Argentina, Chile, and Venezuela (for a list of sample interviews, see Appendix). I also complement my comparative case analysis with evidence from additional Latin American cases, including Brazil and Ecuador, using both primary and secondary sources. These Latin American countries provide an ideal setting for testing my political austerity theory. They are presidential, middle-income South American countries that are similar along economic development indicators,[6] yet maximize the variation in our two main independent variables of interest:[7] a reliance on global capital markets for government financing and an inflation crisis history.

In the following pages, I exploit this variation across twenty different election periods to evaluate both the independent and interactive effects of these two main explanatory variables. These election cases are a subset of the Przeworksi classification of democratically competitive elections discussed in Chapter 3 and are grouped according to their variation in bond market exposure and inflation crisis saliency. For example, Chapters 4 and 5 examine ten election cases characterized by low inflation aversion but varied bond market indebtedness, whereas Chapters 6 and 7 explore another ten cases that are instead characterized by high inflation aversion, but still divergent degrees of bond market dependence. I expect that this variation in debt structure and inflation

---

[6] See footnote 80 in Chapter 1.
[7] King, Keohane, and Verba 1994.

aversion will interact to yield different electoral policy and economic outcomes according to the four hypotheses outlined previously.

By taking advantage of this comparative case design, we can observe whether a high share of bond financing (as a percentage of external debt) increases the likelihood of austerity. Remember that Latin America experienced a key structural financial shock: the 1980s debt crisis, which created both intertemporal and cross-national variation in exposure to decentralized bond markets.[8] Following this shock, many cash-strapped Latin American governments became deeply dependent on international capital markets.

During some elections, governments' vulnerability to sudden financing stops should increase their compliance with market conditionality. For example, during the 1998 Venezuelan presidential elections, a steep fall in oil prices depleted government coffers and increased the country's reliance on global bond market financing, leaving President Rafael Caldera with few options beyond austerity. For other elections, however, non-market revenues (such as windfall commodity income) from state-owned enterprises reduced countries' dependence on debt financing, leaving them with more policy freedom. For instance, if we fast forward by a decade to Hugo Chávez's 2006 reelection bid, booming petroleum prices boosted government revenues and gave Venezuela's president the policy flexibility to fund election-year spending.

Similarly, by exploiting the considerable variation in inflation histories among these South American countries, we can also assess the viability of the inflation aversion mechanism. For example, Argentina, Brazil, and Chile have suffered from very high- and hyperinflations respectively, but Ecuador and Venezuela have never seen inflation reach 100 percent per annum. These contrasting experiences should help us understand whether severe price instability leads to more cautious economic policy making, particularly during election years. For instance, are Venezuelan policy makers more likely to risk inflation-spurring expansionary policies than their crisis-scarred counterparts?

We can also use the intertemporal variation offered by the Argentine, Brazilian, and Chilean cases to further test the effects of policy makers' inflation sensitivity. The massive price shocks of the 1970s and 1980s created a discontinuity in political behavior. Indeed, politicians who crafted macroeconomic policies before these shocks should be more cavalier with policy instruments than their successors. Therefore, political business cycles should be more frequent in earlier decades in these countries.

Finally, we can also use these diverse election cases to examine the interactive effects of these two primary causal mechanisms (Chapter 7). When both constraints – a reliance on bond market financing and inflationary crisis experiences – are simultaneously present, politicians should be compelled by financial

---

[8] Under the Brady Bond restructurings, Latin American governments converted commercial bank debt, which many countries had defaulted on during the 1980s debt crisis, into market-traded debt held by a diversified group of global investors.

market pressures and a popular anti-inflation bias to pursue the most acute type of political austerity cycles.

4.1.1. Economic Policy Choices: A First Glance

How do politicians use macroeconomic policy during election campaigns? Which do they believe is the better electoral strategy? Deficit-spending or macroeconomic discipline? If chief executives behave according to convention, we should observe a high prevalence of expansionary economic policies before elections. By contrast, if political austerity theory is correct, we should observe that economic policy is also often largely neutral and/or contractionary.

In this section, I examine the frequency distributions for Latin American policy stances during elections from 1990 to 2009 to gain a better understanding of the variation in monetary and fiscal policies across the region.[9]

First, I examine fiscal performance, using two different variables: a measure of *election-year fiscal stimulus* that reflects the change in the government's fiscal balance/GDP ratio in the election year relative to the previous year; and an *end-term fiscal stimulus* that measures the change in the balance/GDP ratio in the two years before the election year relative to the previous two years.

I also analyze monetary policy, using two different variables: *election-year monetary stimulus* and *end-term monetary stimulus*. To calculate these variables, it would be ideal to use the central bank's target interest rate. Unfortunately, for many countries in our sample, this policy rate is not publicly available. As a second best-alternative, I employ an interest rate variable, the three-month money markets rate,[10] which theoretically should closely track a country's policy rate. To measure election-year stimulus, I calculate the percentage point change in three-month interest rates in the election year relative to the previous year. In comparison, I compute end-term stimulus by calculating the percentage point change in the three-month interest rate in the final two years before the election.

When evaluating the distribution of fiscal policy stances during Latin American elections, we find a surprising result. Contrary to the developing country literature that anticipates rampant fiscal policy tinkering, governments are often quite disciplined. The histograms in Figures 4.1 and 4.2 show that for about two-thirds of all Latin American elections, macroeconomic policies are either neutral or contractionary. This relationship holds not only during the election year, but also during the final two years of an administration's term. Moreover, we only observe highly expansionary policies, where budget deficits are greater than 2 percent of GDP, in about 15 percent of all Latin American elections.

---

[9] I use histogram analysis, which provides a better understanding of the frequency distribution of Latin American policy stances than regression analysis, which typically yields an average effect.

[10] Global Insight database.

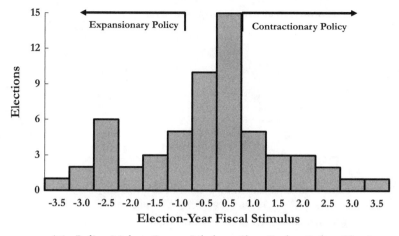

FIGURE 4.1. Policy Makers Just as Likely to Slam Brakes Before Elections.

Notably, we observe a similar trend for monetary policy, which is far tighter than proponents of political business cycle theory would have us believe. We rarely observe aggressive interest rate cuts, either during an election year, or during the final two years of a president's term. The histograms in Figures 4.3 and 4.4 illustrate that monetary policies are contractionary during more than one-half of all Latin American elections.

These results imply that Latin American politicians may not adhere to the spendthrift image offered by the political economy literature and popular press. Rather, their more miserly behavior is straightforwardly in line with the policy variation predicted by political austerity theory. Latin American political

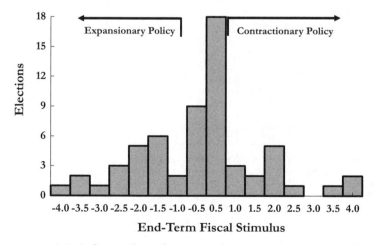

FIGURE 4.2. Policy Makers Slam on Brakes During Final Years of Team.

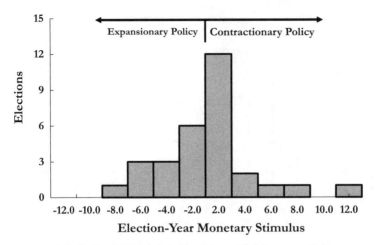

FIGURE 4.3. Policy Makers Are Cautious with Monetary Policy.

leaders may, at times, create a political business cycle, but they often do not broadly manipulate the economy to win elections.

In Chapters 4 to 7, I seek to explain the causes of this variation by adjudicating between the political austerity cycle hypothesis and alternative explanations for the rise of laissez-faire economic policies in Latin America. If political austerity theory is correct, we should observe that pump-priming of the economy only remains an attractive election-year policy when countries are unhindered by the pressures of decentralized debt markets and/or past inflationary crises.

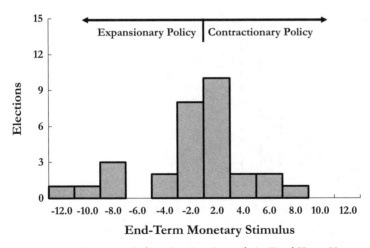

FIGURE 4.4. Monetary Policy Caution Prevails in Final Term Years.

TABLE 4.1. *Macroecomonic Policy Expectations: The Spendthrift or the Miser?*

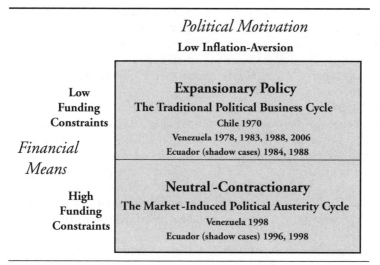

4.2. THE CLASSIC CASE OF ELECTORAL OPPORTUNISM

During the first two case study chapters (Chapters 4 and 5), I assume that chief executives operate in the low inflation aversion dimension, where they exhibit the traditional political behavior. Incumbents see the political benefit of engineering a pre-electoral boom and believe that its inflationary consequences have a low political cost. Hoping to improve their reelection chances, they intend to use macroeconomic policy for redistributive purposes, providing their constituents with economic growth, wage increases, and jobs.

Notwithstanding these political motivations, is a political business cycle feasible? To answer this question, I assess how varied exposure to global bond markets alters debtor governments' policy flexibility. In the following pages, I first examine *the traditional political business cycle hypothesis*, which anticipates that politicians have the financial means to craft an electoral boom. In Chapter 5, I move to the second of the two hypotheses (outlined in Table 4.1) dealing with the feasibility dimension of policy making: the *market-induced political austerity cycle hypothesis*. By contrast, this latter hypothesis instead anticipates that high funding constraints associated with decentralized bond finance promote a political austerity cycle.

4.2.1. Traditional Political Business Cycle (H1)

Earlier in the book, I invoked Tufte's research metaphor of solving a murder mystery. If we hold Tufte's political motive constant (which was reflating the economy before an electoral bid), what clues are essential to proving our suspicions about political tinkering with the economy? If the weapon of choice is economic policy, then government financing is the ammunition. Recall, however, that developing countries often lack firepower. Shallow domestic financial markets and low domestic budget revenues from personal and corporate income taxes frequently leave governments cash-strapped relative to their developed country counterparts.[11] Chief executives often have few alternatives to international financing.

Ironically, political austerity claims that one external funding source – global bond markets – can often be more constraining than liberating for stimulus-minded politicians. Certainly, bond finance can boost fiscal space at low levels of issuance. Recall, that when bond markets account of a low share of public financing, governments are less vulnerable to intense credit swings, capital flight, and interest rate spikes. Indeed, the market enforcement mechanism loses its teeth, and politicians can prioritize economic expansion over economic stability. However, remember that an overreliance can quickly constrain policy freedom.

Should politicians want to expand their policy freedom, they instead have several options. They can tap alternative non-market external financing (such as bank lending[12] and bilateral/multilateral lending), allowing politicians to avoid subjecting their policy decisions to the scrutiny of international bond markets.

Alternatively, windfall non-tax revenues[13] (such as commodity income and foreign aid) can also pad government coffers and reduce their reliance on global markets. In fact, padded public coffers help assuage market fears of debtor default, keeping the cost of government financing low. Rather than funneling resources to foreign interest payments, politicians can leverage the added fiscal space to spend on electoral initiatives – from public works to poverty programs.

Finally, politicians may seek to circumvent institutional constrains on executive power (such as central bank independence and fiscal rules) to gain access to central bank credit and/or fiscal reserves. When governments are unhampered by central bank independence, they can use the central bank to underwrite higher government spending.[14] Employing the printing press to bankroll

[11] Kaufman and Stallings 1991; Gavin and Perotti 1997.

[12] As noted earlier, governments that have a direct, one-to-one banking relationship with their creditors retain greater policy discretion. Banks with high lending exposure to one country have an incentive to keep debtors afloat, given their importance to their profitibility. They will continue to lend, even during credit downturns and domestic economic sluggishness.

[13] See Chapter 3 for a further description of non-tax revenues.

[14] During the 1990s, many Latin American countries adopted laws, establishing central bank independence. These laws sought to curb the region's longstanding inflation problems by prohibiting central banks from funding government spending; and isolating monetary policy from political influence (Jacome, 2001).

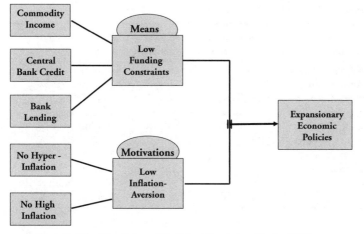

FIGURE 4.5. The Traditional Political Business Cycle (H1).

spending does have its costs, however. Indeed the government typically pays its bills with an inflation tax.[15]

Should we observe any of these phenomena, they are likely to confirm Tufte's expectations of political foul play, or the existence of political business cycles. Figure 4.5 provides an extensive diagram of the causal logic of policy making under these conditions (see Chapter 2 for further details). In the next section, I adjudicate this claim about the importance of financial means against a common alternative explanation: the extent of domestic institutional constraints. I employ a total of seven comparative election cases in Chile, Venezuela, and Ecuador to test for traditional political business cycles. In Chapter 5, I use an additional three election cases in Venezuela and Ecuador to instead examine the prevalence of political austerity cycles. I test my claim that global bond market exposure promotes economic orthodoxy against a common alternative explanation: IMF conditionality. Table 4.2 outlines my expected policy outcomes for all of the comparative cases discussed in the next two chapters (the highlighted cases are for the current chapter; they are also listed in Table 4.1).

4.2.2. An Alternative Argument: Institutional Constraints on Macroeconomic Policy

At first glance, my hypothesis appears to dovetail nicely with the developing-country political business cycle (PBC) literature. It claims that we observe political business cycles when chief executives confront few institutional checks

---

[15] The use of central bank funds expands the money supply, which catazlyes inflation and ultimately eats into citizens' real wages.

TABLE 4.2. *Case Study Overview (H1 and H2)*

Country	Chief Executive	Election Year	Inflation-Aversion?	Market Constraints?	Political Business Cycle?
Chile	Eduardo Frei Montalva	1970	N	N	Traditional PBC
Venezuela	Carlos Andrés Pérez	1978	N	N	Traditional PBC
Venezuela	Luis Herrera Campins	1983	N	N	Traditional PBC
Ecuador	Osvaldo Hurtado	1984	N	N	Traditional PBC
Venezuela	Jaime Lusinchi	1988	N	N	Traditional PBC
Ecuador	León Febres-Cordero	1988	N	N	Traditional PBC
Ecuador	Sixto Durán Ballén	1996	N	Y	Market-Induced PAC
Ecuador	Fabián Alarcón	1998	N	Y	Market-Induced PAC
Venezuela	Rafael Caldera	1998	N	Y	Market-Induced PAC
Venezuela	Hugo Chávez	2006	N	N	Traditional PBC

on their power.[16] For example, in the 1990s, many Latin American countries adopted laws that ostensibly produced autonomous central banks. These laws sought to curb the region's long-standing inflation problems by isolating monetary policy from political influence. Monetary policy was delegated to conservative central bankers who placed a high weight on price stability in the trade-off between growth and inflation.[17] Moreover, government officials were barred from using central bank credit to fund government spending.

More recently, some Latin American countries have extended the commitment to fiscal discipline by adopting fiscal responsibility laws.[18] Many scholars have found that the adoption of such institutional reforms can be welfare enhancing. Central bank independence is often associated with lower inflation[19] and fiscal rules are typically correlated with improved budget balances.[20]

Notwithstanding the importance of these findings, it remains unclear whether the adoption of such institutions is a sufficient condition to improve economic governance. In countries where inflationary crises have helped create a technocratic consensus about macroeconomic governance, they have undoubtedly helped curb inflationary pressures. However, how useful are these institutions when Latin American politicians have different policy aims?

---

[16] See Schuknecht 1996; Schuknecht 2000; Gonzalez 2002; Shi and Svensson 2002; Brender and Drazen 2005; and Shi and Svensson 2006.

[17] See Rogoff 1985.

[18] Since 2000, Argentina, Brazil, Colombia, Ecuador, Panama, and Venezuela enacted fiscal responsiblity laws that featured the adoption of numerical fiscal rules (or ex-ante constraints on deficits, debt, and expenditures). Rather than a fiscal responsibility law, Chile also introduced numerical restrictions, but through a structural balance rule mandating a 1 percent of GDP budget surplus.

[19] Grilli et al. 1991; Cukierman 1992; Alesina and Summers 1993.

[20] von Hagen 1992; von Hagen 1995; Stein, Talvi, and Grisanti 1999; Hallerberg and Marier 2004; Filc and Scartascini 2007.

For example, Venezuela's Hugo Chávez and Argentina's Cristina Kirchner both recently took actions that undermined the integrity of central bank independence laws in their countries. These Latin American presidents redirected reserves from the central bank – which is prohibited by law from underwriting deficit financing – toward domestic political initiatives.

Similarly, many Latin American countries have also adopted fiscal reforms, but compliance has often varied with domestic presidential priorities. For example, Chávez did not uphold his commitment to his fiscal responsibility law – known as the Law of Public Finances – instead veering from its numerical targets when the country benefited from an oil boom. Although Venezuela's fiscal rules had similar limits on deficits, debt, and expenditures as Chile and Colombia, these institutional rules were not sufficient to ensure good macroeconomic governance.

Macroeconomic institutional mechanisms clearly have helped curb fiscal largesse in Latin America. Before the wave of central bank reforms in the 1990s, politicians could freely plunder central bank resources to finance government deficits. For example, during Chile's 1970 elections, a deferential central bank allowed the political guard to capture economic policy. Desperate to win elections, President Frei could use fiscal monetization[21] to prime the economic pump without confronting any notable institutional resistance.

Nonetheless, I claim that the adoption of central bank independence is not a sufficient condition to check a political business cycle. Notwithstanding their legal autonomy, central banks often remained practically dependent on the political apparatus. In fact, many central bank reforms were never fully implemented in Latin America. Reforms often successfully imposed an important check on fiscal policy, prohibiting the funding of deficits with central bank money. However, in many cases, they provided an insufficient check on governments' influence over monetary policy. Government officials could readily remove central bank governors and board of directors, leaving Latin American countries with deferential and impotent central bankers. Fearing job ousters, central bank technocrats often catered to governments' objectives regarding interest rate and credit allocation decisions. Perhaps, for this reason, the scholarly evidence regarding the effect of central bank independence on inflation in Latin America is inconclusive.[22]

In summary, institutions like central bank autonomy and fiscal responsibility laws have helped political and technocratic elites anchor inflation expectations in Latin America. However, they are not a sufficient condition to ensure that governments adhere to economic discipline. Rather, governments must possess the domestic political will to prioritize orthodox macroeconomic governance over deficit-spending.

---

[21] Fiscal monetization, popularly known as "printing money," occurs when the government finances its deficit with central bank credit.

[22] Jácome 2001; Jácome and Vázquez 2005.

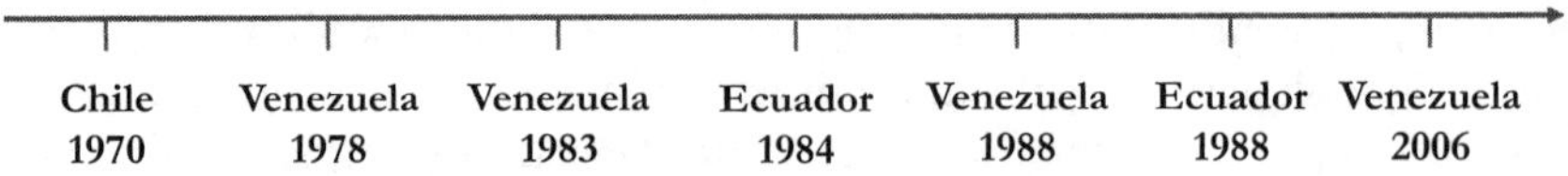

Chile	Venezuela	Venezuela	Ecuador	Venezuela	Ecuador	Venezuela
1970	1978	1983	1984	1988	1988	2006

FIGURE 4.6. The Traditional Political Business Cycle (H1).

Recall that political austerity theory argues that a history of inflation crises cultivates economic risk-aversion and a macroeconomic consensus for price stability. This political will is necessary for sustained institutional reforms. In many cases, institutional designs have effectively discouraged the use of central bank credit to fund government spending. However, they do not preclude governments from heavily intervening in the economy, influencing central bank decision making, or circumventing institutional rules. When stimulus-minded politicians possess alternative, non-market financing means (such as commodity income or bank lending), they often do not hesitate to craft a political business cycle. Institutions may have mitigated O'Donnell's delegative democracies, but the executive retains considerable power in Latin America.[23] Perhaps, Domingo Maza-Zavala, who served on the governance board of Venezuela's central bank from 1994–2007 put it most succinctly, "What can the central bank do and not do? Theoretically, the bank can do lots of things, but practically it can do little."[24]

4.3. COMPARATIVE CASE STUDY EVIDENCE

In testing the first hypothesis (H_1), I employ a comparative case study analysis, using the seven election cases in Chile, Venezuela, and Ecuador that are outlined in Figure 4.6. In these election cases, politicians demonstrated a desire to engineer an economic upturn to improve their party's chances of reelection. In fact, inflation aversion remained low because Chile, Ecuador, and Venezuela had not experienced a severe inflationary shock in the years preceding these elections.

Perhaps most importantly, politicians had the fiscal space to create an electoral boom. Sharing a historic reliance on non-tax revenues (from copper and oil respectively), Chile, Ecuador, and Venezuela possessed an alternative funding source that was insulated from bond market volatility. I expect that this financial independence makes political business cycles more likely. Indeed,

---

[23] For further details, see O'Donnell's (1994–1999) seminal papers about delegative democracies. O'Donnell outlines a "new species" of democracy – observed in many Latin American countries – where presidents enjoy remarkable powers. In many of these newer democracies, chief executives are entitled to govern as they see fit, "constrained only by the hard facts of existing power relations and by a constitutionally limited term of office."

[24] Author's interview with Banco Central de Venezuela (BCV) Board of Director Domingo Maza-Zavala, March 28, 2007.

politicians are more apt to be trigger-happy with the tools of macroeconomic policy when they are empowered with abundant domestic resources.

4.3.1. Chile's 1970 Elections: A Spending Bonanza

Chilean President Eduardo Frei Montalva exemplifies an incumbent who had both the fiscal space and the political will to create an electoral expansion. In light of his low funding constraints, the first hypothesis (H_1) predicts that his party's high priority on economic growth and redistribution (rather than price stability) should yield a PBC.

Frei enjoyed an environment of bountiful financing possibilities before the 1970 elections. As one of the world's premiere producers of copper,[25] the Chilean government possessed an abundant, yet volatile funding source for its expenditures. From the 1960s to 1980s, copper revenues seesawed from 6 to 22 percent of total tax revenues.

During the boom years, the boost in copper income padded government coffers and provided the Chilean government with additional spending flexibility. Indeed, the late 1960s were roaring years for the Chilean copper industry, providing Frei with the income to create an electoral expansion. Global copper prices soared by 85 percent in the second half of the decade (from Frei's inaugural year in 1965 to 1969, when they reached a historic high of US$182.9 per pound).

Several nationalization waves in the 1960s also improved Frei's ability to tap resources from the copper industry.[26] By 1969, the Frei government had acquired a 51 percent majority stake of the mines controlled by U.S. companies, principally Anaconda and Kennecott. Profits from this ownership stake generated additional revenues, beyond the traditional earnings from taxes on foreign companies. Prior to these nationalizations in the early 1960s, the commodity typically accounted for about 7 to 8 percent of total government revenues. Boosted by soaring copper prices, however, Chile's new ownership stake flooded the government's pocketbook with pesos. Copper-related revenues swelled by 19 percent in 1969, amounting to 20.6 percent of Chile's total tax revenues (compared to a mere 12.9 percent of 1968's tax revenues).[27]

This copper windfall could have independently financed considerable new government spending in both 1969 and 1970. Remarkably, however, Frei also drew from a second key financing source: central bank credit. The lack of central bank independence placed few restrictions on Chilean fiscal policy.

The Frei government could freely tap additional resources from a deferential Central Bank of Chile (CBC) to fund its deficits. Before 1989, the state had

---

[25] During the late 1960s, Chilean mines produced about one-sixth of the world's non-Communist copper output (Time 1969; Crowson 2007).

[26] For additional details and data, see Arellano and Marfán (1989).

[27] Arellano and Marfán 1989; Velasco 1994.

extraordinary sway over the CBC. The government appointed all of the CBC's board members, granting Chilean presidents' disproportionate influence over the bank. Legally, not only did the central bank lack an independent monetary policy, but it also provided little check on public finances. When faced with a financing shortfall, chief executives could roll the printing press without facing any CBC resistance. Not surprisingly, public sector deficits were rampant in Chile during this period.[28]

Notably, this relationship would change in later years, with the passage of 1989's basic constitutional law (*Ley Orgánica Constitucional*). Governed by a new set of technical rules and mandates,[29] today's central bank is prohibited from directly or indirectly financing public expenditures. The basic law also insulates the CBC from executive sway by installing independent governors with ten-year terms that outlast the electoral cycle.[30] These measures provide an important cap on Chile's fiscal policy, prohibiting inflationary finance or economic booms funded by central banks. Without the central bank's credit, fiscal deficits must instead be funded by either financial markets or additional government revenues from taxes or state-owned company profits.

During the 1970 election campaign, however, these institutional checks were absent. Frei's finance minister, Andres Zaldívar, oversaw the CBC. The president's close relationship with Zaldívar presented few obstacles to funding an election year expansion with central bank credit. Indeed, Edgardo Boeninger, who was Frei's National Budget Director during this period, reiterates this point.

In the 1960s, ideology determined economic outcomes. There was little concern about inflation. It was not overly important in electoral competition. The government faced high social demand with scarce resources. So, the order of the day was to always obtain money from the central bank; and the budget gap was financed by central bank money.[31]

Not only did Frei have the financial means, but also the political motivation to prime the economic pump. His party, *el Partido Demócrata Cristiano de Chile*, sought to achieve a goal of redistribution with growth.[32] Historically, it drew its electoral support from a range of political parties from right to center. However, with a surge in both political mobilization and union activity in

---

[28] Velasco 1994; Edwards 1995; Corbo 2005; Chumacero, Fuentes, Lüders, and Vial 2006.

[29] The CBC's mission was to "ensure the stability of the value of the national currency and the normal functioning of domestic and foreign payments" (Corbo 2005). This contrasts with its previous mission, which was the "ordered and progressive development of the national economy" (Boylan 1998).

[30] Previously, the executive committee that oversaw the central bank could be ousted at the president's discretion. Therefore, while similar clauses prohibiting central bank financing of the deficit appeared in the 1980 constitution, they were largely ignored by the Pinochet government (Boylan 1998).

[31] Edgardo Boeninger interview, June 6, 2007.

[32] Meller 2000.

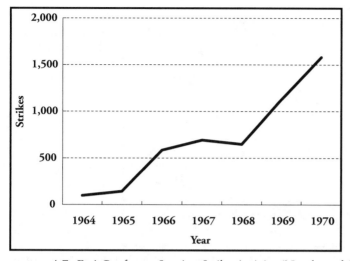

FIGURE 4.7. Frei Confronts Surging Strike Activity (Number of Strikes, 1964–1970). *Source:* Meller 2000

the 1960s, the leadership increasingly focused its attention on blue-collar and peasant workers. At the outset of President Frei's term in 1964, 632 industrial unions occupied the political landscape, representing 14 percent of the work-force. By 1970, the union tally spiked to 1,440 and accounted for about 20 percent of the work force.

Seeing a political opportunity, the Frei government designed a political strategy to win worker support in the prelude to the 1970 elections. Frei not only spent considerable resources on middle-and low-income groups,[33] but also sought to mobilize their political support by encouraging union activity. For example, the Frei administration launched a 1967 promotional campaign in the countryside, known as *juntas de vecinos*, that was designed to union-ize peasant workers. Spurred by this mobilization drive, union membership among peasant workers grew from a mere 2,000 people in 1964 to more than 114,000 by 1970. Voter registration also more than doubled during the Frei government, reaching a total of 3.5 million people by 1970.[34] Frei hoped that political mobilization would strengthen his party's hold on political power, but it instead proved to be its Achilles' heal.

Strike activity surged throughout Frei's term, reaching more than 1,500 manifestations by 1970 (Figure 4.7). Political mobilization led to profound demands on the state, particularly after a fiscal retrenchment in the mid-1960s. Workers clamored for greater redistribution.

[33] Larráin and Meller 1991.
[34] Meller 2000

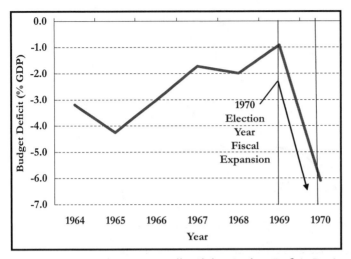

FIGURE 4.8. President Frei Swells Chile's Budget Deficit During the 1970 Elections. *Source:* Oxford Latin America Economic History Database

Clearly, engineering an economic boom was an attractive electoral strategy with little political cost. Indeed, workers were minimally concerned about price stability in a country that had averaged a paltry 1 percent inflation annually over the previous twenty years. The economy had even toyed with deflation in the mid-1960s and most recently registered near-zero inflation in 1969.[35] Under these conditions, workers should clearly reward, rather than punish budget deficits. Frei had a strong incentive to use electoral spending to appease workers' growing demands.

Given the confluence of means and motivations, we should observe expansionary economic policies during the 1970 electoral campaign. Not surprisingly, the Frei administration conducted an election-year fiscal extravaganza, increasing the budget deficit by a whopping 5 percentage points of GDP during 1970 (Figure 4.8). In an astute political move, President Frei used this fiscal expansion to directly target workers with large increases in government employment, pensions, and education and health expenditures.[36]

Possessing two spigots of financing, central bank credit and commodity income, Frei could easily finance his electoral economic boom. Central bank credit funded the deficit, while the boom in copper-related government revenues capped a potentially larger fiscal deterioration.[37] Monetary policy was also accommodative, as evidence by an election-year expansion of domestic credit.[38] Unfortunately for Frei, however, the thundering economy did not pay

[35] Oxford Latin American Economic History Database.
[36] Bitar 1979.
[37] Velasco 1994.
[38] Larraín and Assael 1995.

electoral dividends. The *Demócrata Cristiano* party's candidate, Radomiro Tomic, placed third in the 1970 elections.[39]

Assessing the Alternative Argument: Central Bank Independence. A lack of central bank independence helped fuel Chile's 1970 political business cycle. Indeed, Central Bank Governor José De Gregorio supported this point during our 2007 interview. He further emphasized that central bank autonomy is the key difference between Chile's economic policy today and during the Allende and Pinochet years. I interviewed De Gregorio in the hallowed halls of the Central Bank of Chile, directly across from the Palacio de La Moneda, the former colonial mint where former President Salvador Allende met his demise. De Gregorio explained:

Political incentives were similar, but perhaps there was less accountability because society has become more transparent. Second, there was no central bank independence, and because of that we did not have a strong fiscal policy. We had high inflation and deficits. It was not a mess until Allende, but it was an unstable macroeconomic situation. What makes the difference? Central bank independence makes the difference because monetary policy was subordinated by the fiscal stance.[40]

Although the lack of central bank autonomy contributed to the 1970s spending bonanza, does central bank independence necessarily forestall electoral economic booms? In Chapter 3, I showed that electorally induced inflation cycles are less common today than popularly perceived in Latin America. Proponents of central bank reform might claim that Chile's adoption of a new central bank independence law in 1989[41] led to the demise of the political business cycle.

While clearly an important political reform, I claim that the adoption of this institutional mechanism is not sufficient to explain the lack of a political business cycle in the 1990s. Chile is a country that is widely lauded for its high level of institutional development; nonetheless, the president holds considerable power. For example, the chief executive is constitutionally responsible for the state's daily financial administration, with monopoly-control over all taxation, budget formation, labor regulation, social security, and military affairs. Most importantly, only the president (through his finance minister) has the power to increase government spending or impose budgetary

---

[39] Tomic had 28 percent of the vote, compared to the victorious Allende's 36 percent and second place finisher Jorge Alessandri's 35 percent. Less than 40,000 votes separated Allende and Alessandri.

[40] I interviewed Jose De Gregorio during my field research in Santiago, Chile on April 11, 2007. DiGregorio is the current Governor of the Central Bank of Chile.

[41] On October 10, 1989, the basic constitutional law granted the Central Bank of Chile its operational independence and outlawed the central bank from financing public expenditures.

limits.[42] In light of this concentrated executive power, the president has considerable control over the direction of economic policy in Chile. Notwithstanding central bank deliberations, the president can use his power to create an economic expansion. Ultimately, understanding the political motivations of the executive is absolutely essential to evaluating the intended course of Chilean economic policy.

It's The Economic Crisis Stupid! Political austerity theory claims that Chile's catastrophic inflation experiences during the 1970s altered the executive branch's political motivations. Notwithstanding the onset of legal central bank independence in 1989, I claim that Chile's 1973 inflationary shock changed the traditional electoral emphasis on jobs and growth, making politicians averse to inflation.[43] The severe socioeconomic chaos that led to the breakdown of democracy under President Salvador Allende's leftist *Unidad Popular* (UP) forged a new political consensus regarding the importance of inflation stabilization policies that persisted even after the right-wing Pinochet dictatorship fell from power in 1989.

In evaluating this claim in Chapter 6, I employ a counterfactual analysis[44] establishing that without an inflationary crisis, Chilean politicians would have continued to prioritize economic expansion and job creation before elections at the expense of inflation after elections. Indeed, during the early 1970s, the UP government expressed little concern over inflation, stating that fiscal deficits were not inflationary.[45]

Without the price system's devastating rupture and a breakdown of the political-economic order, I argue that Chile's center-left politicians would not have adjusted their economic views and ushered in an era of orthodoxy during the return of democracy in the 1990s. Indeed, Allende's catastrophic economic failures made budget shortfalls and fiscal monetization taboo in Chile. The country's history of crisis also forged a new consensus among center-left parties, who were determined not only to restore the democratic order, but also to surmount the scarlet letter of economic mismanagement bestowed upon them by Pinochet's right-wing forces.

For example, in my interview with former Foreign Minister Ignacio Walker, who was first elected congressman following Chile's democratic transition, he emphasized the center-left's determination to prove its economic management credentials in the wake of the Pinochet dictatorship. Walker, who until 2008

[42] Aninat et al. 2006.
[43] See Chapters 6 and 7 for further details, where I alter the assumption of low political inflation aversion to test hypotheses 3 and 4.
[44] Fearon (1991) argues that counterfactual propositions play a "necessary and fundamental role in the efforts of political scientists to assess their hypotheses about the causes of the phenomena that they study."
[45] Larraín and Meller, 1991; Cardoso and Helwege, 1992.

served as the Director of CIEPLAN – Chile's most prestigious center-left economic think tank – passionately discussed this challenge:

When we were elected in 1989, after the plebiscite of the 1988, the whole campaign of the right and of the Pinochet people against us was that these people have managed to win a plebiscite, but chaos will be once again here. Because people had this memory of the popular unity government of Allende with hyperinflation and chronic deficits. It was very important for us, this think tank, to manage the economy in terms of fiscal responsibility, it is not for us a concession to the right, or to neoliberals, it is our *own* conviction, we have come to realize that we have to pursue strong social policies, public policies; we have a positive view of the state; in that sense we are not neoliberals; we were 14 years criticizing this dogmatic neoliberal approach of the Chicago Boys during the Pinochet era, but we came to realize, and we came to the conclusion that we wanted to become something like La Force Tranquille of Mitterrand; we had to introduce elements of stability in the country; we had to demonstrate that this center-left coalition could manage to run the country.[46]

In summary, I have argued that the political will of the executive often supersedes the institutional authority of central banks in Latin America. In Chile, we have observed that during the 1990s, presidential ambitions aligned with the inflation aversion that is the hallmark of central bank independence. As a result, it is difficult to separate the importance of politicians who see the benefit in economic discipline from the institutional effect of central bank independence. For this reason, in the next section, I have selected a similar set of cases to Chile's 1970 elections, but where inflation aversion is absent.[47] When chief executives lack inflation aversion, I expect to observe an economic boom before elections, even when executives face strong institutional check and balances such as central bank autonomy.

4.3.2. Venezuela's Petro-PBC Prevails Despite Strong Institutions

Before its considerable institutional decay under Hugo Chávez, Venezuela had long been South America's oldest democracy.[48] Its democratic origins date back to the Pact of Punto Fijo,[49] when the country's two major political parties created an institutional framework designed to limit executive power in the wake

---

[46] I interviewed Ignacio Walker at CIEPLAN's headquarters in Santiago, Chile on April 23, 2007. Walker was a congressional deputy between 1994 and 2002 and Chile's foreign minister between 2004 and 2006.

[47] My strategy follows Fearon's (1991) counterfactual logic for testing hypotheses in small-N cases.

[48] It was not until 2009 not that Venezuela received a negative (autocracy) score in the Polity IV project.

[49] The Pact of Punto Fijo was signed on October 31, 1958, by Venezuela's two major parties, AD and COPEI, with the aim of securing the transition to democracy after the defeat of the Marcos Pérez Jiménez dictatorship. It created a cooperative bipartisan political system that allowed the country to avoid the fate of most other authoritarian oil exporters (Rey 1989; Karl 1997; Monaldi and Penfold 2006; Dunning 2008). The agreement had a strong influence on the

of the dictatorship.[50] Were these institutional checks and balances sufficient to check presidents' temptation to craft political business cycles in Venezuela?

During this era of institutionally constrained executive power, politicians frequently used oil resources to secure reelection for their party. For example, throughout the Punto Fijo period, Venezuela's two major parties – Acción Democrática (AD) and el Partido Social Cristiano de Venezuela (COPEI) – encouraged their presidents to create jobs, growth, and income for their political constituents before elections. Despite the strength of institutions during this period, macroeconomic policy design during this era mimics the pattern witnessed under its most famous dirigiste leader, Hugo Rafael Chávez Frías. Chávez's 1999 constitution may have formally subordinated political actors to the executive branch, but previously presidents and their political parties' expansionary impulses were also rarely restrained by institutional checks and balances. Rather, petroleum dictated their political fortunes.

Oil has been the lifeline of Venezuelan politicos, who have lived and died with oil booms and busts. Indeed, the oil sector plays a dominant role in Venezuela's public life, currently accounting for about 50 percent of government revenues.[51] Steep swings in crude oil prices have produced substantial volatility in Venezuelan fiscal accounts. During boom years, politicians use oil windfalls to ignite electoral spending bonanzas, only to severely retrench their expenditures post-election.

For example, Venezuela witnessed two massive price spikes in per capita oil revenues in 1973–1974 and 1979–1981, which gradually eroded to their pre-boom levels by 1985 (Figure 4.9). Spending surged during each peak, only to retrench again following elections.[52] Notably, before the 1988 elections, oil revenues sank below their pre-boom levels.[53] This income shock should have brought severe fiscal adjustments and spending cuts, but it coincided with yet another election period. Venezuela's politicians instead opted to fuel another economic acceleration. However, this time they funded their electoral expansion with global commercial bank loans rather than oil money. It was only during the 1998 elections, when global bonds supplanted bank loans, that funding disappeared. During the last decade of Chavista rule in Venezuela, the record skips again, yielding yet another rendition of the

---

1961 Constitution, which aimed to limit presidential powers, diminish political polarization, and create cooperation-inducing institutions (Monadli and Penfold 2006).

[50] Monadli and Penfold 2006.

[51] See Baldini (2005) for further details. Historically, oil revenue has also been the main source of budgetary income, but its relative weight in the government budget has been highly volatile, fluctuating between 86 percent of total revenues in 1974 and 38 percent of total revenues in 1998 (DeCosta and Olivo 2008).

[52] Moreno and Shelton 2009.

[53] For further details about commodity booms and busts in Venezuela and their economic and political ramifications, see Naím 1993; Karl 1997; Guerra 2006; Dunning 2008; Monaldi and Penfold 2009; Moreno and Shelton 2009; and Rodríguez and Hausmann 2009.

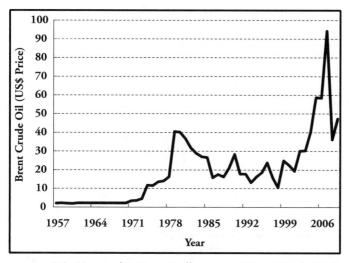

FIGURE 4.9. Venezuela's Petro Rollercoaster (Brent Crude Oil Prices in US$).
Source: Global Financial Data

petro-PBC. During the early Chávez years, oil market doldrums and capital market pressures begot economic austerity, before an oil boom fueled a 2006 electoral spending bonanza.

Venezuela's Punto Fijo Elections: 1968–1988. Venezuela's early election history is dominated by petro-PBCs, even in the face of strong executive constraints. For example, Figure 4.10 highlights the last five major Venezuelan presidential elections that took place during the Punto Fijo period (1958–1988).[54]

Before the 1973–74 oil boom, we do not observe political business cycles in Venezuela. Petroleum prices were not very high, hovering around US$2 per barrel, and the world oil market was relatively stable. Steady growth in oil-related exports spurred economic activity and financed government spending. Without incurring deficits, politicians used oil proceeds to curry favor with key political groups. Oil resources were also heavily invested into infrastructure, educational, and health care spending. Nonetheless, the overall character of fiscal policy remained conservative.[55] Without a source of significant public wealth, "fiscal policy followed an informal rule: governments spent what

[54] The Punto Fijo System begins with the transition to democracy in 1958 but ends with the dissolution of the party system after the 1988 elections. Two major institutional changes contributed to the deconsolidation of the Venezuelan political system: 1) the introduction of direct elections for governors and mayors in 1989 and 2) the modification of the legislature's electoral system from pure proportional representation to a mixed-member system with personalized proportional representation (Monaldi and Penfold 2006).

[55] Hausmann 1995; Bond 2005; Monaldi et al. 2006.

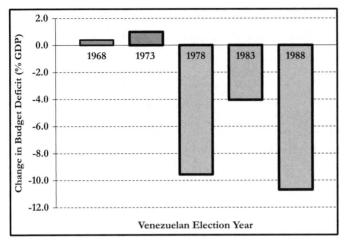

FIGURE 4.10. Punto Fijo's Crude Electoral Expansions (Change in Average Deficit/GDP in Final Two Years Before Elections).
Source: Oxford Latin American Economic History Database

they earned."[56] During the 1968 and 1973 elections, two different incumbent presidents adhered to this miserly behavior, keeping spending in check. Both President Raúl Leoni (AD) and Rafael Caldera's (COPEI) administrations padded moderate budget surpluses, even during election years (Figure 4.10).

By contrast, the oil bonanza of the mid-1970s changed political behavior. With each boom in oil revenues – first in 1973–74, next in 1980–1981, and finally more modestly in 1984–85 – Venezuelan governments feverishly tapped into the country's oil wealth.[57] Unlike the pre-boom calm of the 1960s, presidents and their parties rapaciously devoured windfall revenues before the next elections (Figure 4.11). According to AD party leader Carmelo Lauría, who served in the cabinet of two different governments during this period, "the oil boom created an illusion of endless fiscal expansion possibilities."[58] Indeed, the new oil wealth created a political appetite that could not be quenched, catalyzing successive petro-PBCs in the 1978, 1983, and 1988 elections.

Venezuela's 1978 Elections. During the first oil boom, the price of crude nearly tripled between 1973 and 1974[59] and reached US$16 by the 1978 election year. The massive inflow of resources into public coffers undermined budget rationality. President Carlos Andrés Pérez used the colossal influx of state resources to lead ambitious redistributive efforts and development projects. In the two

[56] Author's interview with José Guerra, February 7, 2007, in Caracas, Venezuela. Guerra was the director of the central bank's research department until 2005 and is currently a professor of economic history in the Escuela de Economía de la Universidad Central de Venezuela (UCV).
[57] García et al. 1997; Karl 1997; and Naím 1993.
[58] Author's interview with Carmelo Lauría, March 5, 2007.
[59] The oil price surged from US$4.6 per barrel in 1973 to US$12 in 1974.

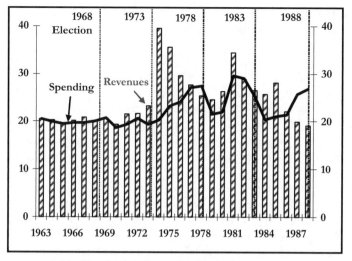

FIGURE 4.11. Venezuela's Petro–PBC (% of GDP).
Source: Oxford Latin American Economic History Database

years before the 1978 elections, Pérez oversaw an enormous fiscal relaxation (Figures 4.10 and 4.11), including massive public works projects[60] and public employment initiatives. Carlos Andrés pilfered historically unprecedented budget surpluses of 13 and 19 percent of GDP in 1974–1975, draining the golden black coffers until they became bleeding red deficits in 1977–1978.[61]

Pérez's massive spending initiatives were nominally aimed at spurring economic development in Venezuela, but more implicitly intended to support his party's presidential candidate, Luis Piñerúa (AD).[62] Pérez also crafted several more clientelistic projects specifically designed to garner electoral gains, including Corpomercadio, a program created to distribute food subsidies to Venezuela's poor.[63]

Inflation was the cost of this substantial stimulus, nearly doubling from an annual average rate of 7.1 percent in 1978 to 12.7 percent by 1979, and vaulting to a 21.5 percent annual rate by 1980. Pérez's efforts to prime the economic pump backfired, allowing COPEI's candidate, Luis Herrera Campins, to win the 1978 elections.[64] Capitalizing on a conservative backlash within the

---

[60] As part of Pérez's "GranVenezuela" initiatives, public investment in Venezuela jumped from 9 percent of GDP in 1973 to 18.6 percent of GDP in 1978 (Guerra 2006).

[61] By 1978, Pérez had eliminated Venezuela's lofty budget surplus, leaving the country with a 2.5 percent of GDP budget deficit (Source: Oxford Latin American Economic History Database).

[62] Pérez's colossal fiscal expansion yielded a considerable build-up in Venezuela's overall public debt. In 1973, the country's total debt was 10 percent of GDP, but reached 30 percent of GDP by the end of Pérez's term in 1978 (García 2006, 2007).

[63] Guerra 2007.

[64] Herrera (COPEI) secured 47 percent of the vote in the 1978 elections, trumping Piñerúa's (AD) 43 percent and the four leftist candidates' combined 8 percent (Ellner 2008).

center-right COPEI, Herrera Campins questioned the feasibility of the Acción Democrática's expansionary economic policies.[65]

Venezuela's 1983 Elections. Nevertheless, a few months after his inauguration, another oil boom amid rising Middle Eastern tensions catapulted prices over US$40 per barrel (Figure 4.9), prompting Herrera to soon forget his campaign promises.[66] Benefiting from a doubling of government revenues by 1981, President Herrera Campins began crafting a classic political business cycle during 1982. He launched a raft of public spending initiatives,[67] virtually eliminating Venezuela's petro-infused budget surplus of 5 percent of GDP by the end of 1982.

Only an oil market correction and exchange rate shock, known as Venezuela's Black Friday in February 1983, slowed government spending (Figure 4.11). Faced with capital flight sparked by falling oil prices, declining export earnings, and large current account deficits, Venezuelan policy makers attempted to defend their fixed exchange rate regime, cutting spending and hiking interest rates.[68] In spite of their best efforts, Venezuelan central bankers lost $10 billion in international reserves and were forced to devalue and abandon the fixed exchange rate on February 18, 1983.[69]

Nonetheless, Luis Herrera's fiscal policy remained more accommodative in the two years before the 1983 elections than during the previous two years (Figure 4.10), characterized by high social spending, subsidies, and economic transfers to politically favored groups.[70] Not surprisingly, however, the devaluation's blow to voters' incomes cost COPEI at the polls. Voters rejected their candidate, Rafael Caldera, instead supporting AD candidate Jaime Lusinchi, who won with 57 percent of the vote, the highest percentage in any presidential election since 1958.[71] The combination of a currency devaluation and expansionary fiscal stimulus again produced rising prices post-election, with inflation doubling from 6.3 to 11.4 percent during the year following the 1983 campaign. The petro-PBC was alive and well in Venezuela.

---

[65] Ellner 2008.

[66] Herrera's mandate switch away from fiscal rectitude is not terribly surprising given the onset of the oil boom and the history of expansionary budget policies in Venezuela's democracy. Indeed, mandate switches in Latin American democracies have been a fairly common occurence (Stokes 2001).

[67] See Guerra (2006) for further details.

[68] This behavior is in line with the Frieden and Stein's (2001) prediction that governments will defend currecy regimes before elections to protect voters' incomes.

[69] From 1961 to 1983, Venezuela's exchange rate was fixed at 4.30 bolivares per U.S. dollar. The fixed exchange rate was replaced with a two-tier system in which the preferential rate stood at 7.5, while on the free market the bolívar slumped to between 12 and 15 to the U.S. dollar.

[70] Guerra, 2006, 2007.

[71] Caldera only pulled in 35 percent of the vote, while the leftist vote was split between Teodoro Petkoff with 4 percent, and José Vicente Rangel with 3 percent (Ellner, 2008).

Venezuela's 1988 Elections. Upon entering office, President Jaime Lusinchi planned his economic and political strategy with a key adviser and AD party-power broker, Presidential Secretary Carmelo Lauría. According to Lauría, they drafted the blueprint for a political business cycle from day 1. They would carry out a much-needed fiscal retrenchment during their early years, in hopes of surfing an economic upturn in the two years before the 1988 elections.[72] They reorganized the public sector, liquidated several state-owned companies, and boosted public salaries for high-caliber government officials. Benefiting from a modest bump in oil revenues in 1984–1985, Lusinchi's administration also closed the budget deficit it inherited from Luis Herrera.[73] By mid-1985, the government had outlined its economic growth plan for 1986–1988, which featured large-scale public investment projects. To Lusinchi and Lauría's dismay, however, oil prices tumbled to half their value by early 1986, leaving their projects unfunded.

Rather than abandoning their plans to secure reelection for their party, they sought out financing from international banks. Like commodity income and central bank credit, accessing these funds placed few restrictions on Lusinchi's policy making flexibility (see Figure 4.5). Recall that political austerity theory holds that before the era of emerging market bond financing, creditors were less apt to pull the plug on debtors. Despite oil's plunge[74] and the economy's turmoil, bank creditors agreed to supply Venezuela with fresh funding, including a partial suspension of its debt payments.[75]

As planned, policy makers boosted spending during 1987 and 1988 (Figures 4.10 and 4.11). Emboldened by the fund injection from its bank creditors, Lusinchi's government crafted a textbook political business cycle. The fiscal accounts swung from an average 4 percent of GDP budget surplus during 1985–1986 to an average 7 percent budget deficit during 1987–1988 (see Figure 4.10).

Notably, Lusinchi expanded the economy in 1988, even amid talks that his political rival Carlos Andrés Pérez was planning on making a presidential bid. With Pérez enjoying broad support among the Venezuelan population in pre-election polling, Lauría believed that Pérez's political brand was key to winning the December elections for Acción Democrática. According to Lauría, although Pérez' candidacy initially met considerable resistance from party

---

[72] Author's interview with Carmelo Lauría, March 5, 2007, in Caracas, Venezuela.

[73] Guerra 2006.

[74] The oil market correction forced yet another devaluation in Venezuela's offical exchange rate in 1986 from 7.5 to 14.5 bolivares per U.S. dollar. Notably, the devaluation ballooned the value of Venezuela's external debt, but creditors were still willing to extend fresh funds. By the end of 1986, Venezuela's external debt had reached 57.8 percent of GDP, compared to 17.8 percent of GDP in 1985 (García et al. 1997).

[75] Since 1983, Venezuela had been in debt restructuring talks with its bank creditors. In light of falling oil prices, these creditors accepted several contigency clauses that allowed the country to postpone a portion of its debt payments in 1987 (Guerra 2006).

faithfuls,[76] they ultimately prioritized keeping the presidency in AD hands over their internal squabbles. In my 2007 interview in his consultancy perched atop the mountains of Caracas, a proud Lauría reflected upon his role, militantly declaring:

I played an important role, because I was the Presidential Secretary...I was the leader of this...I had a lot to do with Perez's candidacy...I made sure everyone in the government, those in favor and those opposed to Pérez, supported him. And the entire party followed! We didn't want to lose power![77]

Ultimately, Lusinchi and Lauría's budgetary bonanza helped secure the December 1988 election for Acción Democrática, but it left incoming President Carlos Andrés Pérez with an economic and political maelstrom. In spite of the AD's soaring popularity, the new Pérez government was straddled with a host of economic woes. Plummeting oil prices, paltry export earnings, and whopping budget gaps magnified Venezuela's balance of payments deficit, causing the country to shed international reserves at an alarming rate. At the same time, the exuberant fiscal stimulus stoked inflation, which catapulted above a 30 percent annual rate by early 1989.[78] Facing an imminent devaluation in February 1989, Pérez adopted a radical neoliberal adjustment program, known as the "great turnabout." On the heels of this announcement, Pérez met a fervent political backlash that erupted into the *Caracazo*, a wave of protests and mass looting that turned deadly.[79] This social uproar eventually fed into Chávez's unsuccessful military coup in February 1992, sowing the seeds for decades of political volatility.[80]

In summary, oil windfalls determined the fate of economic policies during the Punto Fijo era. Surprisingly, an age marked by its institutional strength relative to the Chávez period[81] did not check politicians' expansionary impulses. Rather, electoral booms and busts were simply a product of oil booms and busts.

4.3.3. Central Bank Independence Does Not Check the Political Business Cycle

Does a more direct institutional check on macroeconomic policy, such as central bank independence, influence policy making behavior? Venezuela's central

[76] For example, Lusinchi backed Octavio Lepage, a former Interior Minister and party loyalist, for the presidency in the October primary, even though Pérez enjoyed the support of the party's key labor group constituency (*New York Times*, 1987).
[77] Carmelo Lauría interview, March 5, 2007.
[78] World Bank's World Development Indicators (WDI); CEPAL's Base de Estadísticas de América Latina y El Caribe.
[79] During the week of February 27, 1989, protests and looting were met by massive repression by military troops that resulted in hundreds, and perhaps thousands of deaths.
[80] Lopez-Maya 2005; Ellner 2008.
[81] Monaldi et al. 2006; Monaldi and Penfold 2006; Corrales and Penfold 2007.

bank legally achieved its independence in 1992, but were monetary authorities able to curb Venezuela's long-standing reflationary impulses?

The 2006 elections provide us with an important comparative case. The chief executive is untroubled by inflation but faces an independent central bank with a legal mandate to preserve price stability. Does the presence of an autonomous central bank restrain the president's spendthrift electoral behavior, compelling politicians to choose price stability over jobs and growth? Or, alternatively, with a spendthrift politician at the helm, do we observe the same outcome during 2006 Venezuelan elections as we did in the pre-crisis Chilean 1970 elections?

Importantly, during both of these elections, politicians possess the financial means and political motivations to engage in electoral engineering of the economy. Politically rewarding jobs and growth provide them with their motivation, whereas commodity booms supply their financing. Returning to the first hypothesis (H_1), mapped out in Figure 4.5, we should observe a political business cycle under these conditions. What happens during the 2006 Venezuelan elections? Do we witness a boom-bust electoral cycle in Venezuela? Let us examine the case in more detail in the following section.

Venezuela's 2006 Elections. Facing a contentious reelection bid, President Hugo Rafael Chávez Frías possessed a strong incentive to use macroeconomic policy as a redistributive tool. From the days of his 1998–1999 presidential ascendancy, Chávez had mobilized support on a class basis, championing the causes of the poor. He tapped into widespread voter frustration with clientelism, corruption, and mismanagement. In fact, by the 1998 elections, 63 percent of the population favored radical changes to the current political system.[82] Critical of the old political order,[83] he viewed poverty as a problem of political neglect that could be cured with distribution. Never before in Venezuelan history had the chief of state prioritized the poor over other wealthier sectors of society.

Although scholars continue to debate the efficacy of his spending,[84] Chávez made enormous state investments in health and education through his *misiones* ("mission") programs.[85] Inaugurated in 2003, these *misiones* operate outside existing ministerial and legal structures, funneling government funds into social

---

[82] Hellinger 2003.

[83] The old political order, known as the Punto Fijo political system, was dominated for 40 years by a two-party alliance (between the Partido Social Cristiano de Venezuela, or COPEI, and the Acción Democrática).

[84] A recent series of publications, including Corrales and Penfold (2007), Rodríguez (2007), Ortega and Penfold (2008), and Ortega and Rodríguez (2008) label many of these initiatives as clientelistic (and based on political criteria) rather than programmatic, questioning their capacity to bring long-term sustainable economic development to Venezuela.

[85] For further details about Chávez's economic ideology and policies, see Buxton (2006) and Ellner (2008).

projects, including literacy, educational, and job-training programs and medical clinics and state-run subsidized supermarkets.[86] During the first three years of these programs, Chávez spent an estimated US$20 billion on food, education, and medical care to underserved populations.[87]

A senior executive at the Ministry of Finance, in charge of coordinating economic policy, justified the government's "off-the-books" spending as necessary to circumvent old institutional rigidities and redistribute to the country's most deprived citizens (which account for about two-thirds of Venezuelan households). In his office, ensconced in a modern-day financial fortress with legions of security that could rival Rome, he discussed the government's strong connection with Venezuela's poverty-stricken population.

The goal of the government's political economic model is to make sure provisions of basic services, such as health, nutrition, and education reach the people most in need through the umbrella of the *misiones* programs. Changes were needed in Venezuela's institutions to improve channels of redistribution. Through the law establishing the *consejos comunales*, a new level of government has been created to more directly reach the people with the oil windfalls. Previously, very little funding reached the "pueblo" because it was siphoned off in the higher levels of regional and municipal government. There was no way to implement these programs through the normal budget mechanism because there were too many rigidities. Ninety percent of the budget already flowed to debt payments. The middle class was benefiting far more than the barrios. Therefore, the government constructed a way to get the money directly to the people with the oil windfall of 2003–2004.[88]

The 2006 elections marked an important political challenge to Chávez. Seeking to further build political momentum after a majority of voters rejected a 2004 recall referendum,[89] the Venezuelan President sought to expand his political base with pro-poor spending. Given Chávez's political emphasis on redistributing to Venezuela's poor, he clearly possessed the motivation to create a political business cycle, aggressively spending on social projects, public job

---

[86] These programs include the Robinson, Ribas, Vuelvan Caras, Sucre, Barrio Adentro, and Mercal Missions. The Robinson Mission was a literacy program, which used video cassettes (mainly produced in Cuba) and facilitators in place of classroom teachers. In 2005, the government officially announced that 1.5 million illiterates had been taught reading and writing skills through this program. However, several scholars cast doubt upon this claim (Ortega and Rodríguez 2008). The Ribas Mission provided continuing education for poor adults, whereas the Vuelvan Caras Mission consisted of job-training programs. Sucre Mission sponsored students from "Bolivarian universities" to participate in community programs. The Barrio Adentro Mission established medical clinics across Venezuela's nonafffluent communities, staffed by 12,000 Cuban doctors providing free medical services and medicine. Finally, the Mercal (Mercado de Alimentos) Mission built state-subsidized grocery stores in lower-class communities.

[87] Shifter 2006.

[88] Author's interview on March 7, 2007, at the Ministerio de Finanzas in Caracas, Venezuela.

[89] A revitalized opposition attempted to oust Chávez from power with a recall referendum on August 15, 2004. Aimed at revoking his electoral mandate two years early, the referendum was unsuccessful. Fifty-nine percent of voters wanted Chávez to remain in power.

creation, and economic stimulus. The Venezuelan President firmly rejected neoliberal policies that emphasized a cautious economic policy stance and price stability. In September 2006, a mere three months before his reelection bid, he characteristically delivered a blunt rejection of neoliberal market policies at the United Nations General Assembly and his post-Assembly interviews.

It was shown that the end of history was a totally false assumption, and the same was shown about Pax Americana and the establishment of the capitalist neoliberal world. It has been shown, this system, to generate mere poverty. Who believes in it now?[90]

Capitalism is the way of the devil and exploitation, of the kind of misery and inequality that destroys social values. If you really look at things through the eyes of Jesus Christ – who I think was the first socialist – only socialism can really create a genuine society."[91]

But political motives alone are not sufficient to produce a political business cycle, financial means are also needed. What enables Chávez to take such iconoclastic positions? How can he credibly talk of devoting massive public resources to Venezuela's poor? Chávez possesses the golden key: an alternative financing source independent from global financial markets.

Nevertheless, his ten-year presidency has not always been characterized by enthusiastic government spending. Chávez's leftist political agenda has also been left to the fate of oil booms and busts. Chávez's intrinsic motivations remained steady; he aimed to use government spending to redistribute to his main constituencies: Venezuela's poor and politically excluded. Notwithstanding these leftist impulses, a lack of government funding constrained Chávez's ability to spend during his early presidential years. In 1999, he began his presidency amid a severe fiscal retrenchment, catalyzed by the worst price collapse in world petroleum markets in over fifty years (Figure 4.9). Against the backdrop of a dreary US$10 per barrel price of Venezuelan crude oil, Chávez emphasized prudential economic management and fiscal rectitude in his first speech to the nation in February 1999. Signaling his commitment to fiscal discipline, he also retained as his finance minister Maritza Izaguirre, who oversaw a whopping US$6 billion in budget cuts during President Caldera's final year in 1998.[92]

Chávez maintained this fiscally conservative posture throughout his first four years in office. During this time, his administration approved organic laws that prioritized fiscal frugality, including the Law of Public Finances and the Law of the Investment Fund for Macroeconomic Stabilization. The Law of Public Finances introduced fiscal rules mandating budgetary balance, whereas the Macroeconomic Stabilization Fund invested a portion of the country's oil proceeds into a fund designed to smooth historically volatile oil revenues over

---

[90] For the complete transcript of Chávez's speech to the UN National Assembly, please refer to the UN's webcast archives at http://www.un.org/webcast/ga/61/pdfs/venezuela-e.pdfl.
[91] *TIME magazine*, September 24, 2006.
[92] See Buxton (2003) and Ellner (2008) for further details about Chávez, the economically orthodox politician.

time.[93] Chávez also implemented an economic policy plan, dubbed Consejo Nacional, which featured a fiscal and monetary policy mix that emphasized economic stabilization.[94] With government coffers nearly empty,[95] Chávez hoped such initiatives would help assuage an uneasy international investment community.

Some leftists questioned Chávez's commitment to socialist ideals and proclaimed him a neoliberal.[96] They were puzzled that the president prioritized orthodox economic policies and external debt service over funneling these resources directly to the suffering Venezuelan people. At the time, a pragmatic Chávez understood that his political survival depended on his ability to lure foreign capital and weather the economic storm.

I don't think that, to be revolutionary, a government must inevitably refuse to recognize agreements like its external debt. I do not believe that debt is the key element in classifying a movement as revolutionary. It is about figuring out what is possible in the moment. If our government had refused to pay the external debt, there is no doubt that this would have saved us significant resources – eight or ten million dollars. We could have decided not to pay and instead used the money for development projects. If only it were that simple, everyone would support the decision. It would be a revolutionary, anti-neoliberal act. But what would have happened if that had been our policy? That surely would have led to problems in a range of areas: foreign investments, for example, would have certainly been cut off. These investments total billions of dollars and they are all productive investments . . . none of those projects would have been possible. We need to ask ourselves, given our modest place in the world and variables as overwhelming as the international financial system, how to best confront our reality.[97]

Indeed, without the lofty oil income of previous decades, the government was slow to deliver its promised benefits to the poorest sectors of the population. Venezuela's budget share devoted to social spending surprisingly decreased during the early Chávez years.[98] Despite engineering some economic growth,

---

[93] In addition to promoting budgetary balance, Venezuela's fiscal rules also placed limits on expenditure growth and public debt accrual. At the same time, the Macroeconomic Stabilization Fund sought to reduce volatility in government revenues by investing oil proceeds into a savings fund when oil is above $9 per barrel (based on a five-year average). In the event of an oil market downturn, the government could access additional revenues to pad its spending. For further details, see http://www.bcv.org.ve/ifms/ifmslaw2.htm.

[94] The Consejo Nacional was implemented in 2002 by Chávez's planning minister, Dr. Felipe Pérez.

[95] Chávez finance minister, Tobías Nóbrega, claims that fiscal income had plummeted to 5–8 percent by 1998–2000, compared to 16 percent in the early 1990s (Parker 2007).

[96] Veras 2001.

[97] Chávez and Harnecker 2005.

[98] Social spending's average share of the national budget actually decreased during the Chávez administration. Between 1999 and 2004, it represented 29.3 percent of the budget compared to 31.5 percent between 1990 and 1998 before Chávez was in office (Rodríguez 2007).

unemployment, poverty, and crime all remained stubbornly high on Chávez's watch.[99]

Only with the recovery of oil prices in 2003 did Chávez begin to fundamentally alter his approach to economic policy. Felipe Pérez, Chávez's planning minister between 2002 and 2003, discusses the impressive about-face in Chávez's approach to economic policy following the oil market's resurgence.

In 2002–2003, there were few oil earnings, but when higher earnings began to flow in, Chávez began to use these earnings for political purposes... In 2003, things relaxed a lot and no one worried about fiscal balance. Oil prices began to increase and there were fewer concerns about restrictions. They didn't think rationally. Instead, they thought since they had more money, then they should spend more money in their naïve view of Keynesian economics. They thought increased expenditures would improve economic conditions and increase production. But, the government didn't help create new production capacity and investment... With income from oil, the government started extending credit to *misiones*, etc. And the money should have flown to the poor communities. But, went to individuals in a more corrupt, clientelistic, and politically irresponsible way.[100]

Prior to the December 2006 presidential elections, the government was flush with cash. Booming petroleum markets should have allowed Chávez the fiscal space to return to his anti-neoliberal roots and spend without limitation. But would a legally independent central bank foil the plans of a politician who had both the means and motivation to craft a political business cycle?

I have argued that legally autonomous central banks often do not provide a sufficient check on executive power in Latin America. Venezuela's approved its central bank law in December 1992, imposing an important restriction on the executive branch's fiscal policy by prohibiting the use of central bank financing to fund its deficit. However, in the realm of monetary policy, the central bank continued to defer to government officials who retained the right to sack board members.[101]

Moreover, in the wake of the 2006 elections, Chávez championed a 2005 modification to the central bank law through the National Assembly. The revised law used the country's international reserves to establish the FONDEN development fund, which effectively gave the government "back-door" access to central bank credit. Free of legislative oversight, the executive branch (through the Finance Ministry) oversaw this special development fund. Facing a central bank with legal but not operational independence, Chávez could

---

[99] Buxton 2003.

[100] Author's interview with Felipe Pérez on March 23, 2007, in Caracas, Venezuela. Pérez was planning minister in Chávez's cabinet from May 2002 until April 2003, when he departed because of economic policy differences with Chávez.

[101] Jacome 2001.

tap buoyant petroleum proceeds both directly through the government's oil revenues and indirectly through the off-budget development fund. Indeed, between 2005 and 2006, the government directed more than US$15 billion of international reserves and oil proceeds from state-run Petróleos de Venezuela (PDVSA) into this fund.[102]

Once again, executive prerogative trumped institutional checks in Venezuela. Indeed, Domingo Maza-Zavala, a central bank board member in Venezuela from 1994 to 2007, noted his frustration with the free reign of executive power over the central bank.

What type of impact has the central bank law had? It has had no difference during election periods. Always, in Venezuela, politicians spend more than they earn. Always, they maintain deficits. There are many social, economic, and administrative needs. Leaders always use this as a rationale to increase the size of government and bureaucracies at all levels. What can the central bank do and not do? Theoretically, the central bank can do a lot of things, but practically, it can do little.[103]

Not surprisingly, when a pro-poor spending president finally benefited from an oil boom, he was not going to be thwarted by a legally independent central bank. Chávez tapped oil proceeds to finance his political agenda and craft a political business cycle. Capitalizing on the boom in domestic resources, Chávez spent without increasing the deficit, or tapping external financing markets. In the two years before his 2006 reelection bid, the Venezuelan president extended the size and scope of his *misiones* projects.[104] By 2006, Chávez had a mission for every social ill, from health care and malnutrition to unemployment and illiteracy. As the missions grew, so did Chávez's popularity with his approval ratings soaring by about 15 percentage points in the year after their adoption.[105]

---

[102] In 2005, the National Assembly approved a US$6 billion transfer of international reserves from the central bank to FONDEN. In February 2006, the National Assembly approved another transfer of US$4 billion from the central bank, and the president announced that PDVSA would transfer $100 million dollars a week into FONDEN throughout the year, adding another $5.2 billion (Corrales and Penfold 2007).

[103] The Maza-Zavala interview was conducted at the Banco Central de Venezuela (BCV) on March 28, 2007, during my field research in Venezuela. Dr. Maza-Zavala served on the BCV's board of directors for thirteen years from 1994 through 2007.

[104] In 2004 and 2005, Chávez launched a series of extensions to the original *misiones* programs, including Bario Adentro II (which aimed to construct 100 diagnostic and 100 rehabilitation centers in underserved communities), Robinson II (which sought to provide primary school education), and Vuelvan Caras II (which provided graduates of the government's job-training program with guidance and economic aid for forming cooperatives). For furter details regarding Venezuela's *misiones* programs, see the government's website at http://www.gobiernoenlinea.ve/miscelaneas/misiones.html.

[105] Before the *misiones* programs were launched in 2003, social spending had declined in real terms during the early Chávez years. Not surprisingly, Chávez's approval ratings were a moribund 45 percent. By August 2004, however, profiting from an oil boom and the politically popular *misiones* programs, Chávez had captured 59 percent of the vote during the recall referendum (Corrales and Penfold 2007).

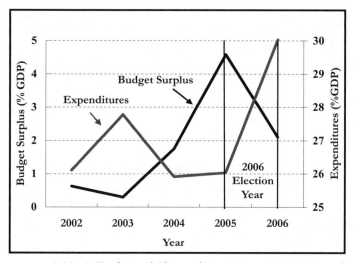

FIGURE 4.12. A Traditional Electoral Expansion (2006 Venezuelan Elections).
Source: CEPAL

During the election year itself, Chávez spent a whopping $7 billion in off-budget discretionary spending on his *misiones* programs. In addition, he slashed Venezuela's lofty budget surplus by half (Figure 4.12). Under pressure from the Venezuelan government, the central bank also marched monetary policy in line with fiscal policy, expanding the supply of credit in the economy.[106] Not surprisingly, following the elections, average annual inflation swelled to 19 percent in 2007 and a staggering 31 percent by 2008, compared to a mere 13 percent in 2006.[107]

Under the 2005 macroeconomic coordination law, the central bank was obligated to harmonize its monetary policy objectives with the executive branch each year. Failure to comply with the annual goals for growth, development, and price stability could lead to punishment and censure for central bank directors.[108] Ironically, the coordination law also reaffirmed legal central bank independence, stating that "the Central Bank of Venezuela shall not be subject to directives from the National Executive and shall not be permitted to endorse or finance deficit fiscal policies."

In summary, Venezuela's monetary policy paradox demonstrates the weakness of Venezuela institutions and the malleability of its laws. Economic

---

[106] Three-month money market rates, a good proxy for the central bank's policy stance, fell by a whopping 24 percentage points from 2002 to 2006 (Estadísticas e indicadores economicos, CEPAL).

[107] CEPAL.

[108] Based on discussion with Maza-Zavala during our March 2007 interview as well as the Constitution of the Bolivarian Republic of Venezuela (Title VI). For further details, see http://www.worldproutassembly.org/archives/2005/05/.constitution_of_5.html.

institutions, such as central bank independence, do not sufficiently check executive power. When commodity-rich governments have ample fiscal space, political business cycles are a product of presidential ambitions, rather than institutional checks and balances. Indeed, even during eras characterized by high institutional strength in Venezuela, electoral booms were quite common. Stimulus-minded politicians crafted political business cycles, whenever they had the financial means, providing considerable support for the first hypothesis (*H*1).

4.3.4. Ecuador's 1984 and 1988 Elections: Bankrolling Economic Populism

Ecuador provides us with another example of a country that never suffered an inflationary crisis. With a similar inflation history to Venezuela, we should expect politicians to place a low weight on inflation control relative to providing jobs and growth. Therefore, we should observe political business cycles in Ecuador before the era of decentralized bond finance.

In the years preceding Ecuador's Brady restructuring, political business cycles were a common phenomenon.[109] Despite repeated oaths of conditionality throughout the 1980s, Ecuador's politicians forged a wide gap between political rhetoric and compliance. They often made neoliberal promises in hopes of assuaging Western global powers,[110] only to unwind those commitments in the prelude to new elections. It's the flip side of the mandate switch, when politicians pursue neoliberal policies that negate prior campaign promises.[111] Instead, before the next election, politicians reverse neoliberal policies that could mar their own or their party's legacy. Therefore, the political motivation is equivalent to the classic political business cycle case where politicians prime the economic pump.

Ecuador's presidents routinely engaged in this electoral behavior in the 1980s. Indeed, in the wake of the debt crisis, Ecuadorians had a tepid acceptance for the need for economic adjustment.[112] Tanking oil markets depleted government revenues. The small agricultural-based country desperately needed financing from its commercial bank creditors. In an external funding environment marred by the debt crisis, creditors tied new loans to market conditionality. To open international funding spigots, it is not surprising that Ecuador's politicians from across the political spectrum openly embraced conservative policies. Leonardo Carrión, a lifelong Ecuadorian foreign ministry official, explains this seeming neoliberal convergence as a response to colossal pressures from the United States.

---

[109] Indeed, in his analysis of political business cycles in Ecuador, Schuldt (1994) finds a strong economic growth expansion during both the 1984 and 1988 elections at the cost of higher inflation.

[110] Stiglitz 2002; Woods 2006.

[111] Stokes 1997; Stokes 2001.

[112] Grindle and Thoumi 1993.

The IMF is largely controlled by the United States. And the United States attempts to get our economy to have a certain type of opening, a type of structure that allows foreign investments.... the Carter era had pressures about human rights. During the Reagan era the pressure was about the liberalization of the economy. There were almost orders from the Government of the United States: 'You liberalize your economy, and if you don't do it, you will have nothing' [in terms of new loans].[113]

Nonetheless, reminiscent of the Venezuelan petro-PBC, Ecuador's voters had become accustomed to receiving the political benefits of oil booms. Since the 1970s oil boom, governments had funneled these windfall gains to key economic sectors and subsidized energy, food, and transportation prices. In some years, oil revenues accounted for 50 to 70 percent of total government revenues[114] Expansive public investment became the norm, allowing government expenditures to eventually outstrip the windfall revenues. Despite achieving unprecedented economic growth,[115] these expansionary policies were unsustainable. They led to massive government borrowing, sowing the seeds for the 1982 debt crisis.[116]

Following the debt crisis, politicians were faced with the unenviable task of pledging austerity to creditors, while delivering expansive political benefits to an economically ailing population. How did politicians manage these divergent goals? Why didn't IMF conditionality reign in their spendthrift impulses? What explains the resilience of government spending despite Ecuador's repeated forays into the world of economic austerity?

A reliance on commercial bank lending allowed governments to maintain this paradox. The promise of new creditor funds, notwithstanding the course of economic policy, created a moral hazard problem (see Chapter 2 for further details). Indeed, global financiers provided a financial backstop to developing countries to avoid an insolvency-related profitability shock to their bottom lines. This defensive lending often eroded conditionality – or the calls for budget discipline – embedded in loan agreements. In fact, it was quite common for Latin American countries to overshoot market conditionality targets and waive out of their IMF programs during this era.[117]

Without a short-term exit option – or conditionality enforcement mechanism – creditors begrudgingly waited for the next administration to renegotiate lending terms. Reminiscent of commodity windfalls, bank lending gave borrowing governments the fiscal space to veer from austerity pledges and pursue their political agendas. Indeed, each new president in the 1980s (Hurtado in March 1983, Febres-Cordero in March 1985, and Borja Cevallos in March 1989) signed an IMF agreements to attain fresh funds from financiers, but drifted from its conditionality clauses in the wake of the next election.

---

[113] Hey and Klak 1999.
[114] Acosta et al. 2006.
[115] Average annual growth rates reach 9.0 to 11.5 percent during the 1970s.
[116] Grindle and Thoumi 1993.
[117] See footnote 37 in Chapter 1.

When their political reputations were at stake, both Osvaldo Hurtado and León Febres-Cordero polished their political images with popular spending policies. Notwithstanding constitutional bans on immediate reelection, these presidents remained concerned about their legacies. Facing social unrest that threatened to oust them from office, they crafted political business cycles to shore up their popularity and avoid an early exit from their presidencies.[118]

Ecuador's 1984 Elections. Early in his term, President Osvaldo Hurtado,[119] a center-left president, pledged his support to a neoliberal agenda. In his first major address in June 1981, he declared that "the era of oil prosperity had come to an end, exports had stagnated and because of that, it was necessary to begin an era of austerity."[120] In March 1983, Hurtado promised the IMF and commercial bankers he would swallow the bitter pill of economic orthodoxy in exchange for rescheduled debt and new loans. Reducing the government deficit was a cornerstone of their conditionality agreement. To garner government revenue, Hurtado vowed to increase public gasoline and transportation prices and raise beer and cigarette taxes.[121]

Facing widespread strikes and street protests against austerity measures, however, Hurtado soon reversed many of the price hikes and spending controls. With the electoral campaign in full swing, his administration used fresh funds from commercial banks and the IMF to boost social spending. They increased public sector wages and launched social programs in education, housing, and health. Hurtado also rewarded a generous subsidy to corporations, known as the *sucretización*, that swapped the bulk of debt payments from the private to the public sector. Not surprisingly, the government oversaw an aggressive credit expansion in the year before elections,[122] while simultaneously easing the pace of its previous budget tightening.[123]

Ecuador's 1988 Elections. Hurtado's presidential successor, León Febres-Cordero, walked a similar path. He professed his neoliberal commitment early in his term, only to reverse course in the prelude to the next elections. Cordero, however, was ostensibly an ideological fiscal hawk. A congressman and prominent businessman from Guayaquil, he proffered an anti-statism platform clothed in the rhetoric of "pan, techo, y empleo" (bread, housing,

[118] Grindle and Thoumi 1993.
[119] Hurtado became president of Ecuador on May 24, 1981, after the former president, Jaime Rodlós was killed in an airplane crash. Hurtado hailed from the small christian democratic party, Democracia Popular (DP). He was also a founding member of Socialist International.
[120] Grindle and Thoumi 1993.
[121] Vicuña 2000; Grindle and Thoumi 1993.
[122] Between April 1983 and May 1984, the money supply (M1) expanded by 115.7 percent, compared to 28.4 percent during the previous period (Schuldt 1994). M1 is a measure of the money supply that incorporates both currency and checking accounts deposits.
[123] Hurtado's fiscal stimulus amounted to about 0.3 percent of GDP between 1983 and 1984 (Oxford Latin American Economic History Database).

and jobs). During his campaign, he demonized Hurtado's leftist tendencies, quipping that "next to Osvaldo Hurtado, Mao Tse-Tung [was] a child."[124] Nonetheless, he too emphasized a social agenda,[125] promising new spending on social programs. Indeed, his political coalition, the Frente de Reconstrucción Nacional (FRN), was instrumental in mobilizing labor strikes against Hurtado.[126]

In his early days in office, Febres-Cordero launched a classic neoliberal agenda, featuring fiscal austerity, deregulation, and a commitment to shrink government's size. In March 1985, his government reached a new agreement with the IMF. Once again, promises of economic austerity brought fresh funding commitments from the IMF and commercial creditors. In 1986, under the Baker Plan, Ecuador repeated the pattern, pledging further orthodoxy for fresh funds.

By 1987, with elections looming, Cordero's political agenda centered on mass appeals once again. Despite his austerity vows, he funded large-scale public works projects, bumped government salaries higher, and froze utility hikes.[127] Like Hurtado, Cordero expanded government credit during the election year, funding new expenditures with central bank funding.[128] Not surprisingly, by 1988's end, inflation had reached a historical pinnacle of 58.2 percent, well above the previous year's average of 29.5 percent.

4.4. SUMMARY

The political economy literature in developing countries assumes that institutions are a key determinant of electoral booms and busts. It claims that checks and balances (such as central bank independence and fiscal rules) temper political ambitions to tinker with the business cycle. These institutional constraints have certainly helped policy makers anchor inflation expectations in Latin America. In many countries, for instance, central bank reforms have effectively discouraged the use of central bank credit to fund government spending.

However, they do not ensure that governments pursue sound macroeconomic governance. Notwithstanding these institutional constraints, Latin America is a region where presidents maintain considerable authority. When they sense a threat to their political objectives, they are often quite willing to use executive power to circumvent laws and institutions.

---

[124] Edgar Terán, President Febres-Cordero's first foreign minister, also smeared Hurtado, asserting he "hates the private sector. He hates businessmen. He hates everyone who is capable of taking a risk and of generating wealth" (Hey and Klak 1999).

[125] Stokes 2001.

[126] Grindle and Thoumi 1993.

[127] Grindle and Thoumi 1993.

[128] Between April 1987 and May 1988, the money supply increased by 37.7 percent compared to a meager 2.8 percent during the previous period (Schuldt 1994).

In this environment, political will is essential to sustaining the commitment to austerity. Over the last several chapters, I have argued that severe income shocks resulting from inflation volatility have cultivated a technocratic climate that uniformly favors economic orthodoxy. However, countries that have never experienced these inflationary crises tend to lack this macroeconomic consensus. Consequently, their policy makers are more likely to aggressively intervene in the economy and create a political business cycle. For these governments, it is simply a question of how to finance political agendas. When presidents can tap the necessary funding resources – from central bank credit and bank lending to commodity windfalls – they tend to create electorally timed economic booms.

Not surprisingly, in a region where the scale of government spending is often dependent on natural resources, even Hugo Chávez has displayed the tendencies of both a thrifty neoliberal and a free-spending socialist. Indeed, political fortunes tend to rise and fall with commodity booms and busts.

5

From Gunboat to Trading-Floor Diplomacy

In the early 20th century, Venezuelan dictator Cipriano Castro borrowed millions of dollars from Great Britain and Germany, but refused to repay the debt. Not surprisingly, these foreign creditors demanded repayment, but how did they make their point clear? In a move reminiscent of Vito Corleone in 1920s New York, they sent their muscle to Venezuela to press their outstanding financial claims. When their warships arrived on the Caribbean coast of Venezuela in December 1901, they delivered an ultimatum to Castro: pay or risk immediate military action. Castro balked, and Britain and Germany blockaded Venezuela's ports, seized its ships, and shelled its harbors for several weeks. In the wake of the war, the United States brokered a settlement, known as the Washington Protocol of 1903, where the creditor nations agreed to lift their blockades in exchange for Venezuelan debt repayment.

The scholarly verdict is out on the success of such gunboat diplomacy,[1] but fortunately, creditor warships no longer appear on debtors' shores. Creditors tend to engage in more civilized tactics now, whether through board room negotiations or trading-floor computers. Nonetheless, in today's more deeply financially integrated world, creditors' choices have an even greater influence on the livelihood of debtor nations.

In Chapter 2, I outlined the foundations of the international component of political austerity theory, arguing that a country's debt structure has important implications for creditor-debtor relations, and ultimately a debtor nation's economic choices. The shift in the structure of lending to developing countries from a centralized banking relationship to a decentralized market relationship altered creditor, and hence, debtor behavior. By diluting lenders' ownership stake across a broad pool of bond market investors, it shifted creditors' horizons from long term to short term. The lack of a direct financial linkage to borrower

---

[1] Marichal 1989; Whitehead 1989; Maxfield 1997; Donnelly 2000; Dornbusch 2000; Finnemore 2003; Mitchener and Weidenmeir 2005; Tomz 2008.

solvency not only removed creditors' vested interest in borrowers' future, but also eased their capital exit.

Ironically, after years of unsuccessfully seeking borrower compliance with lending conditionality, the bond market's capital withdrawal threat finally provided creditors with a viable enforcement mechanism. In a twist of collective action logic, a large, heterogenous group of creditors with little stake in national affairs was more successful at influencing government policy than a small, homogenous cadre of vested bankers.

In this chapter, I explore the effect of these financial market constraints on the political business cycle. I first document the historical underpinnings of political austerity theory, demonstrating how the structural change in global financing affected creditor-debtor relations in Latin America. I then conduct a comparative case study test of the market-induced austerity hypothesis (H_2) against an alternative institutional explanation: IMF conditionality. I find that the 1990's securitization of Latin American debt created a market mechanism that finally made conditionality binding. Before this dispersion of debt ownership, the IMF was not a sufficient constraint on spendthrift behavior. For example, Chapter 4 finds that political business cycles were fairly common in the 1980s. Notwithstanding creditor calls for budget discipline that were embedded into bank lending agreements, electoral booms were often fueled by new bank lending or commodity booms.

5.1. THE CASE OF THE MARKET-CONSTRAINED POLITICIAN

Why do global commercial banks have a longer time horizon than global bond markets? Why do they take significantly longer to sever their lending relationships and cut their financial losses?

Recall from Chapter 2 that a centralized creditor-debtor relationship characterizes bank lending. Centralized systems are defined by a small number of creditors with a large, concentrated debtor exposure. Given the heavy concentration of their loan portfolio, their profitability is directly tied to the financial viability of their borrowers. During difficult economic times, creditors act counterintuitively. Rather than cutting credit, they provide their borrowers with new capital to protect their own balance sheets from a severe profitability shock. In Olsonian terms, as members of a small creditor group, they would rather pay for a portion of a collective good (debtor's financial health) than survive without it.[2] It is worth rescheduling old loans and offering new loans to stave off a potential catastrophic shock to the whole banking consortium.[3]

---

[2] Olson 1965.
[3] The IMF also played a crucial role as an entrepeneur in helping banks overcome the free-rider problem. The Fund pledged to only commit its own multilateral funds if the major creditors also commited to new lending (Cline 1995).

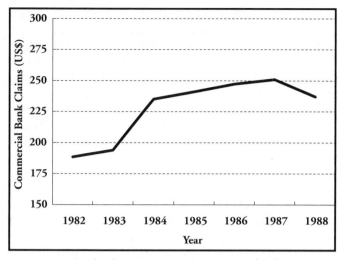

FIGURE 5.1. Bank Claims on Latin America (US$ billion, 1982–1988).
Source: Bank for International Settlements (BIS)

Creditor behavior embodied this logic throughout the 1970s and 1980s in Latin America. During this period, a small number of large global commercial banks were awash in cash. These international banks had received a glut of OPEC deposits following the 1974 and 1979 oil shocks and extended a significant portion of this new financing to Latin American governments.[4]

In fact, global banks, such as Citibank, Chase Manhattan, and Bank of America, possessed the majority of exposure to Latin American borrowers.[5] For example, in 1982, the eight largest U.S. banks had claims on Latin American countries that totaled 10 percent of their assets and 217 percent of their total capital and reserves.[6]

When Mexico ignited the 1982 debt crisis by announcing a 90-day moratorium on its debt, global bankers did not respond by immediately withdrawing their capital and cutting financial ties to the region. Rather, judging the crisis to be one of liquidity and not solvency, bankers collectively responded by providing new loans from 1982 until 1987 (Figure 5.1).[7] Why?

The aim of the new lending was not only to keep debtors afloat, but also to ensure that borrowers paid interest payments that were vital to banks' profitability. In fact, the financial fates of bankers and Latin American governments were strongly linked together. Based on data contained in 1985 financial

---

[4] Frieden 1987.

[5] Latin America accounted for about three-quarters of the total commercial bank claims extended to developing countries in 1982 (Cline 1995). The largest portion of these Latin American claims originated from U.S. banking organizations (FDIC 1997).

[6] FDIC 1997.

[7] The new loans were part of major rescheduling negotiations that began in 1982.

reports, the ratio of bank claims on Mexico, Brazil, and Venezuela amounted to a whopping 131 and 129 percent of shareholder's equity for Bank of America and Chase Manhattan Bank, respectively. In the case of Manufacturers Hanover, Citibank, and Morgan Guaranty Trust Company, their claims on Mexico, Brazil, and Argentina tallied an impressive 154, 114, and 87 percent of shareholder's equity, respectively.[8]

Notwithstanding the incentive to protect individual balance sheets, how did global banks overcome the collective action problem? What forces helped prevent creditor defection, and therefore, avoid a cataclysmic financial shock? How did bankers ensure the common good of borrower solvency?

As reported in the *Wall Street Journal*, the representatives of the major U.S. money center banks, the IMF, and the U.S. government held private meetings to find solutions to the debt crisis. In light of the U.S. banking system's vulnerability to Latin America, the U.S. government and IMF were as concerned about the health of U.S. banks as the major money center banks themselves. Through backroom negotiations, they agreed upon the following implicit compromise. The major commercial banks would extend additional credit to heavily indebted countries to safeguard their own balance sheets from debtor default. However, the U.S. financial authorities paved the way for these new loans by relaxing regulatory conditions.

According to L. William Seidman, Chairman of the Federal Deposit Insurance Corporation (FDIC), senior economic officials pursued a policy of large bank regulatory forbearance during this era. Concerned about bank profitability, the major banks were not required to increase their reserves to offset restructured or past due loans from developing countries. Amazingly, without this forbearance, Seidman believes that seven or eight of the ten largest banks in the United States might have been deemed insolvent.[9] Given banks' precarious financial condition, they were unlikely to survive a severe external shock, including an outright debtor collapse. According to Seidman,

U.S. bank regulators, given the choice between creating panic in the banking system and going easy on requiring our banks to set aside reserves for Latin American debt, had chosen the latter course. It would appear the regulators made the right choice.

The Baker Plan, introduced by U.S. Treasury Secretary James A. Baker in 1985, formalized this government-banker consensus about new lending to heavily indebted countries. Under Baker's scheme, commercial banks pledged a further $20 billion in new lending to heavily indebted countries (and multilateral agencies also committed $9 billion). Some opponents of the plan, including Senator Bill Bradley, worried about the dubious health of the U.S. private

---

[8] Bogdanowicz-Bindert 1986.
[9] For further details, see a *History of the Eighties – Lessons for the Future*, a 1997 study prepared by the FDIC's Division of Research and Statistics at http://www.fdic.gov/bank/historical/history/index.html.

banking system, fearing it would "pile new debt on old."[10] Nonetheless, commercial banks continued their defensive lending from 1986–1988, channeling more than $17 billion in new funds to heavily indebted borrowers.[11]

Market conditionality accompanied the new lending in hopes that debtor countries would improve their finances by pursuing growth and reform initiatives. They advocated for IMF-sponsored market reforms, including balanced budgets and restrictive monetary policies.[12]

The Baker Plan, however, was plagued by moral hazard. Like G.M. executives during the 2008 financial crisis,[13] Latin American political leaders had few incentives to reform, knowing that their creditors feared the consequences of their insolvency. Not surprisingly, it was quite common for Latin American countries to overshoot market conditionality targets and waive out of their IMF programs during this era.[14] Amazingly, in spite of their non-compliance, they often received fresh funds from their creditors. For example, in July 1987, Argentina's Alfonsín government was out of compliance with almost all of its IMF agreement's requirements, yet it managed to secure new credit.

By decade's close, commercial banks and U.S. policy makers began to search for a new resolution to the debt crisis. By this time, the eight major U.S. banks had incurred a devastating shock to their earnings.[15] Fatigued by constant crisis management, they decided to cut their losses. Led by Citibank and Bank of Boston, U.S. financial institutions boosted reserves against bad loans and "wrote off" irrecoverable loans.[16]

By this time, however, the U.S. Treasury had advanced a new, market-oriented approach to debt reduction, known as the Brady Plan.[17] The Brady

---

[10] Roett, 1989.

[11] Cline (1995) suggests the number may be lower, around $13 billion, but also reports that the World Bank claims that "new long term money" from commercial banks was even higher during this period, amounting to $18.1 billion. I chose to report the Global Development Finance Database's $17.5 billion figure because it was the median of the three sources.

[12] In addition to these standard IMF agreements, the Baker Plan also advocated for structural reforms, including privatization and trade and financial liberalization.

[13] Notwithstanding three rounds of government fund injections totaling $19.4 billion from 2008 to 2009, poor management and business practices eventually forced the company into partial nationalization and Chapter 11 bankruptcy.

[14] See footnote 37 in Chapter 1.

[15] In 1989, their net income to total capital and net income to total assets averaged −9.9 and −0.45 percent respectively, returns significantly below the historical industry averages of 9.0 and 0.55 percent (FDIC 1997)

[16] Roett 1989.

[17] The Brady Plan, launched on March 10, 1989, was named after U.S. Treasury Secretary Nicholas J. Brady. This market approach to debt reduction featured at least two basic options for debt holders: 1) the exchange of loans for long-term debt with concessionary interest terms (known as Par bonds), 2) the exchange of loans for a lesser amount of face value in bonds (generally a 30–50% discount), allowing for immediate debt reduction, with a market-based floating rate of interest (known as Discount bonds). The principal of both bonds was backed by the pledge of U.S. Treasury securities. For further details, see the Emerging Market Trader's Association website, http://www.emta.org/emarkets/brady.html.

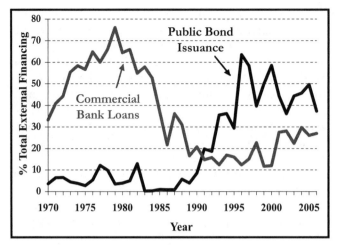

FIGURE 5.2. Bond Issuance Supplants Bank Lending (17 Latin American Countries, Aggregate).
Source: Global Development Finance

restructurings converted outstanding commercial bank loans into market-traded debt. The U.S. Treasury widely touted the plan's debt relief,[18] though some critics questioned its ability to restore debtor creditworthiness.[19]

More importantly, however, the restructurings led to a profound change in developing country financing. It replaced the centralized system of bank lending with a decentralized debt market. Indeed, debt holders surged from a handful of large banks to gaggles of small, decentralized global bond market investors. In fact, new bond issuance grew from US$0.6 billion in 1989 to US$37 billion by 1996, accounting for more than 64 percent of Latin America's total public external financing (Figure 5.2).[20]

Supplanting loans with highly tradeable securities allowed commercial banks to diversify their risk exposure throughout the global financial community. In a new world of numerous and globally dispersed investors, creditors' financial fates were no longer directly linked to the health of developing countries. The system was now characterized by a large number of creditors, who each had only a limited exposure to sovereign borrowers.

---

[18] Between 1989 and 1994, private lenders forgave 32 percent of the total $191 billion in outstanding loans that were restructured under the Brady Plan. These losses, totaling $61 billion, were accrued by the shareholders of the lending banks (Cline 1995).

[19] For example, Jeffrey Sachs suggested that a 40 percent debt reduction was needed for the Brady Plan to reestablish country creditworthiness (Sachs 1989b). Kenneth Rogoff argued that banks benefited at the expense of developing countries. Debt forgiveness not only improved the creditworthiness of borrowers but also inflated the amount banks could be expected to receive from developing countries (Rogoff 1993).

[20] Emerging Markets Trading Association.

These conditions created a perpetual collective action failure. In a decentralized system, propping up borrowers was no longer a worthwhile collective good.[21] Creditors' low financial exposure to sovereign debtors insulated their balance sheets from developing country liquidity crises. Protecting their profitability no longer warranted incurring the costs of rescheduling or extending new money to debtors. Rather, during economic downturns, creditors now could exit without the fear of seriously dampening their own financial welfare. Benefiting from a secondary market backstop, they could sell developing country debt for an acceptable loss, while simultaneously cutting their financial ties with borrowers.

Counterintuitively, the collective action failure among creditors translated into a weakened Latin American state. The Brady Plan, like its predecessors, heralded market conditionality. In the new decentralized system, however, market conditionality stuck.

Straying from the path of market-friendly policies risked igniting a sudden stop of financing, where multitudes of international investors dispose of their debt holdings and restrict new funding.[22] "Sudden stops" have severe repercussions for developing countries, often unleashing a cataclysmic cycle of capital outflows, interest rate spikes, economic distress, and credit downgrades. Hoping to avoid such severe economic repercussions, politicians became more likely to adhere to economic orthodoxy.

A possible critique of this mechanism centers on the logic of procyclicality in Latin America. Rather than markets impelling macroeconomic discipline, expansionary policies in good economic times might beget austere policies in bad economic times.

In response to this critique, I contend that capital market exposure often compels a more conservative policy stance, even under the most benevolent economic circumstances. To avoid investor flight and keep the spigot of foreign financing open, politicians with low capital market exposure often also pursue restrictive economic policies. In a highly interdependent world, international credit evaluations strongly influence the domestic business environment. Domestic firms borrow at rates that are directly linked to a country's credit rating. In light of these market pressures, politicians often avoid aggressive expansionary macroeconomic policies that risk credit downgrades.

---

[21] Under rare circumstances, some segments of the decentralized global bond market have overcome the collective action problem. Indeed, peak bond associations were among the key holdouts from the 2005 Argentina debt exchange. However, the dispersion of ownership among the holdouts was too vast to effectively muster a collective action campaign that benefited the debtor nation. Indeed, the multitudes of individual bondholders (including scores of retail bond investors, global mutual fund managers, investment banks, and hedge funds from across several national and international jurisdictions) had too low of a financial stake in the individual bondholders' debt to warrant acting in the interest of the sovereign borrower (see Chapter 2 for further details).

[22] Calvo 1998; Calvo and Reinhart 2000; Kaminsky, Reinhart, and Vegh 2004; and Edwards 2007.

For example, Chile's government strives to maintain a balance between economic discipline and growth. The country has maintained a healthy fiscal surplus, while growing by an average of 4 percent over the decade. During my 2007 field research interview, the current Central Bank of Chile Governor, José De Gregorio, elaborated on the disciplining effect of financial openness.

We are a very open economy financially. So, although we [currently] do not depend, we are disciplined by external markets. If you are closed economy with a lot of distortions, basically it does not matter what you do. Now, if we do behave like Chávez, we have serious problem with the valuation of a country and the investment climate. So we have a cost. When you are closed, you do not give a damn. So, I think there is an important disciplining effect.[23]

In summary, growth-oriented politicians are unlikely to create political business cycles if they do not have the financial means. In a globalized world, economic policy choices are not the sole realm of politicians and central bankers. International investors can place important financial limitations on political behavior. Indeed, global financial market pressures often check traditional political incentives to use economic policy for electoral gain.

5.1.1. Market-Induced Austerity Cycle (H2)

In the previous chapter, I showed there is often no institutional fix for politics in Latin America. When powerful stimulus-minded executives have the fiscal space, or the availability of budget resources to prime the economic pump, they create a political business cycle regardless of institutional checks and balances, such as central bank independence. Domestic wealth, from oil rigs to copper mines, allows governing elites to circumvent institutional hurdles and achieve political aims.

But, what happens when politicians no longer have the fiscal space to craft an electoral boom? They alleviate this fiscal constraint by borrowing externally. In the wake of the Latin American debt crisis, recall that nations changed the composition of their foreign borrowing, swapping defaulted bank loans for new, government bond issuance. Initially, global capital markets offered a cheap, attractive financing source. Despite this benefit, however, bond markets increasingly placed a large cost on freewheeling political behavior because of borrowing governments' high indebtedness. Although IMF conditionality predated Latin America's heavy foray into global bond markets by several decades, I argue that it was financial market integration that gave conditionality its punch.

In this chapter, I examine the *market-induced political austerity cycle* – the second of two hypotheses dealing with the feasibility dimension of policy

---

[23] Author's interview with current Central Bank President José De Gregorio conducted on April 11, 2007. Prior to becoming central bank president, De Gregorio was both the bank's vice president and policy board member since 2003.

TABLE 5.1. *Macroeconomic Policy Expectations: The Spendthrift or the Miser?*

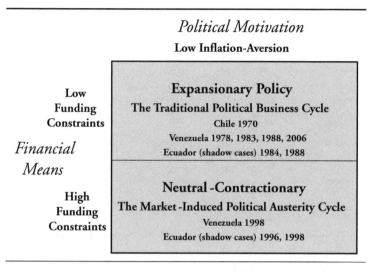

making (shown in the lower box of Table 5.1). I test whether a high dependence on global capital markets for financing blunts spendthrift political behavior (H_2). Once again, I assume that chief executives operate in the low inflation-aversion dimension. Incumbents see the political benefit of crafting a pre-electoral economic boom and believe that its inflationary consequences are minimal. Hoping to improve their reelection chances, they plan in the years preceding an election to use macroeconomic policy to provide their supporters with economic growth, wage hikes, and new jobs.

Notwithstanding these political motivations, when does the market constrain this behavior? At low levels of bond market dependency, debt-powered economic booms are still common. By contrast, when governments' external debt is comprised mostly of bonds and they cannot tap non-market financing alternatives (such as commodity income or bank lending), politicians are likely to restrain their stimulus impulses (Figure 5.3).

Therefore, if the market-induced austerity hypothesis is correct, we should observe that spendthrift behavior is stymied by bond market pressures. Borrower conditionality pledges, a longstanding hallmark of developing country lending, are finally upheld under the ownership dispersion of bond markets. Bondholders' low stake in borrower solvency emboldens their capital exit threat, helping enforce economic orthodoxy. These austerity patterns are further buttressed by elections, when political uncertainty often unnerves international investors. Hoping to avoid credit disruptions that can quickly roil the economy, governments opt for creditor-friendly policies that assuage bondholders worried about debt repayment.

TABLE 5.2. *Case Study Overview (H1 and H2)*

Country	Chief Executive	Election Year	Inflation-Aversion?	Market Constraints?	Political Business Cycle?
Chile	Eduardo Frei Montalva	1970	N	N	Traditional PBC
Venezuela	Carlos Andrés Pérez	1978	N	N	Traditional PBC
Venezuela	Luis Herrera Campins	1983	N	N	Traditional PBC
Ecuador	Osvaldo Hurtado	1984	N	N	Traditional PBC
Venezuela	Jaime Lusinchi	1988	N	N	Traditional PBC
Ecuador	León Febres-Cordero	1988	N	N	Traditional PBC
Ecuador	Sixto Durán Ballén	1996	N	Y	Market-Induced PAC
Ecuador	Fabián Alarcón	1998	N	Y	Market-Induced PAC
Venezuela	Rafael Caldera	1998	N	Y	Market-Induced PAC
Venezuela	Hugo Chávez	2006	N	N	Traditional PBC

In the following pages, I test my claim of a political austerity cycle against an alternative explanation, IMF conditionality and the Washington Consensus' emphasis on fiscal rectitude. To adjudicate between these alternative explanations, I use three comparative election cases in Venezuela and Ecuador. Table 5.2 outlines my expected outcomes for the first set of comparative case studies (from Chapters 4 and 5) that examine a shift in policy makers' means (the highlighted cases are for the current chapter; they are also grouped by their policy making dimensions in Table 5.1).

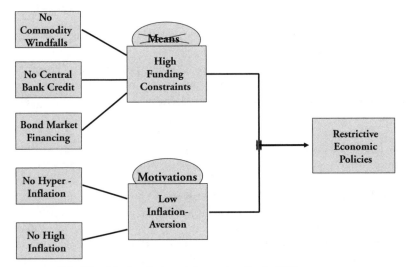

FIGURE 5.3. The Market-Induced Austerity Cycle (H2).

5.1.2. An Alternative Argument: IMF Conditionality

What explains the rise of economic austerity in Latin America? Some scholars point to the ideological dominance of the United States in a post-cold war world.[24] Western governments used the International Monetary Fund and its conditionality arrangements as an instrument to promote a market-oriented economic agenda in the developing world.[25]

Heralding Milton Friedman's revolutionary monetarist manifesto, the Fund emphasized deficit reduction and inflation stabilization as cornerstones of their development agenda during the 1980s. In exchange for the Fund's "stamp of approval," policy makers committed to economic orthodoxy in hopes of tapping much-needed credit from global financial markets.

Notably, however, many scholars have found IMF-backed reform programs were unsuccessful at engineering economic growth in developing countries.[26] Why would countries continue to implement policies that are unfavorable to growth?

Perhaps, governments have little choice because these policies are imposed externally. Indeed, proponents of this hegemonic view have argued that conditionality explains the prevalence of stabilization-minded rather than growth-oriented policies during Latin American election periods.

By contrast, I contend that IMF conditionality was not a sufficient condition to harness spendthrift Latin American politicians. If it were sufficient, we would expect to observe politicians adhering to economic orthodoxy throughout the 1980s. Indeed, IMF agreements called for market reforms, including conservative fiscal and monetary policies, during the post-debt crisis and Baker Plan years. Throughout the decade, however, countries with IMF agreements routinely missed their performance criteria. In fact, between 1980 and 1991, more than two-fifths of countries with IMF agreements did not comply with their conditionality targets.[27]

Rather, I contend that Friedman's monetarist revolution did not take hold until the surge of bond market financing ushered in a new era of economic austerity. With this structural shift in global finance away from traditional bank lending, politicians entered into a Putnam "two-level game." Tapping capital markets to fund domestic spending forced cash-starved governments' hands at home. Aiming to appease foreign investors, they balanced budgets and tightened credit, even at the cost of supplying some jobs and growth to domestic constituents. Rather than creating a broad-based economic boom, they appeased domestic political supporters with line-item budget expenditures

---

[24] Pastor 1987; Stiglitz 2002; Woods 2006.

[25] Dreher, Sturm, and Vreeland (2009) also find that that the IMF uses its economic leverage to gain influence in other institutional forums such as the UN security council. Developing country members of the security council are typically extended IMF agreements with few conditions.

[26] Przeworksi and Vreeland 2000; Vreeland 2003; Easterly 2004.

[27] Edwards 2001.

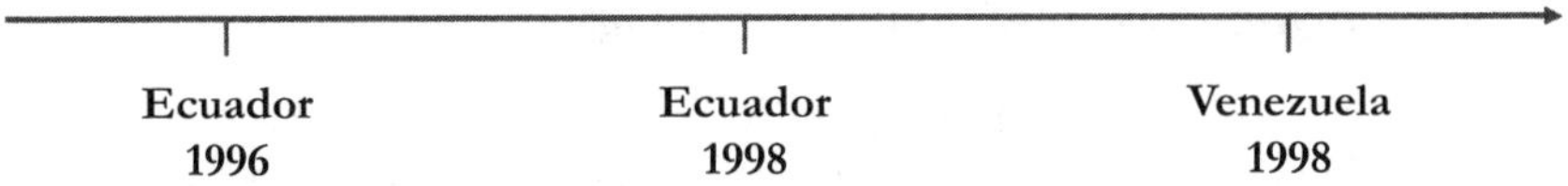

Ecuador	Ecuador	Venezuela
1996	1998	1998

FIGURE 5.4. The Market-Induced Political Austerity Cycle (H2).

and discretionary spending. Counterintuitively, they forged a political austerity cycle, rather than a political business cycle.

5.2. COMPARATIVE CASE STUDY EVIDENCE

In this chapter, I test the market-induced political austerity hypothesis (H_2), employing evidence from the three comparative election cases in Ecuador and Venezuela that are outlined in Figure 5.4.

In the other country cases, such as Argentina, Brazil, and Chile, politicians who were scarred by past economic crises accepted market conditionality early in their democratic experiences. By the 1990s, politicians in these countries recognized the importance of economic discipline and price stability. They valued jobs and growth, but not at the cost of high inflation (see Chapter 6). But, what occurs in countries where historically politicians have placed less emphasis on price stability?

For example, Ecuador and Venezuela have never experienced a severe inflationary crisis (characterized by price increases spiking above 100 percent per annum). Without an inflationary albatross, an inflation-generating boom has a low political cost. Moreover, commodity earnings – from petroleum to agricultural proceeds – help Ecuador and Venezuelan's presidents leverage additional bond market borrowing to finance massive spending sprees.

Nonetheless, when commodity income falls, does a reliance on decentralized bond markets raise the financial cost of stimulus, and therefore, impede the political business cycle? In other words, can financial globalization transform Latin American fiscal doves into fiscal hawks? While market conditionality did not hold in the 1980s, does the growth of international bond markets help enforce conditionality as expected by political austerity theory?

5.2.1. Ecuador's 1996 and 1998 Elections: Market Securitization Defuses the Electoral Boom

If political austerity theory is correct, we should observe a shift to economic orthodoxy following Ecuador's 1994 Brady conversion of its bank loans into bond debt. The market securitization of Ecuador's bank loans not only cut the financial exposure of its major bank creditors, but also provided a swift capital exit threat for its new bondholders, which should theoretically strengthen compliance with conditionality even during elections.

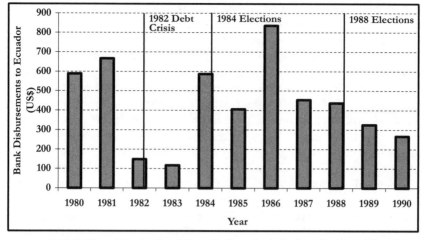

FIGURE 5.5. IMF and Banks Lend Despite Ecuador's Reform Drift (US$ million, 1980–1990).
Source: Global Development Finance

Throughout the 1980s, we have seen that political business cycles were prevalent in Ecuador.[28] In each election cycle, cash-strapped Ecuadorian presidents, including Osvaldo Hurtado, León Febres-Cordero, and Rodrigo Borja Cevallos, tapped the IMF and global commercial banks for fresh funds. Given the difficult-to-dissolve links between Ecuador and its creditors, the IMF and commercial banks repeatedly supplied Ecuador with new cash injections despite its "stop and go" economic reform cycles (Figure 5.5).

Bankrolled by its creditors, the fresh funds gave these governments the fiscal space to deliver new spending and stray from their austerity assurances. Indeed, IMF conditionality alone did not halt politically motivated expansions. Rather, heavily exposed creditors without a short-term exit option – or conditionality enforcement mechanism – awaited the next administration to renegotiate lending terms (See Chapter 4).

The 1990's market securitization of Ecuador's debt, however, altered this pattern. Indeed, market-financed debt placed greater restrictions on Ecuadorian politicians. Under the Brady plan, Ecuador's authorities converted its US$5 billion in outstanding commercial bank loans into market-traded debt. Following this deal, Ecuador's international bonds amounted to more than half the country's total external debt (official multilateral assistance accounted for the remaining share).[29] Even more notably, Ecuador's outstanding bond debt equaled one-third of the country's GDP by the end of 1995.

---

[28] See Chapter 4.
[29] Commercial bank loans now represented a meager 3 percent of Ecuador's external debt in 1995 (World Bank's Global Development Finance).

With bond financing taking center stage during the 1990s, Ecuador became exposed to short-term creditors with less tolerance for bad credits. Veering from market-friendly policies now risked "sudden stops" of financing. When witnessing pre-election policy drift, creditors no longer had to wait to renegotiate loan terms with the next government. The highly dispersed bond market ownership diluted any single creditor's exposure to Ecuador. Creditor profitability no longer warranted endless debt reschedulings. Rather, bond investors had an immediate exit strategy that limited their financial fallout. Without a high stake in borrower solvency, they could either refuse to rollover Ecuador's short-term debt or sell their outstanding bonds in the secondary market. Such actions risked sparking a dramatic capital reversal, sending bond yields higher and posing an immediate threat to both government spending possibilities and the real economy.

In light of these severe economic risks, we should observe a marked change in politicians' electoral behavior compared to the bank lending era. Politicians should be more apt to pursue budget austerity and tight monetary policy to stem capital outflows in the prelude to elections, despite the potential political cost of delivering lower growth and fewer jobs to their constituents.

Ecuador's 1996 Elections. In line with my theoretical expectations, Ecuador's post-Brady restructuring elections are characterized by economic austerity. In 1996, President Sixto Durán Ballén, a right-wing politician from the Partido Unión Republicana (PUR) adhered to his conservative ideological roots. Unlike the last three presidents, including fellow fiscal hawk Febres-Cordero, Ballén avoided election-motivated policy drift.

Why did Ballén resist this political temptation? Facing historically unprecedented levels of unpopularity, Ballén certainly possessed a strong incentive to burnish his presidential legacy before the next elections. Indeed, he enjoyed a paltry 16 percent of voter approval by late 1994.

However, in the prelude to elections, extensive financial market turmoil derailed any political intentions to prime the economic pump. In the wake of Ecuador's 1995 Brady restructuring deal, the government was already paying a heavy price for its access to foreign credit. In fact, public debt service in the 1996 fiscal budget accounted for more than one-third of all government spending.

Concerned about mounting debt, exchange rate overvaluation, and electoral uncertainty, bond investors were hastily withdrawing capital from the country. Compared to its neighbors, interest rates on Ecuador's debt were climbing quickly. In the six months preceding elections, Ecuadorian debt traded at an average premium that was nearly two-thirds higher than interest rates on Argentine, Brazilian, and Mexican debt.[30]

---

[30] Ecuadorian interest rates hovered 13 percentage points above U.S. treasury yields, compared to the more subdued average of 7 to 8 percentage points above U.S. treasury yields in Argentina, Brazil, and Mexico (J.P. Morgan's Emerging Market Bond Index).

Hoping to ease financial market pressures, Ballén used budgetary discipline, along with tight monetary policy, to signal Ecuador's creditworthiness to international lenders.[31] In fact, he championed an election-year balanced budget through Congress, laying the groundwork for a political austerity cycle characterized by neutral fiscal policy. Under Ballén's market-friendly watch, Ecuador's primary budget surplus (about 2 percent of GDP) remained relatively unscathed throughout the electoral campaign.[32] This conservative governance allowed inflation-obsessed investors to take refuge in a stable inflation rate,[33] notwithstanding their concerns about the upcoming change of government.[34]

Ballén, the first president to govern in the new era of decentralized global finance, broke the political trend of macro-level booms and busts around Ecuadorian elections. Notwithstanding his fiscal rectitude, however, he did trumpet many micro-level budget initiatives that were designed to improve his battered political image. Indeed, Ballén hoped to strike a balance between demonstrating economic discipline to markets and appeasing strong pressures for higher wages and new jobs.

In the 1996 election year, Ballén designed several line-item expenditures within the balanced budget framework to help restore his popularity with politically important constituencies. Hoping to curry favor with public workers, for instance, he boosted wages for teachers, hospital employees, and prison workers. In a broader political appeal, Ballén also raised the minimum wage. To offset these new spending commitments and ease market pressures, however, Ballén cut public works projects and vowed to improve tax collection.

Ecuador's 1998 Elections. During the 1998 elections, we observed a similar pattern. Compared to the moral hazard that plagued bank lending in Ecuador, a cash-strapped President Fabían Alarcón had to once again adhere to austerity pledges in the era of decentralized bond finance. Why? In 1998, Ecuador was still highly dependent on international bond markets to finance its government spending. Public officials continued to tap international bond markets to fund more than half of the country's external financing needs.

Why didn't the Alarcón government draw revenues from the proceeds of state-enterprises, such as oil producer Petroecuador? The El Niño devastation and moribund oil markets had left public coffers barren. Between 1996 and 1998, non-tax revenues in Ecuador fell by more than 3 percentage points of GDP, or about one-fifth of the government's total revenues. There were no

---

[31] Hey and Klak 1989.

[32] CEPAL's Estadísticas de América Latina y El Caribe.

[33] Ecuador's average inflation rate only fluctuated minimally in 1996, increasing to 27.2 percent compared to 25.7 percent in the previous year. Moreover, average price increases remained well below their pre-Brady restructuring levels of 50 to 60 percent (World Development Indicators).

[34] Presidential favorites, Jamie Nebot and Rodrigo Paz, attempted to distance themselves from Ballén's market-friendly, but unpopular policies. During the electoral campaign, both contendors underscored a commitment to higher social spending and economic growth (EIU Country Report, 1996).

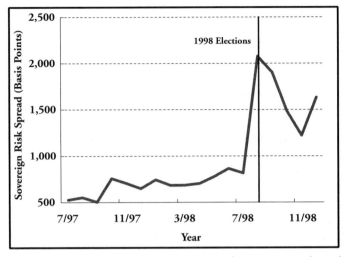

FIGURE 5.6. Ecuador's Credit Plummets Before 1998 Presidential Elections (Bond Yield Differential Between Ecuadorean and U.S. Treasury Debt).
Source: J.P. Morgan

alternative non-market resources that politicians could use to address growing demands for social spending. Rather, Alarcón had to refinance the country's short-term debt obligations solely to maintain the budgetary status quo.

These financing conditions made the Ecuadorean president extremely wary of unnerving international investors who were obsessed with short-term default risk. Ecuador's combined oil and El Niño shocks had already rattled investors. Interest rates on the country's external debt had surged in 1998, reaching more than a 20 percent premium over the yield on U.S. Treasury debt (Figure 5.6). Electoral uncertainty was only making matters worse.

Forced to balance the political vote against the market's vote, the Alarcón government was placed in a precarious political position. On the eve of the 1998 elections, President Alarcón[35] – a center-left politician who intended to run for the presidency again in 2002 – had to calm financial market volatility. Alarcón, who might otherwise stimulate the economy to address strong social demands, was compelled to demonstrate his commitment to fiscal discipline. In an effort to assuage jittery markets, President Alarcón had initially tightened the budget in 1997, but investors still worried about oil-related revenue shortfalls and hefty government outlays that were needed to repair El Niño's latest wreckage. Hence, Alarcón sought an IMF loan agreement, hoping its stamp of approval would ease financial market pressures.

Budget discipline was imperative to getting fresh funds from both financial markets and the IMF. Without such austerity, Alarcón risked igniting a severe

[35] Alarcón hailed from the center-left Frente Radical Alfarista party, which was founded in 1972. He became president in February 1997 because of the impeachment of President Abdalá Bucaram. Though interim president until August 1998, he hoped to make a presidential bid in 2002.

capital withdrawal that could send Ecuador's economy into a free fall. Notably, an Ecuadorian president was facing a sudden stop for the second consecutive election period since its 1994 Brady bond restructurings. Stunningly, Alarcón was willing not only to contract fiscal policy in 1997,[36] but also to promote further belt tightening in 1998. In fact, Alarcón proposed a mid-February fiscal adjustment package to Congress during the 1998 election year.

In spite of impending elections in May and July, the austerity package included spending controls and a potpourri of taxes on cars, corporations, and consumption.[37] Despite his efforts, a politically reluctant Congress eventually rejected Alarcón's unpopular tax increases and spending controls. Why would Alarcón propose legislation that was doomed to fail?

With an eye on the 2002 presidential election, Alarcón hoped to achieve a delicate political balance. The Ecuadorian president wanted to convince financial markets of his commitment to austerity, but without causing the electorate considerable economic harm.

Not terribly different from cash-strapped Greek politicians today, Alarcón played a dangerous political game, hoping to simultaneously appease international investors and domestic voters. Notwithstanding his general support for macroeconomic discipline and budget cuts, there were clear limits on Alarcón's austerity overtures. Like most austerity presidents, he oversaw line-item budget increases in government salaries and public works projects within an orthodox budget framework. In light of his presidential ambitions, Alarcón also took a public stand against some of the most political unpopular parts of the Washington Consensus.[38] Against the backdrop of public outcry and union resistance to IMF reforms, Alarcón openly resisted cutting electricity and gas subsidies and privatizing the state-run social security system. In fact, he hoped to revive his public image in the wake of several corruption scandals that emerged during his final months in office.[39]

5.2.2. 1990s Venezuela: Boom Mentality Persists, But Economy Stalls Without Petrol

A constant in Venezuelan politics is expansive fiscal policy! No politician wants to lose votes. We don't close institutions or businesses because we don't want to lose votes! We don't want to head off inflation because we don't want to lose votes! The state has too much power. I have managed a petrol state. I know.[40]

---

[36] Ecuador's primary budget balance increased by almost one full percentage point to 2.8 percent of GDP during 1997, notwithstanding the upcoming presidential elections.

[37] Alarcón proposed an increase in the value-added tax from 10 to 14 percent, a new 1 to 3 percent vehicle tax, and a 1.25 percent tax on corporate income.

[38] Public opinion surveys indicate very little popular support for privatization throughout Latin America (Baker 2008).

[39] In early April, the Congressional anti-corruption commission issued a report claiming that 2,000 political appointments made under Alarcon's congressional presidency between 1995 and 1997 involved political patronage and nepotism.

[40] Author's interview with Carmelo Lauría, March 5, 2007, in Caracas, Venezuela.

Carmelo Lauría, the Acción Democrática (AD) stalwart who served in the presidential cabinet for three different governments, invokes a common Venezuelan motif: the spendthrift politician and his enabler, the poor citizen clamoring for his share of oil riches. In the absence of a severe inflationary crisis, Venezuelan politicians have rarely wavered from using government intervention to spur jobs and growth.[41]

Former Venezuelan President Ramón José Velásquez, who served as a caretaker chief executive between 1993 and 1994,[42] further quips:

In the end, all that matters is a politician's ability to distribute benefits and carry out development projects. Ideology has little importance.[43]

Though Venezuela has faced some mild inflationary pressures in the post-oil boom era, the country has yet to undergo a massively painful inflationary shock like those incurred elsewhere from Argentina to Nicaragua.[44] Hefty government intervention and expansionary budgets yield little political backlash; rather, a redistributive state is the expected norm in Venezuela. Politicians like Lauría and Velásquez have the freedom to aggressively pursue economic stimulus, without having to fret about inflation stabilization.

If we assume that Venezuelans presidents want to infuse voters' pocketbooks with money, their political behavior should reflect the feasibility of highly interventionist policy choices. Indeed, Gustavo Tarre, a former COPEI Congressman and President of the Congressional Financial Committee, explains this phenomenon.

Ninety percent of Venezuela's politics are rooted in Keynes rather than Hayek. And during election years, even more! But, everything depends on how much you can spend and therefore how much oil income you possess! In Venezuela, no government with oil income from high oil prices has saved even a little bit of money. They spent all of it! And those without money do not spend because they cannot spend, not because they don't want to![45]

As Tarre stresses, Venezuela's recent election history is littered with petro-PBCs during roaring oil markets. When government coffers are bereft of oil income, however, Venezuelan politicians often turn outward for international

---

[41] The clear exception was Carlos Andrés Pérez's second presidency, in which he pursued a neoliberal economic program known as the "great turnabout." Characterized by an indefatigable commitment to market reforms, Pérez unsuccessfully attempted to put an end to the economic model of state intervention established over the previous half-century (Ellner 2008).

[42] Former President Carlos Andrés Pérez was removed from office on corruption charges on May 20, 1993.

[43] Author's interview with President Velásquez in Caracas on March 23, 2007.

[44] Indeed, Venezuela has toyed with double-digit inflation on several occasions over the last three decades, but has never confronted high inflation (above 100 percent per annum) or hyperinflation (well above 1,000 percent per annum).

[45] Author's interview with Gustavo Tarre in Caracas, Venezuela, on March 27, 2007.

financing. As noted above, the structure of this external finance can have important implications for economic policy making.

In a world of commercial bank lending, Venezuelan presidents have crafted electoral booms, even in the absence of oil money. During the 1988 election campaign, President Jaime Lusinchi's (AD) hopes of securing the presidency for his party were almost soured by plunging oil markets. However, Lusinchi famously leveraged fresh global commercial bank funds to aggressively expand government spending and help propel AD to victory.[46] Market conditionality had accompanied this new lending under the Baker Plan, but did not spoil Lusinchi's spending spree. In fact, by the beginning of the ensuing Pérez administration, the new government found only barren public coffers and depleted foreign reserves.[47]

Lusinchi did not heed his lenders' calls for restrictive fiscal and monetary policies, once again demonstrating that IMF conditionality alone is not a successful deterrent. Not surprisingly, the short-term electoral pressures of the office trumped any concerns about complying with creditor calls for conservative, low-inflation policies.

By the next decade, however, the shift in global finance toward market-traded debt emboldened conditionality calls and restricted Venezuela's policy freedoms. In the lead-up to the 1998 elections, yet another oil market collapse besieged Venezuelan politicians. This time, however, new global bank funds were not available because Venezuela had securitized its debt. While commercial banks accounted for almost 90 percent of Venezuela's external debt in 1988, their exposure to Venezuela was almost nil in the mid-1990s.[48] Having to instead tap new funds from an ever-mercurial global bond market left President Rafael Caldera with little choice but to pursue a Hayekian austerity. Indeed, financial markets became the enforcement mechanism for conditionality, prompting historical leftists like Rafael Caldera, Teodoro Petkoff, and Hugo Chávez to all embrace market discipline in the 1990s.

Venezuela's 1998 Elections. During the 1998 election campaign, we can assume that President Rafael Caldera would have liked to craft an economic boom like his presidential predecessors. The political stakes were even higher than normal, with the rise of Hugo Chávez. Caldera was an iconic figure in the old, two-party Punto-Fijo system that Chávez threatened to dismantle.[49] Notwithstanding this clear and present political danger, however, Caldera did not prime the economic pump to win votes. Rather, he administered a highly

---

[46] See Chapter 4 for further details.

[47] According to conversations with Gustavo García, a senior economics professor at Venezuela's Instituto de Estudios Superiores de Administracion (IESA), the central bank had a paltry US$300 million in reserves in the beginning of the Pérez administration.

[48] World Bank's Global Development Finance.

[49] See Chapter 4 for further details.

restrictive set of economic adjustment policies in advance of presidential elections. What explains this surprising behavior?

On the heels of signing an IMF stand-by agreement in 1996, perhaps the Venezuelan president was compelled by IMF officials to implement economic orthodoxy. Indeed, Caldera may have simply complied with the governance standards of the world's most powerful international financial institution, adhering to the conditionality embedded in its IMF stand-by loan agreement.

Certainly, this alternative explanation for the rise of neoliberal policies in Venezuela sheds some light on the power asymmetries between international financial institutions and developing countries. However, the strength of international institutions alone does not sufficiently explain the complete about-face from one of Latin America's most historic leftists. Indeed, even Venezuelan governments that were to the right of Caldera often did not meet their IMF conditionality targets during the halcyon days of bank lending and oil wealth in the 1970s and 1980s.

Rather, I argue that Venezuela's heavy reliance on global bond markets made the country vulnerable to credit shocks that narrowed its policy freedoms. Indeed, 1998's steep fall in oil prices left Caldera with a dearth of available domestic resources to commit to election-year spending. It also sullied Venezuela's credit worthiness. With a high reliance on capital markets for financing, debt-ridden Venezuela was reeling from interest rate spikes and credit downgrades. Fundamentally, a lack of fiscal space forced Caldera to comply with financial market pressures for conservative, low-inflation policies.

In the prelude to the 1998 elections, it is likely that President Caldera wanted to stimulate the economy. Caldera, a left-leaning second-time president from COPEI, was a fervent critic of former President Andrés Pérez's neoliberal reforms. Following Chávez's unsuccessful 1992 coup,[50] the silver and slick haired Caldera revived his political career with a rebuke of Pérez's presidency.[51] He noted that Venezuelans had not poured into the streets to defend Pérez because of democracy's failures.

It is difficult to ask the people to burn for freedom and democracy while they think that freedom and democracy are not able to feed them and impede the exorbitant increase in the cost of subsistence.[52]

---

[50] On February 4, 1992, Chávez and his military supporters, under the banner of the Revolutionary Bolivarian Movement-200 (MBR-200), launched a coup against the Pérez government. The rebels took key strategic points in Caracas, Maraciabo, and Maracay. Without the expected support of the air-force and civilian population; however, Chávez and his comrades were forced to surrender.

[51] Caldera made inroads with Venezuean voters, taking advantage of their lack of support for Pérez's neoliberal ideology. Indeed, a 1993 survey of 1,500 Venezuelans showed strong majorities supported government intervention in the economy, but opposed privatization and price liberalization (Stokes 2001).

[52] Hellinger 2003.

Caldera embraced such social justice principles in his 1993 presidential campaign. Rebuffing economic austerity, he pledged to avoid conditionality demanded by IMF letters of intent. Caldera instead called for a *Carta de Intencíon con el Pueblo de Venezuela*, promising to cure the economic plight of the people.

During his first years in office, Caldera demonstrated he was a president who not only favored government intervention, but was also skeptical of the merits of economic orthodoxy. In fact, the state heavily intervened in the economy, controlling prices and subsidizing goods. In addition to these measures, Caldera revved up the economy by raising Venezuela's government spending by a whopping 5 percentage points of GDP in 1994. The spending, prompted in part by an unexpected banking crisis, erased Venezuela's primary budget surplus and forged a primary budget deficit of more than 3 percent of GDP.[53]

Before the 1998 elections, Gustavo Tarre, a COPEI loyalist and congressional budget chair, contends that the political veteran Caldera wanted to continue his economic interventions.[54]

Philosophically and ideologically, Caldera believed that government spending programs were important. He was also concerned about his legacy and his presidential image in history. I have no doubt that if there was a lot of money, Caldera would have spent a lot of money and Chávez would have never won the election. Chávez would not even have appeared or been a threat. He was only a factor due to the severe economic crisis.

A patriot of the old Punto Fijo system, Tarre conveyed a wistful regret about the lack of oil income to forestall the Chávez threat. It is unclear whether a Caldera spending spree would have squelched Chávez's presidential bid, but Tarre's comments nonetheless underscore an important point. Caldera had the political motivation, but certainly not the financial means to stoke the fires of a political business cycle.

Venezuela's shift from global bank lending to decentralized bond markets had a substantial effect on the government's policy flexibility. In 1990, the Venezuelan authorities negotiated a debt restructuring under the Brady Plan, converting its US$20 billion in outstanding commercial bank loans into market-traded debt. After this swap, Venezuela's international bonds accounted for more than four-fifths of the country's total external debt (compared to bank loans, which now amounted to a paltry 1.5 percent of GDP).[55] By the mid-1990s, Venezuela's outstanding bond debt equaled about two-fifths of the country's GDP.

[53] CEPAL's Estadísticas de América Latina y El Caribe.
[54] Although Caldera had forged a new political party during his 1993 reelection bid, known as Convergence, he still possesed strong ties with many of COPEI's old political guard like Tarre.
[55] Official creditors and other private creditors accounted for the remaining 18.5 percent of Venezuela's external debt in 1990 (World Development Indicators).

Unlike the halcyon days of bank lending under former President Lusinchi, the new decentralized financial system gave Caldera insufficient scope to pursue Keynesian policies under economic duress. When a titanic banking crisis erupted in 1994, investors – without binding financial ties to government borrowers – quickly withdrew their funds. Massive capital flight and spiking interest rates rocked the economy. Real wages slid lower and unemployment surged higher, catapulting Venezuelan families into poverty.[56] Caldera had little choice, but to respond to the crisis with economic orthodoxy.

The weathered president succumbed to the international business community's critiques of his interventionist policies. *The Wall Street Journal*, for example, had publicly rebuked Caldera's determination to "roll back every market-oriented policy implemented to date" in Venezuela.[57] Aiming to assuage skeptical global investors and domestic businesses, Caldera announced an IMF adjustment program, backed by a US$1.4 billion loan. Facing the threat of further capital flight, Caldera grudgingly embraced the neoliberal formula and adopted a set of orthodox economic policies dubbed the "Venezuela Agenda."

Caldera's first policy about-face also foreshadowed yet another turnabout before the 1998 elections. By 1997, the economy had finally stabilized, boosted by privatization proceeds and foreign direct investment following Caldera's oil openings.[58] Before long, however, oil markets took Venezuelans for yet another roller coaster ride. Between 1997 and 1998, moribund global demand depressed the country's crude oil price. It plunged by $6 to US$10 per barrel (Figure 4.9 in Chapter 4), or $5 below the 1998 budget's projected average oil price. Compared to the previous year's budget, revenues sank by a devastating 6 percentage points to a meager 17 percent of GDP by year's end.

Capital outflows yet again exacerbated the funding squeeze. By August 1998, Moody's had wrenched Venezuela's credit ratings down three notches to below investment grade. Foreign investors sold almost US$4 billion in Venezuelan bonds,[59] prompting interest rates on Venezuela's debt to spike five times higher than their January 1998 levels (Figure 5.7).

Pressured by exorbitant funding costs and a tanking economy, Caldera's government yet again adopted austerity measures in hopes of calming jittery markets. Shockingly, they enacted nearly US$6 billion in budget cuts before the 1998 elections,[60] defying the classic political business cycle logic. In fact, the combination of the government's neutral fiscal stance,[61] along with a restrictive

[56] A Congressional report published at the end of 1994 estimated that 79 percent of Venezuelan families were poor, with one in every three families living in conditions of extreme poverty (Buxton 2003).

[57] Ellner 2008.

[58] Caldera introduced legislation in 1995 auctioning oil field operating rights to investors. Foreign direct investment ballooned, reaching US$5.5 billion for the year (Ellner 2008).

[59] International Monetary Fund's International Financial Statistics.

[60] Buxton 2003.

[61] Notwithstanding the government's budget cuts, fiscal policy was not as contractionary as planned because of severe revenue shortfalls.

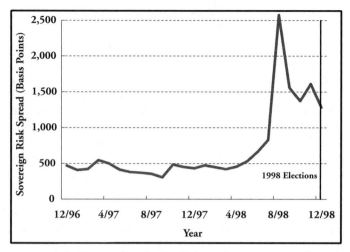

FIGURE 5.7. Venezuelan Credit Sinks Before 1998 Presidential Elections (Bond Yield Differential Between Venezuelan and U.S. Treasury Debt).
Source: J.P. Morgan

monetary policy helped tame inflation throughout the election year, yielding a political austerity cycle. Indeed, inflation steadily declined during the electoral campaign, falling from 52.8 percent in 1997 to 38.6 percent in 1998, and eventually reaching 26.4 percent in 1999.

Teodoro Petkoff, Caldera's influential planning minister, personally believed the massive financial and economic crisis threatened Venezuela's democracy. As the leader of the social-democratic party, Movimiento al Socialismo (MAS), he broke with his party's historic rejection of neoliberalism to help contain the financial hemorrhaging.[62] In the headquarters of anti-Chavista newspaper, *Tal Cual*, Petkoff explained how the scale of the crisis left Caldera and him with few alternatives but to pursue low inflation and economic orthodoxy. The former Marxist guerilla – who today looks like a Venezuelan Magnum PI – brusquely recounted:

It was a terrible situation . . . and our objective was strictly a classic stabilization of the economy. With the fall of oil prices in 1998, we had to bring down public expenditures. We had to cut the fat![63]

Notably, however, Petkoff emphasized that the Caldera government protected education and health-care spending, its constituencies' most-prized possessions. For example, notwithstanding the budgetary belt-tightening, health expenditures (as a percentage of total government expenditures) increased by about 1 percentage point in 1998.[64] Indeed, even during these dire economic

---

[62] Ellner 2008.
[63] Author's interview with Teodoro Petkoff, March 29, 2007.
[64] World Development Indicators.

circumstances, Venezuelan politicians searched for ways to target their supporters within the broader austerity framework.

In summary, the conditionality clauses embedded in loan agreements do not ensure economic orthodoxy. During the era of oil windfalls and bank lending, Venezuelan politicians often strayed from their austerity pledges under IMF conditionality. Rather, commodity booms and busts ultimately determine the fiscal space that politicians have to pursue their political agendas. When chief executives rely on financial rather than oil markets to fund their deficits, conditionality is likely to bind politicians. Gustavo Tarre, President of the Congressional Financial Committee during this period, perhaps best summarizes the pivotal role financing plays in the survival of Venezuelan politicians.

In Venezuela, there are no good governments and there are no bad governments, just governments with money from high oil prices and governments without money. When there is money, they spend a lot... .with the price of oil at nine dollars a barrel, the government of Caldera could not spend! Prices fell during the end of his term, and his spending was restricted, and now we have Chávez.[65]

5.3. SUMMARY

In the first part of the comparative case study analysis, I have assumed that presidents are motivated by a classic electoral calculus: providing jobs and growth to Latin American voters.[66] To achieve these objectives, they hope to stimulate the economy with expansionary macroeconomic policies. In this second case study chapter, we have held this motivation constant, but asked when Latin American politicians veer from their political agendas and pursue a counterintuitive course.

Booming commodity exports, deferential central bankers, and vested global bankers have provided fuel for traditional political business cycles that span time and space in Chile, Ecuador, and Venezuela. When governments have access to such windfall revenues, non-market borrowing resources, and the printing press, Latin American politicians have the fiscal space, or budgetary capacity to pursue aggressive electoral expansions. Notwithstanding institutional constraints, from legal central bank independence[67] to IMF conditionality, presidents often craft such economic booms in hopes of hefty political rewards.

By contrast, Latin America's 1990s securitization of its public debt constricted the political scope for policy action. Facing a constant threat of capital withdrawal, cash-strapped politicians were compelled to slam on the brakes

---

[65] Author's interview with Gustavo Tarre.

[66] In the next chapter, we will relax this assumption in order to examine when a political austerity cycle is instead a deliberate political choice.

[67] Despite legal central bank autonomy, governments may maintain considerable political discretion over monetary policy by retaining the right to sack central bank presidents, or having representatives on the monetary policy board (Cukierman, Webb, and Neyapti 1992; Jacome, 2001). See Chapter 4 for further details.

before elections, as witnessed in two traditionally highly-interventionist countries, Ecuador and Venezuela, in the mid-1990s. When governments must attract considerable capital from decentralized financiers, who have low stakes in their solvency and a quick, viable exit strategy, they quickly change their political tune. The fear of gut-wrenching capital outflows and economic downturns propels debt-ridden governments to narrow budget deficits and hike interest rates, even if they translate into fewer jobs and income gains than hoped during presidential campaigns.

Importantly, however, financial market pressures do not eliminate the political impulse to extend benefits to supporters. Despite less macroeconomic room to maneuver, politicians often reward constituents with line-item budgetary spending. During both Ecuador and Venezuela's political austerity phases, chief executives distanced themselves from aggressive intervention in the economy. However, they simultaneously raised public sector wages, protected social spending programs, and resisted IMF-imposed social security and privatization reforms before elections.

6

When Latin American Grasshoppers Become Ants

"Why not come and chat with me," said the Grasshopper, "instead of toiling and moiling in that way?" "I am helping to lay up food for the winter," said the Ant "and recommend you to do the same." "Why bother about winter?" said the Grasshopper. "We have got plenty of food at present."

In Aesop's classic fable, a carefree grasshopper joyfully chirps throughout a summer's day. By contrast, an industrious ant hauls an ear of corn to his nest. When winter arrives, the ill-prepared grasshopper wrestles with life-threatening hunger, whereas the ants enjoy the fruits of their labor. In the world of economic policy, the grasshopper's chirps are the politician's printing press. Politicians can spend lavishly today or save for a wintery day. Many classic political economy works expect presidents to spend like the profligate grasshopper. Politicians worry about their short-term political survival rather than long-term socioeconomic welfare.[1]

But, when do they instead choose frugality? Developed country scholars contend that fiscally conservative voters promote miserly political behavior.[2] At first, the claim that conservative politics pays electoral dividends does not seem to travel well to Latin America, a region hobbled by high poverty, income inequality, and unemployment. Facing strong redistributive pressures, why would politicians believe that voters are inflation hawks? Why would election-minded incumbents value a seemingly long-run asset such as economic stability? What's the political benefit of low inflation? Presumably, delivering growth and jobs today offers the greatest electoral returns tomorrow.

If this is the case, why do Latin American politicians sometimes drift from this reliable political strategy? Indeed, why might they surprisingly heed the ant's advice and embrace economic orthodoxy?

---

[1] Nordhaus 1975; Tufte 1978; Bates 1981; Sachs 1989a; Dornbusch and Edwards 1991; Kaufman and Stallings 1991.

[2] Lucas 1976; Rogoff 1988, 1990; Brender and Drazen 2008.

Similar to the provision of jobs or growth, inflation also has distributive consequences. Commonly known as an "inflation tax," when governments choose to fund their deficits by printing money, they catalyze inflation and erode real wages. Functionally, policy makers are transferring income from citizens to the government. Moreover, economists sometimes dub the inflation tax as the "cruelest tax of all" because inflation hurts the poor relatively more than the rich. Wealthy individuals are generally sophisticated investors that funnel their earnings into financial assets that hedge against inflation. By contrast, the poor typically keep the majority of their earnings in cash holdings that are eroded by inflation. In addition, the poor are often more reliant on state spending, including income transfers and pensions, that are not indexed to inflation.[3]

Brazil's President Fernando Henrique Cardoso reflects upon the saliency of inflation politics in Brazil during his administration.

The poor in Brazil were the ones most punished by inflation. For decades, no one in Brazil wanted to acknowledge this. It was said that inflation allowed the government to stimulate economic growth, and thus generate jobs for the working class. But, this was a myopic cynical view. In practice, the poor were the only ones who ended up with fistfuls of worthless cash ... inflation acted like a regressive tax that made poor people poorer.[4]

Cardoso's commentary highlights an important Latin American motif: the politics of macroeconomic governance do not conform to traditional partisan cleavages. In light of the region's severe inflation volatility, price stability is a political asset for left-leaning as well as right-leaning politicians.

Recall that in Chapter 2, building on the psychology literature on decision making,[5] I developed the domestic politics component of political austerity theory. In the wake of past inflationary shocks, politicians became more risk-averse, infusing their economic choices with an anti-inflationary bias. They developed a technocratic consensus on macroeconomic governance that blurred partisan lines. Inflation control was not simply the concern of right-wing politicians hoping to please businesses and financiers. Similarly, jobs and social stability were not merely the concern of left-wing politicians hoping to assuage unions and middle-class workers. Rather, following these crises, there was broad-based distress about inflation. According to Cardoso:

The poor would not tolerate inflation any longer, and the wealthy were tired of seeing their business plans and investments destroyed by rising prices.[6]

Consequently, presidents from across the political aisle had to deliver two seemingly contradictory goals: low inflation and high employment. In the classic trade-off between inflation and unemployment, Latin American leaders

---

[3] Easterly and Fischer 2001.
[4] Cardoso 2006.
[5] Kahneman and Tversky 1979; Weber et al. 1993; Hertwig et al. 2004.
[6] Cardoso 2006.

altered their political reasoning from their pre-crisis past. They were more inclined to strike a macroeconomic balance, sacrificing some new jobs to appeal to an expanded low-inflation constituency.

In this chapter, I examine the effect of inflation-aversion on the political business cycle. I first outline how inflation crises bred a political acceptance of economic discipline in Latin America. I then conduct a comparative case study analysis to adjudicate between two competing accounts of the rise of orthodox economic policies in the region: inflation-averse political austerity (H_3) and neoliberal policy diffusion.

6.1. THE CASE OF THE INFLATION-AVERSE POLITICIAN

The first panacea for a mismanaged nation is inflation of the currency; the second is war. Both bring a temporary prosperity; both bring permanent ruin. Both are the refuge of political and economic opportunists.

– Ernest Hemingway

Why does risk-aversion persist beyond the immediate crisis? How do politicians internalize these lessons about inflation's debilitating cost over time? In Chapter 2, I argued that politicians and their economic teams internalized the lessons of macroeconomic mismanagement following severe inflation shocks. To the extent that excessive economic expansions were the root of these crises, it provided a political window of opportunity for macroeconomic policy solutions centered on price stability. Successful inflation-stabilizations not only boosted the credibility of orthodox economic advisors in policymaking circles, but also convinced Latin American leaders of the political merits of austerity.

In the wake of many failed heterodox experiments in inflation control,[7] presidents and ministers who took an orthodox economic turn remedied the political plague of runaway inflation. From Brazil's *real* plan[8] to Argentina's *convertibility* plan,[9] successful inflation stabilization translated into political gold. In Brazil, it catapulted a technocrat, Fernando Henrique Cardoso, to rock star fame and the presidency, causing him to quip: "who am I now, Elvis?"[10] In Argentina, the success of convertibility propelled Carlos Menem into a second presidential term, as proudly noted by the plan's architect, Domingo Cavallo.

The people suffered greatly during the crisis of 89–90, and because Menem successfully stabilized the economy, ended hyperinflation, reformed the economy, and recuperated growth, he reaped the political rewards.[11]

---

[7] Heterodox programs aimed to control inflation with price and wage controls, while maintaining highly expansionary economic policies.

[8] See footnote 55 in Chapter 2.

[9] See footnote 173.

[10] Cardoso 2006.

[11] Author's interview with Domingo Cavallo, May 25, 2007, in Buenos Aires, Argentina. Cavallo was Economy Minister under President Carlos Menem from 1991 until 1996. He served once again as Economy Minister under President De la Rúa in 2001.

By contrast, the inability to cure inflationary ills created political casualties around the region. In 1989, the government of Raúl Alfonsín's struggles with hyperinflation[12] paved the way for a Peronist (PJ) victory against the ruling party, Unión Cívica Radical (UCR). Against the backdrop of shortages, rioting, and looting, the Alfonsín administration left office six months early.[13] This political fallout is not solely a feature of Argentine politics, however. In Peru, Alan García's mismanagement of the economy and an inflation crisis[14] led to his party's (APRA) resounding defeat in the 1990 elections. Similarly, in Bolivia, Siles Zuazo's inability to reign in hyperinflation[15] forced an early exit of his Unión Democrática Popular (UDP) government in July 1985. Finally, steep inflation and severe economic crises in Chile contributed to the breakdown of democracy under President Salvador Allende in 1973.

President Ricardo Lagos, the first Socialist president since Chile's authoritarian turn after Allende, emphasized the political risk of aggressive economic interventions in a refrain that was eerily similar to Hemingway's cautionary tale.

That kind of policy under the Allende government failed at the end. It's very dangerous for democracy to have a general with power ambitions – or a minister of finance with populist ideals. Both of them are a threat to democracy![16]

Following orthodox reformers' stabilization successes, the economic ministries and central banks became more technocratic in Latin America. Post-crisis presidents sought out professionally trained economists for their cabinets, distancing themselves from the pre-crisis potpourri of lawyers, public accountants, and even linotypists and linguistics specialists. In Argentina, Brazil, and Chile, more than three-quarters of the post-crisis presidential cabinets – as measured by the two primary economic positions (finance minister and central bank president) – were professionally trained economists (Figure 6.1).

These economists were schooled in contemporary macroeconomics.[17] Their training was often grounded in a new Keynesian or monetarist approach, but either perspective emphasized inflation control. For example, a Keynesian might deem that macroeconomic policy tools are useful for stabilizing demand shocks, but discourage using these policy levers to craft a temporary

---

[12] By 1989, the annual inflation rate in Argentina was approaching 4,000 percent (CEPAL, 1989).

[13] The outgoing Alfonsín and incoming Menem administrations agreed to move the transition forward to July 1989 from December 1989.

[14] In 1989, Peru's GNP fell by 10.4 percent and inflation rose to 2,775 percent.

[15] During the first half of 1985, Bolivia's annual inflation rate breached 24,000 percent.

[16] Author's interview with President Ricardo Lagos, April 16, 2010.

[17] Contemporary mainstream economics is characterized by a new synthesis, which aims to build a consensus between new Keynesian and monetarist perspectives, emphasizing inflation control and business cycle management through an independent central bank. Traditionally, new Keynesian economics emphasized employing expansionary fiscal and monetary policies to offset demand shocks, whereas monetarists were more wary of the efficacy of government intervention, claiming that it creates an inflationary by-product.

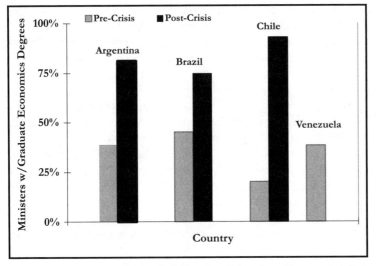

FIGURE 6.1. Latin America's Inflationary Crises Spur Economic Ministry Professionalization (1960–2009).
Source: Index of Economic Advisors (Kaplan 2011)

boom for fear of igniting inflation expectations. Moreover, both schools of thought emphasized the importance of prudent fiscal management. For those more radical economists who favored heterodox interventions, featuring wage and price controls, they were largely discredited after failing to control runaway inflation.

This new band of technocrats, infused Latin American policy with an anti-inflation bias.[18] In a region characterized by a high concentration of executive power, these ministers were often given considerable control of economic choices by their sitting presidents. Alejandro Tomás Foxley, Chile's first finance minister after its democratic transition, discussed his relationship with President Aylwin, for instance, in our 2011 interview.

Aylwin was not an economist; he was a traditional lawyer; he was not into the details; he knew he had a respectable economic team.[19]

In many inflation-scarred countries, economic ministers were given similar latitude with presidential charges ranging from "don't tell me anything, just do it"[20] to "oh, do what you want."[21]

---

[18] I follow in the tradition of other scholars who have emphasized the role of human agency in economic policy choices (Woods 1995; McNamara 1998).

[19] Author's interview with Alejandro Foxley in Washington, DC, on September 29, 2011. Foxley served in multiple cabinet posts in Chile, first as finance minister to President Patricio Aylwin, then as foreign minister to President Michelle Bachelet.

[20] Author's interview with former Economic Minister Juan Sourrouille on May 28, 2007, in Buenos Aires, Argentina.

[21] Cardoso 2006.

Importantly, however their economic prescriptions stood the test of time not solely because of this ministry professionalization, but also because of the tight inner circles that characterized economic policy communities. Post-crisis governance was often characterized by a small group of professional economists who rotated through government and the central bank presidency. In Argentina, for instance, José Luis Machinea, Domingo Cavallo, Roque Fernández, and Roberto Lavagna each served on the economic teams for multiple presidential administrations. Remembering the trauma associated with inflationary crises, these technocratic communities built a governing consensus around macroeconomic discipline, which promised to avoid a repeat of past mistakes.

This technocratic consensus also solidifed a commitment to macroeconomic discipline among politicians who hoped good governance would translate to political rewards. For example, Brazil's Cardoso, who served first as President Itamar Franco's finance minister and later as the nation's president, discusses how an expanded constituency favoring low inflation offered new political gains.

The hope awakened by the Real Plan was the driving force behind my candidacy; it also provided a bond holding together the multiparty coalition with which I ran and I later attempted to broaden as president.[22]

Today, many politicians and economic elites in inflation-scarred countries continue to believe that low inflation is an important economic baseline, if not always the most politically salient issue. Foxley, who was one of the leading forces in Chilean economic policy throughout the post-Pinochet years, highlights the lasting imprint of hyperinflation on Chilean politics.[23]

People in Chile don't like inflation at all, particular lower and middle-class people who are vulnerable to price increases in food, energy, electricity bills and so on ... any country that goes through hyperinflation, people have a long memory because it shocks them in their daily lives.[24]

By contrast, in the years before inflation crises, the political and technocratic merits of inflation control were more questionable. In fact, presidential cabinets tended to be far less populated with professional economists concerned about inflation. About one- to two-fifths of economic teams in Argentina, Brazil, and Chile had graduate degrees in economics or business. Not surprisingly, the historic and current composition of Venezuelan cabinets is quite similar (Figure 6.1), given that the country has never had a severe inflation crisis. Only 38 percent of Venezuelan economic ministers and central bank presidents have been professionally trained in economics or business.

[22] Mainwaring and Scully 2010.
[23] Foxley served in the Aylwin cabinet (1990–1994), the Bachelet cabinet (2006–2009), and as a Chilean senator and member of the Finance Committee from 1998–2006.
[24] Author's interview with Alejandro Foxley, September 29, 2011.

Without inflation scars, Latin American publics do not tend to value price stability either. In the Venezuelan case, even when orthodox reformers entered the policy scene, the lack of historic price volatility left them incapable of sustaining macroeconomic reforms. For example, during the second Pérez administration, the Venezuelan president hired a team of skilled economists with credentials from the best universities. At the beginning of its term, the Pérez team also had extensive discussions with IMF officials as they negotiated an IMF extended fund facility and implemented several economic reforms.

However, austerity never gained widespread political acceptance in Venezuela. Recall that Pérez attempted to launch a series of Washington Consensus initiatives, known as the "great turnabout," to ward off a severe currency crisis in February 1989.[25] Hoping to lure foreign capital amidst oil market doldrums, it instead met severe popular resistance. In fact, the public backlash against the neoliberal adjustment program sparked the *Caracazo*, a sudden outbreak of protests and mass looting that turned bloody.[26] This social tumult eventually cultivated Chávez's political arrival, with an unsuccessful military coup in February 1992.[27]

Without a hyperinflation episode, Venezuela was unable to forge a similar elite and public consensus about the need for inflation control as its South American neighbors. Former Central Bank President Ruth De Krivoy, one of the 1990s economic reformers, supports this notion about the lack of inflation saliency in Venezuelan politics.

There is no support for economic reforms, like central bank independence, unless Venezuelan society goes through an inflationary process that is painful like Argentina, Chile, Peru, and Mexico . . . When you get inflation in the 20–25 percent range, you start feeling the pain, but it's not enough to make people realize inflation is a problem.[28]

Rather, Venezuelan chief executives score political points with the traditional brand of big spending politics. In the earlier Venezuelan electoral cases, remember that politicians created political business cycles whenever they had oil windfalls.[29] If Chilean politics is built on a commitment to macroeconomic stability, Venezuelan politics embodies a macroeconomic commitment to spending and redistribution.

Recall that Rafael Caldera catapulted himself into a second presidency by delivering a reprimand of both Pérez's presidency and IMF conditionality. In fact, a 1993 survey of 1,500 Venezuelans showed strong majorities supported

---

[25] See Chapter 4.
[26] During the week of February 27, 1989, protests and looting were met by massive repression by military troops that resulted in hundreds, and perhaps thousands of deaths.
[27] Lopez-Maya 2005; Ellner 2008.
[28] Author's interview with Central Bank President Ruth De Krivoy in Caracas, Venezuela, on March 9, 2007. She served as central bank president from 1992–1994.
[29] See Chapter 4.

government intervention in the economy, but opposed Washington Consensus reforms such as privatization and price liberalization.[30]

Perhaps former President Ramón José Velásquez best characterizes the state of Venezuelan politics, declaring that:

Venezuelan democracy is about personalistic politics, rather than continuity. There is very little policy continuity. When the state cannot subsidize its people, a crisis results. It does not reflect ideology, but rather the distribution of benefits and resources.[31]

In summary, political austerity theory expects that price stability gains political and technocratic saliency in countries where runaway inflation destroyed the incomes of not only the poor, but also middle classes. A political commitment to low inflation not only provides businesses and investors with a stable, long-run operational environment, but also protects voters' incomes. The public, including its poorest citizens, have a vested interest in low and stable inflation.

Nonetheless, in a new era of Latin American political austerity, how do presidents target their political constituents? In the following pages, we will see that presidents reward their political bases with line-item spending rather than deficit-spending. Within an orthodox budgetary framework, they often reallocate resources, creating new transfers, subsidies, and benefits for politically sensitive constituencies. Politicians also frequently time these benefits strategically to maximize electoral dividends. Most notably, perhaps, I find that presidents often develop new creative ways to exercise their executive power and target supporters that are subject to less scrutiny from voters, markets, and businesses.

6.1.1. Inflation-Averse Austerity Cycle (H3)

Recall that in Chapters 4 and 5, we examined election cases marked by risk-seeking chief executives. Without inflationary scars, these politicians drafted economic blueprints in the years preceding elections with a traditional pump-priming design. The success of these plans, however, often reflected the extent of governments' bond market indebtedness. When bonds accounted for a high share of their financing, governments were more likely to pursue political austerity than political booms. This pattern was most typical in debt-dependent countries that were not able to tap windfall revenues (such as commodity income and privatization proceeds) and non-binding borrowing resources (such as bank lending) to fund new spending.

Over the next two chapters, however, we assume a different set of political motivations (Table 6.1). Rather than aggressively stimulating the economy,

---

[30] Stokes 2001.
[31] Author's interview with President Velásquez in Caracas, Venezuela on March 23, 2007.

TABLE 6.1. *Macroeconomic Policy Expectations: The Spendthrift or the Miser?*

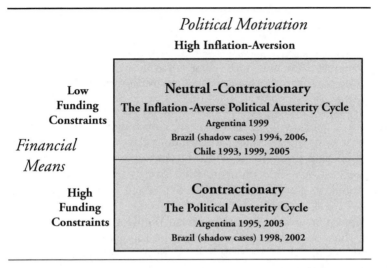

Political Motivation

High Inflation-Aversion

Low Funding Constraints	**Neutral -Contractionary** The Inflation-Averse Political Austerity Cycle Argentina 1999 Brazil (shadow cases) 1994, 2006, Chile 1993, 1999, 2005
High Funding Constraints	**Contractionary** The Political Austerity Cycle Argentina 1995, 2003 Brazil (shadow cases) 1998, 2002

Financial Means

inflation-sensitive politicians voluntarily convert to the neoliberal faith by drafting orthodox budget plans. They make the risk-averse choice of signaling their economic discipline to voters, businesses, and financiers.

In the following pages, I test whether the risk-aversion associated with past inflationary shocks has a mitigating effect on the political business cycle (H_3). If we assume that governments have considerable non-market resources, then they have the fiscal space, or budgetary room to finance an electoral expansion.[32] Political leaders should not be constrained by the interest rate shocks and credit swings that accompany heavy capital market borrowing (Figure 6.2). Rather, any spending limitations are likely to be self-imposed.[33]

If political austerity theory is correct, we should observe that inflation-averse politicians opt for a more measured political strategy than crafting a political business cycle: one that entails a macroeconomic balance of low inflation and moderate economic growth. At the maximum, this involves a tepid budget expansion. If they face strong inflationary headwinds before elections, however, they may even adopt slightly contractionary policies that detract from economic growth.

---

[32] Central bank credit, however, is not a funding option because of laws in Argentina, Brazil, and Chile that legally barred central banks from financing deficits during this time.

[33] In Chapter 7, by contrast, I examine macroeconomic policy when inflation-averse politicians hail from debt-dependent countries. With high funding constraints, politicians plan to deliver the twin policy goals of moderate growth and low inflation to the electorate but are hampered by unexpected credit shocks (Table 6.1).

TABLE 6.2. *Case Study Overview (H3 and H4)*

Country	Chief Executive	Election Year	Inflation-Aversion?	Market Constraints?	Political Business Cycle?
Chile	Patricio Aylwin	1993	Y	N	Inflation-Averse PAC
Brazil	Itamar Franco	1994	Y	N	Inflation-Averse PAC
Argentina	Carlos Menem	1995	Y	Y	Political Austerity Cycle
Brazil	Fernando Henrique Cardoso	1998	Y	Y	Political Austerity Cycle
Chile	Eduardo Frei	1999	Y	N	Inflation-Averse PAC
Argentina	Carlos Menem	1999	Y	N	Inflation-Averse PAC
Brazil	Fernando Henrique Cardoso	2002	Y	Y	Political Austerity Cycle
Argentina	Eduardo Duhalde	2003	Y	Y	Political Austerity Cycle
Chile	Ricardo Lagos	2005	Y	N	Inflation-Averse PAC
Brazil	Luiz Inácio 'Lula' da Silva	2006	Y	N	Inflation-Averse PAC

In testing for these austerity cycles, I adjudicate between two alternative explanations for the choice of economic orthodoxy among political and technocratic elites: political austerity theory and neoliberal diffusion. Table 6.2 outlines the expected outcomes for all of the comparative cases that explore inflation-aversion (they are also grouped by their policy making dimensions in Table 6.1). The six comparative election studies for Argentina, Brazil, and Chile that are examined in this chapter are highlighted.

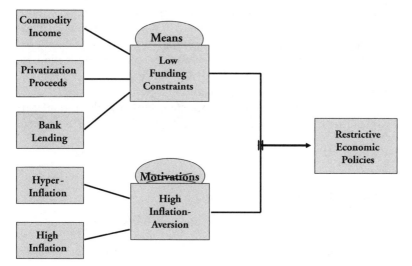

FIGURE 6.2. The Inflation-Averse Austerity Cycle (H3).

6.1.2. An Alternative Argument: Neoliberal Policy Diffusion

The songs of New Zealand's saddleback birds evolve socially. Father and sons twitter different arrangements, yet neighbors often imitate each others' melodies. These inventive songsters even coin new ditties. Like human language, fashion, and art, saddleback songs develop through non-genetic means.[34] P.F. Jenkins, a lifelong observer of saddleback birds, dubbed this musical evolution a cultural mutation. Advancing this idea further, Richard Dawkins, a well-known British evolutionary biologist, spawned the concept of *memes*. Memes, derived from the greek root mimeme, are similar to genes. Like DNA molecules, they survive on the planet because of mutation and replication. Genes move from body to body via sperm and eggs, whereas memes move from brain to brain via books, television, and the Internet. Music, ideas catch phrases, and fashion are all memes.

In the social sciences, diffusion – or the spread of ideas and innovations across societies – embodies this concept of memes. In the wake of the Cold War's final act, countries throughout the globe adopted economic liberalization policies. Many thinkers have claimed that global policy diffusion explained this phenomenon. Indeed, they argue that the prevalence of low-inflation, market-friendly policies reflects a global shift in policy paradigms from Keynesianism to Monetarism.[35] A social construction of knowledge that originated with Thatcher and Reagan spilled into the international arena through Western diplomacy, multilateral institutions, and an Americanized global economics profession.[36]

Other scholars have instead pointed to regional policy diffusion as a more likely explanation for economic orthodoxy. They contend that peer learning and international pressures are often responsible for policy clustering.[37] According to their arguments, governments condition their currency policy choices on other governments' prior policy choices.[38] Why? Policy makers hope to find solutions to pressing development problems from the lessons of regional success stories.[39] Alternatively, diffusion may work through a different channel. International organizations, like the IMF and the World Bank, may persuade or coerce governments into endorsing their economic policy blueprints.[40]

Diffusion theorists correctly identify an important global and regional pattern. Some ideas (or memes) prevailed throughout the 1980s and 1990s. Indeed,

[34] Dawkins 1999; Jenkins 2008.
[35] Hall 1993; Babb 2001.
[36] Hall 1993; Babb 2001; Babb and Fourcade-Gourinchas 2002.
[37] Simmons and Elkins 2004; Barnett and Finnemore 2004.
[38] Simmons, Dobin, and Garrett 2008.
[39] Relying on cognitive shortcuts, however, policy makers often apply second best solutions (Weyland 2006). Hence, peer learning is not always optimal, helping to explain why countries of diverse economic, political, and social structures adopt similar economic programs (Simmons and Elkins 2004).
[40] Barnett and Finnemore, 2004.

the policy pendulum swung toward Hayek[41] and away from Keynes[42] in many, but not all countries. In Latin America, for instance, Chile and Argentine politicians increasingly embraced economic orthodoxy and free-market policies, but in Venezuela politicians preferred highly interventionist policies. What accounts for this variation within Latin America? Why is the diffusion wave so choppy?

The diffusion literature points to policy emulation and interdependent policy making as probable causes. Clearly, secondary learning from neighboring countries' experiences can be important. For example, Chilean politicians, who oversaw one of the region's last democratic transitions in 1989, certainly learned from Argentina, Brazil, and Peru's earlier experiences. Perhaps, at the margin, Chilean leaders were less likely to use macroeconomic policy to redress social debts because they observed these countries' travails with bloated deficits and unforgiving inflation.

Notwithstanding these contributing dynamics, is diffusion a sufficient explanation? I claim that there is no substitute for political leaders' own historical experiences. In the aftermath of macroeconomic policy failures that led to inflationary crises and bred political and social chaos, politicians welcomed alternatives to ineffectual heterodox programs. Orthodox policies that promoted austerity prospered in an economic climate where Latin American leaders gained political credibility through inflation control. Whether rooted in Keynesian or monetarist thinking, governance choices reflected the contemporary macroeconomic idea that budget discipline was the pathway to economic stability. Redistributive politics was no longer a sufficient justification for expansionary economic policies.

Without these traumatic inflationary crises, politicians would have been unlikely to pursue a cautious, non-interventionist course. In Chile, for example, a macroeconomic crisis – of such severity that it plunged the country into autocracy – informed later policy choices. Chile's center-left politicians who oversaw the democratic transition have always been committed to redistribution and poverty reduction. It is unlikely that they would have embraced economic austerity merely because they observed their neighbors' economic hardships or were persuaded by the IMF's all-knowing technocrats. Rather, they internalized the cost of aggressive government intervention in the economy because of their parties' own past policy failures.

Ultimately, policy makers react to their environments, choosing the policies that have the best chance for success. In the world of Darwin, genes propagate in advantageous environments. Similarly, in the world of human culture, memes survive and prosper under favorable conditions. In an environment plagued by very high or hyperinflation crises, stabilization agendas win the

---

[41] Friedrich August von Hayek was an Austrian economist and philosopher who favored free-market non-interventionist government policies.
[42] John Maynard Keynes was a British economist who advocated for government interventionist policies (such as expansionary monetary and fiscal policies) to offset the adverse effects of economic downturns.

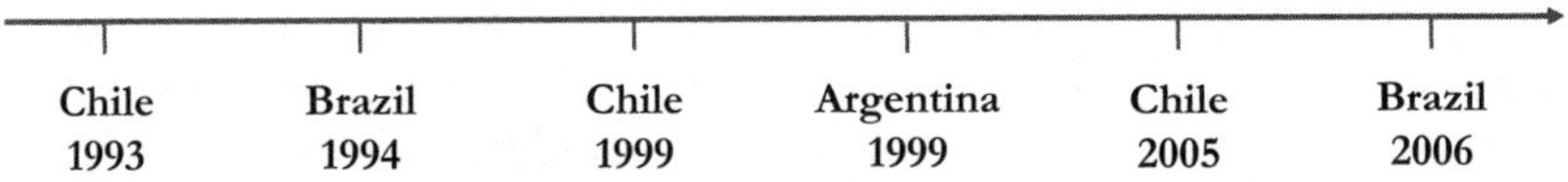

Chile	Brazil	Chile	Argentina	Chile	Brazil
1993	1994	1999	1999	2005	2006

FIGURE 6.3. The Inflation-Averse Political Austerity Cycle (H3).

day. Balanced budgets and tight monetary policies are the best cure for an overheated inflation-ridden economy. If Latin American policy agendas appear similar in the 1990s, it is because countries are responding to common inflationary phenomenon.

Moreover, memes are often sticky. In cultures afflicted by severe inflationary wounds, politicians have lengthy memories. They remember the policy failures – ballooning budget deficits and massive credit expansions – that led to inflationary mayhem. The social unrest, riots, and deaths that followed the price system's rupture are chiseled into their political consciousness. Chief executives choose the prudent macroeconomic course to insure their political lives against a return to an inflationary state.

In summary, the diffusion literature offers several important contributing dynamics to the choice of political austerity in Latin America. Clearly, countries observe and learn from their neighbors' policy successes and failures. They also are often pressured by international organizations and major economic powers to adopt certain policies. However, these experiences are not sufficient to propel presidents toward austerity. Rather, I contend that states' independent economic histories are pivotal to understanding their policy choices.

6.2. COMPARATIVE CASE STUDY EVIDENCE

In the remaining part of this chapter, I test the inflation-induced austerity hypothesis (H_3) that predicts a political austerity cycle, using comparative case study evidence from the six election cases in Argentina, Brazil, and Chile that are outlined in Figure 6.3. Political motivations in these election cases are similar; inflation-averse politicians choose to signal their commitment to economic orthodoxy with budget discipline and sound monetary policy. Politicians in these countries are empowered with the budgetary resources (such as windfall commodity income and privatization proceeds) to engineer electoral expansions. Ironically, however, notwithstanding the financial means to foster a political business cycle, their inflation crisis history prompts them to instead create an inflation-averse political austerity cycle.

What constitutes a past inflationary crisis? At what point does inflation have political saliency? Recall from Chapter 3; I adopt an inflation crisis threshold of 100 percent per annum, based on Sach's definition of "very high inflations."[43] I use a lower cutoff than the standard hyperinflation threshold, commonly

---

[43] Sachs and Larráin 1993.

defined as monthly price increases exceeding 20 percent – the equivalent of almost 800 percent per annum.[44] Why? For the post-World War II era, 800 percent per annum is too high a threshold. Before Latin America's inflation troubles began in the 1970s, the median inflation rate was about 5.9 percent between 1946 and 1970.[45] Moreover, inflation rarely breached 100 percent per annum anywhere in the region. In periods marked by such low-average inflation rates, people do not expect to have high inflation. Therefore, much lower inflation rates than 800 percent could inflict severe economic distress. At the same time, inflation rates that are too low are unlikely to be politically salient. As previously mentioned, there is a relatively strong consensus that levels above 100 percent per annum inflict severe economic harm.[46] As a result, I contend that governments only internalized inflation's political and social costs after struggling with unprecedented shocks that catapulted inflation above this threshold in the 1970s and 1980s.

I expect that a very high or hyperinflation history increases the likelihood that politicians adopt policies geared toward economic stability rather than lofty expansions. In the following pages, I employ a counterfactual analysis to test the effect of severe inflationary crises on policy making[47] asking whether political austerity would have emerged in the absence of a traumatic inflationary shock.

6.2.1. Allende's Policy Failures: When Economic Doves Become Hawks

In the absence of Chile's devastating economic crisis in the 1970s, I claim that Chile's center-left politicians – consisting of the Partido Socialista de Chile (PS) and the Partido Democrata Cristiano de Chile (PDC) – would not have embraced economic orthodoxy during their return to power in the 1990s.[48] Rather, from a counterfactual perspective, Chilean politicians would have continued to prioritize economic expansion and job creation before elections at the expense of inflation after elections.

What was so calamitous about Chile's economic crisis that it could cause life-long socialists to embrace economic orthodoxy? Why are the policy failures that led to this crisis still routinely referenced by Chilean politicians today? Why is it such a defining historical episode? Let me begin by first explaining

---

[44] See footnote 78 in Chapter 2.
[45] Oxford Latin American Economic History Database.
[46] See footnote 43.
[47] See footnote 47 in Chapter 4.
[48] These two parties formed the Concertación de Partidos por la Democracia in 1988. The coalition's roots stemmed from their political opposition to the Pinochet dictatorship. They originally joined forces against the dictatorship in the 1988 plebescite, and were known as the "Concertación de Partidos por el NO" ("Coalition of Parties for NO"). On October 5, 1988, the "NO" vote won with a 54 percent majority; they called a general election for 1989.

the roots of the crisis and then I will discuss how it transformed political thinking in Chile.

For the Salvador Allende government, public spending was the panacea for society's ills. Like Venezuela's Chávez today, he viewed socialism as the salvation of Chile's ailing capitalist democracy, fraught with economic and political inequality. Government spending was aimed at not only redistribution and economic revival, but also the financing of long-term, structural and social reforms. If these government ambitions were not sufficiently expansive, a spike in political activity also intensified distributive pressures. Indeed, almost two-thirds of the 1.4 million new voters who had been registered in the last decade hailed from the center-left.[49]

To address mounting redistributive demands, Allende increased public sector employment and wages, hiking the public payroll by a whopping 5 percentage points of GDP.[50] The Chilean president also boosted social spending by almost two-thirds in just two years.[51] Public utility subsidies, direct handouts of goods, and social security payments accompanied these initiatives.[52] Finally, Allende's long-term structural agenda, which foresaw hefty state intervention in Chile's corporate world, further drained government coffers. Under Allende's nation-alization efforts,[53] the growth of public sector enterprises inflated government expenditures.[54] Allende sunk another 9 percent of GDP in subsidies that were aimed at keeping nationalized firms afloat during production disruptions.[55] In total, Allende's raft of spending initiatives ballooned government expenditures by an exorbitant 15 percent of GDP in a mere two years.

The massive spending spree launched a vicious economic tornado of explod-ing deficits, booming money supply growth, and unbridled inflation. The Allende government funded these budget deficits with central bank financing.

---

[49] Valenzuela 1978.

[50] During 1970 and 1971, employment with the central government and public sector firms expanded by 50 and 35 percent annually (Meller 2000).

[51] Chile's social expenditures increased by 60 percent between 1970 and 1972, mainly driven by real wage hikes in the education and health sectors (Meller 2000).

[52] The real price of electricity fell by 85 percent during the Allende administration, while real fuel prices decreased by 31 percent between 1970 and 1972. At the same time, the Allende government distributed a daily half liter of milk to every child in the country, and 1.8 million breakfasts and 0.56 million lunches to schoolchildren (Meller 2000).

[53] The Allende government, with Congressional approval, approved the nationalization of Chile's Gran Minería del Cobre (GMC) in July 1971, establishing the state as the sole owner of all minerals in Chilean territory (automatically annulling all contracts previously established in the GMC). In addition, Allende created the Area of Social Ownership (APS), which involved bringing the country's main industrial firms under state control. By 1973, fifty-seven of Chile's industrial firms were in state hands. Finally, the Allende government also acquired a majority shareholding in fourteen commercial banks. By 1973, 85 percent of the financial sector was also under state control (Meller 2000).

[54] Public enterprises' purchases of goods and services rose by almost 5 percent of GDP between 1972 and 1973 (Larraín and Meller 1991).

[55] Larraín and Meller 1991.

Refusing to apply orthodox adjustment policies, it "printed money" by ordering a deferential Chilean central bank to conduct an extraordinary money supply expansion. The colossal expansion caused prices to soar without bounds, which eroded real tax revenues and exacerbated budget shortfalls.[56] Allende's government responded by printing more money, which fueled even further inflation.

By 1973, the government's budget deficit reached a mind-boggling deficit of 30.5 percent of GDP and inflation spiraled out of control. Triple-digit price hikes broached a 600 percent annual growth rate, leaving the Chilean economy mired in economic instability, massive shortages, and growing poverty. On September 11, 1973, Chilean democracy collapsed like wooden *Jenga* toy blocks. General Augusto Pinochet and the Chilean military, professing to save the country from destruction, declared it would end the chaos that swept the streets of Santiago.

Pre-Crisis Thinking. This rare, but traumatic event reshaped political thinking. The price system's devastating rupture and the breakdown of social order imprinted the dangers of government stimulus in Chilean political minds. Allende's ruinous economic policies made printing money and running budget deficits taboo in Chile. The country's crisis history also forged a new consensus among center-left parties that prioritized sound economic management. They were determined not only to restore the democratic order, but also to surmount the scarlet letter of economic mismanagement bestowed upon them by General Pinochet's right-wing forces.

Before the crisis, we have seen that the Partido Socialista, which led the Unidad Popular (UP) coalition government, advanced a highly interventionist economic policy. Why did they choose this political path? Chile's stark income inequality led to a high concentration of political power, which reinforced the prevailing economic structure. According to UP officials, Chilean elites benefited disproportionately from the country's economic development. In fact, the wealthiest 10 percent of the population had more than a 40 percent share of total income, compared to the poorest 10 percent of the population that earned a paltry 1.5 percent share.[57]

The UP aimed to break this historical pattern by advancing an economic agenda that benefited the majority of Chileans – blue- and white-collar workers, peasants, and small- and medium-size entrepreneurs. UP leaders believed that Chile's monopolistic structure left the economy with tremendous spare capacity. For them, fiscal deficits and economic expansion were not inflationary. Rather, Allende's government could aggressively spend and inject massive credit into the economy without stoking inflation.[58]

[56] See footnote 79 in Chapter 2.
[57] Larraín and Meller, 1991.
[58] Bitar 1979; Bitar 1986; Larraín and Meller 1991; Cardoso and Helwege 1992.

Sergio Bitar, Allende's former mining minister who has since served as the president of the Partido Por la Democracia (PPD),[59] summarized the UP's view on economic policy in our 2007 interview.

The economic program of the UP had a Keynesian bias that inspired a strong redistributive and stimulative policy ... the existence of idle capacity could be used to redistribute income and accelerate growth ... [the UP] thought it was possible to transform, redistribute, and stimulate the economy without dampening savings or igniting inflation.[60]

Nonetheless, did the Chilean political center embody the same economic thinking? Perhaps, the political transformation was less stark for Chile's centrist party, the Partido Democrata Cristiano de Chile (PDC).

In fact, the PDC shared the UP's general view on the economy during the Allende era. Notwithstanding PDC candidate Radomiro Tomic's loss in the 1970 presidential elections, he advanced a similar economic program as Allende. Tomic hailed from the progressive wing of the PDC, favoring growth with income redistribution. Like Allende, his redistributive proposals featured wage hikes and spending on housing, education, and health care. During the campaign, Tomic appealed to Chile's left-leaning voters by punctuating his progressive politics.

Both juridical order and social reality continue to demonstrate a serious and unjust imbalance. It is imperative to advance a government program which will allow the basic necessities of all Chileans to be satisfied and which will include a significant redistribution of income, opportunities, and power.[61]

Notwithstanding these similarities, the Christian Democrats did favor a somewhat less interventionist response. They preferred to gradually implement structural reforms to avoid upsetting economic stability.[62] By contrast, Allende had called for a highly expansive state aimed at empowering workers through government redistribution and nationalization. The UP capitalized on these differences during the 1970 presidential campaign, branding President Eduardo Frei Montalva and the Christian Democrats as reformers who failed to break with the past.[63] Indeed, the majority of workers, who did not fret about inflationary pressures at the time, supported Allende's bold reform over

---

[59] The Partido Por la Democracia (PPD) is a social democratic party founded by Ricardo Lagos during the Pinochet dictatorship. The PPD is one of the principal members of the La Concertación de Partidos por la Democracia. The PPD's roots are in the Chilean socialist movement. Today, the party is also a member of Socialist International.

[60] Author's interview with Sergio Bitar in Santiago, Chile in 2007; Bitar referenced this passage in the interview (Bitar 1979).

[61] Bitar 1986.

[62] Although Tomic contemplated copper and bank nationalizations, he placed more emphasis on income redistribution through economic policies than long-term structural reform (Bitar 1986).

[63] Meller 2000.

Tomic's guarded reforms, helping catapult Allende to the presidential seat in La Moneda.[64]

Without the severe economic crisis that followed, it is hard to imagine that these two parties would have arrived at an economic consensus that touted economic stability as the hallmark of social welfare. The UP government had expressed little concern over inflation, believing that the economy's spare capacity allowed them to pursue an aggressive stimulus. Notwithstanding a more cautious approach, the Christian Democrats also favored using monetary and fiscal policy for redistributive purposes. In Chapter 4, we saw that President Frei and the Christian Democrats fashioned an election-year spending extravaganza in 1970, without much regard for inflation. They injected the economy with massive stimulus, targeting workers with increased spending on government employment, pensions, education, and health care. In the absence of inflationary woes, the holy political trinity of jobs, growth, and redistribution ruled the day.

The Post-Crisis Thinking. After a seventeen-year governing hiatus, Chile's center-left parties returned to power during the resumption of democracy with a new respect for economic orthodoxy. The coalition's economic team sounded a harmonious chord written from the lessons of the past. Acknowledging the importance of economic stability, they promised not to veer from the military's neoliberal model. The center-left would adhere to budget discipline and price stability. Within this framework, however, they agreed to pursue redistribution and poverty alleviation.

On the heels of a plebiscite victory[65] against the Pinochet dictatorship, the "Coalition of Parties for NO" ("Concertación de Partidos por el NO") cemented their alliance for the 1989 election campaign. The newly minted Democratic Alliance (Concertación de Partidos por la Democracia) featured a coalition between the Partido Socialista de Chile (PS), the Partido Por la Democracia (PPD), and the Partido Democrata Cristiano de Chile (PDC). Their presidential candidate, PDC member Patricio Aylwin, campaigned on a slogan of "crecimiento con equidad" ("growth with equity"). Riding a wave of popular support, they would eventually win the 1989 elections and topple General Pinochet from power.[66]

In the prelude to these elections, Aylwin and the Concertación strived to redress the hefty social debt left in Pinochet's wake, but without sacrificing

---

[64] Tomic mustered a mere 28 percent of the vote, compared to the victorious Allende's 36 percent and second place finisher Jorge Alessandri's 35 percent. Less than 40,000 votes separated Allende and Alessandri.

[65] On October 5, 1988, the "NO" vote won with a 54 percent majority, paving the way for general elections in 1989.

[66] Aylwin won the 1989 presidential election with 57 percent of the vote, compared to his right-wing opponents, Hernán Büchi Buc and Francisco Javier Errázuriz, who garnered 29 and 15 percent of the vote, respectively.

economic growth and stability. Aylwin hoped to improve the plight of Chilean workers, embattled by rising poverty and unemployment under the dictatorship.[67] His campaign promised new social spending, but also pledged not to reverse the sound macroeconomic management of the Pinochet years. For example, the Concertación's platform advocated for workers' economic rights and called for minimum wage hikes, but "in line with the possibilities of the economy."[68]

Manuel Marfán, a socialist party member, canvassed for Aylwin before holding several senior positions in Chile's Finance Ministry. Marfán would later become Finance Minister in 1999 and a Central Bank Board Member in 2003. In his office chambers in the executive wing of Chile's Central Bank, we discussed the challenge of overcoming Allende's stigma of economic mismanagement.

Forty-five percent of the population was below the poverty line! What do you do with 45 percent? How do you solve this problem without imposing a threat to macroeconomic stability? You need to spend efficiently and you need to try and raise resources as much as possible through tax hikes. Usually, you don't do this to win an election! But, we had to invest in reputation and credibility . . . Aylwin and the center–left coalition had all the credibility on social issues, but did not have legitimacy on how to manage the economy because of the country's continual macroeconomic crises, such as high inflation, fiscal deficits, and balance of payments crises . . . Most of our effort was devoted to gaining credibility that we would have good economic governance."[69]

The Concertación hoped that pledging a commitment to budgetary balance would erase longstanding memories of Allende's bloated deficits, roaring inflation, and economic devastation. By raising taxes, they could promise voters new social spending efforts without widening the government's deficit.

They were particularly concerned about assuaging the business community, who fretted that the center-left's return could renew economic distress and threaten private property. Without the private sector's support, the Concertación was vulnerable to a challenge from the Chilean right. The Concertación labored to convince the business sector of its economic management credentials. Alejandro Tomás Foxley, a PDC economist who would later serve as Aylwin's finance minister, noted the importance of maintaining business confidence at the time:

We had to reduce government expenditures to show the private sector that we were serious, that we were not populists, that we could control inflation, that the government would do its part.[70]

---

[67] Poverty hit a peak of 45 percent during the Pinochet years. Unemployment also spiked from 9 percent in 1974 to a high of 21 percent in 1985 (though it subsided to pre-Pinochet lows in the remaining years of his rule). See Meller et al. (1993) for further details.

[68] Angel and Pollack 1990; Stokes 2001.

[69] Author's interview with Manuel Marfan in Santiago, Chile on April 20, 2007, and again June 28, 2007.

[70] Author's interview with Alejandro Foxley, September 29, 2011.

The Concertación had learned from Allende's failures and recognized Pinochet's successes in stabilizing the economy, promoting growth, and taming inflation.[71] According to Foxley, Aylwin and the Concertación understood that the "social effort had to be gradual in order to avoid worsening inflation and nullifying the positive effect of social policy."[72] The coalition's leaders publicly acknowledged the achievements of the military's economic model. In the 1989 presidential debates, Aylwin lauded the military regime for preserving economic stability and containing inflation.[73] In that same year, Foxley laid out the Concertación's economic platform in a publicly available paper prepared by CIEPLAN, the coalition's main economic think tank.

We, opposition economists, who were very critical of the management of the economy by the military regime, especially during the first ten years of this experience, have also learned the positive lessons offered by such experience, in particular during its most recent phase.[74]

Surprisingly, even UP officials – who had once labored for Allende's socialist experiment in the 1970s – embraced the neoliberal model's call for economic discipline in the 1990s. Sergio Bitar, who prior to being secretary general of the social democratic party was Allende's mining minister, echoes Foxley's sentiments.

Expansion of social expenditures shouldn't undermine the incomes of the poor classes in the longer-term. In the experience of the Popular Unity, not only did they fail to generate an improvement in the income of the poor, but also they created political costs in terms of supply shortages and fiscal solvency. With the return of democracy, the private sector had to have confidence in the left and the left had to create that confidence that we were going to pursue a serious policy to stimulate investment.[75]

Bitar spoke with me from the Partido Por la Democracia's modestly outfitted headquarters in Santiago. In an office shrouded with photos of Bitar and a who's who of world leaders, the coalition chief talked about his party's dedication to "a serious and stable political economy." His central message about the Concertación's economic agenda could be summarized in one word: discipline. Seventeen years since the transition to democracy and one of the Concertación's most well known public faces was still pitching the center-left's sound economic management.

---

[71] A steep recession in 1982–1983 was the notable exception to Pinochet's broad success in promoting economic growth with price stability. In addition, these policies yielded a hefty social cost of rising poverty and unemployment (Meller et al. 1993; Stokes 2001).

[72] Foxley 1993.

[73] Stokes 2001.

[74] I translated the original Spanish transcript into English from Foxley's economic policy platform published by CIEPLAN (Foxley 1989).

[75] Sergio Bitar interview, June 20, 2007.

In a later interview with Bitar's fellow Concertación heavyweight, Edgardo Boeninger, he elaborated on the center-left's conversion to economic orthodoxy. Boeninger, who served as Aylwin's Presidential Secretary for four years, believes that "all parties at the core of the Concertación had undergone a substantial ideological shift during the Pinochet years." According to Boeninger, both Socialists and Christian Democrats learned from Allende's economic mismanagement.

While socialists never admitted it openly, they confided in private that they were responsible for the coup d'etat; the economy was a mess under Allende. The socialist party is very conscious about this, and wanted to try and avoid the idea that they lacked the ability to govern the economy, they are still traumatized by the Allende years...By 1973, Chile was experiencing chronic inflation and was caught in a vicious populist cycle of higher salaries and higher prices. The state was simply playing the role of arbiter between social groups. They learned the hard way that inflation was hardest on the worker; and that the lowest income groups suffer the most.[76]

Notably, when I interviewed Jorge Arrate, the Secretary General of the Socialist Party from 1989 to 1992, he also spoke candidly about both the Allende years and the challenge of governing through the democratic transition. Arrate, who joined the Aylwin cabinet as Minister of Education in 1992, discussed this tumultuous socialist party history with me in his hacienda-style home in the Providencia neighborhood of Santiago.

For an important part of Chilean population, we were not legitimate people to be governing because we had failed in 1973, particularly in the business community. They still feared us because they recall when the workers came and took over the factories. This was tough for me to understand at first. They had this memory, the same as we have memories of Pinochet and the dictatorship. The social and economic confrontation in Chile of 1973 was tremendous. I say social and economic because there were not only the Allende government mistakes in economics, but also that the economy became a battlefield.[77]

In summary, traumatic events have clearly shaped economic policymaking in Chile. The country's left and centrist politicians, scarred by past economic crises, pledged their commitment to sound economic management throughout the democratic transition. Impressively, almost two decades after the dictatorship, the Concertación's top officials are still fixated on the importance of a disciplined economic policy approach.

Assessing the Alternative Argument: Neoliberal Policy Diffusion. Regional diffusion scholars pose an alternative explanation for the prevalence of economic orthodox policies in Latin America in the 1990s. Rather than policy

---

[76] Edgardo Boeninger interview, June 6, 2007.
[77] I interviewed former Secretary General of the Socialist Party, Jorge Arrate, on June 28, 2007, during my field research in Santiago, Chile.

makers independently responding to common inflationary phenomena, they suggest that peer learning or international economic coercion account for policy outcomes.[78] Latin American politicians either adopt economic policies because they learn from regional success stories or are compelled by IMF conditionality.

During my field research, I found evidence of peer learning within Latin America. For example, when crafting their economic policy blueprints, Chile's politicians learned from the region's earlier democratic transitions. Argentina, Brazil, and Peru's tumultuous transitions underscored the dangers of aggressively expanding the economy to meet pent-up redistributive demands. Budget deficits financed by massive credit creation produced unrelenting inflation that plunged their economies into crisis.

For example, in my open-ended interviews with Chilean policy makers, they mentioned the importance of peer learning. Manuel Marfán, who was a young member of the Socialist Party during the democratic transition, explained that the Concertación had to overcome its credibility challenge. According to Marfán, who would later serve as Chile's finance minister under the Eduardo Frei administration, the credibility challenge had two dimensions: one international and one domestic. The Socialists and Christian Democrats accepted the neoliberal model not only because of previous governance blunders, but also because of the policy mistakes of neighboring countries.

Chile was the last country to make the transition to a democratic regime; and in all the other cases, the main problem of the transition had been bad governance, or the loss of control over the economic situation; they all ended up in fiscal crisis with hyperinflations.[79]

In my interview with Mario Marcel, who was a young member of the Christian Democrats during the democratic transition, he shared Marfán's thoughts. According to Marcel, who would later become Chile's budget director under the Lagos administration, Chile learned from earlier democratic transitions, including the utter failure of President Alfonsín to bring inflation under control during Argentina's transition.[80]

Macro disequilibrium was the Achilles heel of the new democracies. We learned a lot about what to avoid from the experience of other countries.[81]

I also found some evidence of global diffusion, supporting the notion that elite views reflected a global shift in policy paradigms.[82] Chile's *socialist*

---

[78] Barnett and Finnemore 2004; Simmons and Elkins 2004; Weyland 2006.

[79] Manuel Marfán interview, April 20, 2007.

[80] Chumacero, Fuentes, Luders, and Vial 2006.

[81] I interviewed Mario Marcel, who served as budget director under President Ricardo Lagos in Chile between 2000 and 2006 at CIEPLAN's headquarters in Santiago, Chile, on June 21 and June 28, 2007.

[82] Hall 1993; Babb 2001; Babb and Fourcade-Gourinchas 2002.

renewal in Europe provides a good example. While in exile, many leaders of the Chilean Socialist Party had front-row seats to the economic collapse of Europe's socialist system. On the heels of these political and economic transitions, the Chilean Socialist Party experienced its own ideological renovation.

Indeed, Ricardo Lagos, who openly embraced austerity politics as the first Socialist President since Allende, acknowledges that some of the roots of Chile's political transformation date back to the end of the Cold War.

I think that for socialism the fall of the Berlin Wall was like the fall of Wall Street in 2008 for neoliberalism. The time of dogmas concluded on both sides.[83]

Jorge Arrate, the former Socialist Party leader and recent national president candidate, directly lived these experiences. In our 2007 interview, Arrate discussed how European politics influenced the evolution of Chilean socialist thought in the 1970s and 1980s. During the Pinochet years, Arrate had lived in exile in Rome, East Berlin, and Rotterdam. According to Arrate, the socialists were among the few people who were permitted on both sides of the Berlin Wall.

Observing the failures firsthand of the socialist model in Europe (including its lack of political freedoms in East Germany and Russia), they shifted their political thinking toward social democracy and the political center in Chile. Some of the leading socialists, including Arrate, Carlos Altamirano,[84] and Ricardo Núñez,[85] hoped to form an alliance with the Christian Democrats. This rightward shift caused a rupture among party elites. The hardline Marxist-Leninist members refused to veer from the communist's doctrine of "violent popular insurrection." By contrast, Arrate, Altamirano, and Núñez's movement rejected the communist doctrine. Dubbed the socialist renewal, it instead prioritized the displacement of the Pinochet dictatorship. They "defined democracy as the limitation of their political agenda; this meant leaving out any violent component."[86] In the following passage, Arrate elaborates on the socialist renewal.

In the 1980s, for the socialists, the question was how to displace the dictatorship. Everyone wanted an agreement with Christian Democrats – even the communists – but we could not attain an agreement while at the same time pushing a policy of violent insurrection. Such a policy scared the Christian Democrats... We thought by that time, although some component of violence would occur, the main way of displacing the dictatorship was a political and not a military solution. We needed to seek an agreement with the moderate opposition to Pinochet (the Christian Democrats).[87]

[83] Author's interview with President Ricardo Lagos, April 16, 2010.
[84] Altamirano was general secretary of the Chilean Socialist Party (PS) between 1971 and 1979.
[85] Núñez was the leader of the socialist renewal while in exile in Western Europe.
[86] Author's interview with Jorge Arrate, June 28, 2007.
[87] Author's interview with Jorge Arrate, June 28, 2007.

Notwithstanding these instances of global diffusion and peer learning, they were not sufficient explanations for Chile's rightward macroeconomic shift. Without their traumatic, inflationary struggles, left-leaning politicians would have been unlikely to embrace conservative macroeconomic policies. Given both the Socialists' and Christian Democrats' historical emphasis on state control and government redistribution, it is hard to imagine they would have adopted economic austerity without living through a devastating economic crisis. Similarly, in the absence of neighbors' inflationary crises or the fall of the Berlin Wall, Chilean policy makers would have still opted for restrictive economic policies. It was Chile's historical experiences, rather than secondhand experiences of other countries, that influenced its economic policy. Learning from their policy failures, politicians internalized the cost of aggressive economic intervention and became more risk-averse economic managers. Embracing economic orthodoxy was a strategy designed to demonstrate the center-left's managerial competence in the wake of its past economic travails. It was not a reaction to external events. Alejandro Foxley, in fact, notes the gravity of the learning process for the Socialist Party in Chile.

People who had been very involved with the Unidad Popular government knew what reckless macroeconomic policy led them into; they knew they had done it terribly bad. If they were seen as again supporting those type of populist strategies of the Allende years, they risked losing public opinion.[88]

Indeed, much of Chile's left had been severely traumatized by the economic and social consequences of the chaotic Allende period. By the end of the 1980s, both left and right politicians believed that the goal of social equity could only be achieved through macroeconomic orthodoxy.[89]

Perhaps, Boeninger best summarizes the importance of personal experience in the policy making process.

It's one thing to read papers and books; it's another thing to live through it.[90]

6.2.2. Chile's Post-Pinochet Elections

In the following pages, I demonstrate the saliency of these policy lessons by exploring economic decisions when political stakes are the highest: election campaigns. During these periods, I show that political elites prioritize economic stability over aggressive economic stimulus. The commitment to economic discipline is exemplified by the professionalization of the finance ministry and central bank presidency posts.

---

[88] Author's interview with Alejandro Foxley, September 29, 2011.

[89] See Muñoz (1990) for further details. The main political and economic beliefs of the Concertación are summarized in the proceedings of a seminar, held at CIEPLAN (the center-left's main economic think tank) in early 1990 before the Aylwin government's inauguration. Key cabinet officials, including Boeninger and Foxley, officially presented the government's views.

[90] Author's interview with Edgardo Boeninger, June 6, 2007.

TABLE 6.3. *Chile's Economic Ministry Professionalization under Democracy (1960–1973; 1990–2010)*

Economic Minister	Term	Education
Pre-Inflation Crisis		
Eduardo Figueroa Geisse	1960–61	BA, Civil Engineering, Universidad de Chile
Luis Mackenna Shiell	1961–63	Graduate Studies, Princeton University
Sergio Molina Silva	1964–67	BA, Economics, Universidad de Chile
Andrés Zaldívar Larraín	1968–69	BA, Law, Universidad de Chile
Américo Zorrilla Rojas	1970–71	Secondary education, linotypist
Orlando Millas Correa	1972	BA, Law, Universidad de Chile
Fernando Flores	1973	PhD, Linguistics, University of California-Berkeley
Post-Inflation Crisis		
Alejandro Foxley	1990–1993	PhD, Economics, University of Wisconsin
Eduardo Aninat	1994–1999	PhD, Economics, Harvard University
Manuel Marfán Lewis	1999	PhD, Economics, Yale University
Nicolás Eyzaguirre Guzmán	2000–2005	ABD, Economics, Harvard University
Andrés Velasco Brañes	2006–2009	PhD, Economics, Columbia University
Felipe Larraín Bascuñan	2010–current	PhD, Economics, Harvard University

Table 6.3 highlights the pre- and post-crisis differences in the training of presidents' finance ministers under democracy. Before Chile's 1973 inflation shock, none of the country's finance ministers had advanced graduate degrees in economics. Beginning with the post-crisis governance of the "Chicago Boys" during the Pinochet years,[91] every minister's credentials featured doctoral economics training. Central bank presidents followed a similar trend, with 85 percent of post-crisis presidents having an advanced graduate degree in economics or business, compared to only one-quarter of the pre-crisis presidents.

In light of Chile's past inflation scars, center-left presidents opted to appoint skilled technocrats to these parts in hopes of demonstrating their ability to govern the economy. Not surprisingly, with such technicians at the helm, politicians were more likely to use tailored initiatives within a balanced budget framework to reward supporters than jeopardize economic discipline with a spending bonanza.

Chile's 1993 Elections. Early in the democratic transition, the new Concertación government cemented its reputation as a careful steward of the economy. Foxley and the economic team pursued macroeconomic stability and

---

[91] The "Chicago Boys" were a group of young Chilean economists schooled in monetarist economics at either the University of Chicago, or its Chilean affiliate Catholic University of Chile.

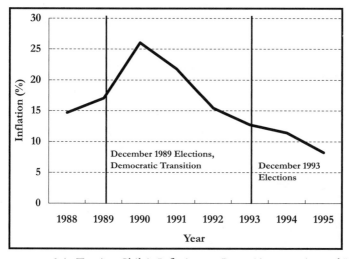

FIGURE 6.4. Taming Chile's Inflationary Beast (Average Annual Inflation, % Change). *Source:* CIEPLAN

tamed the inflationary beast that had been stirred by the transition. Throughout its term in office, the Aylwin administration steadily guided prices lower, bringing annual inflation near single digits by the 1993 elections (Figure 6.4).

Before these elections, Aylwin's coalition government possessed sufficient resources to engineer an electoral economic boom. However, his party preferred to signal its anti-inflation credentials to voters and markets with balanced budgets and stable credit creation. According to my third hypothesis (*H3*), this combination of high inflation aversion and low-funding constraints should yield an inflation-averse political austerity cycle.

Aylwin could have ignited an economic boom had he desired during the 1993 elections. Chile was producing one-quarter of the world's copper output, compared to one-sixth of the world's output in the late 1960s.[92] With prices reaching historically high levels (Figure 6.5),[93] copper revenues were steadily flowing into government coffers.[94]

At the same time, the Chilean government had a strong credit standing in international capital markets. In 1992, Standard & Poor's rating agency assigned Chile the only investment grade rating (BBB) in Latin America. The

[92] See Spilimbergo 1999; Crowson 2007; and World Metal Statistics for further details.
[93] In 1992, high-grade copper prices hovered around 115 U.S. cents per pound, well above the historical average of 56 cents per pound (Global Financial Data).
[94] The Chilean government received about $1 billion per year throughout the 1990s from the state-owned oil company, CODELCO (Coporación Nacional del Cobre de Chile). On average, these copper-related receipts represented about 11 percent of Chile's fiscal revenues (Dirección de Presupuestos de Chile, Estadísticas Fiscales 2009; Spilimbergo 1999). Additional tax income also flowed into government coffers from direct taxes of private mining companies.

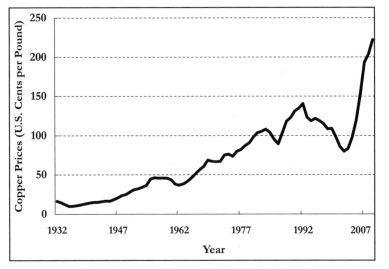

FIGURE 6.5. Global Copper Prices, 1932–2009 (Higher Grade Copper Prices, 5-Year Moving Average).
Source: Global Financial Data

country also benefited from historically low international borrowing rates. Notwithstanding a brief interest rate spike before Aylwin took office, Chile's U.S. dollar interest rates had reached thirty-year lows in 1992–1993.[95] In light of these propitious conditions, Chile had attracted a steady inflow of private capital throughout the early years of its democratic transition.[96] Certainly, the government could have tapped international creditors for additional financing had it wished.

The Aylwin government, however, wanted to break with the boom-bust cycles of the past. Its overwhelming political priority was securing macroeconomic stability.[97] Rather than relying on foreign funds or volatile copper proceeds to finance new social spending, it chose to raise revenue through domestic tax reform. The government's tax reform would give a solid footing to public finances before introducing new expenditures. Aylwin and his economic team believed that maintaining a balanced budget would help them avoid past mistakes. Indeed, facing intense demands for redistribution, Aylwin did not want to risk creating budget deficits that might stoke the inflationary fire.

Aiming to solve Chile's longstanding battle between redistribution and economic stability, Aylwin instead chose a "change in continuity." The Concertación-led government planned to maintain budget surpluses, while altering

[95] Ffrench–Davis 2000.
[96] Foreign direct investment, and to a lesser extent, short-term private inflows were responsible for the capital surge of about $2.5 billion per year between 1990 and 1993 (Ffrench-Davis 2000).
[97] Chumacero, Fuentes, Luders, and Vial 2006.

the composition of government spending to redress the country's hefty social debt. In the early days of his administration, the Aylwin government proceeded as planned, hiking both the value-added and corporate taxes to expand the social effort.[98] Notably, Aylwin's economic team raised the share of social spending in the government budget by 3.4 percentage points in 1990 compared to the previous year.[99]

Alejandro Foxley, Aylwin's economic minister, discussed the political balance between inflation control and social stability in a radio and television address in April 1990.

Inflation is the worst enemy of economic growth and social progress. In countries with high inflation, the workers lose all of the time... products disappear from the stores and supermarkets and lines emerge to buy the necessities. When there is much inflation, each family lives in the daily distress of constant chaos... With runaway inflation, people are demoralized; conflicts and strikes increase, ultimately rupturing the social peace. For this reason, the government has to have the objective of maintaining low inflation... The government's priorities are clear. The social effort comes first, but this social effort should be done without increasing inflation. The President and all of his cabinet support a policy of austerity in the public sector.[100]

In light of Aylwin's strong emphasis on price stability, his economic team pursued restrictive economic policies before the 1993 election. With inflation still hovering above a 20 percent annual rate at the end of 1991, the government slowed both monetary policy and fiscal policy. It halved the pace of credit expansion and halted the deterioration of the budget surplus.[101] As a result of these policies, inflationary pressures relented before the 1993 elections (Figure 6.4), but at the cost of slowing economic growth. The annual real GDP growth rate decelerated from a lofty 12 percent in 1992 to a more modest 7 percent pace in 1993. Notably, however, falling growth did not hurt Aylwin in the election polls. His approval ratings spiked from 60 to 70 percent between 1992 and 1993.[102]

---

[98] The legislature approved Aylwin's tax reform during his first year in office. The value-added tax rose from 16 to 18 percent and corporate taxes increased from 10 to 15 percent.

[99] Velasco 1994.

[100] Foxley's economic address to the nation is included in a collection of economic speeches and dialogues from his 1993 book, *Economía Política de la Transición*. I translated the original Spanish transcript into English.

[101] The rate of money supply expansion (M1) – the best available proxy for monetary policy at the time – fell from 45 percent annual rate in 1991 to a 21 percent rate by 1993. The pace of budget's deterioration also slowed. Between 1989 and 1991, the budget surplus fell by 2.4 percentage points. In comparison, the surplus only fell by 1.1 percentage point between 1991 and 1993 (Estadísticas e indicadores economicos, CEPAL).

[102] The survey was conducted by Barómetro de Centro de Estudios de Realidad Contemporánea (CERC) between 1990 and 1993. The survey question read, ¿Usted aprueba o no aprueba la gestión del gobierno que encabeza el Presidente Aylwin? ("Do you approve or not approve of President Aylwin's management of the government?")

For the most part, the economy followed the path of the government's economic plan during the transition to the next election. Aylwin's economic team wanted to address powerful social pressures in the wake of the Pinochet dictatorship, but incrementally. Before assuming his cabinet post as Treasury Secretary, Foxley cautioned Aylwin about "yielding to social pressures, particularly the need to demonstrate too many things in a very short time." Foxley feared that if Aylwin had attempted to address redistributive demands too quickly, he would have propelled Chile into Latin America's "traditional cycle of populist politics," characterized by an overheating electoral economy and inexorable inflation.[103]

The 1993 elections were a popular referendum on the Concertación government. The main business organizations and even the right had to concede that the coalition's disciplined economic program had been generally successful.[104] Indeed, not only did the Concertación's candidate Eduardo Frei Ruiz-Tagle win the elections,[105] but he began his term in office in 1994 with a whopping approval rating of 84.7 percent.[106] Despite possessing the financial means to craft a political business cycle, Aylwin's risk-aversion led him to prioritize inflation control over an electoral boom. In a country still traumatized by its inflationary past, this electoral strategy was a tremendous success.

Chile's 1999 Elections. The 1999 elections posed an important challenge to the Concertación leadership. In the wake of a global credit crisis, rooted in East Asia, Chile plunged into recession at the end of 1998. The economic downturn complicated the Concertación's ideological compromise between economic and social stability. Risk-averse technocrats still prioritized economic stability, but loosened fiscal and monetary policy to offset the downturn. They did not jeopardize igniting inflation, however, with prices falling throughout the election year (Figure 6.6).

After fifteen years of consecutive economic growth, mounting job losses had eroded the coalition's popularity.[107] By the end of 1998, President Eduardo Frei's approval ratings had plunged from their 1994 highs to 54 percent; and

---

[103] Foxley summarized his views about the inflationary dangers of massive social spending in the proceedings of a Concertación seminar, held at CIEPLAN (the center-left's main economic think tank) in early 1990 before the Aylwin government's inauguration (Foxley 1990; Muñoz 1990). I translated the original Spanish transcript into English.

[104] Author's interview with Alejandro Foxley, September 29, 2011.

[105] The Christian Democrat won 58 percent of the vote in the 1993 elections, 3 percent more than his predecessor Patrico Aylwin obtained in the first post-Pinochet elections in 1989. Arturo Alessandri, the right-wing candidate, secured second place with only 24 percent of the vote.

[106] The survey was conducted by Barómetro de Centro de Estudios de Realidad Contemporánea (CERC) in 1994.

[107] By the end of the 1999 December elections, unemployment approached 9 percent, amounting to a 4 percentage point increase in unemployment in just two years.

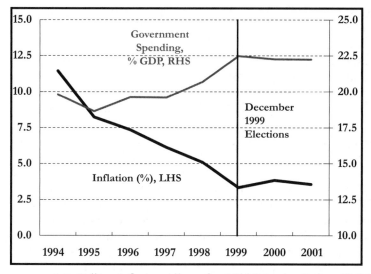

FIGURE 6.6. Falling Inflation Allows for Mild Stimulus Before Chile's 1999 Elections (Average Annual Inflation, % Change).
Source: CEPAL

they would fall further by September 1999, reaching a low of 45 percent.[108] The Christian Democrats (PDC) not only had a president with corroding political capital, but they had also fared more poorly than anticipated in the 1997 legislative elections.[109]

With the electorates' concerns about social issues intensifying, Ricardo Froilán Lagos Escobar's popularity grew in 1999. Lagos, who served in the cabinets of the first two Concertación governments,[110] was also a long-time leader of the Socialist Party (PS) and democracy advocate under the Pinochet dictatorship. Riding a wave of popularity, Lagos would eventually score a

---

[108] These surveys were conducted by Barómetro de Centro de Estudios de Realidad Contemporánea (CERC) in 1998 and 1999.

[109] The Christian Democrats (PDC) won only 23 percent of the vote in the 1997 Chamber of Deputies elections, compared to 27 percent in the 1994 legislative elections. Its 23 percent total was lower than the combined performance of its coalition partners, Partido por la Democracia (PPD) and the Partido Socialista (PS). The poor performance in the legislative elections was compounded by the lackluster showing of its two leading presidential hopefuls, Alejandro Foxley and Andrés Zaldívar, in the battle for Senate seats. That said, the PDC still won the most votes overall, increasing its congressional representation by one deputy and one senator.

[110] Lagos served as Minister of Education for the Aylwin administration and Minister of Public Works for Frei's government. He was also associated with the Allende government; Lagos was the first Ambassador to the United Nations and was later appointed Ambassador of the Soviet Union just before the 1973 coup.

decisive victory over PDC candidate Andrés Zaldívar in the Concertación's presidential primaries.[111]

In preparing for the 1999 elections, the Concertación faced a dilemma. Should they abandon their pledge of economic stability to address growing social demands and rising unemployment? Or, should they maintain their commitment to economic stability? In other words, should they use economic austerity to assuage fears about a socialist candidate reviving Allende's economic chaos?

The Concertación continued to strike a balance between economic and social stability. In his campaign, Lagos tried to overcome his socialist stigma, reassuring the business community that he would not change economic policy.[112] At the same time, he emphasized equity and social justice, with a campaign slogan that promised "growth with equality" ("Crecer con Igualdad").

Like most politicians, President Frei made many political promises before the 1999 elections. He pledged to maintain a macroeconomic equilibrium, while spending to curb rising job losses. Although Frei hailed from the PDC, maintaining the Concertación's hold on power was essential. In fact, Frei's budget director and fellow PDC member, Joaquín Vial, was surprised by the extent of Frei's determination to reelect the coalition.[113]

For Frei, the continuity of the coalition was very important. It was more than I was expecting. I was expecting that he was concerned about his own political future. He was very much concerned about the coalition. For him, his legacy would be judged by the Concertación's continuation. Securing the continuity of the coalition came first; having a Concertación government coming after him was very important. And then came this how do you want to go into the history books; you know, this legacy stuff.

Frei believed that sound economic management was essential to maintaining the Concertación's hold on the presidency. It may have been ten years after the democratic transition, but the Concertación was still preoccupied with avoiding inflation. According to Vial, "Frei was not willing to have one iota of additional inflation."

---

[111] Amid a historically high turnout, Lagos won an impressive 71.3 percent of the vote compared to Zaldívar's 28.6 percent. The turnout was more than 1.4 million voters, about half the Concertación's total vote in the 1997 elections (Angell and Pollack 2000).

[112] Angell and Pollack 2000.

[113] Author's interview with Joaquín Vial on April 23, 2007, at the Spanish bank BBVA's headquarters in Santiago, Chile. Vial has been chief economist at BBVA since 2004. Previously, he was Frei's Budget Director at the Ministry of Finance (Director de Presupuestos del Ministerio de Hacienda de Chile) between 1997 and 2000. Vial was also the executive director of CIEPLAN, the center-left's think tank, between 1993 and 1997, and the economic policy coordinator at the Ministry of Finance between 1992 and 1993.

During the budgetary planning phase of 1998, Frei's government put forth a very restrictive budget compared to previous years.[114] From his executive office at BBVA's Santiago headquarters, Vial recalled his 1999 budget discussions with President Frei during the summer of 1998. Notably, the former budget director again underscored Frei's commitment to price stability.

President Frei was not a very vocal guy, but he was very clear that he wanted a balanced budget! Many people believed strongly that one of the reasons for economic instability and the 1970's poor economic performance was massive budget deficits; the president did not want to break the record of good fiscal management, at least he did not want to go into history as being the one that caused this problem. For people who have lived through the traumas of Allende and the early years of Pinochet, they had the memories of runaway inflations and massive budget deficits, they know they cannot fool around with economics. They were not willing to take risks with inflation. Politicians learned from the past. Fear of inflation is something that is a major deterrent against of crazy fiscal policies. In the case of Chile, the history of crisis helped curb inflationary cycles.[115]

Notwithstanding Frei's lack of desire to create a political business cycle, he did possess the funds. Benefiting from a decade of budget surpluses and windfall privatization revenues,[116] the Chilean government had some policy flexibility.[117] Utility and port privatizations offset the impact of the global downturn on government revenues.[118] At the same time, a lack of external public debt freed Chile from the market conditionality faced by other Latin American countries, enabling it to borrow during the downturn.[119]

Taking advantage of this financial ammunition, Chile used its additional funding to offset the 1998–1999 economic recession. The authorities engaged in a budgetary expansion, but fell short of a political business cycle. Recall that such a cycle is characterized by an aggressive government-led expansion before elections that yields inflation. In comparison to the whopping pro-cyclical

---

[114] Frei submitted a 1999 budget that called for a real rise in government spending of 2.8 percent, compared to a 7.4 percent real increase in the 1998 budget (Economic Intelligence Unit Country Reports, 1997–1998).

[115] Joaquín Vial interview, April 23, 2007.

[116] Beginning in December 1998, Chile privatized thirteen regional water utilities, including a 35 percent stake in Emos, the water company serving the Santiago metropolitan area. The government also sold three of its biggest ports in 1999, including Valparaiso, San Antonio, and San Vicente.

[117] According to Chile's budget law, in the event of unexpected revenue receipts, the government can exceed its initial total budget investments by 10 percent (Vial 2007).

[118] The state-owned Codelco copper consortium's eroding profits and sinking corporate tax revenues had depressed government revenues.

[119] Chile's investment grade rating (S&P rated its debt at A- in 1998) afforded the country more flexibility than its neighbors when it finally borrowed from international markets. Chile had its first public bond emissions in 1998–1999, but it was "not driven by a need for financing." Rather it was seen as "a way to develop a long-term debt market for the private sector" (Vial 2007).

budgetary expansions explored in Chapter 4, the Concertación's counter-cyclical stimulus took place during an economic freefall, making inflation less likely.[120] Moreover, the scale of the stimulus was also smaller. Frei's father's ballooned the budget deficit by 5 percentage points of GDP during the 1970 election year, whereas the younger Frei expanded the deficit by 2.5 percentage points of GDP.

According to Vial, the fiscal stimulus was also designed to compensate for the monetary policy contraction in 1998.[121] Following the 1997–98 Asian crisis, the central bank had increased interest rates to defend the Chilean peso from currency speculators.[122] From Vial's perspective, during 1999, the economic team was "basically trying to pick up the pieces."[123]

I also interviewed Frei's Finance Minister, Manuel Marfán, about the economic policy program during the 1999 elections. Marfán talks of the importance of the counter-cyclical response, or "saving in good times, to have more degrees of freedom in bad times." He surmised that without this fiscal savings, it would have been difficult to spend during the downturn. Moreover, he believed that without this spending, "the recession would have been much worse."[124] Despite strong election-year social pressures, however, Marfán underscored Chile's commitment to economic orthodoxy.

There were more strikes prior to elections, because the unions thought that the government would be more willing to pay concessions to avoid political costs. In my negotiations with the public sector unions, I didn't want to make a mistake with the macroeconomic equilibrium that we would pay to heavily for after the elections. I would not go beyond a 5 percent wage increase![125]

As budget director during this time, Vial also acknowledges the difficulty in balancing economic stability and rising social discontents. Like Marfán, Vial admits that political concessions were made within the context of maintaining economic discipline. In spending to offset the downturn, the Frei cabinet allocated new expenditures for infrastructure projects and public salaries, which increased by about 6 and 8 percent, respectively, during the election year.[126]

We concentrated investment mostly in small projects done at the municipal level that were very labor intensive to ameliorate the impact of the recession. Let's put it this way,

---

[120] In the prelude to the election year, real GDP growth slowed from 6.6 to 3.2 percent, and would fall to −0.8 by the end of 1999 (CEPAL).

[121] Chile's three-month money market rates, a proxy for central bank monetary policy, rose by about 1.1 percentage points during 1998, but were reversed going into the election year (CEPAL).

[122] The result was tighter domestic liquidity, with the money supply, as measured by M1, declining by 5.9 percent in 1998, compared to a 16.6 percent increase in the previous year (World Development Indicators).

[123] Joaquín Vial interview, April 23, 2007.

[124] Author's interview with Manuel Marfán, June 28, 2007.

[125] Manuel Marfán interview, June 28, 2007.

[126] Estadísticas e indicadores economicos, CEPAL.

I would have done this thing independent of an election cycle because it was counter-cyclical fiscal policy. We did have spare, unused capacity, and we did have ample cash available... It made a lot of sense to spend more money. It was a traditional Keynesian response to a transitory shock... But, it coincided with the elections. And there are strong municipal machines, so I'm pretty sure it had an electoral effect; but it's difficult to discern this effect from normally good macroeconomic intervention.[127]

In summary, President Frei possessed the financial means, but not the political motivation to prime the economic pump before the 1999 elections. Although a huge external shock to domestic growth necessitated a counter-cyclical response, it did not stoke inflation in the bleak economic environment.[128] Notwithstanding the moderate stimulus, economic growth and inflation fell throughout the election period (Figure 6.6). Rather than delivering an electorally timed boom, macroeconomic policies were mainly designed to offset the economic downturn. Electoral pressures mostly manifested on the micro level through line-item budgetary targeting, such as public sector wage hikes and municipal spending projects.

Chile's 2005 Elections. During the 2005 elections, Chile's incumbent government had the financial means, but not the political motivation to create a political business cycle. Booming copper markets padded government coffers with cash. A strong external debt profile also limited external market constraints on policy making. Nonetheless, austerity politics persisted throughout the election period. In line with the inflation-averse hypothesis, Chile once again avoided the electoral boom-bust cycle that had been historically associated with Latin American democracies.

In 2000, under the stewardship of President Ricardo Lagos, the Socialist Party took the reins of government for the first time since the Allende period. Aiming to quell critics who were concerned about the left's ability to govern the economy in a globalized world, the Lagos economic team enacted two important institutional reforms: a structural balance rule and an inflation target.

These reforms were designed to reduce executive discretion and institutionalize the left's commitment to sound economic management. For example, the budget rule sought to formalize the Concertación's longstanding, but informal observance of fiscal discipline, pledging that the government would maintain a budget surplus of at least one percent of GDP.[129]

Mario Marcel, who served as Lagos's budget director between 2000 and 2006, spoke about the importance of demonstrating sound economic management in a globalized world during our 2007 interview. Ironically, our discussion about globalization's constraints took place at CIEPLAN headquarters,

---

[127] Author's interview with Joaquín Vial, April 23, 2007.

[128] In Chapter 3, I account for such counter-cyclical responses during the election year by using the output gap as a control variable in the large-N statistical tests.

[129] The rule was a discretionary policy self-imposed by the Lagos administration (Aninat, Landregan, Navia, and Vial 2006).

which is adjacent to the UN's Economic Commission for Latin America and the Caribbean (ECLAC), where Raúl Prebisch governed for thirteen years. Prebisch had been a well-known dependency theorist and seminal skeptic of globalization.

Globalization imposes a lot of discipline; especially on the fiscal side. You may be prudent, but when you operate in a globalized environment, you have to prove that you're prudent. That's the advantage of any fiscal rule. It works as a signaling device. It's relevant for Chile because the budgetary institutions are very presidential. The executive has full control over public finances. Having all that control means you have a lot of discretion. Economic agents don't know how you will use that discretion. You can use it to be very responsible or you can use it to be very populist. So, limiting discretion in the Chilean case was very important.[130]

Under Lagos, the central bank also moved to an inflation-targeting framework in 2001 (though it was initially conceived in 1999). Within this framework, the central bank committed to an annual inflation target of 2 to 4 percent. While inflation aversion had long been a primary policy objective of Concertación governments, it was now formalized; ironically, this was done by a Socialist government that once rejected the neoliberal economic model. These institutional rules were an effective signaling device for communicating the left's commitment to sound economic management. For many years, the Chilean left had believed that economic stability was a necessary condition for social equity, but it had not held Chile's top leadership post since the Allende era.

According to Ernesto Ottone and Carlos Vergara, two of Lagos's main political advisors, the Chilean president adopted these institutional rules to convey his belief that "macroeconomic stability was the basis for progress." In my interview with Vergara, who now resides at the European Commission for Latin America and the Caribbean (ECLAC), he emphasized the importance of the structural balance rule in both cementing his historical legacy, but also bolstering the left's economic management credentials.

The structural surplus rule was a key strategic element in the economic plan. Now, saving in boom times allowed us to spend during bad times. In other words, we could define counter-cyclical policy in terms of social spending... Lagos ended the suspicion in Chile that a man from the left could not govern and unite the country, and could not combine social stability, social progress, and democracy with good governance.[131]

In his final Presidential Address in May 2005, Lagos also underscored this point, declaring that economic growth and social stability are not mutually exclusive. Rather, they are the twin pillars of a successful modern capitalist

---

[130] Author's interview with Mario Marcel, June 21 and June 28, 2007.
[131] Author's interview with Carlos Vergara on April 26, 2007, during my field research in Santiago, Chile. I translated these excerpts from his book, titled *Ampliando Horizontes*, that summarizes the main political strategies of the Lagos government (Ottone and Vergara 2006).

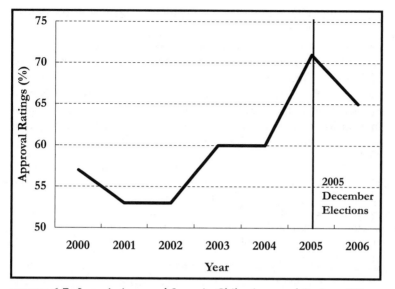

FIGURE 6.7. Lagos's Approval Soars in Chile, Approval Ratings (%).
Source: CERC

democracy. Allende's redistributive efforts had been associated with runaway inflation and economic failure. However, Lagos insisted that redistribution can accompany price stability and economic growth.

It is a false dilemma "to grow or redistribute." Growth without redistribution or redistribution without growth ends in fatal social and political crises and the loss of liberties. Balanced distribution and growth is the only responsible and durable path to social progress.[132]

In the 2005 electoral campaign, the Concertación nominated yet another Socialist candidate, Michelle Bachelet.[133] Bachelet, the former Health and Defence Minister under Lagos, benefited enormously from his popularity. After six years in office, Lagos had a 71 percent approval rating.[134] Moreover, Lagos's popularity improved dramatically during the final years of his presidency (Figure 6.7). His popular acclaim mainly reflected his socioeconomic legacy. Indeed, Lagos was able to achieve tremendous progress in meeting his twin goals of economic and social stability. During his tenure,

---

[132] Ricardo Lagos, Mensaje Presidencial, 21 de mayo de 2005. I translated the original Spanish language text into English.

[133] The Concertación did not have a primary election because the only serious rival Soledad Alvear, a Christian Democrat and former Minister of Justice and of Foreign Affairs, withdrew her candidacy after polling poorly (Angell and Reig 2006).

[134] The survey was conducted by Barómetro de Centro de Estudios de Realidad Contemporánea (CERC) between 2000 and 2006. The survey question read, ¿Usted aprueba o no aprueba la gestión del gobierno que encabeza el Presidente Lagos? ("Do you approve or not approve of President Lagos's management of the government?").

per capita income, minimum salaries, and educational attainment improved, while poverty and unemployment both fell dramatically.[135]

Given these successes, Bachelet campaigned on a message of continuity. Senator Sergio Bitar, who was Michelle Bachelet's campaign advisor, stressed the importance of fiscal discipline when I interviewed him about the Concertación's 2005 electoral strategy. Recall that Bitar also served as Salvador Allende's mining minister. He put forth a view that marks a pronounced shift in the Socialist Party's economic attitude since Allende's massive budgetary expansion that ended in an inflationary spiral, recession, and a 1973 coup.

> In order to understand today's political economy; one has to understand what happened with the Popular Unity government in the 1970s. One of the most important conclusions for the entire Chilean left from this period, was the use of an expansive political economy can have gigantic political costs. Rather, the major electoral and political benefits come from a serious, stable, and responsible political economy. For fifteen years, we have maintained a high level of political discipline, knowing that populism doesn't pay.[136]

Alejandro Foxley, Bachelet's economic spokesman and original architect of the Concertación "growth with equity" strategy, echoed Bitar's words on the campaign trail. Not surprisingly, he and the Bachelet economic team advocated not only for continued sound economic management, but also for a reduction in income inequality. Bachelet proposed a range of social policies, including universal pre-school education, flexible hours for working women, and pension reform.[137]

Given the Concertación's unwavering commitment to social policy within an orthodox macroeconomic framework, Lagos did not possess the political motivation to fashion an inflation-jeopardizing electoral economic boom. If he desired, he could have created a political business cycle (PBC). The Chilean president had bountiful resources, but chose to stay the course of prudent economic management. Copper prices reached historically high levels in 2005 (Figure 6.5), helping Codelco, the state copper company, register a boom in annual profit growth.[138] Codelco's profits, along with taxes on private copper companies, stuffed government accounts with cash.[139] Chile also met

---

[135] GDP per capita rose during Lagos's term from US$4,860 in 2000 to US$5,903 in 2004. At the same time, the minimum salary went up by 29 percent and the number of students enrolled in higher education rose from 411,000 to 600,000. Unemployment also fell from 9.7 to 8.1 percent and poverty decreased from 45.1 to 18.8 percent of the population in 2003 (author's interview with Ricardo Lagos on April 16, 2010; Angell and Reig 2006).

[136] Author's interview with Senator Sergio Bitar, June 20, 2007.

[137] Angell and Reig 2006.

[138] Codelco reported a forty percent increase in annual profits in the first nine months of 2005, compared to the previous period.

[139] The Comisión Chilena del Cobre (Cochilco) estimated the Treasury's copper revenue in 2005 at US$7.3 billion, including US$5.3 billion from Codelco – which transfers all of its profits to the Treasury – and US$2 billion in income tax from private copper companies. The budget director, Mario Marcel, indicated that two-thirds of the surplus was saved, mostly through

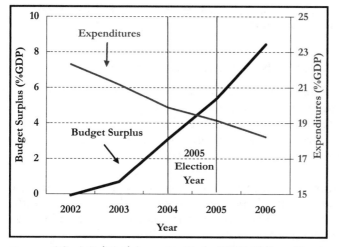

FIGURE 6.8. A Political Austerity Cycle (2005 Chilean Elections).
Source: CEPAL

few funding constraints in international debt markets, given its Standard & Poor's investment grade rating (A) and its ability to borrow at interest rates as low as 2 percent in 2004.[140] Notwithstanding these advantageous funding conditions, the Chilean government instead paid down its external debt in 2005.[141]

In summary, contrary to Chilean presidents' earlier behavior during commodity booms,[142] Lagos refrained from creating a spending bonanza before the 2005 elections. Rather, he cut spending and oversaw a hefty boost to the budget surplus before the 2005 elections (Figure 6.8). The central bank followed suit, raising interest rates a whopping 11 times in one year to curb inflationary pressures, moving the target interest rate from 3.5 percent in December 2004 to 5.6 in November 2005.

Lagos and his economic team's contractionary policy stance signaled the Socialist Party's continued commitment to economic stability in an election year. In light of the economy's previous brisk pace,[143] however, the Lagos government still delivered more than five percent growth in 2005. The result

---

pre-payments of government debt, and the rest was allocated to a long-term fund to guarantee the payment of the minimum statutory pensions (Economist Intelligence Unit, January 2006).

[140] Global Development Finance.

[141] The Chilean government's foreign debt decreased by US$700 million in 2005, reaching a total of US$4 billion (Global Development Finance; Economist Intelligence Unit, July, 2006).

[142] See Chapter 4.

[143] This rapid growth rate translated into a positive output gap (or a positive difference between actual and potential GDP), risking inflation and further justifying the government's restrictive policy stance before elections.

was an inflation-averse cycle, characterized by moderate rates of economic growth and contained inflation during both 2005 and 2006.[144]

6.2.3. Hyperinflation Creates a New Brand of Argentine Politics

During the post-World War II era, Argentina had its bouts of economic volatility, but inflation remain relatively confined. From 1946 to 1975, average inflation increased by 21 percent per annum, a rate that was tamed by developing country standards.[145] Throughout the next decade, however, Argentina's economic history was bursting with tales of big budget deficits, lofty inflation, and eventually hyperinflation.

This cataclysmic shock had a profound effect on the political and technocratic elite in Argentina. After hyperinflation destroyed the incomes of the poor and middle classes in Argentina, the ability to control inflation and protect people's income became a priceless political asset. Without this price shock, political austerity theory argues that big budget spending that padded voter incomes would have continued to rule the day.

Perhaps, diffusion may once again be a contributing dynamic. In fact, Argentine policy makers occasionally point to peer learning as a factor that contributed to the political acceptance of neoliberal policies. For example, José Luis Machinea, who served for two different Argentine presidential cabinets and as Executive Secretary of the United Nations' Economic Commission for Latin America and the Caribbean, is ideally suited to observe regional trends.[146] In our conversation during my field research, Machinea highlighted that much of the region has become fiscally responsible, after "learning from history and learning from governments that have collapsed from grave economic crises."[147]

We would expect that political leaders are careful observers of their neighbors' economic successes and failures. The diffusion of these ideas helps explain the availability of some policy options, but not the choice of economic policy. Neoliberal paradigms, for instance, existed throughout the 1980s, but had little resonance with Argentine politicians and voters who generally preferred experimenting with more interventionist heterodox policies. It was only after these policies failed at taming inflation that politicians gravitated toward neoliberal solutions.

---

[144] Inflation remained in the middle of the central bank's inflation target range in 2005, finishing the year at an average annual rate of 3.1 percent (compared to a band of 2–4 percent). In 2006, inflation's rate of expansion did not budge either, registering a 3.4 percent gain for the year (World Development Indicators).

[145] Oxford Latin American Economic History Database.

[146] Machinea was central bank president (1986–1989) and economic minister (1999–2001).

[147] Author's interview with José Luis Machinea, June 2007 in Santiago, Chile. I conducted the original interview in Spanish during my field research in Santiago, Chile, and translated the text of the interview into English.

In the absence of hyperinflation, Argentina's political class would have been unlikely to accept economic orthodoxy, judging from their behavior during the early days of the democratic transition, before the inflation crisis reached its peak.

Pre-Crisis Thinking. Before the inflationary storm of the late 1980s, economic stability received little political and technocratic weight in the ruling elites' choices. In the early days of democracy, Argentina's left-wing politicians were consumed by traditional redistributive concerns. However, the political quest to hastily boost people's earnings led to the eventual erosion of their incomes.

In the wake of the Videla military dictatorship,[148] President Raúl Alfonsín's government faced tremendous pressures for social spending and redistribution. The political opening unleashed a deluge of economic demands that were previously repressed by the Videla dictatorship. Unions clamored for higher wages and better social services, whereas industrial entrepreneurs and agricultural producers lobbied for tax breaks and subsidies. In an effort to assuage these pressures, the Alfonsín government promoted economic expansion through massive public investment and easy private credit. Firing the dual cylinders of monetary and fiscal policy, Alfonsín hoped to create new jobs and bolster his middle and working-class support.[149]

In my 2007 field research interview, Juan Sourrouille, who served as Alfonsín's Minister of Economy, discussed Argentine economic policy during the democratic transition. Sourrouille suggested that politicians did not draft economic blueprints, or fret much about inflation.

From a technical standpoint, there was *not* a comprehensive view in Argentina about the best economic strategies... There was *not* an important difference in political parties with respect to their economic policy... The Peronists were traditionally more interventionist than the Radicales. But, no one had an alternative plan. There is an important reason. The reason is that the conventional anti-inflationary plan was recessive; the way of controlling inflation was reducing demand. The left had the idea that this program was anti-popular, and that the popular sectors would reject attempts at controlling demand... In Argentina, democracy was new, and from this perspective, el Peronismo y Radicalismo had a *common front against recession*; the right was not going to win the elections; and they were the only ones who were open to austerity programs and IMF recommendations.[150]

---

[148] Jorge Rafael Videla took over the Argentina presidency in 1976 in a coup d'état that deposed Isabel Martínez de Perón. After the return to democracy in 1983, he was prosecuted for large-scale human rights abuses and crimes against humanity that took place under his rule.

[149] Alfonsín also hiked real wages, courtesy of a price freeze, hoping to boost the average Argentine's earning power.

[150] Author's interview with Juan Sourrouille in Buenos Aires, Argentina on May 28, 2007. Sourrouille served as Minister of the Economy from February 1985 to March 1989. I conducted the original interview in Spanish and translated the text of the interview into English.

Alfonsín's hope of meeting redistributive demands with wage hikes, easy credit, and public investment caused inflation to rear its ugly head. Between December 1983 and June 1985, the monthly inflation rate had more than doubled, reaching an eye-popping 42 percent. The alarming spike in prices sparked fears of hyperinflation.[151]

As a result, the political landscape showed signs of a tepid acceptance for stabilization by the mid-1980s. Facing historically unprecedented inflation levels, Alfonsín brought Juan Sourrouille and his team of technocrats into government to stabilize the economy. According to Sourrouille, their stabilization plan – dubbed the Austral Plan[152] – had the full-backing of the President. Invoking the famous Nike slogan before its time, Alfonsín told Sourrouille "no me diga nada, haga!" (don't tell me anything, just do it!).[153]

Notwithstanding considerable criticism from the Radical party's (UCR) old guard and the unions,[154] Alfonsín boldly advanced the Austral Plan's stabilization agenda. In addition to the typical price and wage freezes that characterized heterodox plans, he also called for fiscal and monetary discipline and agreed to a new IMF program.[155]

With the November 1985 Congressional elections approaching, Sourrouille recounted Alfonsín's political concerns when he entered the cabinet. "There was not only an inflation problem, but an electoral problem." Inflation could have caused the UCR to lose the Congressional elections. Despite the protests of UCR hardliners who clamored for more spending, Alfonsín's remained committed to inflation stabilization.

Surprisingly, the political choice of austerity did not harm the President's support. The Austral Plan was politically popular. Alfonsín's approval ratings reached 80 percent, and the UCR kept its absolute majority in the Chamber of Deputies. Pollsters interpreted the electoral victory as a vote of confidence for the administration.[156]

---

[151] Fernández 1991.

[152] The Austral Plan, launched on June 14, 1985, was a heterodox stabilization plan that aimed to break the inflationary inertia with freezes on salaries and prices. Other measures including military spending cuts, the cessation of central bank financing of budget deficits, and the establishment of a new currency, the austral. The Argentine peso was replaced by the Argentine austral at 1,000 to one with freezes on salaries and prices.

[153] Author's interview with Juan Sourrouille, May 28, 2007.

[154] Most unions and the other left-wing parties, such as the Peronists (PJ), openly opposed the program. The unions, for example, called for a half-day strike in May before the program's launch. The strike rebuked Alfonsín with the slogan, "don't pay the foreign banks with the hunger of the people."

[155] In January, the IMF had provided the country with a new standby loan of US$1.39 billion that opened the door for US$4.2 billion in new commercial bank loans. In exchange for the funding, Argentina commited to IMF austerity measures and commercial bank debt renegotations. With the onset of hyperinflation, the IMF revised the program's targets and approved the heterodox economic program (Manzetti 2001).

[156] Manzetti, 2001.

The central government's preoccupation with inflation continued beyond 1985. Although Alfonsín's stabilization attempt initially kept inflation at bay,[157] the economic menace struck again in 1986. Indeed, throughout the rest of the 1980s, Sourrouille and his economic team focused on stabilization, rather than traditional political calculus of priming the economic pump. In my interview with Sourrouille from his Buenos Aires apartment, he discussed Alfonsín's political obsession with controlling inflation.

The fundamental concern was inflation. All of our focus was on controlling inflation, and improving the fiscal situation... The President of the Republic had more than one opportunity to spend before elections, but he understood the danger of inflation. He was focused on controlling the fiscal situation and controlling the wage problem.[158]

Sourrouille's emphasis on inflation stabilization foreshadows Argentina's economic policy in the coming decade. Similar to Chile, Argentina's policymakers learned from their personal trauma of taming the inflationary beast. Indeed, once released from its cage, inflation was hard to subdue. For example, despite Sourrouille's heterodox measures during the end of the decade, controlling the gaping budget deficit proved economically and politically difficult. When the government ended the Austral Plan's initial price freeze, repressed inflationary pressures resurfaced.[159] At the same time, public enterprises and provincial governments were slow to balance their books.[160] The government printed money to fund its deficit, entering into a vicious cycle of widening deficits and spiraling inflation.

In a later interview with José Luis Machinea, Alfonsín's central bank president[161] discussed the government's failed stabilization attempt. Echoing Sourrouille's view, Machinea emphasized the government's commitment to stabilization. Despite its effort, however, he believes stabilization flopped because "a low inflation rate was never a public good."[162]

Rather, political resistance from unions, provinces, public enterprises, private entrepreneurs, and the Peronist opposition doomed their stabilization attempt. The provinces and public enterprises failed to control spending, private entrepreneurs resisted subsidy cuts, the Peronist Party criticized the government's "excessive inflation preoccupation," and the Confederación

---

[157] Inflation declined from 28.4 percent in the second quarter of 1985 to 3.8 and 2.5 percent in the third and fourth quarters of that same year.

[158] Sourrouille interview, May 28, 2007.

[159] In April and June 1986, the government allowed a wage increase of 5 percent for state employees and 8.5 percent for private employees. The elimination of wage and price freezes were intended to break the disequilibrium between seasonal goods prices (not covered by the price freezes) and administered prices. But, a series of uncontrolled price and wage hikes in the wake of the price deregulation ignited further inflation.

[160] Fernández 1991; Manzetti 2001.

[161] Machinea also later served as Minister of the Economy under the Fernando de la Rúa administration from December 1999–February 2001.

[162] Author's interview with José Luis Machinea on June 13, 2007.

General del Trabajo (CGT) launched thirteen general strikes between 1984 and 1988.[163] According to Machinea, these pressures produced "a classic, electoral cycle pattern during this period that ended in crisis." Indeed, both the fiscal deficit and inflation ballooned before the 1989 elections, sowing the seeds for a post-election economic maelstrom.[164]

By mid-decade, however, Argentina was mired in an inflationary storm. Severe food shortages sparked riots, looting, and bouts of social violence. Shopkeepers guarded their barricaded doorways with guns, and security forces brutally killed fourteen rioters. Unable to halt inflationary turbulence, Alfonsín became an "exhausted president, without any authority."[165] Jettisoned from office five months early, he left Argentina near anarchy.[166]

Living through hyperinflation and the collapse of public order traumatized Argentines. In the wake of the economic and political collapse, their concerns for economic stability and public order dominated public opinion.[167] For the next decade, the socioeconomic chaos also shifted Argentina's elites closer toward the political center. Indeed, inflation aversion became a foremost political concern, often elevated to the level of more classic political priorities such as job creation and economic growth.

Like in Chile, these political concerns manifested in the professionalization of presidents' economic teams post-crisis. Table 6.4 summarizes the divergence in ministers' economic credentials in the immediate pre- and post-crisis Argentina.[168] Presidents swapped ministers with bachelor's degrees in public accounting and civil engineering for technocrats with economic doctorates from prestigious universities. A similar phenomenon occurred with Argentina's central bank credentials. Following inflation-stabilization, 86 percent of central bank presidents had advanced graduate degrees in economics or business, compared to less than half of the pre-crisis presidents.

After the sacking of Roberto Lavagna in 2005, Néstor Kirchner appeared to initially drift from budgetary discipline under the stewardship of Felisa Miceli, the former president of the state-owned Banco de la Nación. However, Argentina maintained a primary budget surplus, along with a tight monetary

---

[163] Traditionally, Radical governments have confronted vicious opposition from Peronist trade unions (Machinea 1990; Di Tella 1999).

[164] Notably, given the government's stabilization efforts, the final election year stimulus was fairly tame. In the final two years of Alfonsín's term, the average fiscal deficit declined by 1.3 percentage points. It was 1987's whopping expansion that ultimately led to the overheating of the economy (Bases de Datos y Publicaciones Estadísticas del CEPAL).

[165] O'Donnell 1989; Echegary and Elordi 2001.

[166] In the May 1989 presidential elections, Alfonsín's party, the Unión Cívica Radical (UCR) and their presidential candidate Eduardo Angeloz, were punished by voters for the economic turmoil. The UCR won only 32 percent of the vote, compared to the Peronist's (Partido Justicialista) strong 47 percent victory.

[167] Echegaray and Elordi 2001.

[168] Finance ministers with terms lasting fewer than four months were not included given the political volatility and economic ministry turnover during both 1989 and 2001.

TABLE 6.4. *Argentina's Economic Ministry Professionalization under Democracy (1983–2005)*

Economic Minister	Term	Education
Pre-Inflation Crisis		
Bernardo Grinspun	1983–1985	BA, Economics, Universidad de Buenos Aires
Juan Vital Sourrouille	1985–1989	BA, Public Accounting; Doctor in Economic Science
Néstor Rapanelli	1989	BA, Civil Engineering
Antonio Erman González	1989–1991	BA, Accounting, Universidad Nacional de Córdoba
Post-Inflation Crisis		
Domingo Cavallo	1991–1996	PhD, Economics, Harvard University
Roque Fernández	1996–1999	PhD, Economics, University of Chicago
José Luis Machinea	1999–2001	PhD, Economics, University of Minnesota
Domingo Cavallo	2001	PhD, Economics, Harvard University
Roberto Lavagna	2002–2005	Graduate Degree, Economics, University of Brussels

policy stance, even during the 2007 presidential elections.[169] While revenues from the commodity boom helped preserve the budget surplus, President Kirchner also valued fiscal surpluses as a political asset. By accumulating pesos in the Treasury, he had an arsenal of patronage resources to direct to politically important provinces. Economic discipline ultimately served two political ends. It signaled good governance, but behind the veil of budget austerity, he could deliver considerable discretionary spending without any congressional oversight.[170]

Post-Crisis Thinking. In a refrain strikingly similar to the Chilean Concertación's chorus, Machinea claims that Argentina's policy makers have learned an important lesson from 1989's severe economic and political crisis. In the 1980s, stabilization emanated from the center, but was repelled from the periphery in a somewhat similar fashion to the Venezuelan case. In comparison, Machinea believes that inflation stabilization became more widely accepted in the 1990s, following the brunt of the inflation crisis. Indeed, by January 1990, 67 percent of the people interviewed in a Buenos Aires survey identified inflation as the most important problem for them and their families.[171]

---

[169] CEPAL's Bases de Datos y Publicaciones Estadística.

[170] Recall that the "superpoderes" law granted Kirchner the power to spend extra-budgetary revenues without congressional approval. This law allowed him to control redistributive resources to cash-strapped provincial governments who were restricted from borrowing externally following the crisis (see Chapters 1 and 8 for further details).

[171] Echegary and Elordi 2001.

Machinea elaborated on the importance of this popular transformation during our interview.

> Everyone has realized that conducting populist macroeconomic policies can destroy a government. The theme of fiscal responsibility is much more valued than in the past; governments have learned their lesson and fiscal responsibility is now an important objective... Policy learning is a result of severe crises. Everyone realizes that populism or macroeconomic disorder risks creating tremendous political opposition, and ultimately political volatility. Hence, governments have been more cautious... In addition, inflation has more weight with the citizenry now. Because of past suffering, neither the politicians nor the citizenry request very expansive fiscal policies. The people remember traumatic periods very strongly. Traumatic economic situations have generated a learning process among the citizenry.[172]

Under President Carlos Saúl Menem, Argentina's policy makers formalized their commitment to price stability through *convertibility* in the 1990s. By an act of Congress, the convertibility plan sought to maintain exchange rate stability, and hence domestic price stability, by pegging the Argentine peso to the U.S. dollar. The law guaranteed peso-U.S. dollar parity and barred money supply increases that were not backed by foreign exchange reserves.[173]

President Menem marketed his austerity plans as "surgery without anesthesia,"[174] cautioning the public to prepare for tough times. Convertibility created a policy bias toward deflation; workers lost jobs and real wages stagnated.[175]

However, convertibility's success at ending Argentina's inflationary turmoil boosted its political popularity. Hyperinflation, which sparked three consecutive years of negative growth and rising poverty, nurtured the political demand for economic stability.[176] Fueled by the saliency of inflationary trauma, austerity slowly gained political acceptance. Indeed, price stability was an important political commodity. In a twist of political logic, restrictive monetary and fiscal policies signaled economic competence rather than aggressive government expansion. Against this backdrop, the political business cycle fell out of fashion during the 1990s.

6.2.4. Argentina's 1999 Elections

Argentina's inflation aversion produced disciplined macroeconomic policies, even amid an environment of funding availability. During the 1999 Argentine

---

[172] Author's interview with José Luis Machinea, June 13, 2007.

[173] The convertibility plan was crafted by Minister of the Economy Domingo Cavallo. It also included such measures as budget cuts and a massive reduction in public sector employment.

[174] Cited in Echegaray and Elordi (2001), 191.

[175] The average unemployment rate rose from 10.1 percent in 1993 to almost 19 percent by 1995 (CEPAL).

[176] By 1990, inflation crossed the thousand percent level for the second consecutive year and poverty rates had more than doubled in five years. GDP growth also fell for the third consecutive year, declining by 1.8 percent in 1990 compared to a 1.9 and 6.9 percent contraction in 1988 and 1989, respectively (Wiesner 2008).

elections, windfall privatization proceeds gave policy makers the added fiscal space, or budgetary capacity to fund an electoral expansion. Moreover, Argentina could have borrowed additional funds externally to further alleviate its budget constraints. With a good credit standing in international markets, Argentina was the first country to issue new global debt in the wake of the 1998 Russian default.

Despite these low-funding constraints, political austerity theory anticipates that Argentina's inflationary scars placed a political premium on price stability. In fact, I find scant evidence of an electoral boom-bust cycle in 1999, with national-level policy makers as concerned about preserving voters' incomes through inflation control as spurring higher wages and new jobs. Notably, there is evidence of local-level political business cycles in provinces like Buenos Aires, where the Peronist presidential candidate, Eduardo Duhalde, had governed for eight years.

What accounts for the discrepancy between political motivations on the national and provincial level? It reflects the political success of convertibility nationally at the time. Menem voluntarily imposed austerity because it was necessary to maintaining low inflation through the country's exchange rate peg. At the same time, however, he furtively revamped domestic laws to allow provincial governors to finance their deficits externally and spend freely on their constituents. Let us examine how Menem played the game of austerity politics: signaling national austerity to international investors while removing spending constraints sub-nationally.

Facing few funding constraints, the Menem government used new privatization earnings and foreign borrowing to offset the 1999 economic downturn.[177] For example, privatization proceeds helped compensate for depleted recession-year tax revenues. The government had sold shares in Banco Hipotecario Nacional, the national mortgage bank, and Yacimientos Petroliferos Fiscales (YPF), the national oil company. These privatization windfalls boosted government income by US$2.6 billion, equivalent to about 5 percent of total 1999 revenues, helping rebuild its income-squeezed coffers.[178]

In addition to privatization windfalls, bond financing gave the government access to additional cash. Notwithstanding a global credit shock, the government's lower external funding needs in 1999 partly insulated it from rising interest rates, helping to preserve some financial maneuverability. The global credit squeeze – catalyzed by the 1997–98 Asian crisis – boosted Argentina's cost of international borrowing. However, it did not cut the country's credit access. Throughout 1998 and 1999, Argentina tapped global markets without much difficulty, outside of a brief negative credit shock related to Brazil's

---

[177] In 1999, real GDP growth declined by 3.4 percent, compared to a 3.9 percent increase a year earlier (CEPAL's Bases de Datos y Publicaciones Estadí sticas).

[178] Privatization income boosted government revenues by 1.6 percent in 1999 compared to 1998 (Economist Intelligence Unit, March 2000).

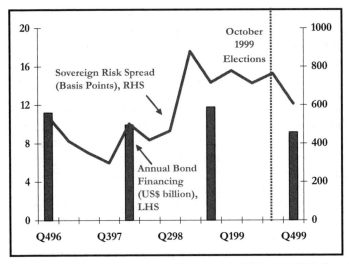

FIGURE 6.9. Argentina Taps Market Despite Tight Credit Before 1999 Elections.
Source: J. P. Morgan and Global Development Finance

January 1999 devaluation.[179] Figure 6.9 shows that Argentina's sovereign risk spread (or the premium it paid for its borrowing above U.S. treasury bonds yields) steadily rose throughout the year. Nevertheless, the country continued to issue bonds. Argentina's bond financing only fell in 1999 because the country's funding needs were one-fifth less than during 1998.

In light of its reduced borrowing needs, Argentina faced little friction raising funds from financial markets.[180] By April 1999, Menem's economic team had tapped more than US$4.5 billion, or sufficient funds to cover the government's financial requirements through September 1999.[181] Moreover, Argentina continued to readily borrow throughout the year. When the recession drove revenues lower, Menem padded government coffers with US$2 billion more of bond financing than initially planned.

In fact, Menem could have opened the spigot of international financing to fund even further expenditures, had he wished. Argentina had maintained its favorable high-yield investment ratings (BB and Ba3 for S&P and Moody's respectively)[182] since the height of the credit boom in 1997. These credit

---

[179] The collapse of Brazil's exchange-rate based stabilization effort, the Real Plan, in early 1999 temporarily shut Argentina out of global capital markets (Mussa 2002).

[180] Though credit markets temporarily closed following the Russian August 1998 default, Argentina was the first country to return to global financial markets, borrowing US$2.3 billion in the final quarter of 1998 (Economist Intelligence Unit, April 1999).

[181] IMF Letter of Intent, May 1999.

[182] Moody's, however, did place Argentina on credit watch on August 20, 1999, noting the potential for a future downgrade.

ratings were buoyed by strong economic fundamentals, including a decade-long economic expansion, averaging almost 6 percent per annum.[183]

While Argentina had the credit access to fund a politically timed expansion, its reliance on bond financing in part prevented it from deviating from IMF conditionality at the national level. Indeed, Argentina's credit standing was tied to its IMF "poster child" status, earned for eagerly embracing neoliberal reforms. In March 1999, the IMF gave the country its formal stamp of approval, commending Argentina's economic team. In its yearly Article IV consultation, the IMF executive directors praised the authorities' "prudent economic management, which helped the country withstand the recent turmoil affecting emerging market countries." The Fund also noted that "Argentina's fiscal situation improved markedly over the past two years, reflecting the strength of economic activity as well as tight expenditure control."[184] The Heritage Foundation, a conservative Washington think tank, also ranked Argentina's economy as among the "freest" in the world.[185]

Given Argentina's access to global capital markets, why didn't Menem engage in a pre-electoral spending spree? Was a savvy political operator like Menem intimidated by the risk of capital exit? With its IMF stamp of approval, capital withdrawal was unlikely before the next election. Menem could have likely tapped additional financing without unnerving markets.

The Argentine president maintained a tight budgetary belt to sustain convertibility. It was Menem's political gold, popularly credited for ending the country's tumultuous hyperinflation. Convertibilty's success relied on a credible commitment to parity between the U.S. dollar and Argentine peso. Price stability was thus linked to exchange rate stability, with budgetary discipline being the bedrock of the currency peg. This coupling meant that Menem not only had to send a signal of sound economic management to inflation-sensitive voters, but also global bond investors concerned about Argentina's ability to service its debt.

Pablo Guidotti, who served as Menem's Deputy Minister of the Economy and Treasury Secretary, discussed the link between investor confidence and inflation control under convertibility. As a member of Menem's economic team in 1999, Guidotti claimed the cabinet's priority was ensuring a smooth political transition under the currency board system to avoid a "fall back into instability."

Our main preoccupation was how to deal with the external situation that was developing after the Russian and Brazilian crises... In 1999, we were trying to reassure capital markets that the transition in Argentina would not change the economic program... We had joint seminars abroad to promote a view that anyone who would win would be

---

[183] Comisión Económica para América Latina y Caribe, *Anuario Estadístico de América Latina y Caribe 2006, Cuentas Nacionales en Dólares*.

[184] IMF Article IV, 1999.

[185] Corrales 2002b.

reasonable in economic terms ... At some point, this implied that we actually preferred to defend the image of Machinea [Presidential Candidate De La Rúa's chief economic advisor]. Because he was central bank president during hyperinflation, many people doubted that he was the right guy. So, we had to say to capital market that Machinea was a friend. We had to make sure that the election did not add any risk to the external environment.[186]

Guidotti's boss was Roque Fernández, who served as Menem's Minister of the Economy from 1996–1999. In our 2007 interview, Fernández admits that he did not support convertibility, but he feared its removal would stoke inflationary pressures. During his tenure, he recalled taking many politically unpopular stances to maintain austerity, including refusing to award a salary hike to teacher unions protesting in the Plaza de Mayo, Buenos Aires's central square. He also strongly dismissed the characterization of some Menem critics that the president's lack of budgetary discipline led to Argentina's 2001 crisis.

If you look at the statistical records, contrary to the official history let's say, you will notice that primary expenditures during the 1990s were almost constant during the whole periods in relation to GDP. Nothing from the statistical record supports that there was increase in primary expenditures during this period. Obviously, nominal expenditures increased, but not in terms of GDP. It's not true that there was a blow up in expenditure![187]

The official record supports Fernández's claims. According to the United Nation's Economic Commission for Latin America and the Caribbean, a trusted Latin American data hub since the days of Raúl Prebisch, primary government expenditures (net of interest payments) held fairly steady during the 1990s. Moreover, primary spending decreased during the second term of the Menem government, compared to his first term, which ended in 1995 (Figure 6.10). At the same time, Menem consistently met IMF fiscal targets during the final two years of his second term, with the exception of the third quarter of 1999.[188]

Moreover, notwithstanding the upcoming presidential elections, the authorities proposed spending cuts of US$0.5 billion in 1999. With the hopes of meeting Argentina's year-end fiscal target, the government unsuccessfully targeted cuts in teacher's salaries and educational programs.[189] Instead, public investment projects and ministerial operational budgets were the ultimate

---

[186] Author's interview with Pablo Guidotti conducted on May 28, 2007. Today, Guidotti is the Dean of the School of Government at Universidad Torcuato Di Tella, where I was a research affiliate during the Argentine phase of my field work.

[187] I interviewed former Economy Minister Roque Fernández on May 23, 2007, at the Universidad de CEMA. Fernández was Economy Minister under President Carlos Menem from August 1996 until December 1999. He also served as Menem's central bank president between February 1991 and August 1996.

[188] Guidotti Interview, May 2007; Economist Intelligence Unit's Country Reports 1998–1999.

[189] Strong opposition forced the government to withdraw some of the proposed cuts in education and social programs in 1999 (Economist Intelligence Unit, April 1999; Economist Intelligence Unit, December 1999).

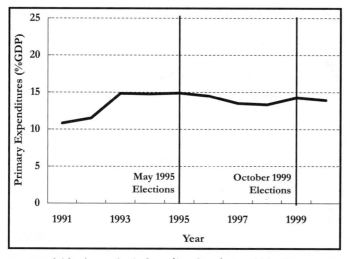

FIGURE 6.10. Argentina's Spending Steady in 1990s (Primary Expenditures, % GDP). *Source:* ECLAC and CEPAL

budgetary casualties.[190] Certainly, this belt-tightening behavior does not fit the classic electoral economic expansion.

Austerity paid dividends with voters. In a 1997 poll, 60 percent of Greater Buenos Aires residents wanted to maintain convertibility, compared to a mere 12 percent who instead favored its abolishment.[191] Not surprisingly, voters with painful memories of hyperinflation continued to support the institutional commitment to price stability. That said, austerity had a clear cost. During 1998 and 1999, 44–48 percent of national-level survey respondents rated their "personal economic situation as worse."[192] Although the employment situation had improved since 1995, Menem had clearly not achieved his 1995 campaign promise to "pulverize unemployment as [he] pulverized inflation."[193]

In the wake of a new recession, economic policy featured heavily in the 1999 campaign. Eduardo Duhalde, the governor of the politically important Buenos Aires province, battled Menem for control of the Peronist Party. Menem had unsuccessfully tried to reform the constitution to run for a third-term and prevent Duhalde's presidential bid.[194] Even after his constitutional reform was thwarted, however, Menem declined to back Duhalde's candidacy. In light

---

[190] IMF Letter of Intent, May 1999.
[191] The remaining 28 percent of residents who were polled did not voice an opinion (Weyland 2004).
[192] Graciela Römer 1999 as cited in Weyland 2004.
[193] Unemployment had fallen from its 18 percent peak in 1995, but continued to hover around 13–15 percent in 1998 and 1999 (World Bank's World Development Indicators).
[194] In 1998, in spite of the unconstitutionality of a third-term presidency, Menem fruitlessly tried to gain a court ruling permitting his candidacy (Levitsky 2000).

of their power struggle, President Menem gave little support to Duhalde's campaign and often appeared to "actively undermine" it.[195]

In response, Duhalde attempted to distance himself from Menem, harking back to more traditional *Justicialista* policies. The Buenos Aires governor supported higher government spending, rebuked the IMF's austerity, and called for a debt default.[196] He criticized the Fund for "strangling Argentina year after year" and complained that debt payments were "bleeding Argentina."[197]

By contrast, the FREPASO-UCR coalition, known formally as the Alianza por el Trabajo, la Justicia y la Educación, took a more conservative approach. It was careful to avoid criticizing convertibility, given the UCR's past leadership failures during the 1980's hyperinflation crisis.[198] Rather, the alliance sought to assuage voters, businesses, and markets that it had learned from past policy mistakes.

Capitalizing on Duhalde's misreading of the Argentine electorate, Alianza's presidential candidate, Fernando De la Rúa, sharply chastised Duhalde's irresponsibility. The Alianza candidate declared that "Argentina should honor the payment of its foreign debt and comply with its international obligations."

Regrettably for Duhalde, most voters opposed default in 1999 and De La Rú a eventually won the elections by a healthy margin.[199] Indeed, a July 1999 Gallup survey of 1,677 people nationwide found that only 11 percent of the voting age population supported a debt default.[200]

Duhalde also undermined domestic confidence with his comments, unnerving businesses and financial institutions with global operations. The presidential candidate caused a temporary surge in Argentina's sovereign risk premium, jolting the country's borrowing rates in international markets more than 1,000 basis points over U.S. Treasury debt during August 1999.[201]

In light of the split between Menem and Duhalde, Menem had little incentive to use macroeconomic policy to improve the election chances of his party rival. Even if we were to assume that Menem and Duhalde were more aligned than popularly perceived, it's unlikely policy would have been much different considering Menem's vested interest in maintaining his commitment to low inflation through convertibility.

According to Guidotti, their rivalry just made it easier for Menem to be fiscally conservative. In fact, in his role as Treasury Secretary, Guidotti claims that "he never received any requests to spend money to help the Peronist campaign."[202]

---

[195] Levitsky 2000.

[196] Di Tella 1999.

[197] Tomz 2001.

[198] Di Tella 1999.

[199] De La Rúa won the 1999 elections with 48.4 percent of the vote, compared to Eduardo Duhalde's 38.3 percent and Domingo Cavallo's 10.2 percent.

[200] Tomz 2001.

[201] J. P. Morgan's Emerging Market Bond Index.

[202] Author's interview with Pablo Guidotti 2007.

Over the course of the election year, there was some government stimulus, but not of the magnitude of a political business cycle.[203] The Menem government was never in danger of creating an electoral boom-bust cycle on the national-level. Argentina's small primary surplus shifted into deficit, but the overall fiscal balance deteriorated by a paltry 0.6 percentage points of GDP compared to the previous year.[204] This was a tepid fiscal expansion, particularly in a recession year. Under the currency board, credit conditions also remained very restrictive.[205]

In spite of Menem's relatively neutral policy stance, his Economy Minister Roque Fernández acknowledged that there were some line-item, election-year spending increases. They were aimed at assuaging political pressures from government ministers, who were active in party politics, and provincial politicians.

People in the cabinet were saying, look why are we going to leave US$30 billion in international reserves? The next government will spend it and why don't we spend it ourselves? That was the discussion in the cabinet. The political motivation was that even though many of them knew that the president was not going to be re-elected, many of them were participating in politics and they wanted to go on in the system with some other guys. There was a lot of pressure to spend in order to benefit the [Peronist] party, particularly in the province of Buenos Aires.[206]

In line with Fernández characterization of election-year spending pressures, line-item budgetary spending on public transfers to the provinces increased by about 0.7 percentage points of GDP.[207] Most importantly, however, national politicians also found clever new ways of delivering public goods to their political supporters within an ostensibly balanced budget framework.

Menem devised a strategy for simultaneously signaling national austerity to inflation-wary businesses and voters, while allowing local-level politicians to spend on their most important constituencies. Before the 1999 elections, Menem lifted the restriction that impeded provinces from using co-participation funds, or national economic transfers, as collateral to secure private bank loans. This allowed local governors to finance their deficits directly from private banks and global capital markets. By eliminating this restriction, the central government effectively removed the ceiling on provincial spending.[208]

---

[203] By contrast, the IMF had suggested that "an election-driven increase in public spending led to a sharp deterioration in fiscal discipline in 1999" (Weisner 2008).

[204] CEPAL's Estadísticas de Finanzas Públicas.

[205] M1, a measure of money supply that proxies the government's credit stance, increased by a meager 1.6 percent in 1999 (CEPAL's Bases de Datos y Publicaciones Estadística).

[206] Fernández interview, 2007.

[207] CEPAL's Estadísticas de Finanzas Públicas.

[208] Fernández and Cavallo disagreed about the relaxation of this restriction. Cavallo thought the restriction should be maintained to keep provincial spending in check, while Fernández

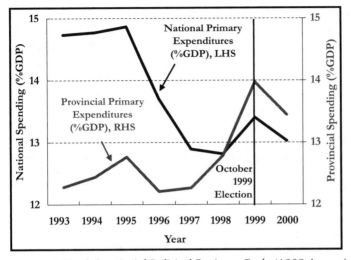

FIGURE 6.11. A Provincial Political Business Cycle (1999 Argentine Elections).
Source: Secretaría de Política Económica

Not surprisingly, without this ceiling, local governors spent considerably in the prelude to the 1999 elections.[209] Between 1997 and 1999, local provinces increased their spending by 2 percentage points of GDP (Figure 6.11).[210] For example, Eduardo Duhalde, the Peronist candidate and governor of Buenos Aires province, oversaw a massive expansion of public spending, transforming a small fiscal deficit in 1996 to a considerable deficit by 1999.[211] Most of the new spending was related to personnel increases – traditionally, a proxy for clientelism.[212] By contrast, national-level expenditures fell by more than 2 percentage points from mid-decade to the end of 1998, before undergoing a short and mild pre-election spurt in 1999.[213] While this spending erased the country's modest budget surplus, inflation rates declined throughout the

believed it was not the federal government's responsibility to dictate directives to autonomous provinces (based on author's interviews with Roque Fernández, Domingo Cavallo, and Jorge Baldrich in Buenos Aires, Argentina during May 2007).

[209] Indeed, Mussa (2002) finds that Argentina's fiscal problems arose from high levels of spending and a lack of fiscal discipline in the provinces, for which the central government ultimately had to assume responsibility.

[210] Dirección de Gastos Sociales Consolidados, Secretaría de Politica Económica.

[211] In 1996, the Province of Buenos Aires, where Duhalde was governor, had an average fiscal deficit of 7 percent of current revenues, which by 1999, increased to 25 percent of current revenues (Corrales 2002a).

[212] Between 1995 and 2000, personnel spending in the province of Buenos Aires increased by 61 percent; the overall increase of the other provinces was 10.2 percent (Corrales 2002a).

[213] MVA-Macroeconomía; Dirección de Gastos Sociales Consolidados, Secretaría de Politica Económica.

election period. Therefore, this modest countercyclical stimulus fell considerably short of an inflation-inducing, political electoral cycle.[214]

In summary, Menem's economic stance is best characterized as neutral during the 1999 election year. In spite of recessionary pressures, the political motivation of preserving price stability via convertibility trumped political pressures for new jobs and higher growth. Surprisingly, the government allowed unemployment to tick up (from 12.8 to 14.1 percent) in 1999 notwithstanding that year's presidential election.[215] Notably, Menem could have leveraged privatization windfalls and global markets to finance a political business cycle, but he chose not to use this policy latitude. The 1999 Argentine case lends support to the inflation-averse hypothesis (*H3*) that governments with a history of inflation crisis typically hope to achieve a combination of measured economic growth and inflation control. They generally do not fashion an electoral boom, even when they possess the financial means. Rather, shrouded in a cloak of austerity, they often find inventive methods of funneling benefits to political supporters in particular sectors of the economy, or in Argentina's case through clientelism at the local provincial level.

6.2.5. Brazil's 1994 and 2006 Elections: A New Macroeconomic Consensus

Unrelenting inflation and economic instability also sparked a shift in political logic in Brazil. Like Argentina and Chile, politicians who once supported aggressive government intervention to create jobs and growth, instead opted for greater policy prudence in the wake of inflationary mayhem. Following the steep political costs associated with hyperinflation, the politics of macroeconomic policy became less contentious and more technocratic. Presidents' economic teams increasingly consisted of professionally trained economists rather than political insiders. For instance, University of California-Berkeley economist Pedro Milan led the finance ministry for the first eight years following hyperinflation.

In the wake of the crisis, Brazil did not implement legal central bank independence under its fixed exchange rate system. However, over the course of the first several post-crisis years, President Cardoso granted greater operational autonomy to the central bank, particularly once it had swapped an exchange rate anchor for an inflation-targeting system. A new technocratic leadership was charged with the task of cementing the executive branch's commitment to price stability through the daily management of interest rates. Table 6.5 demonstrates the post-crisis shift in central bank president's professional training. Between 1993 and 2010, all of Brazil's central bank presidents possessed

[214] Argentina had a negative output gap (or a negative difference between actual and potential economic growth), providing a justification for countercyclical policies according to Keynesian thought.
[215] CEPAL's Bases de Datos y Publicaciones Estadística.

TABLE 6.5. *Brazil's Central Bank Professionalization under Democracy (1985–2010)*

Central Bank President	Term	Education
Pre-Inflation Crisis		
Fernão Carlos Botelho Bracher	1985–1987	BA, Law, Universidade de São Paulo
Francisco Roberto André Gros	1987	BA, Economics, Princeton University
Fernando Milliet de Oliveira	1987–88	N/A
Elmo de Araújo Camões	1988–89	N/A
Wadico Waldir Bucchi	1989–90	PhD, Business, Universidade de São Paulo
Ibrahim Eris	1990–91	PhD, Economics, Vanderbilt University
Francisco Roberto André Gros	1991–92	BA, Economics, Princeton University
Gustavo Jorge Laboissière Loyola	1992–93	PhD, Economics, Fundação Getulio Vargas
Paulo Cesar Ximenes Alves Ferreira	1993	Centro de Estudios Monetarios Latinoamericano
Post-Inflation Crisis		
Pedro Sampaio Malan	1993–1994	PhD, Economics, University of California-Berkeley
Persio Arida	1995	PhD, Economics, Massachusetts Institute of Technology
Gustavo Jorge Laboissière Loyola	1995–1997	PhD, Economics, Fundação Getulio Vargas
Gustavo Henrique de Barroso Franco	1997–1999	PhD, Economics, Harvard University
Arminio Fraga Neto	1999–2002	PhD, Economics, Princeton University
Henrique de Campos Meirelles	2003–2010	MBA, UFRJ; Advanced Management Program, Harvard University

advanced graduate training in economics and business, compared to only three presidents with such credentials in the pre-crisis period.

These technocratic communities internalized the lessons of Brazil's hyper-inflation years, operating with a mission of managing inflationary expectations to avoid a repeat of past policy mistakes made during the Sarney and Collor de Mello administrations.

José Sarney, Brazil's first president following the Figueiredo military dicta-torship, took office in 1985.[216] In response to massive redistributive pressures during the democratic transition, he followed a highly interventionist economic policy, even after igniting inflation. Notwithstanding a neoliberal doctrine that was en vogue in the West, the Brazilian president believed that austerity was an ineffective solution to the country's inflationary woes. Sarney maintained that tight monetary and fiscal policies had little traction over inflationary inertia, instead producing the twin troubles of recession and inflation,

---

[216] The opposition candidate, Tancredo Neves, initially won the November 1984 elections, but his untimely pre-inaugural death propelled Sarney into the presidency.

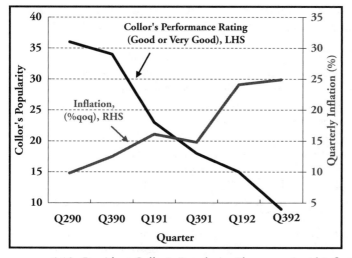

FIGURE 6.12. President Collor's Popularity Plummets Amid Inflationary Chaos.
Source: Datafolha Opinião Pública; Oxhom and Cuatenzeiler 1998

popularly known as stagflation.[217] His rejection of economic orthodoxy suggests that neoliberal diffusion was not a sufficient condition to explain the adoption of austerity. Otherwise, Sarney would have caved to international pressures for fiscal rectitude from the IMF and global bankers.

Rather, before the November 1986 elections, Sarney oversaw a classic political business cycle, massively expanding the public deficit to boost the economy. The central bank covered the fiscal deficit by printing money. To control inflation, the Sarney economic team designed the heterodox Cruzado Plan[218] that featured wage and price controls.

At first, this policy mix of lax monetary and fiscal policies provided Sarney with considerable political gains. The governing coalition, Partido do Movimento Democrático Brasileiro (PMDB), won an absolute majority in the Chamber of Deputies and all but one gubernatorial race.[219]

Despite these short-run political gains, inflation soon reared its ugly head. Once unleashed, inflation was a beast that Sarney and his successor, Fernando Collor de Mello,[220] tried to tame albeit unsuccessfully.

As inflation accelerated, both presidents' popularity declined. Figure 6.12 shows the inverse relationship between President Collor's job approval and

[217] Rabello de Castro and Ronci 1991.
[218] The Cruzado Plan was a heterodox economic stabilization program, similar to the Austral Plan in Argentina. Combining initial wage readjustments with price and wage freezes and the creation of a new currency, it hoped to control inflation (Rabello and Ronci 1991; Fishlow 1997).
[219] PMDB won 48 percent of the seats in the Chamber of Deputies.
[220] Collor defeated Lula of the Workers' Party in the 1989 presidential elections.

inflation. Despite multiple stabilization attempts,[221] hyperinflation emerged by the end of the decade, leaving the broken reputations of political parties and presidents in its wake.[222]

Brazil's 1994 Elections. Given Brazil's ongoing inflationary bedlam, it is not surprising that economic stabilization took center stage during the 1994 elections. Fernando Henrique Cardoso, President Itamar Franco's finance minister, was making a presidential bid.

Should Cardoso have desired, he could have used macroeconomic policy tools to create a political business cycle. Without an independent central bank,[223] he could have continued the political practice of financing government deficits with central bank credit. But, Cardoso instead opted for a disciplined economic policy that provided inflation control in an election year, even if it meant fewer new jobs. Why?

In countries with a history of economic volatility, protecting voter incomes with price stability often proves more successful at securing the economic vote than electoral expansions. In fact, repeated bouts of hyperinflation had instilled a societal acceptance of economic austerity among political elites and the broader population. During the fall of 1993, polls showed that 91 percent of respondents rated Brazil's economic situation as "poor or very poor," and Brazilians perceived the inflationary menace as the "single gravest problem" confronting them.[224]

Capitalizing on this shift in voter priorities, Finance Minister Cardoso implemented the Real Plan on July 1, 1994. Although it was a mere three months before elections, the plan bravely heralded a fiscal adjustment. It also called for a new currency, the real, which was initially anchored to the U.S. dollar.[225]

---

[221] Under the Collor Plan, the administration began to focus on fiscal adjustment in order to get inflation under control. However, the economic team met widespread resistance among interest groups, state governors, and congressional politicians (Weyland 2004).

[222] The failure of Collor's stabilization efforts and his weak base of support increased his political vulnerability. Accused of fraud and corruption, Collor resigned in December 1992 amid a wave of peaceful demonstrations calling for his ouster.

[223] The Brazilian Central Bank typically followed the guidelines of the National Monetary Council, which was headed by Cardoso, the Minister of Finance. Brazil had approved a constitutional amendment in the 1980s prohibiting the monetization of budget deficits. Nonetheless, short-term financing of budgetary shortfalls was permitted, leaving the central bank vulnerable to political pressures to spend (Ribeiro 2002).

[224] Weyland 2004.

[225] The new currency unit was created by first establishing a dual domestic price system. One set of prices was linked to the old cruzeiro, which continued to circulate. At the same time, a new monetary unit, called the unidade real de valor (URV), was created. The URV's value rose by 40 percent or more per month (it was readjusted daily and pegged to the dollar), whereas the cruzeiro did not change in value. The government also urged economic actors to adopt the URV in order to smooth the transition. The URV was eventually translated into the Real in July of 1994. Compared to previous stabilization plans, the Real Plan was unique because it used the market for monetary conversion, rather than price and wage freezes (Fishlow 1997).

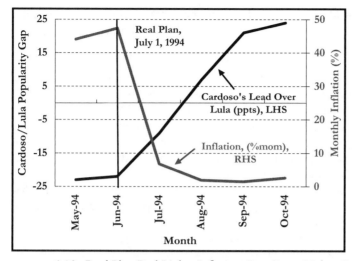

FIGURE 6.13. Real Plan Red Lights Inflation, But Green Lights Cardoso's Candidacy.
Source: Datafolha Opinião Pública and EIU Country Data

Reminiscent of Argentina's convertibility scheme, tight monetary policy and a stable currency were designed to rein in inflation.

In line with the plan, Franco's economic team tightened both monetary and budgetary policy during the election year. In fact, they built up the budget surplus by a whopping 3 percentage points of GDP in 1994 compared to one year earlier.[226] In response to this austerity, inflation plummeted during the second half of 1994.

Cardoso, the candidate of continuity, witnessed his popular support boom in the weeks following the introduction of the Real Plan. Before its introduction, the former finance minister had trailed Luiz Inácio "Lula" da Silva of Brazil's Partido dos Trabalhadores (PT)[227] by as much as 22 percentage points in mid-June.[228] In contrast to Cardoso's focus on inflation stabilization, Lula ran a more traditional campaign, criticizing stabilization and promising social spending, jobs, and growth. In light of the Real Plan's success in curbing inflation, however, Cardoso displaced Lula as vote leader by mid-August[229] (Figure 6.13). Cardoso's team not only tamed inflation, but also delivered moderate economic growth of nearly 5.5 percent, helping boost real incomes (Figure 2.5 in Chapter 2).[230] With Lula in his rearview mirror, Cardoso secured

---

[226] They ended the year with a budget surplus of 5.6 percent of GDP, withdrawing about 3 percentage points of stimulus from the economy compared to 1993 (CEPAL's Bases de Datos y Publicaciones Estadística).

[227] The PT is a center-left social democratic party, originally founded by intellectuals, artists, and workers in 1980.

[228] Datafolha Opinião Pública 1994.

[229] Datafolha Opinião Pública 1994.

[230] World Development Indicators.

an impressive landslide victory in the October 1994 elections.[231] Ironically, inflation stabilization and a political austerity cycle helped propel Cardoso to victory.

Brazil's 2006 Elections. In a twist of fate, by the 2006 elections, Lula was making a reelection bid with a platform that promised a continuation of the economic discipline he first inherited from Cardoso in 2002. It was a departure from his radical discourse from earlier unsuccessful presidential campaigns that featured fiery anti-capitalist rhetoric. Rather, his first victorious presidential campaign in 2002 had supplanted talk of debt defaults and re-nationalizations with market-friendly banter about maintaining economic orthodoxy.

After governing Brazil with budget surpluses and inflation targeting for four years, Lula pledged to maintain these economic policies during the 2006 elections. He only slightly radicalized his political discourse, rebuffing talk of any privatization initiatives. It was difficult to differentiate between Lula and his rival PSDB candidate, Geraldo Alckmin, who ran under the drab slogan of "same policies, but better managed."

Like Cardoso – a left-leaning sociologist turned financial market poster child – Lula had transformed into a president that supported both fiscal responsibility and social activism. Similar to the post-Pinochet Chilean compromise, Lula hoped to reduce income inequality, unemployment, and poverty, but within the context of economic stability. The Brazilian president's economic team was careful to signal to inflation-averse voters and markets that he would not tolerate complacency about budget deficits nor inflation.[232] Lula did not want to be associated with the return of the inflationary menace. Indeed, twelve years after Cardoso's real plan successfully curbed inflation, price stability and economic discipline continued to yield a hefty political reward.

Recall that the long-lasting embrace of economic discipline is an important part of political austerity cycle theory. Whereas other political economy scholars have implied that budget discipline is a short-term phenomenon, I have argued that even during periods of economic stability, politicians choose austerity to signal their sound economic management to inflation-averse markets and voters.[233]

---

[231] Cardoso (PSDB) won a first-round victory against Lula (PT), taking 54.3 percent of the votes, compared to Lula's 27 percent.

[232] Santiso 2006; Cardim de Carvalho 2007; Amann and Baier 2009.

[233] Weyland (2004), for instance, makes an important contribution to the economic reform literature. Employing prospect theory, Weyland suggests that when policy makers face crisis conditions, they are more likely to be in a domain of losses, and hence, exhibit risk-seeing behavior. Under these conditions, goverment leaders choose drastic neoliberal measures, with hopes of restoring economic growth. In contrast to Weyland, I suggest that the saliency of past inflationary crises makes both voters and politicians more cautious; and hence, they choose safer, market-friendly policies that do not risk inflation or capital flight. Hence, austerity policies are often the risk-averse, and not the risk-oriented choice.

If Lula wanted to prime the economic pump, hefty budget surpluses and a strong currency awarded the Brazilian president sizeable policy maneuverability. Greater electoral spending would not have gravely eroded the government's surplus or undermined a resilient Brazilian real. Moreover, windfall oil and gas royalties yielded stronger-than-expected 2005 revenues, further bolstering public finances.[234]

Capital markets also presented Lula with a possible funding source. Unlike the 1998 and 2002 elections where external credit markets posed tight policy restrictions (which I examine in Chapter 7), Lula could have tapped international investors for more financing. Brazil's standing in international credit markets had improved substantially during Lula's first term. Between 2003 and 2006, the country's credit rating jumped several notches on both Standard & Poor's and Moody's long-term credit rating scales.[235] Brazil's sovereign risk spread (or the premium it paid for its international borrowing above U.S. treasury bonds yields) also declined dramatically since Lula's first days in office.[236] In fact, benevolent market conditions in late 2005 allowed Brazil to pre-finance its 2006 external debt payment obligations.[237]

Whereas Brazil nominally had the credit access to fund a politically timed expansion, its reliance on bond markets (which held almost two-thirds of Brazil's external financing), only raised the importance of signaling price stability during elections. Lula may have liked to deliver political rewards through broad-based aggressive stimulus, but would have risked raising Brazil's risk premium and undermining economic confidence in the nation. Lula had learned from Brazil's past, instead reinforcing the left's commitment to inflation control. In fact, the Brazilian president publicly highlighted that "controlled inflation represents an extraordinary gain for salaried workers."[238]

In the final two years of Lula's term, Finance Minister Antonio Palocci and his economic team oversaw a steady rise in the primary budget surplus, climbing by about one-half percentage point to 3.9 percent of GDP.[239] At the same time, Brazil handily met its inflation target in 2005, the year before elections. The Comitê de Política Monetária (or Copom, Brazil's monetary policy committee) took advantage of some of the country's policy flexibility. It steadily cut interest

---

[234] Economist Intelligence Unit Country Report, December 2005.

[235] S&P increased Brazil's sovereign rating by two credit notches from B+ in 2003 to BB in 2006; Moody's raised Brazil's sovereign rating by three notches from B2 in 2003 to Ba2 in 2006.

[236] Brazil's sovereign risk spread fell from a 13 percentage point premium over U.S. treasury bonds in January 2003 to a mere 2 percentage point premium in 2006.

[237] Brazil issued US$1.5 billion in real-denominated foreign bonds (the first issue on international markets) to help cover its 2006 foreign debt service. Indeed, after new global bond issuance in Brazil fell by almost half in 2002 (or by US$3.1 billion), reaching a mere US$4.8 billion, it averaged US$7.3 billion during the first three years of the Lula administration (Global Development Finance; Economist Intelligence Unit Country Report, December 2005).

[238] *Reuters*, June 18, 2007.

[239] CEPAL's Bases de Datos y Publicaciones Estadística.

rates between 2005 and 2006, but not enough to undercut the government's tight fiscal policy stance.[240]

The continuity of his economic team's fiscal austerity commitment and its reluctance to engage in budgetary populism, prompted former President Cardoso, his fiercest political competitor in the 1990s to remark:

Only Nixon could go to China and only Lula could show the world that the Latin American left could run a stable modern economy.[241]

Although we do not observe a political business cycle in Brazil in 2006, we do see some minor tinkering with the timing of public expenditures. For instance, in a political maneuver straight from the pages of U.S. President Nixon's playbook, Lula front-loaded December pension payments to September – one month before the first-round of elections.[242] The Brazilian president also oversaw mild line-item increases in public salaries and public works projects, amounting to less than 1 percent of total government expenditures.[243] Notwithstanding the lack of a political business cycle, however, Lula won the 2006 election in a second-round landslide victory, capturing 61 percent of the vote.

In summary, both Cardoso (a leftist thinker) and Lula (a leftist activist) prioritized inflation stabilization over more rapid job and growth creation. In fact, the combined Lula and Cardoso years (1995–2006) produced an average economic growth rate of 2.7 percent, almost half of Brazil's 5.0 rate of trend growth.[244] Both leaders preferred to tackle Brazil's outstanding development difficulties – poverty, income inequality, and unemployment – within a context of budgetary discipline, even during election periods.

6.3. SUMMARY

In this chapter, we have examined inflation-averse political behavior. Notwithstanding a political economy literature that expects a political business cycle in newer democracies, Latin American presidents often surprisingly choose austerity. With their political survival at stake, why would politicians pursue such a policy goal?

In developed countries, rational expectation scholars have suggested that politicians might fear retribution from fiscally conservative voters. But, why

---

[240] The Comitê de Política Monetária cut Brazil's key interest rate, the SELIC rate, by 6 percentage points to 13.75 percent between May 2005 and October 2006 (Economist Intelligence Unit Country Report, December 2005).

[241] Cardoso 2006.

[242] Economist Intelligence Unit Country Report, December 2005.

[243] CEPAL's Bases de Datos y Publicaciones Estadística.

[244] Brazil's trend growth was calculated using the Hodrick-Prescott filter on the change in real GDP growth.

would politicians in a developing region characterized by leftist tendencies believe voters are fiscally conservative? What is austerity's political payoff?

Political austerity theory anticipates that the saliency of past inflationary crises has shifted economic policy toward the right in Latin America. Viewing economic policy through the lens of their own macroeconomic histories, politicians have avoided highly expansionary policies that risk a return of the political horrors associated with hyperinflation.

What explains the political saliency of inflation aversion even years after economic crises? What is the political benefit of preserving these policy lessons? Political and technocratic elites believe that a commitment to low inflation reaps significant political rewards. Price stability protects the incomes of middle-class and poor voters that were previously devastated by hyperinflation. Not surprisingly, public opinion polls in the wake of these crises often show that inflation is a top national concern. Even years beyond a crisis, however, the severity of past price shocks prompts political elites to signal their governance credentials to an expanded constituency that has a low inflation tolerance. Notwithstanding the expected macroeconomic partisan divide in the political economy literature, partisan lines are blurred in Latin America. Left-leaning elites believe they too can earn political credibility by anchoring inflation.

To test inflation-aversion's effect on the electoral boom-bust cycles, I first relaxed the assumption that presidents are risk-seeking, or willing to gamble with inflation to improve the election-year economy. I then examined the effect of the financing availability on presidents' ostensible frugality, asking if politicians veer from economic discipline when states have resources.

I find that inflation-averse politicians across time and space maintain their commitment to economic discipline, and often most pronouncedly during election years. They govern within the confines of an orthodox budgetary framework that delivers growth, but also tempered inflation. Moreover, booming commodity exports, deferential central bankers, and privatization proceeds do not alter their commitment. Rather, they are more likely to target political supporters by reallocating spending (such as public sector wage hikes, public works projects, and social transfers) within the budget or altering their timing to coincide with elections. Alternatively, politicians also sometimes take a less transparent course, feigning macroeconomic balance while delivering discretionary spending to important economic sectors, or in Argentina's case politically sensitive provincial levels of government.

7

The Political Austerity Cycle

In the fall of 2008, Dublin-based Depfa Bank flapped its funding wings, creating a financial tornado in Wisconsin's 900-student Whitefish Bay High School. Depfa, an Irish bank specializing in municipal bond investments, had lent US$165 million to Wisconsin's school district. When Depfa stumbled into a cash-crunch, the Irish bank immediately withdrew funds from many of its U.S. municipal investments, including Whitefish Bay. Without funding from creditors like Depfa, the Wisconsin school district resigned to its fate of budget cuts, slashing spending initiatives and teacher retirement payouts.

A financial motif for U.S. municipalities, the 2008 global financial crisis tightened foreign financial spigots for many cash-strapped local governments.[1] For instance, the New York Metropolitan Transit Authority (MTA), deeply dependent on external financing from creditors like Depfa, approved a 7.5 percent increase in subway fares and tolls between 2010 and 2015 to plug its funding deficit.[2] Ironically, the 2008 credit crisis that rippled through the United States is a familiar plight for many Latin American governments that repeatedly incurred "sudden stops" to their financing during the 1990s.[3]

Global finance has become a key player in domestic politics. The Whitefish Bay school district and the New York MTA did not want to cut teacher pensions or raise subway fares, but without funding from foreign creditors, they were left with few alternatives. These quandaries parallel the predicament of many Latin American countries during periods of high dependence on international bond markets.

National and local politicians are often compelled by financial market pressures to make undesirable political choices. Even when the most left-leaning

---

[1] *Morning Edition*, National Public Radio, November 4, 2008.
[2] *MTA Press Release*, July 28, 2010.
[3] See Chapters 1 and 2 for a more extensive discussion of the economics literature on sudden stops.

Latin American politicians rely on bond markets for a large share of their financing needs, they become vulnerable to swift capital reversals and interest rate shocks. Investors often become most skittish during periods of electoral uncertainty, prompting politicians to be cautious stewards of the economy. They implement conservative policies that promise market-friendly low inflation, rather than high-growth, high-inflation electoral cycles.

For instance, Hugo Chávez, who led a 1992 coup against Venezuela's neoliberal reforms, adopted orthodox policies when faced with a commodity crash and credit crunch early in his presidency in 1999. Argentine President Carlos Menem also cut public salaries during his 1995 election campaign when a regional credit crunch terrorized an already inflation-sensitive electorate. Similarly, when contagion pressures from the East Asian Crisis threatened to shut down financial markets, Brazilian President Fernando Henrique Cardoso announced an economic adjustment package. He raised taxes and reduced spending notwithstanding his 1998 reelection bid.

If austerity is sometimes a prudent economic choice, when is austerity a wise political choice? Throughout this book, I have argued that inflation control is an important public good in countries that have suffered from very high and hyperinflations. After these devastating distributive shocks, politicians and their economic teams internalized the dangers of runaway inflation, becoming more tempered in their approach to macroeconomic policy. They searched for alternative ways to target their political supporters beyond aggressive macroeconomic intervention. As a result, these inflationary crises created the space for elite and popular acceptance of inflation-curbing monetarist policies. In such an environment, providing jobs and growth remains an important political goal, but deflation becomes more politically palatable. That said, politicians certainly want to avoid a grim deflationary spiral of falling inflation and growth. If this is the case, what explains the advent of the most severe form of the political austerity cycle?

7.1. THE CASE OF THE CASH-STRAPPED, INFLATION-SCARRED POLITICIAN

Remember that politicians typically plan electoral economic strategies years in advance because of the lag between economic policy choices and outcomes. In light of inflation's political saliency, however, they choose a more measured political strategy than crafting a political business cycle. Presidents and their economic teams voluntarily opt for austerity to control inflation. Pursuing such policies necessitates a delicate balance, however.

It hinges on governments' fiscal space, or their financial means to fund additional expenditures. When they can tap alternative non-market revenues and funding (such as commodity income, privatization proceeds, and bank lending), they can avoid the interest rates swings and credit downturns that are characteristic of high bond market indebtedness. Governments have the

TABLE 7.1. *Macroecomonic Policy Expectations: The Spendthrift or the Miser?*

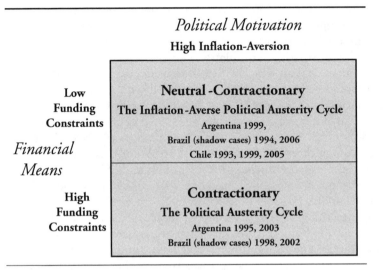

Political Motivation	
High Inflation-Aversion	

Financial Means	
Low Funding Constraints	**Neutral -Contractionary** The Inflation-Averse Political Austerity Cycle Argentina 1999, Brazil (shadow cases) 1994, 2006 Chile 1993, 1999, 2005
High Funding Constraints	**Contractionary** The Political Austerity Cycle Argentina 1995, 2003 Brazil (shadow cases) 1998, 2002

capacity to target moderate growth and low inflation with a neutral mix of economic policies.

During the last chapter, for instance, we observed that inflation-averse politicians with ample fiscal space were successful at delivering these public goods to the electorate. If the economy slowed more than initially planned, windfall commodity and privatization revenues helped fund new spending and support growth. However, politicians were careful to keep their interventions to a minimum and avoid igniting inflation (see Table 7.1 for a review of these cases).

By contrast, when politicians are highly reliant on global markets for their financing, they risk sudden cessations of financing that rapidly channel through to the real economy. To regain market confidence and reattract capital flows, politicians must convince creditors of their debt servicing capacity, often signaling their creditworthiness by complying with conditionality. They slash spending and hike interest rates, even if these actions slow economic growth and destroy jobs.[4] During a credit shock that threatens to debilitate growth, such orthodox policies often appear to be the lesser of two evils.

How do governments contain the political fallout from such a severe brand of austerity? When facing such intense market pressures, Latin American presidents must appease two levels of "constituents": international investors and key domestic supporters. To achieve these seemingly conflicting policy goals,

---

[4] See Chapter 2.

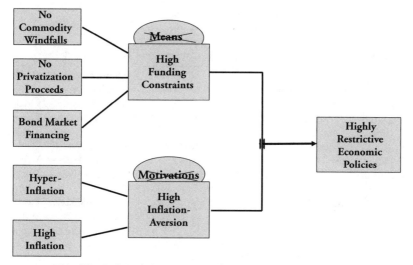

FIGURE 7.1. The Political Austerity Cycle (H4).

politicians often govern with macroeconomic orthodoxy, while using their considerable executive powers to extend micro-level benefits. For example, Chile is the region's epitome of institutional development, yet the president has substantial control over public finances. Not surprisingly, Chilean leaders often use this extensive policy discretion to target line-item expenditures (such as public salaries or public works spending) to key supporters within an orthodox budget framework.

7.1.1. Political Austerity Cycle Hypothesis (H4)

The political austerity hypothesis (H_4) examines the most constraining electoral circumstances, when politicians possess neither the financial means nor the political motivation to fashion a political business cycle. Politicians who prefer stability-oriented policies are compelled by financial market pressures to intensify their economic orthodoxy. Their economic agendas are highly restrictive, characterized by contractionary macroeconomic policies.

Figure 7.1 provides a diagram of the causal logic of policy making under these conditions. Reliant on bond market financing, politicians pursue miserly economic policies in hopes of placating both their creditors and a perceived inflation-sensitive electorate.

In the following pages, I test this most acute form of the political austerity cycle. Employing four comparative election cases, I adjudicate between the *political austerity hypothesis* and competing explanations for Latin America's fiscal rectitude: IMF conditionality, neoliberal policy diffusion, and central bank independence. I find that institutional checks and balances and policy

TABLE 7.2. *Case Study Overview (H3 and H4)*

Country	Chief Executive	Election Year	Inflation-Aversion?	Market Constraints?	Political Business Cycle?
Chile	Patricio Aylwin	1993	Y	N	Inflation-Averse PAC
Brazil	Itamar Franco	1994	Y	N	Inflation-Averse PAC
Argentina	Carlos Menem	1995	Y	Y	Political Austerity Cycle
Brazil	Fernando Henrique Cardoso	1998	Y	Y	Political Austerity Cycle
Chile	Eduardo Frei	1999	Y	N	Inflation-Averse PAC
Argentina	Carlos Menem	1999	Y	N	Inflation-Averse PAC
Brazil	Fernando Henrique Cardoso	2002	Y	Y	Political Austerity Cycle
Argentina	Eduardo Duhalde	2003	Y	Y	Political Austerity Cycle
Chile	Ricardo Lagos	2005	Y	N	Inflation-Averse PAC
Brazil	Luiz Inácio 'Lula' da Silva	2006	Y	N	Inflation-Averse PAC

diffusion are contributing, but not sufficient explanations for the prevalence of conservative policy making.

Table 7.2 outlines the expected outcomes for these comparative cases, along with the inflation-aversion case results from Chapter 6 (the highlighted cases are for the current chapter; they are also grouped by their policy making dimensions in Table 7.1).

7.2. COMPARATIVE CASE STUDY EVIDENCE

The four comparative case studies of Argentine and Brazilian elections are also mapped chronologically below (Figure 7.2). In all of these cases, inflation-rattled politicians want to deliver the foundations of a sound, stable political economy featuring balanced growth and inflation control. Notwithstanding these modest economic goals, the structural shift from a centralized to a decentralized financing regime has created formidable funding obstacles. When highly indebted governments have a strong reliance on bond market financing, they are vulnerable to election-induced "sudden stops," or abrupt foreign credit reversals. If political austerity theory is correct, the combination of these high-external funding constraints and domestic economic risk-aversion should yield a deflationary electoral cycle.

Argentina 1995	Brazil 1998	Brazil 2002	Argentina 2003

FIGURE 7.2. The Political Austerity Cycle (H4).

7.2.1. Argentina's Political Plight: A Credit-Crunch Heightens the Anti-Inflation Bias

Riding a wave of popularity as an inflation hawk, President Carlos Saúl Menem faced a political dilemma heading into the 1995 Argentine elections.[5] After taming hyperinflation during his first term yielded political gold, the Peronist President's reelection bid presented a paradox of success. Should Menem reinforce his commitment to the economic orthodoxy that allowed him to squash inflation? Or, should he instead drift from economic discipline to contain convertibility's negative side effects: rising unemployment and falling wages? In light of the high popular approval for the government's anti-inflation plan known as convertibility, President Menem and his economic team pursued a tempered policy mix that prioritized inflation control and moderate growth. Within this austere framework, they also hoped to alleviate some growing discontent by directing line-item spending to popular poverty programs and public works projects.

However, an unexpected financial maelstrom forced the government into a more deflationary policy stance than initially planned. A global credit crunch, dubbed the Tequila crisis for its Mexican origin, threatened to catapult Argentina back into crisis, renewing economic austerity's high political premium. It also temporarily shut down Argentina's spigot of international financing. In order to assuage wary bondholders of the Argentine government's good credit standing, Menem had to intensify his government's restrictive policy stance. Inflation aversion ultimately combined with bond market funding constraints to yield the most severe form of a political austerity cycle in the prelude to the 1995 elections.

Argentina's 1995 Elections. Menem's popularity throughout his first term reflected his success with inflation stabilization. In March 1991, when Finance Minister Domingo Cavallo first implemented the convertibility plan,[6] inflation fell dramatically,[7] and popular support for Menem's economic policies nearly doubled.[8]

---

[5] Under the Pacto de Olivos, Raul Alfonsín and Carlos Menem cut a political deal. The UCR opposition would support a constitutional amendment permitting Menem (PJ) to run for a second-term. In exchange, Menem would accept some institutional constraints on the presidency, including limitations on executive decrees.

[6] Beginning April 1, 1991, the convertibility plan allowed the Argentine peso to be freely convertible into dollars at parity. To support the peso, the Congress enacted a law prohibiting the central bank from printing money to cover budget deficits without the backing of gold or currency reserves.

[7] Inflation fell from a 27 percent month over month rate in February 1991 to a paltry 0.6 percent by December 1991.

[8] The proportion of people who approved of Menem's job performance climbed from 32 percent in April 1991 to 65 percent by the end of that year (Echegary and Elordi 2001; Stokes 2001).

Indeed, price stability was an important determinant of Menem's political support. During Menem's first administration, inflation was inversely correlated with the president's approval ratings; the lower the inflation rate, the greater Menem's popular appeal.[9]

Notably, public opinion polls also showed surprisingly high levels of support for Menem's economic austerity. In 1995, 43 percent of respondents supported "controlling the public deficit even if it means reducing personnel and social expenditures."[10] Moreover, the convertibility plan itself garnered more than 45 percent approval during late 1994.[11]

Menem and his economic team hoped to benefit from austerity. By avoiding the trauma of past inflation, they could build support among a widespread domestic coalition favoring low inflation. Many middle-class families and private sector firms had accumulated debts in foreign currency,[12] prompting Menem to wager that many voters would cheer price stability, even at the cost of some potential new jobs.

Capitalizing on these inflation fears, Menem's political rhetoric often emphasized the perils of high inflation. For example, in April 1990, Menem declared "I have certainty that we are on the right path," warning that the only other alternative was a return to "a system that drove us to the depths of hyperinflation and worse still, to the depths of national hyper-frustration, to hyper-poverty."[13]

During my 2007 field research, I interviewed Domingo Cavallo, Menem's economic advisor and architect of convertibility,[14] who underscored the political importance of taming inflation.

In Latin America, inflation is the most important determinant of public opinion. Inflation poses the gravest political risk. The inflation, stagflation, and hyperinflation phenomenon is very Latin American . . . with [our] hyperinflation history, parties that allow inflation lose elections and parties that control inflation win elections . . . populism only works in the context of economic stability.[15]

After taming inflation, however, Menem was faced with a political catch-22 before the 1995 elections. He could strengthen his commitment to convertibility, the hallmark of his political success. Alternatively, the Argentine president could address convertibility's weaknesses, namely rising unemployment and falling real wages (Figure 7.3). Aggressively pursuing the economic growth

---

[9] Echegaray and Elordi 2001; Stokes 2001.

[10] Survey participants were asked, "Which aspects of the economic model do you agree with, and which do you disagree with?" (Romer & Associates 1995 as cited in Stokes 2001.)

[11] Mora y Araujo & Asociados, 1999 as cited in Weyland (2004).

[12] The private sector issued almost $9 billion in bonds denominated in foreign currencies between 1992 and 1995. Credit in dollars in the banking system also increased by 12.5 billion pesos between 1992 and 1995, or 65 percent of all banking credit (Diaz-Bonilla and Schamis 2001).

[13] Echegaray and Elordi 2001; Stokes 2001.

[14] I conducted the original interview with former Economy Minister Domingo Cavallo on May 25, 2007, during my field research in Buenos Aires, Argentina. I translated the text from our conversation.

[15] Cavallo interview, May 2007.

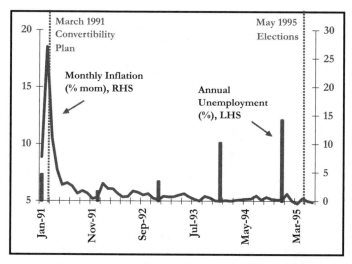

FIGURE 7.3. Menem's Political Dilemma: Inflation Stabilization vs. Unemployment.
Source: International Financial Statistics and World Development Indicators.

path, however, threatened to undermine Menem's convertibility commitment, which was premised on fiscal discipline. It was a delicate policy pendulum, swinging between jobs and price stability.

Not surprisingly, Menem chose to preserve convertibility, a vital political asset. Before the Tequila crisis, an *inflation-averse political austerity cycle* (*H3*) seemed likely. President Menem was clearly inflation-averse, but when possible he also sought to deliver jobs, growth, and social benefits.

Within the overall macroeconomic framework, the Argentine president tried to mitigate social pressures. Worried about worsening the fiscal burden, the Menem government understood that large-scale employment programs or government-administered wage hikes were out of the question.

His economic team instead implemented low-cost social-assistance programs to help quell social discontents. These programs were comprised of about US$1 billion in new spending on anti-poverty and public infrastructure initiatives.[16] They had important political rewards, including reinforcing clientelistic networks of the Peronist movement that were crucial to "getting out the vote" among Argentina's poor populations.[17] In fact, scholars have found that Argentine politicians often direct material benefits to poorer citizens in return for their votes.[18]

---

[16] They included US$200 million for anti-poverty programs administered by the Secretaría de Dearrollo Social and US$700 million from the federal government used by Eduardo Duhalde, the Peronist Governor of Buenos Aires province, to create a new infrastructure and social program called the Fondo de Reparación Histórica del Conurbano Bonaerense.

[17] Weyland 2004.

[18] Levitsky 2003; Stokes 2005.

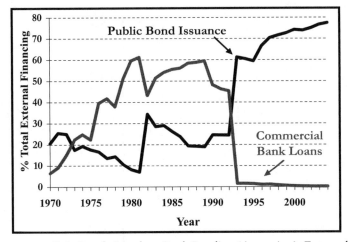

FIGURE 7.4. Bonds Supplant Bank Lending (Argentina's External Financing).
Source: Global Development Finance.

Notwithstanding these line-item initiatives, Menem oversaw a tempered budgetary expansion. Against the backdrop of growing social demands for wage hikes and redistribution, the new spending – along with a fall in government revenues – cut Argentina's humble budget surplus in half.[19] At the same time, however, Argentina's currency board ensured a commitment to tight monetary policy. The combination of tight monetary policy and mildly stimulative fiscal policy yielded a neutral-to-contractionary overall economic policy mix.

The Tequila shock changed this policy picture, however, restricting the government's scope for policy action. Under Menem, Argentina had become the poster child for emerging market bond markets. In April 1993, Argentina's Brady restructuring converted the country's US$25.5 billion in defaulted commercial bank loans into market-traded debt. Following this deal, Argentina's international bonds amounted to about two-thirds of the country's total external debt (Figure 7.4).[20] In nominal terms, Argentina, along with Brazil and Mexico, becomes one of the most indebted emerging market countries.

The shift to decentralized finance renewed Argentina's access to global finance in an era of diminished bank lending. However, credit access came at a high cost. In contrast to the long-term view of vested international bankers that looked beyond economic downturns, bond market investors often withdrew their financing immediately during hard times.

---

[19] Argentina's primary fiscal surplus of 1.4 percent of GDP shrank by 1.0 percentage point between 1993 and 1994, compared to a more modest 0.5 percentage point decline the previous year (CEPAL's Bases de Datos y Publicaciones Estadística).

[20] Commercial bank loans now represented a meager 1.5 percent of Argentina's external debt in 1993. Official multilateral assistance accounted for the remaining share (World Bank's Global Development Finance).

Roque Fernández, who served in President Menem's cabinet during this global financing shift, notes the stark difference in creditor behavior between the two funding methods.

Previous to Brady bonds, if you had a problem, the only thing you had to do was meet with five to six important banks – including Citibank, Bank of America, and J.P. Morgan. This steering committee would represent the rest of the banking community in negotiations. They would discuss the restructuring of overdue debt...and then the banks would produce a refinancing. For the first time during the Tequila Crisis, there was no steering committee![21]

Creditors, who were now dispersed across the globe, could sell their bonds in the secondary market, or refuse to rollover existing debt. Such "sudden stops" of financing had harmful economic effects. They triggered higher interest rates that threatened not only growth, but also cash-strapped government's ability to fund their domestic spending. The Tequila crisis posed such a danger to Argentina in 1995.

The collapse of the Mexican peso in December 1994 rippled through Latin American bond and currency markets. Capital departed Argentina amid fears that the government would devalue its currency and abandon convertibility. With a growing trade deficit and an overvalued currency peg, investors surmised Argentina's currency board would crumble. As a result, Argentina's sovereign risk spread (or the premium it paid for its borrowing above U.S. treasury bonds yields) nearly doubled by February 1995 (Figure 7.5).

In order to reassure capital markets of Argentina's commitment to economic austerity and its exchange rate peg, Menem's economic team pursued conservative fiscal and monetary policies. Why? According to Menem's Central Bank Governor, Roque Fernández, who was in charge of the government's 1995 creditor negotiations, "when you have an open economy to capital flows, you are at the mercy of public expectations."[22]

Notwithstanding the election year, Fernández and the rest of Menem's economic team announced an austerity plan featuring budget cuts. By executive decree, the economic team pledged to slash the budget by US$1 billion in 1995, including public salary reductions.[23] As Figure 7.5 shows, we do not observe the classic increase in expenditures during the 1995 election-year. Rather, government spending plateaus in an environment of deteriorating Argentine credit risk (as evidenced by the higher sovereign risk premium in Figure 7.5). Fernández

---

[21] Author's interview with Roque Fernández in Buenos Aires, Argentina on May 2007. Fernández was both central bank president (1991–1996) and later finance minister (1996–1999) for President Carlos Menem.

[22] Author's interview with Roque Fernández, May 2007.

[23] The budget cuts were part of a March austerity plan, announced by the finance ministry intended to avoid a projected budget deficit for 1995. In addition to the budget cuts, the plan also called for bolstering revenues by US$2.5 billion by eliminating tax deductions and tax evaders (*New York Times*, 1995).

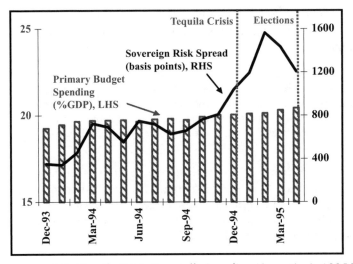

FIGURE 7.5. Tequila Crisis Forestalls Spending (Argentina's 1995 Elections).
Source: MVA-Macroeconomía and J. P. Morgan.

elaborated on the government's non-traditional political thinking from his Universidad del CEMA office in Buenos Aires.

> In 1995, we announced a wage decrease by decree, which is contrary to traditional expectations. The usual thought is that you would have relaxed fiscal and monetary policy during an election period. Normally, what you will observe in the executive branch is that all different levels of government – federal, provincial, municipal, local – all of them will go to the executive branch to ask for more money for the election. However, we were being really attacked, or let's say under the pressure of capital flight. And it was necessary to signal to the population and the rest of the world that the government will take some effective fiscal austerity measures. Given that the budget was 80 percent public salaries, we had to cut salaries.[24]

In addition to this moderate fiscal tightening, the economic team also made monetary policy more restrictive, boosting domestic interest rates to substantially higher levels than U.S. rates.[25] Their commitment to economic orthodoxy also helped Argentina raise emergency funds from multilateral institutions that praised neoliberal virtues, including the International Monetary Fund, the Inter-American Development Bank, and the World Bank. During my field research in Buenos Aires, I had the opportunity to discuss Argentina's economic management of the 1995 Tequila Crisis with the father of convertibility, Menem's Economy Minister Domingo Cavallo. Like Fernández, Cavallo

---

[24] Author's interview with Roque Fernández, May 2007.
[25] Mussa 2002.

emphasized the absolute necessity of pursuing stabilization policies during the 1995 election year.

Obviously, in March 1995, Menem could not follow a populist economic path. Rather, he had to take very restrictive measures. Menem had to present the image that we would have fiscal discipline in the future and avoid contagion from the Tequila crisis. In this case, it was not possible to use economic populism to win the 1995 election. It was the complete contrary. Menem's electoral strategy was to say that it was necessary to re-elect him because he needed to complete the economic reforms that had greatly benefited the people of Argentina, including providing stability and ending hyperinflation . . . Menem won this election because he was a successful stabilizer and reformer.[26]

Cavallo and the Menem administration believed their austerity would be rewarded by voters. Pablo Guidotti, who during this period was serving as a member of the Central Bank's Board of Directors, discussed the expected political payoff of preserving convertibility during the crisis. In our interview in the peaceful confines of the Universidad Torcuato Di Tella, Guidotti employed a war metaphor to managing the Tequila shock.

And suddenly, you get hit by the Tequila out of nowhere. In a certain sense, this situation forced everybody, even the people that didn't believe in Menem to defend convertibility and recognize the ability of the economic team to deal with this external shock . . . everyone was supporting them, even the opposition. It's a little bit like what happens during a war. It generated the idea among the population at large that convertibility had to be defended. When the war was won, everyone had this feeling that Argentina had overcome the crisis. Anyone that would criticize the government in the middle of the crisis was seen as almost unpatriotic.[27]

If politicians had to live within their means, how did they target their political supporters? In addition to the clientelistic spending programs discussed earlier, politicians tinkered with the timing of public works projects to reap electoral rewards. For example, Jorge Baldrich, who served as the Undersecretary of Economic Policy Program for the Provinces under President Carlos Menem, discussed this phenomenon. Baldrich, who later became the Secretary of the Congressional Budget Commission and Argentina's Treasury Secretary under the De La Rúa administration, claims that public works expenditures are commonly synchronized to the Argentine political calendar. In fact, he asserts that the highest infrastructure disbursements generally occur two months before election dates.

For public works projects, there is more of an independent announcement, or timing effect. More so than crossing the actual budget threshold itself, the problem is the timing and allocation of spending before elections. We are not talking about huge infrastructure projects; rather, a relatively low amount of money that is sufficient to cover the cost

---

[26] Author's interview with Domingo Cavallo, May 2007.
[27] Author's interview with Pablo Guidotti, May 2007.

of political campaigns, political brokers, etc. To finance these expenditures, you don't need a lot of money.[28]

In summary, Menem and his economic team initially pursued a neutral policy mix in the prelude to the election year. It featured a modest narrowing of the country's budget surplus and ongoing commitment to price stability through convertibility. Menem's economic team also increased social spending in 1994 in hopes of assuaging socioeconomic pressures, including rising unemployment and poverty.

However, even this line-item tinkering with social expenditures quickly dissipated when the 1994–95 Mexican crisis unleashed a wave of investor panic throughout Latin America in early 1995. Under a system of decentralized bond finance, Argentina rallied to assuage the concerns of the international investment community and prevent another catastrophic crisis.

With international capital quickly withdrawing, the government had little choice but to pursue a more restrictive policy stance. At this point, even if Menem had wanted to create a political business cycle, his government lacked the financing. Rather, an already inflation-averse policy stance was intensified by a severe credit disruption, creating a *political austerity cycle* (*H4*). Notably, economic stability paid hefty political dividends in the 1995 crisis year, propelling Menem to an impressive electoral victory.[29]

Assessing the Alternative Argument: IMF Conditionality. Perhaps, Latin America's adoption of conservative economic policies does not reflect its inflation history or a shift to decentralized global finance. Rather, countries may adopt neoliberal policies because they are compelled by IMF conditionality.[30]

Throughout this chapter, I have argued that the main determinants of Latin America's neoliberal policy shift are past inflationary crises and a structural shift in global finance. Certainly, the IMF had an important consultancy role in outlining the various measures available to Latin American nations, but this is not a sufficient explanation for understanding the domestic policy choices of sovereign nations. Rather, I contend that even in the absence of IMF conditionality, countries often opt for austerity. In order to further examine this counterfactual, I explore a comparative case where IMF conditionality is not present: the 2003 Argentine elections.

---

[28] I interviewed Jorge Baldrich at Universidad Torcuato Di Tella in Buenos Aires, Argentina on May 23, 2007. Baldrich served in Menem's Cabinet from 1994–1996 as the Undersecretary of Economic Policy Program for the Provinces. As a Mendoza congressman from 1999–2000, he was the Secretary of the Budget Commission for the House of Representatives. Baldrich also became Secretary of the Treasury in 2001.

[29] Menem won his 1995 reelection with 49.8 percent of the vote compared to José Octavio Bordón's (FREPSAO) 29.2 percent.

[30] Stiglitz 2002; Barnett and Finnemore 2004; Woods 2006.

This election occurred in the wake of Argentina's 2001 crisis and debt default. For much of the period before elections, Argentina's IMF negotiations for a new funding package were deadlocked. Though Argentina finally accepted an IMF agreement three months before the April 2003 election, it did not involve the release of new funds. Rather, Argentina merely restructured outstanding debt with multilateral institutions coming due in 2003. At this juncture, the IMF had considerably less influence in Argentine policy making compared to the 1990s. Therefore, if we find that economic policy remains restrictive, it bolsters the evidence against IMF conditionality being a necessary condition to check electoral economic expansion.

It would also lend further support to Chapter 4's finding, showing that the presence of IMF conditionality was an insufficient constraint on Latin American politicians' spending behavior. In that chapter, I explored cases where IMF conditionality was present (such as Latin America's economic policy making during the 1980s), rather than absent (such as Argentina 2003) during elections. I found that conditionality often did not have any teeth. Large budget deficits and hefty credit expansions were quite common during this period. For example, notwithstanding a deteriorating fiscal position that caused Argentina to be out of compliance with almost all of its IMF agreement's requirements, the Alfonsín government still managed to secure US$6 billion in new financing from its creditors in 1987. Whereas this evidence suggests that IMF conditionality is not a sufficient condition for government austerity, perhaps it is a necessary condition. To investigate this prospect, let us examine the 2003 election case.

Argentina's 2003 Elections. Before the 2003 elections, Argentina did not receive any IMF disbursements and was not subject to new conditionality. The government simply restructured its multilateral debt under a January 2003 IMF agreement.[31] To the authorities' dismay, Argentina did not have any alternative funding options beyond global financial markets and international institutions.[32] Following the 2002 currency board collapse and debt default, the interim Duhalde government[33] was shut out from international credit markets. Argentina was not able to issue debt on global capital markets again until

---

[31] The IMF agreement had a short shelf-life, providing a temporary restructuring until August 2003. Under the agreement, Argentina refinanced US$11.6 billion in public external debt commitments due in 2003 (including US$6.6 billion owed to the IMF; and US$5.0 billion owed to the World Bank and the IDB). The agreement enabled Argentina to avoid default on its multilateral obligations that were due in the first eight months of 2003 (Economist Intelligence Unit 2002–2003 Country Reports).

[32] Nonetheless, a new export tax generated limited government revenues. In addition, the cessation of interest payments following the debt default also provided some relief (Economist Intelligence Unit, 2002–2003 Country Reports).

[33] Following the fall of the De La Rúa government, Argentina cycled through three different presidents in a mere twelve days amid street protests and riots. On January 2, 2002, Eduardo Duhalde took office as interim president. During his first days in office, Duhalde confirmed

2005. Rating agencies had downgraded Argentina's credit to default status[34] and Argentine debt was trading at a whopping 50–70 percentage point premium above U.S. treasury bond yields.[35]

If President Duhalde global had wanted to give the economy a pre-election boost to help his Peronist candidate, Santa Cruz Governor Néstor Kirchner, depleted government coffers would have presented a serious obstacle. According to Duhalde's Central Bank Governor, Alfonso Prat-Gay,

> There was a complete absence of degrees of freedom for policymakers around elections. There was no room to maneuver on the fiscal side; the only option was a tighter fiscal stance . . . There was little fire power![36]

Notwithstanding these funding constraints, Argentina's policy makers had no interest in crafting a political business cycle in 2003; their efforts were entirely focused on managing the fallout from the 2001 economic crisis. In spite of convertibility's demise, their commitment to economic stability continued to rule the day.

Prat-Gay, who I interviewed in Buenos Aires, emphasized the importance of preserving price stability a full decade after hyperinflation. He shared this view with his predecessor, Mario Blejer, who summarized their mission as "diminishing the relative inflationary consequences of devaluation and default."[37]

In an office with walls that were covered with financial-sector awards, including Euromoney's prize for Central Bank Governor of the Year, Prat-Gay also discussed the challenge of balancing price stability against interest group pressures for financial support.[38]

> Inflation was a more important variable than economic growth to both elites and the electorate because highly volatile past inflation created high economic and social costs . . . when I took office, Duhalde agreed to stringent conditions about central bank independence and currency stability. Banks were lobbying for a more permissive agenda with the central bank, hoping we would make massive loans to help the financial sector recover from massive losses. Banks wanted the central bank to solve their solvency

---

Argentina's debt moratorium, abandoned the currency board, and devalued the peso (Mussa 2002).

[34] In November 2001, S&P shifted Argentina's long-term debt rating six full notches lower from CCC+ to D. In December 2001, Moody's followed suit, moving Argentina's rating to the highest speculative category, (Ca) which also reflected the country's default.

[35] J.P. Morgan's Emerging Market Bond Index.

[36] I interviewed Alfonso Prat-Gay during my field research in Buenos Aires on May 24, 2007. Prat-Gay served as Duhalde and Kirchner's Central Bank Governor from 2002–2004.

[37] I interviewed Mario Blejer in the United States on December 4, 2007. Blejer served as Deputy Central Bank Governor and Central Bank Governor of Argentina between 2001–2002. He previously worked at the International Monetary Fund from 1980–2001.

[38] Notably, the IMF had lobbied for a more hawkish policy stance, believing Prat-Gay was too accommodative. According to Prat-Gay, he ignored the Fund's recommendations believing their extremely orthodox advice would have choked-off economic growth (Prat-Gay Interview, May 2007).

problem by reducing the market mechanism. I disagreed, believing we needed to create a profitable financial system based on market incentives to improve balance sheets and asset and liability exposures...[As a result] inflation came down after elections, rather than going up, increasing the central bank's credibility. The inflation-target for 2004 was in single digits compared to the 30 percent that people had predicted![39]

The belief in the importance of economic discipline was not exclusive to central bankers. Roberto Lavagna, the Minister of the Economy for both Duhalde and his successor Néstor Kirchner, also prioritized budget rectitude. Lavagna's protégé and principal advisor, Ricardo Delgado, outlined the economic team's priorities during our 2007 interview. He also reflected on Argentina's political transformation to macroeconomic orthodoxy.

There was a clear commitment to fiscal health. Under Lavagna, Argentina realized that politics of permanent debt are not good politics. Politicians understood that fiscal health was necessary. It became a preoccupation for politicians. Fiscal surplus was part of the political fortification!...They understood that it was a necessary condition. Many politicians were very worried about the fiscal surplus. If they allowed the central bank to underwrite government spending again, we would be in a situation of very high inflation...It's difficult to think of Argentina's current political model without a fiscal surplus. Argentina cannot return to the international financial world to finance the deficit. The fiscal surplus allows Argentina to have very little financial needs-less than 1 percent of GDP.[40]

In the post-convertibility world, Delgado also mentioned that politicians embraced fiscal surpluses for another benefit beyond price stability and financial independence. Financing shortages had been a problem at the provincial, as well as the national level ever since the central bank reestablished restrictions prohibiting private bank lending to provincial governments.[41] Hence, with a budget surplus, "the nation could dominate the provinces by controlling the redistribution resource."

The president was very focused on maintaining the fiscal surplus; he had a vision that was almost mercantilist. He wanted to ensure that he had pesos in the treasury, and dollars in the central bank. He wanted money to accumulate![42]

In the prelude to Kirchner's eventual 2003 electoral victory,[43] we observe restrictive economic policies, even in the absence of IMF conditionality. Indeed,

---

[39] Prat-Gay interview, May 2007.

[40] Author's interview with Ricardo Delgado, May 2007. We met at Lavagna's consulting firm, *Ecolatina*, where Delgado was the director.

[41] Recall that the abolition of these limitations contributed to the provinces' fiscal problems in the 1990s; they used private bank lending, secured against co-participation proceeds (central government transfers), to fund higher expenditures (Economist Intelligence Unit Country Reports, 2002–2003).

[42] Delgado interview, May 2007.

[43] Kirchner won the 2003 elections in a tight battle with former President Menem. Kirchner secured 22.2 percent of the vote, a slim victory over Menem's 19.5 percent of the vote.

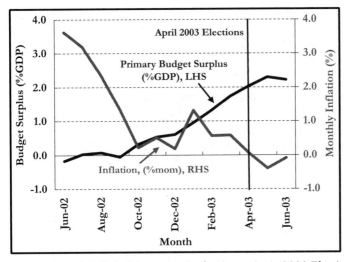

FIGURE 7.6. A Political Austerity Cycle (Argentina's 2003 Elections).
Source: MVA-Macroeconomía and EIU Country Data.

a political austerity cycle unfolds in 2003, marked by a rising budget surplus, contractionary monetary policy, and falling inflation (Figure 7.6). During the election year, Duhalde and Lavagna surprisingly cut the government's expenditures by 1 percentage point of GDP.[44] They also raised new revenues through an export tax, initially implemented in 2002. Moreover, Prat-Gay's central bank pursued a restrictive monetary policy stance,[45] while simultaneously providing sufficient liquidity to "reestablish the foundational elements of a broken monetary and financial system."[46]

In summary, Argentina policy makers prioritized low inflation and economic discipline throughout the 1990s, even when it meant cutting spending and salaries during an election year. Sudden cessations of financing and capital outflows intensified this trend. The failures of convertibility to function as a long-term political commitment mechanism are well documented. However, in the wake of convertibility's collapse, Argentina's economic team continued to operate under the premise that economic stability was a necessary condition for long-term development.

[44] MVA-Macroeconomía; Secretaria de Hacienda 2006.
[45] The pace of credit expansion slowed in 2003 compared to 2002, as measured by the percentage change in M1, a proxy for money supply growth (CEPAL's Bases de Datos y Publicaciones Estadística). The central bank also enforced a weekly deposit withdrawal limit to curb money supply growth (Economist Intelligence Unit, Country Report, 2002–2003).
[46] Prat-Gay had to restore liquidity in the system, regain monopoly control over the currency, and recreate prudential regulations for the banking system. When he took over the central bank, "banks had not turned in their balance sheets in more than one year." (Prat-Gay interview, May 2007).

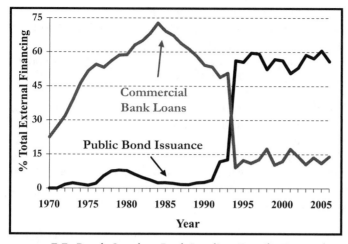

FIGURE 7.7. Bonds Supplant Bank Lending (Brazil's External Financing).
Source: Global Development Finance.

7.2.2. Markets and Politics in Brazil: When Leftists Become Economic Hawks

What explains Fernando Henrique Cardoso or Luiz Inácio Lula da Silva's embrace of economic austerity in Brazil? Cardoso was a sociologist and world-renowned dependency theorist, trained at the Universidade de São Paulo. Lula was a shoe shiner, factory workers, and union activist. In Chapter 6, we observed how politicians internalized the lessons from hyperinflation and shifted their policies toward the political center.

In a similar pattern to Argentina, a shift in the global financial architecture intensified this preexisting tendency toward inflation-aversion. A new era of decentralized finance ushered in tighter funding restrictions in Brazil relative to the country's bank borrowing past. Fears of capital outflows and "sudden stops" of financing shifted Brazilian economic policy to the right.

The 1998 elections mimicked the 1994 elections,[47] with price stability once again emerging as a top political objective. This time, however, Brazil's high global bond market exposure magnified the political trend toward inflation control. Brazil's 1994 Brady restructuring had converted a whopping US$50.6 billion in defaulted commercial bank loans into market-traded debt. Following the restructuring, Brazilian bonds amounted to about 55 to 60 percent of the country's total international indebtedness (Figure 7.7).[48]

The newly created emerging bond markets provided the government with a key funding source, but it also increased Brazil exposure to global financial

---

[47] See Chapter 6.

[48] Official multilateral assistance accounts for the remaining share of external financing beyond public bond issuance and commercial bank loans (World Bank's Global Development Finance).

market turbulence. In the wake of the 1997–1998 East Asian crisis, Brazil's growing external bond debt profile subjected the country to the dark side of capital markets. Brazil faced intense financial market pressures that raised the cost of expansionary economic policies. The conditions were ripe for a Brazilian political austerity cycle during the 1998 elections.

Brazil's 1998 Elections. In his first term (1994–1998), President Cardoso attempted to contain government spending to appease two important actors: domestic voters who worried about a return of hyperinflation and international investors who fretted about Brazil's ability to service its international debt. To meet his economic stability goals, the Brazilian president launched several fiscal initiatives, including social security, tax, and administrative reform. However, Cardoso's reform agenda was obstructed by considerable resistance from Congressional opposition parties.[49]

Without these reforms, Brazil's primary fiscal deficit deteriorated significantly between 1996 and 1997, making the country a prime target for financial contagion from the 1997–1998 East Asian crisis. Privatization windfalls[50] temporarily alleviated Brazil's fiscal woes. Ultimately, however, a growing fiscal deficit, coupled with a gaping current account deficit, unleashed a severe credit crunch. Fearing Brazil's weak economic fundamentals would incite a devaluation, international investors withdrew capital from the South American country.

Before this latest round of turmoil, the political payoff to economic stability had been impressive. The initial success of Cardoso's inflation stabilization had boosted his popularity in opinion polls. Capitalizing on approval ratings near 50 percent in early 1997,[51] the Brazilian president had proposed a constitutional amendment to allow for his reelection.

Immediately after its successful passage, however, the 1997–1998 East Asia crisis struck global financial markets. Fearing the crisis might not only force a devaluation but also a return of inflation, the founding member of Brazil's social democratic party (PSDB) would spend his remaining days in office desperately defending Brazil's currency. Throughout his first term, Cardoso never strayed from economic orthodoxy. In a November 1997 radio address, for instance, Cardoso assuaged Brazilians' concerns about the global crisis, reiterating his resolve to maintain the real's value and win the war against inflation.

You can be sure of one thing; we will not let the real lose value and let inflation come back! We may even have to pay a temporary price for this, but it's better to have higher

---

[49] Cardoso also struggled to win support for reform from many of the state-level administrations within Brazil's federal structure. Notably, however, during his second term, he would eventually persuade Congress to pass the Fiscal Responsibility Law, which sought to restrict state and municipal spending.

[50] During Cardoso's first term, the government received US$72.7 billion by privatizing public enterprises and services from the mining and telecommunications sector (Weyland 2004).

[51] Datafolha Opinião Pública, 1996–1997.

interest rates for a while than to have salaries lose their value again. The real, and therefore the purchasing power of your salaries, will be protected![52]

Mired in a financial maelstrom, Cardoso's primary political goal was preserving Brazil's U.S. dollar peg,[53] the bedrock of Brazilian price stability. Notably, Cardoso's behavior matches the behavior predicted by the politics of exchange rates literature, which expects politicians to avoid currency devaluations during election periods.[54] In fact, within months of his reelection in January 1999, Cardoso would eventually devalue the real.

A mere one year before his reelection, however, Cardoso announced an adjustment package in the autumn of 1997 to defend the currency. Contrary to the traditional political business cycle, the austerity package raised taxes and reduced public spending. Under the peg, sound economic fundamentals were necessary to maintain the fixed exchange rate's stability and avoid an inflation-spurring devaluation. Although the package failed to win Congressional support, it demonstrated the depth of Cardoso's commitment to economic stability. In fact, the president forged forward with stabilization, defending the Brazilian currency with tight monetary policy, including a near doubling of interest rates.

However, Cardoso's policy actions produced a financial catch-22. Higher interest rates helped attract foreign capital and maintain exchange rate stability, but the soaring cost of government borrowing simultaneously worsened the fiscal deficit and intensified Brazil's financial contagion vulnerability. This vicious cycle deepened in the summer of 1998, following the August 1998 Russian default. Figure 7.8 shows the massive shock to Brazil's international borrowing rates. They mushroomed to 10 to 15 percentage points above U.S. treasury yields, significantly higher than the more subdued average of 4 to 5 percent over the previous two years.

Without another wave of global financial market turbulence in 1998, Cardoso may have pursued an *inflation-averse political business cycle* (H_3), or a neutral election-year policy mix. The Brazilian president had already been using fiscal stimulus to offset the tight monetary policy stance associated with defending the currency.

However, the August 1998 Russian default produced a secondary and more severe credit shock. To avoid a devaluation, Cardoso had to pursue a more aggressive austerity. Benefiting from a crisis-related boost in his political capital, Cardoso tightened fiscal policy without the resistance he met in 1997.

---

[52] *New York Times*, November 5, 1997.

[53] Following the success of the Real Plan in taming inflation, Cardoso's economic team created a crawling peg fixed exchange rate regime designed to allow for a steady, but modest depreciation of the Brazilian real against the U.S. dollar.

[54] This literature assumes that currency depreciation or devaluation is politically unpopular because it reduces the purchasing power of the population and the wealth of tradeable producers. Hence, politicians defer devaluations until following elections (Frieden and Stein 2001; Schamis and Way 2003).

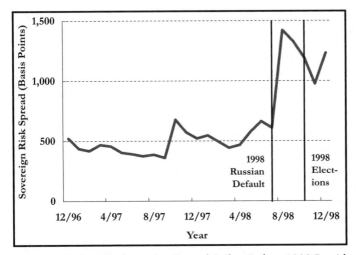

FIGURE 7.8. Brazil's Sovereign Spread Spikes Before 1998 Presidential Elections (Bond Yield Differential Between Brazilian and U.S. Treasury Debt). *Source:* J. P. Morgan.

Indeed, opinion polls reflected Cardoso's renewed political capital. In the months preceding the Russian financial crisis, polls had shown a dead heat between Cardoso and Lula de Silva (PT), the neoliberal critic who was his second-time challenger. Following the crisis, however, Cardoso took a significant lead in the polls amid renewed Brazilian financial market turmoil (Figure 7.9).

Solidifying his track record as the guarantor of stability, Cardoso crafted a *political austerity cycle* (H_4) in the months before his reelection, using tight monetary and fiscal policies to defend the currency and avoid a renewed inflationary crisis.[55] Despite his previous difficulties balancing the budget, Cardoso swung Brazil's primary fiscal deficit back into surplus by year's end.[56] He also promised long-awaited fiscal reforms, including preserving a budget surplus throughout his next term and streamlining the bureaucracy.[57] While price stability translated to political gains in urban sectors, Cardoso's alliance with the Liberty Front Party (PFL) and its clientelist network helped him secure electoral support from poor, uneducated, and largely unorganized sectors of the less developed areas of Brazil.[58]

---

[55] In exchange for these adjustments, Cardoso was able to muster US$41.5 billion in financial support from the U.S. government and the International Monetary Fund.

[56] Cardoso tightened fiscal policy in 1998, narrowing the fiscal deficit by 1.3 percentage points of GDP, compared to a 1 percentage points widening of the deficit in 1997. By 1998's end, Brazil had a primary budget surplus of 0.3 percent of GDP (CEPAL's Bases de Datos y Publicaciones Estadística).

[57] Bustani 2001.

[58] Weyland 2004.

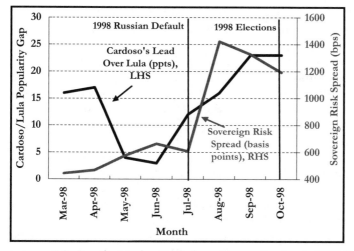

FIGURE 7.9. Brazil's Market Turbulence Boosts Cardoso's 1998 Reelection Bid.
Source: Datafolha Opinião Pública and J. P. Morgan.

On net, voters rewarded Cardoso's stabilization record, catapulting him to a decisive first round victory over Lula, and presenting him with a mandate to shield Brazil from international market turmoil.[59]

Assessing the Alternative Argument: Central Bank Independence. The adoption of legal central bank autonomy in Latin America in the 1990s is often touted as an explanation for the region's shift to more conservative economic policies. For example, the political business cycle (PBC) literature predicts that institutions, such as central bank independence, are the primary check against government excess and political preferences to spend before elections.[60] According to this literature, politicians aiming to profit from an electoral boom create a time-inconsistency problem, where their short-term political myopia produces long-term economic distortions. In order to constrain these opportunistic chief executives, institutional checks and balances are necessary.

If the PBC literature is correct, we should observe a greater tendency toward electoral economic stimulus in Brazil, a country that did not implement central bank independence. Brazil had approved a constitutional amendment in the 1980s prohibiting the monetization of budget deficits. However, short-term financing of budgetary shortfalls was permitted, leaving the central bank vulnerable to political pressures to spend.[61]

Notwithstanding the absence of legal central bank autonomy, however, I found that Cardoso enacted restrictive economic policies during Brazil's 1998

---

[59] Cardoso grabbed a healthy 53.1 percent of the vote compared to Lula's 31.7 percent.
[60] See Schuknecht 1996; Schuknecht 2000; Gonzalez 2002; Shi & Svensson 2002; Brender & Drazen 2005; and Shi & Svensson 2006.
[61] Ribeiro 2002.

election year. For many countries, central bank independence is an important institutional anchor that facilitates the political goal of price stability. Nevertheless, the evidence suggests that central bank autonomy is not a necessary condition for economic policy austerity. In Brazil's case, the executive branch was in charge of the institutional anchor for inflation, first the fixed exchange rate and then inflation-targeting. Therefore, it was the political will of the chief executive rather than an executive constraint, that was the most important driver of austerity.

In Cardoso's case, a commitment to low inflation earned him a political reputation as an economic reformer. His ability to curb hyperinflation helped him win his 1994 presidential bid.[62] Moreover, when financial market stress threatened to delve Brazil back into inflationary chaos, President Cardoso voluntarily defended Brazil's exchange rate peg throughout the 1998 election period. Although the global credit crunch made his policies more deflationary than planned, he did not stray from a credible commitment to economic stability.

Perhaps, economic frugality is a rare electoral event, driven by the unique circumstances of the 1998 election. In order to shed light on this possibility, let us examine the next Brazilian presidential election in 2002. Does President Cardoso behave any differently this time in the continued absence of central bank independence, yielding to his political impulse to spend? Or, does political austerity theory prove robust? Might the combination of his inflation aversion and vigorous market constraints once again produce orthodox election-year policies?

Brazil's 2002 Elections. In the prelude to the 2002 elections, Cardoso once again prioritized stabilization. This time, however, he changed his commitment device from an exchange rate anchor to inflation targeting. Cardoso hoped to maintain price stability, but without the fixed exchange rate that exposed Brazil to global financial contagion. Why?

On the heels of his 1998 electoral victory, Cardoso was forced to abandon Brazil's U.S. dollar peg. The costs of using an exchange rate anchor to curb inflation had become clear. Preserving the peg meant subjecting Brazil to a vicious financial cycle. The dollar peg yielded an overvalued currency that eroded Brazil's export competitiveness.[63] Deteriorating external fundamentals, along with a fiscal deficit, subjected Brazil to the severe financial volatility and capital outflows that could only be mitigated with interest rate hikes. Ironically, however, higher interest rates increased the government's borrowing costs and ballooned its budget deficit, generating a fresh round of market speculation.

---

[62] See Chapter 6.

[63] A strong Brazilian real weakened the country's balance of payments position, creating a current account deficit. Much of Brazil's current account deterioration between 1994 and 1999 reflected a serious decline in the country's trade and services balance from a surplus of US$5 billion in 1994 to a deficit of more than US$7 billion in 1998 (Coes 2009).

Hoping to exit this quagmire, Cardoso pledged to avoid fiscal deficits and ensure price stability through a different mechanism. In June 1999, the Brazilian president adopted an inflation targeting framework. Without formal central bank independence, this price stability initiative was rooted in the political will of the executive branch. Pedro Milan, the Minister of Finance at the time, proposed the inflation target, while the Monetary Policy Committee (COPOM) of the Central Bank of Brazil merely managed daily interest rates fluctuations to fulfill the executive's goals.[64] Moreover, if the target was breached, the Central Bank Governor was required to write an open letter to the Minister of Finance explaining the reasons and proposing remedies for the missed target.[65]

Cardoso employed this monetary policy initiative, along with large primary budget surpluses, to restore confidence in Brazil and right the ailing economy. However, Brazil's ongoing economic travails opened a political window of opportunity.

Beginning in his 2002 election campaign, Lula seized on Cardoso's weaknesses: slow growth, high unemployment, and stagnant real wages.[66] Cardoso's first-term price stability mission had improved the poor's standard of living, but their income growth had stalled under his second-term economic austerity.[67] Lula harshly criticized Cardoso's primary budget surpluses, intimating that wage payments should trump credit payments. Two of his key advisors, Federal Deputy Alóizio Mercadante (cited as Lula's possible Finance Minister) and Guido Mantega (who later became his planning minister), also critiqued Cardoso's economic model. Mercadante voiced support for a plebiscite on foreign debt payments and Mantega characterized primary budget surplus of 3 percent as "suicidal."[68]

Riding the wave of economic volatility to political prosperity, Lula (PT) became the frontrunner for the 2002 presidential contest. By December 2001, public opinion polls showed Lula had a more than 20 percentage point lead over presidential rivals, José Serra of Cardoso's PSDB party and Ciro Gomes (PPS), a PSDB defector and former Ceará Governor.[69]

Investor concern for Lula's ostensibly unorthodox economic policies sparked a confidence crisis. The popularity of the leftist politician contributed to

---

[64] The daily interest rate, known as the Selic rate (or Sistema Especial de Liquidação), is set by the COPOM.

[65] Arestis et al. 2007.

[66] Over the course of Cardoso's two administration, unemployment increased from 6.0 to 9.1 percent (World Development Indicators).

[67] The 1994 Real Plan increased the monthly income of the lowest 50 percent of income earners in Brazil from a R$175 annual average (in September 2004 prices) before the plan to a R$234 annual average during Cardoso's first term. In his second term, however, wages stagnated, falling slightly to an annual average of R$232 (Coes 2009).

[68] Coes 2009.

[69] In the December 2001 survey, 36 percent of Brazilian respondents who were polled intended to vote Lula, compared to 16 percent for Gomes and 11 percent for Serra (Datafolha and Eleições 2002).

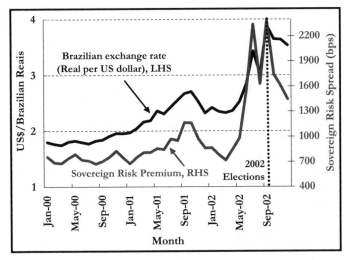

FIGURE 7.10. Lula's Impending Presidential Victory Sparks Financial Market Fears. *Source:* Datafolha Opinião Pública and EIU Country Data.

capital withdrawals, a weakening currency and a surging Brazilian sovereign risk premium during the election year (Figure 7.10).[70]

Given these market pressures, the government had little room to maneuver. Facing steep interest rates on its international borrowing, Cardoso had limited scope for additional election year spending. New expenditures could have propelled the country's borrowing rates even higher and jeopardized its ability to service its lofty external debt during the second half of the year. Further spending could have also intensified the vicious cycle of higher interest rates, fiscal deterioration, and capital outflows. This scenario risked shattering Cardoso's economic management credentials by sparking a debt default and an economic crisis. To avoid such a fate, Cardoso secured new IMF funds during the 2002 summer.[71]

In the 2002 election year, not only did President Cardoso lack the financial means, but he also lacked the political motivation to create a political business cycle. Rather, Cardoso wanted to reassure voters and financial markets of the PSDB's commitment to economic stability. Concerned about budding inflationary pressures – inflation had already breached the government's 2001 target[72] – Cardoso pledged to maintain Brazil's primary budget surplus and meet its 2002 inflation target.

In addition, Cardoso sought to assuage international investor concerns about the next administration's economic policies. Similar to the actions of Menem's

[70] During the summer of 2002, Moody's and S&P also downgraded Brazil's sovereign credit rating one full notch each, from B1 to B2 and BB− to B+.

[71] In August, Brazil immediately withdrew US$6 billion from a new US$30 billion IMF package to help cover its remaining 2002 debt payments and ease economic volatility during the presidential transition.

[72] Inflation rose by 7.7 percent in 2001, outside the target range of 4 to 6 percent.

economic team during the Argentine 1999 elections, Cardoso vouched for the incoming government. In an effort to calm jittery markets, the Brazilian president brokered a deal between the IMF, financial markets, and all of the presidential candidates. In fact, both leftist candidates, Lula and Gomes, promised to shed their anti-globalization images in support for ongoing IMF funding.

In a letter entitled *Carta ao Povo Brasileiro (Letter to the Brazilian People)*, the frontrunner Lula promised to continue Cardoso's macroeconomic policies. The former union activist pledged that he would not forsake macroeconomic discipline, price stability, or timely debt service to boost redistribution and employment.[73] Further helping to calm markets, PT party centrist and Riberão Preto Mayor Antonio Palôcci emerged as Lula's key economic advisor and choice of finance minister. As mayor of Riberão Preto, Palôcci was a strong advocate of economic austerity. In a series of further important market overtures, Lula selected millionaire textile magnet José Alencar of the center-right Liberal Party to be his vice presidential running mate, and Henrique Meirelles, formerly a Bank of Boston executive, as the new central bank president. Lula's shift to the center helped assuage investor concerns and propel him to a resounding second round victory in the 2002 presidential elections.[74]

In summary, Brazil's 2002 elections were characterized by an incumbent president determined to preserve his legacy as an economic stabilizer and forestall a financial market confidence crisis. In the absence of legal central bank independence, Cardoso opted for price stability during yet another election. Cardoso's commitment to economic austerity suggests that central bank autonomy is not a necessary condition for macroeconomic rectitude. In fact, the Brazilian president used a variety of institutional tools – from exchange rate anchors to inflation-targeting – to help achieve his price stability goals. His unyielding determination to cage the inflationary menace was the most important driver of austerity over his two administrations. According to Cardoso, for instance:

We needed a state capable of fulfilling the promises of democracy without burdening those promises – workers, retirees, the poor – with the weight of an inflation tax.[75]

In line with the expectations of political austerity theory, this economic risk-aversion along with high funding constraints from international bond markets bred election-year austerity. During the 2002 elections, Cardoso bolstered the primary budget surplus by about one-quarter to 2.2 percent of GDP[76] and hiked interest rates by almost 2 percentage points.[77]

---

[73] Cardim de Carvalho and Ferrari-Filho 2007; Coes 2009.

[74] Lula (PT) garnered a whopping 61.3 percent of the vote compared to Serra's (PSDB) mere 38.7 percent in the 2002 presidential elections.

[75] Mainwaring and Scully 2010.

[76] CEPAL's Bases de Datos y Publicaciones Estadística.

[77] Brazil's average Selic interest rate increased by almost 2 percentage points from 17.5 to 19.1 percent in 2002 (CEPAL).

Notably, Lula kept his campaign pledge to govern with sound economic management, maintaining both Cardoso's inflation targeting framework and his primary budget surpluses. In an unexpected turn of events, the leftist politician, affectionately dubbed "Lula Lite" for his shift to market-friendly policies, became the darling of international financial markets. Indeed, within days of his electoral victory, Lula reiterated his electoral promise:

Our government will not neglect the control of inflation and will maintain a posture of fiscal responsibility. The difficult course that Brazil will be confronting is going to demand austerity in the use of public monies![78]

After two of Brazil's most notable leftists, Cardoso and Lula, became economic hawks, today's policy debate has shifted to the social costs of economic stability. In fact, a growing disenchanted chorus of Brazilians have called for greater redistribution, more jobs and improved wages. Nevertheless, Lula maintained his commitment to budget surpluses throughout the 2006 and 2010 elections. Moving forward, will the 2014 elections revive the political business cycle, or will inflation aversion and market pressures continue to rule the day?

7.3. SUMMARY

Over the last two chapters, I have relaxed the classic political economy assumption that politicians are most concerned about providing jobs and growth to their supporters before elections. Rather, I have claimed that past inflationary wounds often curb spendthrift instincts, prompting governments to instead pursue restrictive economic policies before elections. They tend to slam on the brakes even when they are free from the surveillance of independent central bankers and conservative international institutions, such as the IMF. In fact, a countervailing institutional force is not a necessary condition for disciplined economics. Rather, politicians often willingly deliver austerity in countries with volatile inflation histories.

In this chapter, we saw that external funding shocks in highly indebted countries frequently magnify this miserly behavior. When faced with sudden cessations of bond market financing, as experienced by Argentina and Brazil during the 1990s, politicians often intensify their deflationary stances. In fact, the political austerity cycle appears in its most binding form, when inflation-averse presidents, from Brazil's Cardoso to Argentina's Menem, must attract funding from decentralized investors with mobile capital.

---

[78] *New York Times*, October 2002.

8

Conclusion

A safety-first Volvo, or a sleek Porsche speedster? In crafting economic policy, speed often trumps caution. Chief executives step on the economy's gas pedal, hoping to jolt jobs and economic growth higher. Political economy theorists expect this behavior to be most intense before elections, when politicians' survival is at risk. Indeed, electoral engineering can be an attractive political tool. Notwithstanding its potential economic costs, voters often reward free-spending governments and a booming economy.

In the United States, there are many examples of politicians engineering an election-time economic boost, widely known as a *political business cycle*. Most recently, George W. Bush engaged in a spending spree in the prelude to the 2004 presidential elections. Courting elderly voters, Bush championed a huge Medicare subsidy for prescription drug purchases. The president also slashed taxes before his reelection campaign. Coupled with the Iraq War and homeland security spending, the government's budget balance swung from surplus to a sizable deficit between 2002 and 2004.[1]

A similar pattern occurred during the 1972 presidential election campaign. In spite of the Vietnam War's assault on government coffers, President Richard M. Nixon cut taxes and hiked social security benefits by a whopping 20 percent in the year preceding the election. In addition to ballooning the budget deficit, Nixon also pressured the Federal Reserve to fire up the printing presses and expand the money supply. The Fed lowered its key monetary policy target at the time – the discount rate – by 1.5 percentage points between 1970 and 1972.

Political business cycles are also a common phenomenon beyond U.S. borders. Scholars have found evidence of electoral boom-bust cycles across the globe, from Japan and Russia to Turkey, Italy, and Mexico.[2] For example,

---

[1] Bureau of Economic Analysis, Department of Treasury.

[2] Kohno and Nishizawa 1990; Krueger and Taran 1993; Limosani and Navarra 2001; Gonzalez 2002.

Russian president Boris Yeltsin ensured his 1996 reelection with a spending boom that was largely mortgaged by the privatization of Russia's natural resources.[3]

Stepping on the economic accelerator, however, often carries a cost. Electorally timed expansionary policies can overheat the economy and ignite inflation.[4] For both Nixon and Yeltsin, the inflation rate surged in the years following their reelection stimulus, creating serious long-term problems for their economies.[5]

In newly democratized regions like Latin America, a rich political economy scholarship expects electoral engineering to be a frequent occurrence.[6] Presidents often face high social debts from an authoritarian past. Widespread income inequality and poverty typically translate into strong popular pressures for jobs and growth. At the same time, presidents in young democracies face few institutional checks and balances. Without independent central banks, strong legislatures, or free media, the political economy literature assumes that chief executives use fiscal and monetary to address these redistributive pressures.

Strikingly, however, I find that Latin American politicians are just as likely to hit the brakes as step on the accelerator. Rather than engaging in expansionary policy before elections, many Latin American governments pursue restrictive economic policies. Their economic discipline yields a *political austerity cycle* characterized by measured growth and stable or falling inflation. What explains this surprising fact? If budgetary largesse is the hallmark of democratic transitions, why do we observe such a dogged embrace of austerity in newly democratizing regions like Latin America?

8.1. THE POLITICAL ROOTS OF AUSTERITY

This book develops a new framework, dubbed political austerity theory, to account for the prevalence of "yellow light" economic policies in Latin America. It offers a dual-level explanation for inflation's political saliency that has both international and domestic roots.

First, I argue that a history of inflationary crises prompts politicians to search for policy alternatives to inflation-spurring economic expansions, opening the door to orthodox policies that are centered on inflation control. Neoliberal

---

[3] See footnote 5 in Chapter 2.

[4] Electorally motivated stimulus is most problematic when the economy has a small output gap – or little spare capacity – and therefore, is at risk of overheating. For a more extensive discussion of economic policy, output gaps, and inflation, please see Chapter 2.

[5] After Nixon's 1972 reelection campaign, the inflation rate jumped from 3 to 6 percent in 1973, reaching 11 percent by 1974. For Yeltsin, inflation emerged as a problem again following the 1996 elections notwithstanding earlier efforts to stabilize the economy. In 1999, inflation surged by 86 percent, more than doubling 1996's rate of inflation (IMF's International Financial Statistics).

[6] Ames 1987; Schuknecht 2000; Acosta and Coppedge 2001; Block 2002; Gonzalez 2002; Shi and Svensson 2002, 2006; Brender and Drazen 2005; Barberia and Avelino 2011.

policies ideas may disseminate from Western powers and the International Monetary Fund (IMF)[7]; however, politicians are careful tacticians that adopt policies to fit their independent economic structures.[8]

In countries where hyperinflation has destroyed middle-class and lower-incomes, protecting voters from income shocks becomes an important political commodity. Anchored by these transformative crises, Latin American politicians gravitate toward the economic center, preserving the lessons of unsustainable fiscal stimulus in their technocratic communities. They avoid loose spending and credit policies that once contributed to inflationary mayhem, instead opting for conservative, risk-averse economic policies. Fostering new growth and jobs surely are political assets, but only in the context of price stability. If growth is too rapid, inflation threatens to undercut its political benefits by crushing wages.

Second, I contend that a structural shift in the global financial architecture from cross-border bank loans to global bond issues reduced the economic autonomy of highly indebted countries. In the political fallout from bank-funded, break-neck expansions that produced hyperinflation, governments searched for funding alternatives to the inflation tax that had eroded voter incomes. Ironically, politicians tapped international bonds to finance their political agendas, a move that ultimately created an external check on powerful executives who traditionally faced few domestic institutional constraints.

Recall that when governments fund a large share of their financing with global bonds rather than bank loans, it is more difficult for sovereign debtors to tap new funds when they veer from austerity. Whereas centralized bank lending is plagued by a moral hazard problem that undermines conditionality's potency, decentralized bond market's exit threat serves as a conditionality enforcement mechanism. Failure to meet the market's economic policy demands (such as maintaining low inflation, fiscal discipline, or debt servicing capacity) can rattle investors, leading to capital flight that almost instantaneously results in higher sovereign risk premiums and soaring interest rates. In fact, the economics literature on sudden stops finds that such cessations of financing create two important economic risks in emerging market countries. Prohibitively high interest rates not only thwart governments' capacities to deliver an economic boost, but also choke economic activity and shrink incomes.[9] Not surprisingly, these financial market pressures compel politicians to adhere to austerity. Former Venezuelan Planning Minister Ricardo Hausmann, for instance, quips about the power of market discipline.

When I was in government, markets could discipline you, so you wanted to be good to markets. If you are good to markets, markets reward you. If you are bad to markets,

---

[7] Hall 1993; Babb 2001; Babb and Fourcade-Gourinchas 2002.
[8] Woods 1995; McNamara 1998.
[9] Calvo 1998; Calvo and Reinhart 2000; Calvo, Izquierdo, and Talvi 2003; Kaminsky, Reinhart, and Vegh 2004.

markets punish you. In the end, god is in control, god is great, god is all powerful, but he is a busy man, or woman. And in order to do his work, he has capital markets. If you behave well, god rewards well. If you behave poorly, god punishes you.[10]

Notably, the market enforcement mechanism does not function as well at low levels of bond market indebtedness. When governments possess non-market financing alternatives – from commodity and privatization revenues to bank loans and foreign aid – they have the fiscal space[11] to fund their spending without outside checks and balances. A reliance on bond markets to finance expenditures, however, subjects governments to the threat of capital flight, and therefore, the scrutiny of external evaluation.

In summary, the political austerity cycle's foundations lay in these political and economic features of developing countries. Inflation aversion breeds a new set of political incentives that diverge from the traditional political business cycle motivation. Politicians, who wish to avoid repeating inflationary horrors, seek a more measured balance between growth and inflation control. Notwithstanding these choices, either political strategy – stimulus or austerity – can yield a more deflationary outcomes than first hoped.[12] When governments are highly indebted to global bond markets, their best-laid political plans may be hastily derailed by credit disruptions and interest rate shocks.

8.2. IMPLICATIONS: QUALITY OF DEMOCRACY AND GROWTH

Given the market's ability to shatter domestic political agendas, my findings raise important questions about the compatibility of markets and democracy in an age of deepening financial integration. They raise the question of whether developing country citizens are able to prosper socially, politically, and economically in a financially globalized world? Or, does the weight of globalization's demands – from balanced budgets to economic orthodoxy – crush governments' ability to respond to the basic needs of their citizenries?

The scholarship on politics and markets has exploded in recent years. For some scholars, deepening global market integration represents a setback for democracy. Faced with a constant threat of capital withdrawal, governments pursue policies that favor capitalists over other social groups.[13] By contrast, other scholars have argued that markets and democracy can amicably coexist. Government policies that boost investment often favor wage-earning citizens. Markets create wealth, which then stabilizes democracies.[14] Most

---

[10] Author's interview with Ricardo Hausmann in Caracas on February 15, 2007.
[11] See footnote 39 in Chapter 1.
[12] See Chaper 2 for a full description of the variants of the political austerity cycle.
[13] Cardoso 1973; Cardoso and Faletto 1979; Block 1977; Lindblom 1982; Bates and Lien 1982; Frieden 1991; Kurzer 1993; Andrews 1994; Helleiner 1994; Cerny 1995; Keohane and Milner 1996; Strange 1996; Pauly 1997; Rodrik 1997; Garrett 1998a; Garrett 1998b; Rodrik 2000; and Boix 2003.
[14] Przeworksi and Wallerstein 1982, 1988; Przeworski et al. 2000.

recently, political economy scholars have sought to advance the globalization debate by exploring both the nature of the external constraint and the ability of governments to insulate their populace from international market pressures.[15]

This book brings a new set of considerations to this debate by examining how different types of international credit affect government policy choices in developing countries. When borrowers move from backroom negotiations with vested bankers to an impersonal dialogue with publicly traded markets, their bargaining power is often diluted relative to their creditors. Ironically, by compelling greater budgetary discipline, financial markets may be more effective at promoting good governance than traditional institutional checks such as central bank independence and IMF programs.

These patterns also hold during periods of political survival, where I claim that the advent of political business cycles is conditional on governments' foreign debt structures. For highly indebted developing nations, bank lending often enables electoral booms while bond markets instead impose economic orthodoxy. This analysis gives us important new insights into the political business cycle literature in developing countries.

For new democracies with few institutional checks on executive power, markets may enhance presidential accountability in the economic policy realm. In fact, market conditionality may improve developing country governance, helping politicians avoid the pitfalls of deficit finance and inflation. Fashioning an electoral spending bonanza was once a familiar motif in developing countries, notwithstanding its often harmful economic effects. However, global debt securitization has reduced the prevalence of political booms and busts in Latin America.

Notwithstanding this market disciplining effect, I have also argued that austerity is a political choice. In countries where runaway inflation destroyed popular living standards, price stability is a public good. Providing a low inflation environment appeases not only the international and domestic business communities, but also middle and working class voters. Price stability can protect the purchasing power of citizens that were previously plagued by inflation crises. Indeed, inflation-traumatized voters often demand economic stability and low inflation, as demonstrated in my comparative case studies in Aylwin's Chile, Cardoso's Brazil and Menem's Argentina. While public sector job cuts grab the headlines, the majority of workers benefit from the stable prices provided by sound economic management.

Counterintuitively, powerful executives that face few institutional constraints may still be responsive to the degree that their actions yield low inflation and economic stability. On the other hand, governments' efforts to stabilize the

---

[15] McNamara 1998; Mosley 2000; Swank 2002; Rudra 2002; Bearce 2003; Mosley 2003; Wibbels and Arce 2003; Wibbels, 2006; Tomz 2007; Pepinsky 2008; Rudra 2008.

economy could also flare tensions between markets and democracy. If politicians achieve discipline by shrinking the welfare state, a balanced budget may not be in the interest of domestic constituents.

Indeed, the compatibility of markets and democracy ultimately depends on how politicians address the composition of spending within an austerity framework. If political elites decide to slash social security, education, and pension benefits, the losses from social instability may quickly erase the gains from economic stability.

8.2.1. Targeting Political Supporters within an Austerity Framework

If politicians decide to live within their means, how do they target supporters in an age of budget austerity? During my open-ended elite interviews, many politicians and members of presidential technocratic teams noted a new pattern emerging in economic policy during election years: the prevalence of micro-level rather than macro-level targeting of voters.

Politicians signal fiscal responsibility with balanced budgets, yet direct budgetary line-item spending to key supporters. How do they accomplish this goal without surpassing their budget constraints? Throughout the book, we have seen that political elites have several options. They can finance new spending by raising taxes on exports, consumption, and corporations, and even renationalizing state-owned enterprises.[16] Politicians can also streamline expenditures on the other side of their balance sheets. They can reallocate expenditures toward social spending that targets a broader segment of the population (such as education), or more efficiently channels funds to the most vulnerable sectors (such as conditional cash transfers). On the heels of elections, politicians can also funnel resources to some of the most politically expedient line-item categories, such as public work projects and public salaries.

Public works projects, for instance, can deliver sizeable proceeds to key political sectors.[17] During Chile's 1999 elections, President Frei oversaw a mild fiscal stimulus to offset slower growth. Within the context of a disciplined macroeconomic policy; however, he funneled money toward municipal public works projects to boost the Concertación's electoral support.[18] In Argentina, public works expenditures were commonly synchronized to the political calendar throughout the 1990s, with funding sometimes diverted to paying for political campaigns and brokers.[19] During the 2006 Brazilian elections, President Luiz

---

[16] The World Bank estimates that state-owned enterprises account for more than 10 percent of the region's GDP.

[17] Rose-Ackerman 1999.

[18] See Chapter 6.

[19] See Chapter 7.

Inácio Lula da Silva maintained macroeconomic discipline, but allowed for some tinkering with the timing of pension payments.[20]

Line-item expenditures on public personnel, a traditional proxy for clientelism,[21] is yet another technique developing country politicians employ to target voters.[22] For example, during the 1995 elections, President Menem directed $1 billion into new spending on anti-poverty and public infrastructure projects that were used to reinforce clientelistic networks.[23] A similar phenomenon occurred during the 1999 elections, when Eduardo Duhalde, Governor of Buenos Aires province was running as the Peronist Party's presidential candidate. In the prelude to these elections, personnel spending in the province of Buenos Aires increased by about two-thirds between 1995 and 2000.[24] Finally, many scholars of Venezuelan politics have argued that Chávez's mission projects, inaugurated in 2003, are based on clientelistic rather than programmatic criteria.[25]

Ironically, throughout the book, we have also observed that financial markets give politicians not only an incentive to reach macroeconomic balance, but also the motivation to deploy several off-balance sheet methods for exploiting their executive power for electoral gains. For example, notwithstanding overseeing a primary budget surplus throughout his tenure, former President Néstor Kirchner readily directed subsidies and price controls to the energy and transportation sectors in Argentina. By maintaining low consumer prices, he boosted his popularity with middle and working-class voters before his wife and fellow Justicialist party candidate, Cristina Fernández de Kirchner, was successfully elected in the October 2007 presidential campaign. Recall that the 2005 *superpoderes* law also empowered Kirchner to spend extra-budgetary revenues without congressional approval. Indeed, the Argentine president could proclaim fiscal austerity, while discreetly funneling political favors.[26] During the 1999 Argentine elections, President Menem accomplished a similar feat. He signaled national-level austerity, while lifting local government spending restrictions that allowed local governors to spend freely in politically sensitive provinces.[27]

The use of administrative controls and discretionary spending has not been confined to Argentine borders. In the mid-1990s, politicians in both Venezuela and Ecuador used micro-level initiatives to curry favor with the

---

[20] See Chapter 6.
[21] The transfer of material benefits to poor constituencies.
[22] Levitsky 2003; Stokes 2005.
[23] See Chapter 7.
[24] See Chapter 6.
[25] Corrales and Penfold 2007; Rodríguez 2007; Ortega and Penfold 2008; Ortega and Rodríguez 2008.
[26] See Chapter 1.
[27] See Chapter 6.

electorate. During political austerity phases, presidents raised public sector wages, extended electricity and gas subsidies, and safeguarded social spending initiatives.[28] More recently, President Hugo Chávez modified Venezuela's 2005 central bank law to tap foreign currency and oil reserves to establish FONDEN, an off-budget development fund. In the 2006 election year, Chávez spent an estimated $7 billion from this fund on state mission programs that invested in health, education, and job-training programs.[29]

8.2.2. A Political Exit Threat from Capital's Exit?

Notwithstanding these political tools, the capacity of governments to stimulate their economies ultimately depends on their ability to develop alternative forms of financing that are less susceptible to speculative market pressures. Without such diversification, future financial turbulence threatens to intensify austerity politics. Currently, Asian demand for Latin American commodities might pad government coffers, but what happens to governments' policy flexibility during a prolonged global downturn? Cross-border bank lending, the traditional external financing backstop against recessionary pressures, wallows at less than a third of its pre-market securitization height.

Concerns about capital market volatility have prompted many governments to reduce their exposure to foreign bond markets in recent years. Notwithstanding its initial benefits, from fostering efficiency gains to serving as a conduit for cheap financing, unfettered capital has a crisis-prone downside. As famously noted by economic historian Charles Kindleberger, financial markets are susceptible to panics and manias. Therefore, excessive borrowing leaves governments vulnerable to financial booms and busts that have devastating economic consequences. Financing long-term development with shorter-term capital risks unleashing income shocks that can quickly undermine the economic vote. Hoping to insulate their nations from global financial volatility, developing country governments have reduced their external debt burdens, fortified their stocks of foreign currency reserves, implemented capital controls, and developed local bond markets that are less susceptible to speculative pressures from foreign investors.

These actions, along with the region's adherence to fiscal discipline following its inflation crises, have granted Latin America more room to maneuver. They have produced a positive spillover effect in global markets, with sovereign risk premiums steadily declining in recent years. Latin America's improved debt profile has also left many countries better equipped to weather external credit shocks. In response to the 2008 global financial crisis, for instance, many Latin American countries employed countercyclical fiscal policies to offset the

---

[28] See Chapter 5.
[29] See Chapter 4.

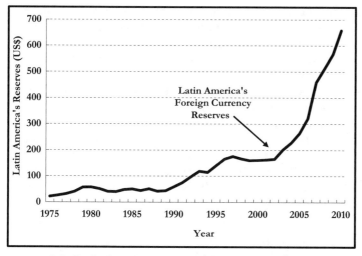

FIGURE 8.1. Latin America's Financial Insurance (US$ billion, 1975–2010).
Source: World Development Indicators.

economic downturn – marking a noteworthy departure from their historic pro-cyclical bias.[30]

Global Financial System's Inequities. Among the reform initiatives discussed above, the choice of strengthening Latin America's reserve arsenal has been particularly controversial. Seeking an insurance policy against market instability, Latin American countries built an impressive war chest of foreign currency reserves between 2006 and 2010, nearly tripling their total reserves in a mere four years (Figure 8.1). This financial artillery helps battle global financial volatility and insulate domestic economic policy from the abrupt credit swings and rate hikes known as sudden stops.

In exchange for this insurance, Latin American governments have unfortunately paid a high opportunity cost. They hold reserves in low-yielding U.S. assets, rather than investing in high-return projects in their own domestic economies. In fact, the current reserve system inherently benefits U.S. firms, offering them a massive amount of foreign financing at cheap interest rates.

According to textbook economic fundamentals, this result is puzzling. Developed country capital should chase the higher relative interest rates offered by developing country debt. In today's international financial system, however, the tide often is reversed. Developing country capital chases the financial security of U.S. treasury bonds. Notwithstanding the recent increase in global investment to Latin America, future global financial volatility threatens to intensify the search for such safe-haven assets, and thus, reverse

---

[30] Gavin and Perotti 1997; Kaminsky, Reinhart, and Végh 2004; Lupu 2006; Pinto 2010.

these regional capital inflows. Foreign currency reserves provide protection against such volatility, but also finance cheap mortgages, corporate subsidies, and government bailouts in the United States. Is this insurance policy optimal, when Latin American countries could use these funds to address their own domestic economic travails?

Beyond this inequity, Latin America's insurance policy may not adequately shelter the region from future global financial turmoil. While Latin America's improved debt profile and more pragmatic governance helped insulate it from the 2008 global financial crisis, it is not clear that the region will have sufficient room to maneuver moving forward. The wave of financial panic that quickly spread across the globe in 2008–2009 offered the following lesson: even developed countries with ostensibly lower default risk are still vulnerable to sudden stops of financing.

8.3. IMPLICATIONS: PARTISAN POLITICS AND ECONOMIC POLICY

This book also makes an important contribution to our understanding of partisan politics in developing democracies. Recall that the political economy literature on macroeconomic policy traditionally segments partisan politics into two worlds.[31] Right-leaning politicians use economic policy to provide a low-inflation environment to businesses and financial constituencies, even at the cost of fewer jobs and lower growth. By contrast, left-leaning politicians are expected to win favor with middle-class and working families by fostering more jobs and higher growth, notwithstanding the potential inflationary cost. Do we find a similar ideological divide in the developing world?

I have explored this question by examining macroeconomic policy making in Latin America, a region where scholars have identified broad ideological and partisan swings, including the emergence and decay of a neoliberal consensus.[32] Political austerity theory contends that in the realm of macroeconomic policy making, however, the neoliberal consensus has not unraveled. Austerity politics has replaced partisan politics, as leftists have become centrists throughout much of the region.

Rather than macroeconomic policy choices reflecting the ideologies of political parties, they are the product of governing in a world of capital mobility and historical inflation volatility. Learning from their past struggles, political leaders and technocratic policy communities have gravitated toward conservative macroeconomic policies that are unlikely to repeat economic shocks or precipitate capital flight.

For instance, Brazil's most famous historical leftists, Fernando Henrique Cardoso and Luiz Inácio Lula da Silva, both embraced economic austerity

---

[31] Hibbs 1977; Alesina 1987; Alesina and Rosenthal 1995; Bartels 2008.
[32] Roberts 1998; Stokes 2001; Murillo 2001; Murillo 2002; Levitsky 2003; Bruhn 2004; Roberts 2012.

during their post-hyperinflation presidencies. Cardoso was a sociologist and world-renowned dependency theorist, trained at the Universidade de São Paulo. Lula was a shoe shiner, factory workers, and union activist. After governing Peru into inflationary mayhem during the late 1980s, President Alan García, once an ardent skeptic of neoliberalism,[33] also became a follower of IMF orthodoxy during his 2006 political reincarnation. Chilean President Ricardo Lagos, a long-time socialist party leader and opposition organizer under the conservative Pinochet dictatorship, formalized a commitment to low inflation by establishing a central bank inflation target and an institutional fiscal surplus rule. Even Hugo Chávez, who led a 1992 coup d'état against Venezuela's neoliberal reforms, adopted economic austerity when faced with a commodity crash and credit crunch early in his presidency.[34]

Future of Partisan Politics in Latin America. If politicians adopted orthodox policies during an era characterized by inflation anxiety and financial market dependency, why has mild inflation and booming commodity markets not swung the region's economics back to the left? The fate of the Latin American political business cycle ultimately rests with the region's financial means and political motivations. Perhaps, Latin American politicians will continue to preserve crisis governance lessons in their technocratic communities, partly to ensure that a rising middle class can profit from growing economic stability. Alternatively, inflation-aversion might instead fade with new generations of policy makers. Hyperinflation may have simply unleashed a *recency effect* on the region's politics, where leaders place a high political premium on current political and economic trauma.[35] How potent is inflation saliency in Latin America?

The German hyperinflation experience shows that inflationary crises can leave a permanent imprint on national psyches. Dreading that aggressive stimulus could lead to a re-emergence of runaway inflation, German society has developed a broad-based consensus in favor of economic discipline. In fact, the political and economic chaos associated with the Weimer Republic's trillion-fold inflation between 1914 and 1923 endures in the collective German technocratic and political consciousness. Notwithstanding the economic fallout from the global financial crisis, Chancellor Angela Merkel's efforts to limit government outlays are widely popular.[36]

Certainly, there are Latin American countries, such as Chile and Brazil, where political and technocratic elites may follow in Germany's unwavering footsteps. However, the political importance of inflation control shows

---

[33] See Chapter 2.

[34] See Chapter 4.

[35] Weber et al. 2004; Hertwig et al. 2004.

[36] The German government passed a constitutional law requiring the government deficit to be capped at 0.35 percent of GDP in 2016 and eliminated by 2020 (James 2009).

signs of receding in other countries. Recall that during Argentina's 2007 presidential election, for example, President Néstor Kirchner had an unwavering commitment to fiscal discipline. However, Kirchner simultaneously infused the economy with a heterodox mix of exchange rate stimulus and price controls, reflecting the complexity of the inflation issue in Argentina today. His administration claimed to be guardians of low inflation, with price increases hovering below 10 percent throughout the election year.[37] Ironically, however, many economists, investors, and opposition politicians questioned the integrity of the government's statistical reports.[38]

This behavior suggests that inflation-aversion may be more mitigated in Argentina currently than elsewhere in the region. After experiencing a severe deflationary spiral and massive unemployment (or the exact opposite of an inflationary shock) that culminated in the 2001–2002 debt crisis, there appears to be more political scope for aggressive macroeconomic intervention. Moreover, shunned from global capital markets since the debt crisis, Argentina's policy actions are no longer subject to the scrutiny of global bond investors. During the 2011 elections, for instance, President Cristina Kirchner fired the twin cylinders of monetary and fiscal policies, notwithstanding the brisk pace of economic growth.

Notably, however, the Kirchner government has aimed to curb inflation through administrative means, including its ongoing tinkering with official inflation statistics. Most likely, it hopes to contain the public outcry over a return of inflation that erodes popular living standards – implying that hyper-inflations' shadow may have receded to some extent, but still looms large.

8.4. IMPLICATIONS: AUSTERITY IN THE DEVELOPED WORLD

In light of recent global financial turbulence, do any of these developing country patterns translate to the developed world? Do markets still perceive the risk of default to be lower in developed country settings, leaving them with greater policy discretion?

The recent financial pandemic has certainly demonstrated that developed countries are no longer immune to the ills of market contagion. High levels of foreign indebtedness have placed the developed world, from Greece and Portugal to the United Kingdom and the United States, under the microscope of global capital markets. Mounting debt burdens have left Southern Europe in a cloud of speculative contagion and prompted Great Britain to impose the biggest cuts in state spending since World War II.

Austerity, however, is not solely a brand of conservative prime ministers such as David Cameron. In the early years of the euro-zone crisis, left-leaning prime ministers, such as Greece's Papandreou, Portugal's José Sócrates, and

---

[37] In 2007, average inflation rose by 8.8 percent in Argentina (EIU Country Database).
[38] See footnote 10 in Chapter 1.

Spain's José Luis Rodríguez Zapatero, also proposed several rounds of austerity in hopes of quelling sovereign default fears among bond investors. Perhaps, the power of creditors is best summarized by former Senator Alan Simpson, the Joint-Chairman of the President Obama's U.S. National Commission on Responsibility and Reform.

Bond markets don't have any thoughts about compassion – it's not your favorite Uncle Henry trying to get an extension on a mortgage, it's hammer time!

Notwithstanding these similarities, two important characteristics of developed world debt leave many policy makers with greater room to maneuver than their developing world counterparts. First, developed country governments have the ability to issue long-term debt in their own currencies, allowing them to reduce both foreign exchange and default risk. A lower financing cost provides these governments with greater policy flexibility than developing country governments.

Second, those governments with global reserve currency status such as the United States benefit from borrowing from public institutions rather than private investors. Compared to myopic portfolio investors, Asian central banks from China, Hong Kong, Malaysia, Taiwan, and Japan possess a long-term stake in the system, making them likely to purchase dollar assets for the foreseeable future. Buying dollar-denominated debt not only allows for cheap currencies that bolster East Asian export competitiveness, it also creates a low-interest rate facility in the United States. Despite "currency war" headlines, both the United States and East Asia have a strong incentive to preserve the status quo in the global financing system.

By contrast, those developed countries without global reserve currency status are more likely to suffer from high funding costs during periods of financial volatility, as demonstrated most crudely by several waves of recent austerity measures in Greece, Italy, Portugal, and Spain. In theory, these countries should benefit from the euro's reserve currency status; however, fears of a eurozone split have led to capital flight from these peripheral countries to core economies like Germany.

Compared to Southern Europe, the United States' global reserve currency status affords it a longer time horizon to solve its budgetary woes. However, even in this unique case, the United States' heavy reliance on foreign capital to fund its budget deficits has raised the country's credit risk. After borrowing trillions of dollars from foreign creditors to fund lofty tax cuts, a hefty stimulus package, and a dual-front war in Iraq and Afghanistan, foreigners today hold about two-thirds of the U.S. government's total debt. Moreover, the United States has taken a page from the Latin American playbook, amassing debt with an average maturity of a mere five years compared to almost fourteen years in Great Britain. U.S. politicians have thus infused higher refinancing risk into their credit rating by facilitating such a short-term debt structure.

Notwithstanding S&P's recent downgrade of U.S. debt, the United States should continue to readily attract foreign capital for the foreseeable future. Against this backdrop, however, President Obama has emphasized the need to reverse the country's "legacy of deficit spending," saying it is "only going to get harder, so we might as well do it now. Pull off the band-aid. Eat our peas."

Without a doubt, tough budgetary choices mount for an increasingly politically polarized United States. Fiscal adjustment is essential to preserving the dollar's global reserve status over the long run. The risk is that the country will not be able to overcome its political gridlock and solve its budgetary woes. But, how will political elites manage this painstaking process amid growing social unrest and class resentment? In confronting similar tensions this past decade, the forging of an elite-governing consensus on macroeconomic policy helped lay the groundwork for Latin America's economic success. Will the United States be able to achieve a similar governing consensus and avoid a looming credit crisis? Or, will its domestic discourse descend deeper into discord, unable to transition from the politics of hope to the politics of austerity?

Field Research Interviews

A sampling of the 100 Latin American field research interviews.

Presidents and Government Ministers

Daniel Artana, Asdrúbal Baptista, Domingo Cavallo, Imelda Cisneros, Alejandro Foxley, Ricardo Hausmann, Ricardo Lagos, Roberto Lavagna, Ricardo López Murphy, Rolf Lüders, Daniel Marx, Moisés Naím, Guillermo Ortega, Luis Palacios, Andrés Palma, Felipe Pérez, Teodoro Petkoff, Miguel Rodríguez, Roberto Smith, Juan Sourrouille, Ramón José Velásquez, and Ignacio Walker.

Budget Directors, Presidential Secretaries and Advisers, and Party Chiefs

Jorge Arrate, Genaro Arriagada, Jorge Baldrich, Sergio Bitar, Edgardo Boeninger, Nicolas Gadano, Ricardo Hormázabal, Carmelo Lauría, Mario Marcel, Francisco Rodríguez, Gustavo Tarre, Humberto Vega, Carlos Vergara, and Joaquín Vial.

Central Bank Presidents, Board Members, and Research Directors

Mario Blejer, José De Gregorio, Ruth De Krivoy, Roque Fernández, Javier González Fraga, José Guerra, Pablo Guidotti, Miguel Kiguel, José Luis Machinea, Felipe Morandé, Manuel Marfan, Domingo Maza Zavala, Alfonso Prat-Gay, and Harold Zavarce.

Bibliography

Abrams, B. A. 2006. How Richard Nixon Pressured Arthur Burns: Evidence from the Nixon Tapes. *Journal of Economic Perspectives* 20, no. 4: 177–88.

Abrams, B. A., and Butkiewicz, J. L. 2012. The Political Business Cycle: New Evidence from the Nixon Tapes. *Journal of Money, Credit and Banking, Blackwell Publishing* 44: 385–99.

Acosta, A., Araujo, M., Liñan, A., and Saiegh, S. 2006. Veto Players, Fickle Institutions and Low-quality Policies: The Policymaking Process in Ecuador (1979–2005). In *Inter-American Development Bank*. Latin American Research Network. Working Paper R-523. Washington, D.C.

Agenor, P. 1998. Stabilization Policies, Poverty, and the Labor Market. Mimeo, *IMF and World Bank*, 1–60.

Agénor, P. C., and Montiel, P. 1999. *Development Macroeconomics*. Princeton, N.J.: Princeton University Press.

Ahlquist, J. S. 2006. Economic Policy, Institutions, and Capital Flows: Portfolio and Direct Investment Flows in Developing Countries. *International Studies Quarterly* 50: 681–704.

Akerlof, G., and Shiller, R. 2009. *Animal Spirits*. Princeton, N.J.: Princeton University Press.

Alesina, A. 1987. Macroeconomic Policy in a Two-Party System as a Repeated Game. *Quarterly Journal of Economics* 102: 651–78.

Alesina, A., and Perotti, R. 1997. Fiscal Adjustments in OECD Countries: Composition and Macroeconomic effects. *IMF Staff Papers* 44, no. 2: 210–48.

Alesina, A. 1988. Macroeconomics and Politics. *National Bureau of Economic Research Macroeconommics Annual* 3: 13–61.

Alesina, A., and Roubini, N. 1992. Political Cycles in OECD Economies. *Review of Economic Studies* 59: 663–88.

Alesina, A., and Summers, L. 1993. Central Bank Independence and Macroeconomic Performance: Some Comparative Evidence. *Journal of Money, Credit, and Banking* 25: 151–62.

Alesina, A., and Rosenthal, H. 1995. *Partisan Cycles, Divided Government, and the Economy*. Cambridge: Cambridge University Press.

Alesina, A., Roubini, N., and Cohen, G. 1997. *Political Cycles and the Macroeconomy*. Cambridge: MIT Press.

Alonso, J. F. Socialism Has Emerged from Scarcity. *El Universal*. 2 April 2009.

Alt, J., and Chrystal, A. 1983. *Political Economics*. Berkeley: University of California Press.

Alt, J., and Lassen, D. 2006. Transparency, Political Polarization, and Political Budget Cycles in OECD Countries. *American Journal of Political Science* 50, no. 3: 530–550.

Alt, J., and Rose, S. 2007. Context-Conditional Political Budget Cycles. *Handbook of Comparative Politics*. In S. Stokes and C. Boix, eds. Oxford: Oxford University Press.

Amann, E., and Baer, W. 2009. The Macroeconomic Record of the Lula Administration, the Roots of Brazil's Inequality, and Attempts to Overcome Them. In *Brazil under Lula: Economy, Politics, and Society under the Worker-President* J. L. Love and W. Baer, eds. New York: Palgrave Macmillan.

Ames, B. 1977. The Politics of Public Spending in Latin America. *American Journal of Political Science* 21, no. 1: 149–176.

Ames, B. 1987. *Political Survival*. Berkeley: University of California Press.

Andrews, D. 1994. Capital Mobility and State Autonomy: Toward a Structural Theory of International Monetary Relations. *International Studies Quarterly* 38: 193–218.

Angell, A., and Pollack, B. 1990. The Chilean Elections of 1989. *Bulletin of Latin American Research* 9, no. 1: 1–24.

Angell, A., and Pollack, B. 1995. The Chilean Elections of 1993: From Polarization to Consensus. *Bulletin of Latin American Research* 14, no. 2: 105–125.

Angell, A., and Pollack, B. 2000. The Chilean Presidential Elections of 1999–2000 and Democratic Consolidation. *Bulletin of Latin American Research* 19:357–378.

Angell, A., and Reig, C. 2006. Change or Continuity? The Chilean Elections of 2005/06. *Bulletin of Latin American Research* 25, no. 4: 481–502.

Aninat, C., Londregan, J., Navia, P., and Vial, J. 2006. Political Institutions, Policymaking Processes, and Policy Outcomes in Chile. In *Inter-American Development Bank*. Latin American Research Network. Working Paper R-521. Washington, D.C.

Arellano, M., and Bond, S. 1991. Some Specification Tests for Panel Data: Monte Carlo Evidence and an Application to Employment Equations. *Review of Economic Studies* 58, no. 2: 277–298.

Arellano, P., and Marfán, M. 1989. Twenty-five Years of Fiscal Policy in Chile. In *The Political Economy of Fiscal Policy*. M. Urrutia, S. Ichimura, and S. Yukawa, eds. United Nations University Human and Social Development Programme: United Nations University Press.

Arestis, P., Fernande de Paula, L., and Ferrari-Filho, F. 2007. Inflation Targeting in Emergin Countries: The Case of Brazil. *Political Economy of Brazil*. P. Arestis and A. Saad-Filho: eds. New York: Palgrave, MacMillan.

Argentina, A Victim of Mexico's Fall, Tries to Recover. *The New York Times*. 12 March 1995.

Argentina Breathes Easier as Crisis Eases in Brazil. *The New York Times*. 5 November 1997.

Argentina's Menem Implements Stern Austerity Plan. *The Washington Post*. 1 March 1995.

Arriagada, G. 1997. *Hacia Un 'Big Bang' del Sistema de Partidos?* Santiago, Chile: Editorial Los Andes.

Avant, D., Finnemore, M., and Sell, S. 2010. *Who Governs the Globe?* Cambridge: Cambridge University Press.

Avelino, G., Brown, D., and Hunter, W. 2005. The Effects of Capital Mobility, Trade Openness, and Democracy on Social Spending in Latin America: 1980–1999. *American Journal of Political Science* 49, no. 3: 625–41.

Babb, S., and Fourcade-Gourinchas, M. 2002. The Rebirth of the Liberal Creed: Paths to Neoliberalism in Four Countries. *American Journal of Sociology* 108, no. 3: 553–79.

Babb, S. 2001. *Managing Mexico: Economists from Nationalism to Neoliberalism.* Princeton, N.J.: Princeton University Press.

Baldini, A. 2005. Fiscal Policy and Business Cycles in an Oil-Producing Economy: The Case of Venezuela. *IMF Working Paper.* No. 05/237.

Baker, A. 2009. *The Market and the Masses in Latin America.* New York: Cambridge University Press.

Baker, A., and Greene, K. 2011. The Latin American Left's Mandate: Free Market Policies and Issue Voting in New Democracies. *World Politics* 63, no. 1: 43–77.

Barberia, L., and Avelino, G. 2011. Do Political Business Cycles Differ in Latin American Countries? *Economia* Spring, 101–46.

Barnett, M., and Finnemore, M. 2004. *Rules for the World: International Organizations in Global Politics.* Ithaca: Cornell University Press.

Barro, R., and Gordon, D. 1983. A Positive Theory of Monetary Policy in a Natural Rate Model. *Journal of Political Economy* 91, no. 4: 589–610.

Barro, R. 1996. Determinants of Economic Growth: A Cross-Country Empirical Study. *NBER Working Paper 5698, National Bureau of Economic Research.*

Bartels, L. 2008. *Unequal Democracy: The Political Economy of the New Gilded Age.* Princeton, N.J.: Princeton University Press.

Bates, R. H., and Lien, D. D. 1985. A Note on Taxation, Development and Representative Government. Working Papers 567, *California Institute of Technology*, Division of the Humanities and Social Sciences.

Bearce, D. H. 2003. Societal Preferences, Partisan Agents, and Monetary Policy Outcomes. *International Organization* 57, Spring, 373–410.

Bernhard, W., Broz, J. L., and Clark, W. R. 2002. The Political Economy of Monetary Institutions. *International Organization* 56, no. 4: 1–32.

Bickers, K., and Stein, R. 1996. The Electoral Dynamics of the Federal Pork Barrel. *American Journal of Political Science* 40, no. 4: 1300–1326.

Bitar, S. 1979. *Transición, Socialismo, y Democracia: La Experiencia Chilena.* Mexico: Siglo Veintiuno Editores.

Bitar, S. 1986. *Chile: Experiment in Democracy.* Philadelphia: Institute for the Study of Human Issues.

Block, F. 1977. *The Origins of International Economic Disorder: A Study of the United States International Monetary Policy from World War II to the Present.* Berkeley: University of California Press.

Block, S. 2002. Political Business Cycles, Democratization, and Economic Reform: The Case of Africa. *Journal of Development Economics* 67: 205–228.

Block, S., and Vaaler P. 2004. The Price of Democracy: Sovereign Risk Ratings, Bond Spreads and Political Business Cycles in Developing Countries. *Journal of International Money and Finance* 23: 917–946.

Boeninger, E. 1990. El Marco Político General y el Marco Institucional del Próximo Gobierno. *Transición a la Democracia.* CIEPLAN: 43–69.

Bogdanowicz-Bindert, C. A. 1986. The Debt Crisis: The Baker Plan Revisited. *Journal of Interamerican Studies and World Affairs* 28, no. 3: 33–45.

Boix, C. 2003. *Democracy and Redistribution.* Cambridge: Cambridge University Press.

Bond, R. V. 2005. *Lecciones Aprendidad de Política Económica en Venezuela: 1936–2004.* Caracas, Instituto Latinoamericano de Investigaciones Sociales.

Bonvecchi, A., and Giraudy, A. 2007. Argentina: Crecimiento Económico y Concentración del Poder Institucional. *Revista de Ciencia Política* Vol. Especial, 29–42.

Borenzstein, E., Eichengreen, B., and Panizza, U. 2006. Building Bond Markets in Latin America. *Unpublished manuscript.* University of California, Berkeley and Inter-American Development Bank, 1–36.

Bosworth, B. P., Dornbusch, R., and Labán, R., eds. 1994. *The Chilean Economy: Policy Lessons and Challenges.* Washington, D.C.: Brookings Institution.

Boylan, D. 1998. Pre-emptive Strike: Central Bank Reform in Chile's Transition from Authoritarian Rule. *Comparative Politics* 30, no. 4: 443–462.

Boylan, D. 2001. *Defusing Democracy: Central Bank Independence and the Transition from Authoratarian Rule.* Ann Arbor, MI: University of Michigan Press.

Brazil Victor Moves to Calm Nervous Markets. *The New York Times.* 29 October 2002.

Brazil's Lula Says Low Inflation As Vital As Growth. *Reuters.* 18 June 2007.

Brazil's Presidential Election: Lula's Legacy. *The Economist.* 30 September 2010.

Brender, A., and Drazen, A. 2005. Political Budget Cycles in New Versus Established Democracies. *Journal of Monetary Economics* 52, no. 7: 1271–1295.

Brender, A, and Drazen, A. 2008. How do Budget Deficits and Economic Growth Affect Reelection Prospects? Evidence from a Large Cross-section of Countries, *NBER Working Paper* No: 11862.

Bresser-Periera, L. C. 2009. *Developing Brazil: Overcoming the Failure of the Washington Consensus.* London: Lynne Rienner Publishers.

Brown, D., and Hunter, W. 2004. Democracy and Social Spending in Latin America: 1980–1992. *American Political Science Review* 93, no. 4: 779–90.

Broz, J. L. 2002. Political System Transparency and Monetary Commitment Regimes. *International Organization* 56, no. 4: 863–89.

Broz, L., and Plouffe, M. 2010. The Effectiveness of Monetary Policy Anchors: Firm-Level Evidence. *International Organization* 64, no. 4: 695–717.

Bruhn, K. 2004. Globalization and the Renovation of the Latin American Left: Strategies of Ideolgoical Adaptation. Paper presented at the annual meeting of the Midwest Political Science Association, Chicago.

Bustani, C. 2001. The 1998 Election in Brazil. *Electoral Studies* 20: 305–309.

Burdick, J., Oxhorn, P., and Roberts, K., eds. 2009. *Beyond Neoliberalism in Latin America: Societies and Politics at the Crossroads?* New York: Palgrave Macmillan.

Buxton, J. 2003. Economic Policy and the Rise of Hugo Chávez . In *Venezuelan Politics in the Chávez Era: Class, Polarization, and Conflict.* S. Ellner and D. Hellinger, eds. London: Lynne Rienner Publisher.

Cagan, P. 1956. The Monetary Dynamics of Hyperinflation. In *Studies in the Quantity Theory of Money.* M. Friedman, ed. Chicago: University of Chicago Press.

Calvo, G. 1998. Capital Flows and Capital-Market Crises: The Simple Economics of Sudden Stops. *Journal of Applied Economics (CEMA)* 1, no. 1: 35–54.

Calvo, G., and Reinhart C. 2000. Fixing Your Life. In *Brookings Trade Forum 2000: Policy Challenges in the Next Millennium*. S. Collins and D. Rodrik, eds. Washington, D.C.: Brookings Institution.

Calvo, G., and Mendoza, E. 2000a. Capital-Markets Crises and Economic Collapse in Emerging Markets: An Informational-Frictions Approach. *American Economic Review* 90: 59–64.

Calvo, G., and Mendoza, E. 2000b. Rational Herd Behavior and the Globalization of Securities Markets. *Journal of International Economics* 51, no. 1: 79–113.

Calvo, G., Izquierdo, A., and Talvi, E. 2003. Sudden Stops, the Real Exchange Rate and Fiscal Sustainability: Argentina's Lessons. In *Monetary Unions and Hard Pegs*. V. Alexander, J. Mélitz and G. M. von Furstenberg, eds. Oxford, United Kingdom: Oxford University Press.

Calvo, G., Izquierdo, A., and Mejia, L. 2004. On the Empirics of Sudden Stops: The Relevance of Balance Sheet Effects. *NBER Working Paper 10520. Washington D.C.: National Bureau of Economic Research.*

Cameron, D. 1978. The Expansion of the Public Economy: A Comparative Analysis. *American Political Science Review* 72, no. 12: 1243–61.

Canes-Wrone, B., and Park, J. 2012. Electoral Business Cycles in OECD Countries. *American Political Science Review* 106, no. 1: 103–22.

Cardim de Carvalho, F. J. 2007. Lula's Government in Brazil: A New Left or the Old Populism? In *Political Economy of Brazil*. P. Arestis and A. Saad-Filho, eds. New York: Palgrave, MacMillan.

Cardim de Carvalho, F. J., and Ferrari-Filho, F. 2007. The Twilight of Lula's Government: Another Failed Experiment with Left-Wing Administrations? In *Political Economy of Brazil*. P. Arestis and A. Saad-Filho, eds. New York: Palgrave, MacMillan.

Cardoso, E. 1992. Inflation and Poverty. *National Bureau of Economic Research Working Paper* 4006, 1–52.

Cardoso, E., and Helwege, A. 1992. *Latin America's Economy: Diversity, Trends, and Conflicts*. Cambridge: MIT Press.

Cardoso, F. H. 1973. Associated Dependent Development: Theoretical and Practical Implications. In *Authoritarian Brazil*. A. Stepan, ed. New Haven: Yale University Press.

Cardoso, F. H., and Faletto, E. 1979. *Dependency and Development in Latin America*. Berkeley: University of California Press.

Cardoso, F. H. 2006. *The Accidental President of Brazil: A Memoir*. Cambridge, MA: Public Affairs.

Carey, J. M. 2003. The Re-election Debate in Latin America. *Latin American Politics and Society* 45, no. 1: 119–133.

Castañeda, J. 2006. Latin America's Left Turn. *Foreign Affairs*. May/June.

Chávez, H., and Harnecker, M. 2005. *Understanding the Venezuelan Revolution: Hugo Chávez Talks to Marta Harnecker*. Monthly Review Press.

Chinn, M. D., and Ito, H. 2008. Forthcoming. A New Measure of Financial Opennness. *Journal of Comparative Policy Analysis* 10, no. 3: 309–32.

Chinn, M. D., and Frieden, J. 2011. *Lost Decades: The Making of America's Debt Crisis and the Long Recovery*. New York: W. W. Norton & Company, Inc.

Cerny, P. 1995. Globalization and the Changing Logic of Collective Action. *International Organization* 49: 595–626.

CESOP (Centro de Estudos de Opinião Pública. Universidade Estadual de Campinas). 1994. O Brasil através de Pacotes Econômicos. *Opinião Pública: Encarte de Dados* 2, no. 1: 1–16.

Chumacero, R., Fuentes, R.,Lüders, R., and Vial, J. 2006. Understanding Chilean Reforms. In *Global Research Project on Understanding Reform*. Global Development Network. Working Paper. New Delhi.

Clamor Over Chilean Copper. *Time*. 27 June 1969.

Clark, W. 2003. *Capitalism, Not Globalism: Capital Mobility, Central Bank Independence, and the Political Control of the Economy*. Ann Arbor, MI: University of Michigan Press.

Cline, W. R. 1995. *International Debt Reexamined*. Washington, D.C.: Institute for International Economics.

Coes, D. V. 2009. Exchange Rate Policy, Perceptions of Risk, and External Constraints under Lula. In *Brazil Under Lula: Economy, Politics, and Society under the Worker President*. J. L. Love and W. Baer, eds. New York: Palgrave Macmillan.

Cohen, B. 1986. *In Whose Interest? International Banking and American Foreign Policy*. New Haven: Yale University Press.

Cohen, B. 1996. Phoenix Risen: The Resurrection of Global Finance. *World Politics* 48, no. 2: 268–296.

Coppedge, M. 1997. A Classification of Latin American Political Parties. Working Paper Series 244. *The Helen Kellogg Institute for International Studies*, University of Notre Dame.

Corbo, V. 2005. "Monetary Policy and Central Bank Independence in Chile." Prepared for the *Banco de Mexico Conference*, November 14–15.

Corrales, J. 2002a. *Presidents Without Parties: The Politics of Economic Reform in Argentina and Venezuela in the 1990s*. University Park: The Pennsylvania University Press.

Corrales, J. 2002b. The Politics of Argentina's Meltdown. *World Policy Journal*. 19, no. 3: 29–42.

Corrales, J., and Penfold, M. 2007. Venezuela: Crowding Out the Opposition. *Journal of Democracy* 18, no. 2: 99–113.

Corrales, J., and Penfold, M. 2011. *Dragon in the Tropics: Hugo Chavez and the Political Economy of Revolution in Venezuela*. Washington, D.C.: Brookings Institution Press.

Coursol, A., and Wagner, E. 1986. "Effect of Positive Findings on Submission and Acceptance Rates: A Note on Meta-Analysis Bias." *Professional Psychology* 17: 136–137.

Cox, G., and McCubbins, M. 1986. Electoral Politics as a Redistributive Game. *The Journal of Politics* 48: 370–89.

Crowson, P. 2007. The Copper Industry, 1945–1975. *Resources Policy* 21, no. 1–2: 1–18.

Cukierman, A. 1992. *Central Bank Strategy, Credibility, and Independence*. Cambridge: MIT Press.

Cukierman, A., Webb, S., and Neyapti, B. 1992. Measuring the Independence of Central Banks and Its Effect on Policy Outcomes. *World Bank Economic Review* 6, no. 3: 353–98.

Cutler, D. M., and Katz, L. 1991. Macroeconomic Performance and the Disadvantaged. *Brookings Papers on Economic Activity* 2: 1–66.

DaCosta, M., and Olivo, V. 2008. Constraints on the Design and Implementation of Monetary Policy in Oil Economies: The Case of Venezuela. *IMF Working Paper* 8, no. 142.

Dahl, R. A. 1971. *Polyarchy: Participation and Opposition*. New Haven: Yale University Press.

D'Anieri, P. J., Kravchuk, R., and Kuzio, T. 1999. *Politics and Society in the Ukraine*. Colorado: Westview Press.

Davis, C. 2012. *Why Adjudicate? Enforcing Trade Rules in the WTO*. Princeton, N.J.: Princeton University Press.

Dawkins, R. 1999. *The Selfish Gene*. Oxford: Oxford University Press.

DeLong, J. B., and Lang, K. 1992. Are All Economic Hypotheses False? *Journal of Political Economy*. 100:1257–72.

Diamond, L., and Linz, J. 1989. Introduction: Politics, Society, and Democracy in Latin America. *Democracy in Developing Countries*. Boulder, CO: Lynn Rieyner Publishers.

Diamond, L.1999. *Developing Democracy: Toward Consolidation*. Baltimore, M.D.: The Johns Hopkins University Press.

Díaz-Bonilla, E., and Schamis, H. E. 2001. From Redistribution to Stability: The Evolution of Exchange Rate Policies in Argentina, 1950–1998. In *The Currency Game: Exchange Rate Politics in Latin America*. J. Frieden and E. Stein, eds. Baltimore, M.D.: The Johns Hopkins University Press.

Dickersin, K. 1990. The Existence of Publication Bias and Risk Factors for Its Occurrence. *Journal of the American Medical Association* 263: 1385–89.

Di Tella, T.S. 1999. Argentina Becoming 'Normal': the 1999 Elections. *Government and Opposition* 35, no. 1: 67–76.

Donnelly, J. 2000. *Realism in International Relations*. Cambridge: Cambridge University Press.

Dornbusch, R., and Edwards, S. 1989. The Macroeconomics of Populism. In *The Macroeconomics of Populism in Latin America*. R. Dornbusch and S. Edwards, eds. Chicago: University of Chicago Press, 15–44.

Dornbusch, R. 2000. *Keys to Prosperity: Free Markets, Sound Money, and a Bit of Luck*. Cambridge, MA: MIT Press.

Dornbusch, R., Fischer, S., and Startz, R. 2001. *Macroeconomics*. New York: McGraw-Hill Higher Education.

Drazen, A. 2000. The Political Business Cycle After 25 Years. *NBER Macroeconomic Annual*. Cambridge: MIT Press.

Drazen, A. 2000. *Political Economy in Macroeconomics*. Princeton, N.J.: Princeton University Press.

Drazen, A., and Brender A. 2005. Political Budget Cycles in New Versus Established Democracies. *Journal of Monetary Economics* 52, no. 7: 1271–95.

Drazen, A., and Eslava, M. 2010. Electoral Manipulation via Voter-Friendly Spending: Theory and Evidence. *Journal of Development Economics* 92, no. 1: 39–52.

Dreher, A. 2005. IMF and Economic Growth: The Effects of Programs, Loans, and Compliance with Conditionality. *Working Paper*. Zurich, Switzerland. Swiss Federal Institute of Technology.

Dreher, A., Marchesi S., and Vreeland, J. 2008. The Politics of IMF Forecasts. *Working Paper.*

Dreher, A., Sturm, J., and Vreeland, J. 2009. Global Horse Trading: IMF Loans for Votes in the United Nations Security Council. *European Economic Review* 53, no. 7: 742–757.

Duch, R., and Stevenson, R. 2004. The Economy: Do they get it Right? Paper presented at the 2004 Annual Meeting of the Midwest Political Science Association, Chicago, April 15–19, 2004.

Dunning, T. 2008. *Crude Democracy: Natural Resource Wealth and Political Regimes.* New York: Cambridge Studies in Comparative Politics, Cambridge University Press.

Dunning, T. 1790. Engodenous Oil Rents. *Comparative Political Studies* 43, no. 3: 379–410.

Duverger, M. 1954. *Political Parties: Their Organization and Activity in the Modern State.* Trans. by B., and R. North. New York: Wiley Press.

Easterly, W., Rodríguez, C., and Schmidt-Hebbel, K. 1994. *Public Sector Deficits and Macro Economic Performance.* New York: Oxford University Press.

Easterly, W., and Fischer, S. 2000. Inflation and the Poor. *World Bank Policy Research Working Paper* 2335.

Easterly, W. 2001. *The Elusive Quest for Growth: Economists' Adventures and Misadventures in the Tropics.* Cambridge, MA: MIT Press.

Easterly, W. 2004. What Did Structural Adjustment Adjust? The Association of Policies and Growth with Repeated IMF and World Bank Adjustment Loans. *Journal of Economic Development* 76, no. 1: 1–22.

Echegaray, F., and Elordi, C. 2001. Public Opinion, Presidential Popularity, and Economic Reform in Argentina 1989–1996. In *Public Support for Market Reforms in New Democracies.* S. Stokes, ed. New York: Cambridge University Press.

Economic Commission for Latin America and the Caribbean 1988–06. *Statistical Yearbook for Latin America and the Caribbean.* New York: The United Nations.

Economic Commission for Latin America and the Caribbean. 1989. Preliminary Overview of the Economy of Latin America and the Caribbean. Santiago: The United Nations.

Edwards, S. 1989. The International Monetary Fund and the Developing Countries: A Critical Evaluation. *Carnegie-Rochester Conference Series on Public Policy: IMF Policy Advice, Market Volatility, Commodity Price Rules and other Essays*, North-Holland: 7–68.

Edwards, S. 1994. The Political Economy of Inflation and Stabilization in Developing Countries. *Economic Development and Cultural Change* 42: 235–66.

Edwards, S. 1995. *Crisis and Reform in Latin America: From Despair to Hope.* Published for the World Bank. Oxford: Oxford University Press.

Edwards, S. 2001. *Crime and Punishment: Understanding IMF Sanctioning Practices.* Mimeo: Rutgers University.

Edwards, S. 2007. Capital Controls, Capital Flow Contractions, and Macroeconomic Volatility. *Journal of International Monetary and Finance* 26, no. 5: 814–840.

Eichengreen, B., and Mody, A. 1998. What Explains Changing Spreads on Emerging Market-Debt: Fundamentals or Market-Sentiment? NBER Working Paper 6408. Washington, DC: National Bureau of Economic Research.

Eichengreen, B., Hausmann, R., and Panizza, U. 2004. The Mystery of Original Sin. In *Other People's Money: Debt Denomination and Financial Instability in Emerging Market Economics*. B. Eichengreen and R. Hausmann, eds. Chicago: University of Chicago Press.

Eichengreen, B. 2003. *Capital Flows and Crisis*. Cambridge: MIT Press.

Ellner, S. 2008. *Rethinking Venezuelan Politics: Class, Conflict and the Chávez Phenomenon*. London: Lynne Rienner Publishers.

Engel, E., and Meller, P., eds. 1993. *External Shocks and Stabilization Mechanisms*. Washington, D.C. and Baltimore: Inter-American Development Bank and John Hopkins University Press.

Farrell, H. 2009. *The Political Economy of Trust: Interests, Institutions, and Inter-Firm Cooperation in Italy and Germany*. New York: Cambridge University Press.

Fearon, J. D. 1991. Counterfactuals and Hypothesis Testing in Political Science. *World Politics* 43, no. 2: 169–95.

Federal Deposit Insurance Corporation. 1997. *A History of the Eighties–Lessons for the Future*. Washington, D.C.: FDIC's Division of Research and Statistics.

Fernández, R. 1991. What Have Populists Learned from Hyperinflation? In *The Macroeconomics of Populism in Latin America*. R. Dornbusch and S. Edwards, eds. Chicago: University of Chicago Press, 121–49.

Ffrench-Davis, R. 1973. *Politicas Economicas en Chile, 1952–1970*. Centro de Estudios de Planificacion Nacional, Universidad Catolica de Chile.

Ffrench-Davis, R. 2002. *Economic Reforms in Chile: From Dictatorship to Democracy*. Ann Arbor, MI The University of Michigan Press.

Finnemore, M. 2004. *The Purpose of Intervention: Changing Beliefs about the Use of Force*. Ithaca, New York: Cornell University Press.

Fishlow, A. 1997. Is the *Real* Plan for Real? In *Brazil under Cardoso*. S. K. Purcell and R. Roett, eds. Boulder, CO: The Americas Society and Lynne Rienner Publishers, Inc.

Filc, G., and Scartascini, C. G. 2007. Budget Institutions. In *The State of State Reform*. E. Lora, ed. Palo Alto: Stanford University Press and the World Bank.

Foxley, A. 1989. Bases Para El Desarrollo de la Economía Chilena: Una Visión Alternativa. *Colección Estudios, CIEPLAN* 26, no. 6: 175–85.

Foxley, A. 1990. La Política Económica para la Transición. *Transición a la Democracia, CIEPLAN: 101–36*.

Foxley, A. 1993. *Economía Política de la Transición*. Santiago, Chile, Ediciones Dolmen.

Frankel, J. A., and Orszag, P. R. 2002. *American Economic Policy in the 1990s*. Cambridge: The MIT Press.

Frankel, J. A. 2005. Contractionary Currency Crashes in Developing Countries. *National Bureau of Economic Research Working Paper* 11508, 1–60.

Franzese, R. 2002. Electoral and Partisan Cycles in Economic Policies and Outcomes. *Annual Review of Political Science* 5, 369–22.

Frieden, J. 1987. *Banking on the World*. New York: Harper & Row.

Frieden, J. 1991. *Debt, Development, and Democracy: Modern Political Economy in Latin America, 1965–1985*. Princeton, N.J.: Princeton University Press.

Frieden, J., and Stein, E. eds. 2001. *The Currency Game: Exchange Rate Politics in Latin America*. Washington, D.C., Baltimore, M.D.: The Johns Hopkins University Press.

Frieden, J., Ghezzi, P., and Stein, E. 2001. Politics and Exchange Rates: A Cross-Country Approach. J. Frieden and E. Stein, eds. In *The Currency Game: Exchange Rate Politics in Latin America.* Baltimore, M.D.: The Johns Hopkins University Press.

Friedman M. 1968. The Role of Monetary Policy. *American Economic Review* 58, no. 1: 1–17.

Friedman, M. 1970. A Theoretical Framework for Monetary Analysis. *The Journal of Political Economy* 78, no. 2: 193–238.

Galiani, S., Heymann, D., and Tommasi, M. 2003. Great Expectations and Hard Times: The Argentine Convertibility Plan. *Economia: Journal of the Latin American and Carribean Economic Association* 3, no. 2: 109–60.

García Osio, G., Penfold, R., Balza R. R., Marcano, L, and Sánchez, G. 1997. La Sostenibilidad de La Política Fiscal en Venezuela. *Banco Interamericano de Desarollo*, Documento de Trabajo No. R-317 y *Revista del Banco Central de Venezuela*, Volumen XI (2).

Garreton, M. A. 2000. Chile's Elections: Change and Continuity. *Journal of Democracy* 11, no. 2: 78–84.

Garrett, G. 1998a. *Partisan Politics in the Global Economy.* New York: Cambridge University Press.

Garrett, G. 1998b. Global Markets and National Politics: Collision Course or Virtuous Circle? *International Organization* 52, no. 4: 787–824.

Garrett, G., and Mitchell, D. 2001. Globalization and the Welfare State. *European Journal of Political Research* 39, no. 2: 145–177.

Gavin, M., and Perotti, R. 1997. Fiscal Policy in Latin America. *NBER Macroeconomic Annual.* Cambridge: MIT Press.

Gerber, A., Green, D., and Nickerson, D. 2001. Testing for Publication Bias in Political Science. Political Analysis 9, no. 4: 385–392.

Gonzalez, M. 2002. Do Changes in Democracy Affect the Political Budget Cycle?: Evidence from Mexico. *Review of Development Economics* 6, no. 2: 204–224.

Greif, A., Milgrom, P., and Weingast, B. R. 1994. Coordination, Commitment, and Enforcement: The Case of the Merchant Guild. *Journal of Political Economy* 102: 745–76.

Grilli, V., Masciandaro, D., and Tabellini, G. 1991. Political and Monetary Institutions and Public Finance Policies in the Industrial Countries. *Economic Policy* 13: 341–392.

Grindle, M., and Thoumi, F. 1993. Muddling Toward Adjustment: The Political Economy of Economic Policy Change in Ecuador. In *Political and Economic Interactions in Economic Policy Reform: Evidence from Eight Countries.* R. Bates and A. Krueger, eds. Cambridge: Blackwell Publishers.

Green, D., Kim, S. Y., and Yoon, D. 2001. Dirty Pool. *International Organization* 55, no. 2: 441–468.

Guerra, J. 2006. *Venezuela Endeudada: De Carlos Andrés Pérez a Hugo Chávez.* Caracas, De la A a la Za Ediciones.

Guidotti, P. E. 2004. Global Finance, Macroeconomic Performance, and Policy Response in Latin America: Lessons from the 1990s. *Working Paper, Buenos Aires: Universidad Torcuato Di Tella.*

Guisinger, A., and Singer, D. A. 2010. Exchange Rate Proclamations and Inflation-Fighting Credibility. *International Organization* 64, no. 2: 313–337.

Gupta, S., Clements, B., Baldacci, E., and Mulas-Granados, C. 2005a. Fiscal Policy, Expenditure Composition, and Growth in Low-Income Countries. *Journal of International Money and Finance* 24, April: 441–63.

Gupta, S., Baldacci, E., Clements, B., and Tiongson, E. 2005b: What sustains fiscal consolidation in emerging market countries? *International Journal of Finance and Economics* 10, no. 4: 304–21.

Guttman, W., and Meehan P. 1976. *The Great Inflation, Germany 1919–23*. Gordan and Cremonesi. Printed by Clifford Frost Ltd.

Hacker, J., and Pierson, P. 2005. *Off Center: The Republican Revolution and the Erosion of American Democracy*. New Haven: Yale University Press.

Haggard, S. 1985. The Politics of Adjustment: Lessons from the IMF's Extended Fund Facility. *International Organization* 39, no. 3: 505–34.

Haggard, S., and Kaufman, R. 2008. *Development, Democracy, and Welfare States: Latin America, East Asia, and Eastern Europe*. Princeton, N.J.: Princeton University Press.

Haggard, S., and Kaufman, R. 2008. *Development, Democracy, and Welfare States: Latin America, East Asia, and Eastern Europe*. Princeton, Princeton University Press.

Hall, P. 1993. Policy Paradigms, Social Learning, and the State: The Case of Economic Policymaking in Britain. *Comparative Politics* 25, no. 3: 275–96.

Hallerberg, M., and Marier, P. 2004. Executive Authority, the Personal Vote, and Budget Discipline in Latin American and Caribbean Countries. *American Journal of Political Science* 48, no. 3: 571–87.

Hawkins, K. 2003. Populism in Venezuela: The Rise of Chavismo. *Third World Quarterly* 24, no. 6: 1137–60.

Heath, R.M. 2007. Presidential and Congressional Elections in Chile, December 2005 and January 2006. *Electoral Studies* 26: 507–33.

Helleiner, E. 1994. *States and the Remergence of Global Finance*. Ithaca: Cornell University Press.

Hellinger, D. 2003. Political Overview: The Breakdown of Puntofijismo and the Rise of Chavismo. In *Venezuelan Politics in the Chávez Era: Class, Polarization, and Conflict*. S. Ellner and D. Hellinger, eds. London: Lynne Rienner Publishers.

Heller, P. 2005. Understanding Fiscal Space. *IMF Policy Discussion Paper 5*, no. 4: 1–18.

Hertwig, R., Barron, G., Weber, E. U., and Erev, I. 2004. Decisions from Experience and the Effect of Rare Events. *Psychological Science* 15: 534–39.

Hey, J. A. K., and Klak, T. 1999. From Protectionism Towards Neoliberalism: Ecuador Across Four Administrations, (1981–1996). *Studies in Comparative International Development* 34, no. 3: 66–97.

Hibbs, D. 1977. Political Parties and Macroeconomic Policy. *American Political Science Review* 71: 1467–87.

Hibbs, D. 1987. *The American Political Economy*. Cambridge, MA: Harvard University Press.

Hojman, D. E. 1993. *Chile: The Political Economy of Development and Democracy in the 1990s*. London: MacMillan Press.

Huber, E., and Stephens, J. D. 2001. *Development and Crisis of the Welfare State: Parties and Policies in Global Markets*. Chicago, University of Chicago Press.

Huber, E., Mustillo, T., and Stephens, J. D. 2008. Politics and Social Spending in Latin America. *Journal of Politics* 70, no. 2: 420–436.

International Monetary Fund. 2001. *A Manual on Government Finance Statistics*. Washington, D.C.: International Monetary Fund.

Iverson, T., Pontusson, J., and Soskice, D. 2000. *Unions, Employers and Central Banks: Macroeconomic Coordination and Institutional Change in Social Market Economies*. New York: Cambridge University Press.

Jácome, L. I. 2001. Legal Central Bank Independence and Inflation in Latin America During the 1990s. *IMF Working Paper* 01, no. 212.

Jácome, L. I., and Vázquez, F. 2005. Any Link Between Legal Central Bank Independence and Inflation? Evidence from Latin America and the Caribbean. *IMF Working Paper* 05, no. 75.

James, H. 2009. Germany's Fiscal Follies. *Project Syndicate*. 3 July 2009.

Jenkins, P., and Baker, A. 2008. Mechanisms of Song Differentiation in Introduced Populations of Chaffinches Fringilla Coelebs in New Zealand. *The International Journal of Avian Science* 126, no. 4: 510–24.

Jervis, R. 1976. *Perceptions and Misperceptions in International Politics*. Princeton, N.J.: Princeton University Press.

Kahneman, D., and Tversky, A. 1979. Prospect Theory: An Analysis of Decision under Risk. *Econometrica* 47, no. 2: 263–92.

Kaminsky, G., Reinhart, C., and Végh, C. 2004. When It Rains, It Pours: Procyclical Capital Flows and Macroeconomic Policies. *Working Paper 10780*. Cambridge: National Bureau of Economic Research.

Kaplan, S. B. 2006. The Political Obstacles to Greater Exchange Rate Flexibility in China. *World Development* 34, no. 7: 1182–1200.

Kaplan, S. B. 2008. How Globalization Transformed Macroeconomic Policymaking in Latin American Elections. Paper presented at the Annual Meeting of the American Political Science Association, August 30, Boston, Massachusetts.

Kaplan, S. B. 2009. *From Spendthrifts to Misers: Globalization and Latin American Politicians*. Ph.D. Dissertation, Department of Political Science, Yale University.

Karl, T. L. 1997. *The Paradox of Plenty: Oil Booms and Petro-States*. Berkeley: University of California Press.

Katzenstein, P. J. 1985. *Small States in World Markets: Industrial Policy in Europe*. Ithaca, New York: Cornell University Press.

Kaufman, R., and Stallings, B. 1991. The Political Economy of Latin American Populism. In *The Macroeconomics of Populism in Latin America*. R. Dornbusch and S. Edwards, eds. Chicago, University of Chicago Press, 15–44.

Kaufman, R., and Segura-Ubiergo, A. 2001. Globalization, Domestic Politics, and Social Spending in Latin America: A Time-Series Cross-Section Analysis, 1973–1997. *World Politics* 53 (July): 553–87.

Keefer, P. 2005. Democratization and Clientelism: Why Are Young Democracies Badly Governed? *World Bank Policy Research Working Paper* 3594. Washington, D.C.: World Bank.

Keefer, P., and Khemani, S. 2005. Democracy, Public Expenditure, and the Poor: Understanding Political Incentives for Providing Public Services. *World Bank Research Observer* 20, no. 1: 1–27.

Keohane, R. 1984. *After Hegemony: Cooperation and Discord in the World Political Economy*. Princeton, N.J.: Princeton University Press.

Keohane, R., and Martin, L. 1995. The Promise of Institutionalist Theory. *International Security* 20, no. 1: 39–51.

Keohane, R., and Milner, H. 1996. Internationalization and Domestic Politics: An Introduction. In *Internationalization and Domestic Politics*. R. Keohane and H. Milner, eds. Cambridge: Cambridge University Press, 25–47.

Khong, Y. F. 1992. *Analogies at War*. Princeton, N.J.: Princeton University Press.

Kiguel, M. A., and Liviatan, N. 1992. Exchange-Rate-Based Stabilization in Argentina and Chile. *World Bank Policy Research Working Paper 1318*. Washington, D.C.: The World Bank.

King, G., Keohane, R., and Verba, S. 1994. *Designing Social Inquiry: Scientific Inference in Qualitative Research*. Princeton, N.J.: Princeton University Press.

Kohno, M., and Nishizawa, Y. 1990. A Study of the Electoral Business Cycle in Japan: Elections and Government Spending on Public Construction. *Comparative Politics* 22: 151–66.

Kravchuk, R. 2002. *Ukrainian Political Economy: The First Ten Years*. New York: Palgrave Macmillan.

Krueger, A., and Turan, I. 1993. The Politics and Economics of Turkish Policy Reform in the 1980s. In *Political and Economics Interactions in Economic Policy Reform: Evidence from Eight Countries*. R. Bates and A. Krueger, eds. Oxford: Basil Blackwell.

Krugman, P. 1994. LDC Debt Policy. In *American Economic Policy in the 1980s*. M. Feldstein, ed. Chicago: University of Chicago Press, 691–722.

Krugman, P. R., and Obstfeld, M. 2003. *International Economics: Theory and Policy*. Boston, MA: Addison Wesley.

Kurtz, M. J. and Brooks, S. M. 2008. Embedding Neoliberal Reform in Latin America. *World Politics* 60: 231–80.

Kurzer, P. 1993. *Business and Banking: Political Change and Economic Integration in Western Europe*. Ithaca: Cornell University Press.

Lake, David. 1996. Anarchy, Hierarchy, and the Variety of International Relations. *International Organization* 50, no. 1, 1–33.

Lapper, R. Kirchner's Ruse. *Financial Times*. 17 September 2006.

Larraín, F., and Meller, P. 1991. The Socialist-Populist Chilean Experience: 1970–73. In *Macroeconomic of Populism in Latin America*. R. Dornbusch and S. Edwards, eds. Chicago: National Bureau of Economic Research and University of Chicago Press: 175–222.

Larraín, F., and Meller, P. 1991. The Socialist-Populist Chilean Experience: 1970–1973. In *The Macroeconomics of Populism in Latin America*. R. Dornbusch and S. Edwards, eds. Chicago: University of Chicago Press, 175–214.

Larraín, F., and Assael, E. 1995. Cincuenta Años de Ciclos Político Económico en Chile. *Cuadernos de Economía* 32, no. 96: 129–150.

Leblang, D., and Bernhard, W. 2000. The Politics of Speculative Attacks in Industrial Democracies. *International Organization* 54: 291–324.

Leblang, D. 2002. The Political Economy of Speculative Attacks in the Developing World. *International Studies Quarterly* 46: 69–91.

Levitsky, S. 2000. The Normalization of Argentine Politics. *Journal of Democracy* 11, no. 2: 56–69.

Levitsky, S. 2003. *Transforming Labor-Based Parties in Latin America: Argentine Peronism in Comparative Perspective*. New York: Cambridge University Press.

Levitsky, S., and Roberts, K. 2011. *The Resurgence of the Latin American Left.* Baltimore, M.D.: The Johns Hopkins University Press.

Levy, J. 1994. Learning and Foreign Policy: Sweeping a Conceptual Mind Field. *International Organization* 48, no. 2: 279–312.

Lewis-Beck, M. 1988. *Economics and Elections.* Ann Arbor: University of Michigan Press.

Limosani, M., and Navarra, P. 2001. Local Pork-Barrel Politics in National Pre-Election Dates: The Case of Italy. *Public Choice* 106, no. 3–4: 317–326.

Lindbeck, A. 1976. Stabilization Policies in Open Economies with Endogenous Politicians. *American Economic Review* 66, 1–19.

Lindblom, C. 1977. *Politics and Markets: The World's Political-Economic Systems.* New York: Basic Books.

Lindblom, C. 1982. The Market as Prison. *The Journal of Politics* 44, no. 2: 324–336.

Lohmann, S. 1998. Federalism and Central Bank Independence: The Politics of German Monetary Policy, 1957–1992. *World Politics* 50, no. 3: 401–446.

López Maya, M. 2005. *Del Viernes Negro Al Referendo Revocatorio.* Caracas, Venezuela: Alfa Grup Editorial.

Lucas, R. 1976. Econometric Policy Evaluation: A Critique. *Carnegie-Rochester Conference Series on Public Policy.* 1: 19–46.

Lupu, N. 2006. Cyclical Tolerance for Inequality: Explaining the Procyclicality of Fiscal Policy in Middle-Income Democracies. Unpublished typescript, Princeton University.

Lupu, N. and Pontusson, J. 2011. The Structure of Inequality and the Politics of Redistribution. *American Political Science Review* 105, no. 2: 316–36.

Lynch, N. 2007. What the "Left" Means In Latin America Now. *Constellations* 14, no. 3: 373–83.

Machinea, J. L. 1990. *Stabilization Under Alfons ín's Government: A Frustrated Attempt.* Buenos Aires, CEDES.

Mainwaring, S. 1993. Presidentialism, Multipartism, and Democracy: The Difficult Combination. *Comparative Political Studies* 26, no. 2: 198–28.

Mainwaring, S., and Sully, T., eds. 2010. *Democratic Governance in Latin America.* Stanford: Stanford University Press.

Manzetti, L. 1991. *The International Monetary Fund and Economic Stabilization: The Argentine Case.* New York: Praeger Publishers.

Mankiw, N. G. 2003. *Macroeconomics.* New York: Worth Publishers.

Marichal, C. 1989. *A Century of Debt Crises in Latin America: From Independence to Great Depression, 1820–1930.* Princeton, N.J.: Princeton University Press.

Maug, E., and Naik, N. 1996. Herding and Delegating Portfolio Management: The Impact of Relative Performance Evaluation on Asset Allocation. Unpublished Manuscript, London Business School.

Maxfield, S. 1997. *Gatekeepers of Growth: The International Political Economy of Central Banking in Developing Countries.* Princeton, N.J.: Princeton University Press.

Mayhew, D. 1974. *Congress: The Electoral Connection.* New Haven: Yale University Press.

McNamara, K. R. 1998. *The Currency of Ideas: Monetary Politics in the European Union.* Ithaca: Cornell University Press.

Mejía Acosta, A., and Coppedge, M. 2001. Political Determinants of Fiscal Discipline in Latin America, 1979–1998. Paper presented for the *International Congress of the Latin American Studies Association.* Washington, September 5–8.

Meller, P., Lehmann, S., and Cifuentes, R. 1993. *Los Gobiernos de Aylwin Y Pinochet: Comparación de Indicadores Económicos y Sociales.* Apuntes CEIPLAN, 118.

Meller, P. 2000. *The Unidad Popular and the Pinochet Dictatorship.* A Political Economy Analysis. New York: St. Mantzńs Press.

Meller, P. 2005. *La Paradoja Aparente.* Santiago, Chile: Taurus Press.

Milgrom, P. R., North, D., and Weingast, B. R. 1990. The Role of Institutions in the Revival of Trade: The Law Merchant, Private Judges, and the Champagne Fairs. *Economics and Politics* 2, no. 1: 1–23.

Mitchener, K. J., and Weidenmier, M. D. 2005. Empire, Public Goods, and the Roosevelt Corollary. *Journal of Economic History* 65, no. 3: 658–92.

Monaldi, F., González, R. A., Obuchi, R., and Penfold, M. 2006. Political Institutions, Policymaking Processes, and Policy Outcomes in Venezuela. In *Inter-American Development Bank.* Latin American Research Network. Working Paper R-507. Washington, D.C.

Monaldi, F., and Penfold, M. 2009. Institutional Collapse: The Rise and Decline of Democratic Governance in Venezuela. In *Venezuela: Anatomy of a Collapse.* F. Rodríguez and R. Hausmann, eds. Center for International Development and the David Rockefeller Center for Latin American Studies at Harvard University, the Instituto de Estudios Superiores de Administración (IESA), and the Andean Development Corporation (CAF).

Moreno, M. A., and Shelton, C. 2009. Sleeping in the Bed One Makes: The Venezuelan Fiscal Response to the Oil Boom. In *Venezuela: Anatomy of a Collapse.* F. Rodríguez and R. Hausmann, eds. Center for International Development and the David Rockefeller Center for Latin American Studies at Harvard University, the Instituto de Estudios Superiores de Administración (IESA), and the Andean Development Corporation (CAF).

Morrison, K. 2009. Oil, Non-tax Revenue, and the Redistributional Foundations of Regime Stability. *International Organization* 63:107–138.

Mosley, L. 2000. Room to Move: International Financial Markets and National Welfare States. *International Organization* 54: 737–773.

Mosley, L. 2003. *Global Capital and National Governments.* New York: Cambridge University Press.

Muñoz, O., ed. 1990. *Transición a la Democracia. Marco Político y Económico.* Santiago, Chile: CIEPLAN.

Murillo, M. V. 2001. *Labor Unions, Partisan Coalitions, and Market Reforms in Latin America.* New York: Cambridge University Press.

Murillo, M. V. 2002. Political Bias in Policy Convergence: Privatization Choices in Latin America. *World Politics* 54, no. 4: 462–93.

Murillo, M. V., and Martinez-Gallardo, C. 2007. Political Competition and Policy Adoption: Market Reforms in Latin American Public Utilities. *American Journal of Political Science* 51, no. 1: 120–39.

Mussa, M. 2002. *Argentina and the Fund: From Triumph to Tragedy.* Washington, D.C.: Institute for International Economics.

Naím, M. 1993. *Paper Tigers and Minotaurs: The Politics of Venezuela's Economic Reforms.* Washington, D.C.: Carnegie Endowment for International Peace.

Nooruddin, I., and Vreeland, J. 2008. The Effect of IMF Programs on Public Wages and Salaries. Paper prepared for the *Workshop on Global Governance, Poverty and Inequality.* Waterloo, Ontario.

Nooruddin, I. 2011. *Coalition Politics and Economic Development*. Cambridge: Cambridge University Press.

Nordhaus, W. 1975. The Political Business Cycle. *Review of Economic Studies* 42, 169–90.

North, D. 1990. *Institutions, Institutional Change, and Economic Performance*. New York: Cambridge University Press.

Obstfeld, M., and Rogoff, K. 1996. *Foundations of International Macroeconomics*. Cambridge: MIT Press.

Obstfeld, M. 1998. The Global Capital Market: Benefactor or Menace? *Journal of Economic Perspectives*. 12, no. 4: 9–30.

Obstfeld, M., and Taylor, A. 2005. *Global Capital Markets: Intergration, Crisis, and Growth*. Cambridge: Cambridge University Press.

O'Donnell, G. 1989. Transitions to Democracy: Some Navigation Instruments. In *Democracy in the Americas: Stopping the Pendulum*. R. A. Pastor, ed. New York: Holmes & Meier.

O'Donnell, G. 1994. Delegative Democracy. *Journal of Democracy 5*, 55–69.

O'Donnell, G. 1999. Delegative Democracy. *Counterpoints: Selected Essays on Authoritarianism and Democratization*. Notre Dame: University of Notre Dame Press.

O'Donnell, G., Mainwaring, S., and Valenzuela, S. 2002. *Issues in Democratic Consolidation: The New South American Democracies in Comparative Perspective*. Notre Dame: University of Notre Dame Press.

Olson, M. 1965. *The Logic of Collective Action*. Cambridge: Harvard University Press.

Ortega, D., and Rodríguez, F. 2008. Freed from Illiteracy? A Closer Look at Venezuela's Robinson Campaign. *Economic Development and Cultural Change*. 57, no. 1: 1–30.

Ortega, D., and Penfold, M. 2008. "Does Clientelism Work?: Electoral Returns of Excludable and Non-Excludable Goods in Chávez 's Misiones Programs in Venezuela." Presented at *Yale University's Popular Sectors and the State in Chávez 's Venezuela Conference*. March 6–7.

Ottone, E., and Vergara, C. 2006. *Ampliando Horizontes: Siete Claves Estratégicas del Gobierno de Lagos*. Santiago: Random House Mondadori S.A.

Padgett, Tim. The Sound and the Fury. *Time*. 24 September 2006.

Panizza, F. 2005. Unarmed Utopia Revisited: The Resurgence of Left-of-Centre Politics in Latin America. *Political Studies 53*, no. 4: 716–34.

Parker, D. 2007. Chávez and the Search for an Alternative to Neoliberalism. In *Venezuela: Hugo Chávez and the Decline of an "Exceptional Democracy."* S. Ellner and M. T. Salas, eds. London: Rowman & Littlefield Publishers, Inc.

Pastor, M. 1987. The Effects of IMF Programs in the Third World: Debate and Evidence from Latin America. *World Development* no. 15: 365–91.

Pauly, L. W. 1997. *Who Elected the Bankers? Surveillance and Control in the World Economy*. Ithaca: Cornell University Press.

Pepinsky, T. 2009. *Economic Crises and the Breakdown of Authoritarian Regimes: Indonesia and Malaysia in Comparative Perspective*. New York: Cambridge University Press.

Persson, T., and Tabellini, G. 2003. *The Economic Effects of Constitutions*. Cambridge, M.A.: MIT Press.

Peru's New President: Second Time Sober? *The Economist*. 27 July 2006.

Pinto, P. 2010. The Politics of Hard Times: Fiscal Policy and the Endogeneity of Economic Recessions. In *Politics in the New Hard Times: The Great Recession in Comparative Perspective*. M. Kahler and D. Lake, eds. Cornell, Cornell University Press, forthcoming.

Polillo, S., and Guillén, M. 2005. Globalization Pressures and the State: The Worldwide Spread of Central Bank Independence. *American Journal of Sociology* 110, no. 6: 1764–802.

Pop-Eleches, G. 2009. *From Economic Crises to Reform: IMF Programs in Latin America and Eastern Europe*. Princeton, N.J.: Princeton University Press.

Powell, B., and Whitten, G. 1993. A Cross-National Analysis of Economic Voting: Taking Account of the Political Context. *American Journal of Political Science* 37, no. 2: 391–414.

Przeworski, A., and Wallerstein, M. 1982. The Structure of Class Conflict in Democratic Societies. *American Political Science Review* 76, no. 2: 1235–69.

Przeworski, A., and Wallerstein, M. 1988. The Structural Dependence of the State on Capital. *American Political Science Review* 82:11–30.

Przeworski, A., Alvarez, M., Cheibub, J. A., and Limongi, F. 1996. What Makes Democracies Endure? *Journal of Democracy* 7, no. 1: 39–55.

Przeworski, A., Alvarez, M., Cheibub, J. A., Limongi, F. 2000. *Democracy and Development: Political Institutions and Well-Being in the World, 1950–1990*. Cambridge: Cambridge University Press.

Pzeworksi, A., and Vreeland, J. 2002. The Effect of IMF Programs on Economic Growth. *Journal of Development Economics* 62, no. 2: 385–421.

Purcell, S. K., and Roett, R. eds. 1997. *Brazil under Cardoso*. Boulder, CO.: The Americas Society and Lynne Rienner Publishers, Inc.

Rabello de Castro, P., and Ronci, M. 1991. Sixty Years of Populism in Brazil. In *The Macroeconomics of Populism in Latin America*. R. Dornbusch and S. Edwards, eds. Chicago: University of Chicago Press, 121–49.

Reinhart, C., Rogoff, K. S., and Savastano, M. 2003. Debt Intolerance. *Brookings Papers on Economic Activity* 1:1–62.

Reinhart, C., and Rogoff, R. 2004. Serial Default and the Paradox of Rich to Poor Capital Flows. *American Economic Review* 94, no. 2: 53–58.

Reinhart, C., and Rogoff K. S. 2009. *This Time Is Different: Eight Centuries of Financial Folly*. Princeton, N.J.: Princeton University Press.

Remmer, K. 1991. The Political Impact of Economic Crises in Latin America in the 1980s. *American Political Science Review* 85, no. 3: 777–800.

Remmer, K. 1993. The Political Economy of Elections in Latin America, 1980–1991. *American Political Science Review* 87: 393–407.

Remmer, K. 2002. The Politics of Economic Policy and Performance in Latin America. *Journal of Public Policy* 22: 29–59.

República de Chile. 1925. *Constitución Política de 1925, Artículo 62*. Santiago, Biblioteca del Congreso Nacional de Chile.

República de Chile. 2005. *Constitución Política de 1980, Artículo 25*. Santiago, Biblioteca del Congreso Nacional de Chile.

Rey, J. 1989. *El Futuro de la Democracia en Venezuela*. Caracas: IDEA.

Rezende, F. 1998. Prospects for Brazil's Economy. *International Affairs* 74, no. 3: 563–76.

Ribeiro, F. 2002. Central Bank: Independence. Governance, and Accountability. *Institute of Brazilian Issues*. The George Washington Unversity.

Riding, Alan. In Venezuela, Ex-President Seeks Old Job. *The New York Times*. 28 June 1987.

Roberts, K. M. 1998. *Deepening Democracy? The Modern Left and Social Movements in Chile and Peru*. Stanford: Stanford University Press.

Roberts, K. M., and Moisés, A. 1998. Neoliberalism and Lower-Class Voting Behavior in Peru. *Comparative Political Studies* 31, no. 2: 217–46.

Roberts, K. M., and Wibbels E. 1999. Party Systems and Electoral Vulnerability in Latin America: A Test of Economic, Institutional, and Structural Explanations. *The American Political Science Review* 93, no. 3: 575–90.

Roberts, K. M. 2012. Market Reform, Programmatic (De-)Alignment, and Party System Stability in Latin America. *Cornell University Typescript*.

Roberts, K. M. Forthcoming. *Changing Course: Parties, Populism, and Political Representation in Latin America's Neoliberal Era*. New York: Cambridge University Press.

Rodríguez, F. 2007. Why Chávez Wins. *Foreign Policy*. Washington, D.C.: The Slate Group, Newsweek Interactive, LLC.

Rodríguez, F., and Hausmann, R. 2009. Why Did Venezuelan Growth Collapse? In *Venezuela: Anatomy of a Collapse*. F. Rodriguez and R. Hausmann, eds. Center for International Development and the David Rockefeller Center for Latin American Studies at Harvard University, the Instituto de Estudios Superiores de Administración (IESA), and the Andean Development Corporation (CAF).

Rodrik, D. 1997. *Has Globalization Gone Too Far?* Washington, D.C.: Institute for International Economics.

Rodrik, D. 2000. How Far Will International Economic Integration Go? *The Journal of Economic Perspectives* 14, no. 1: 177–86.

Roett, R. 1989. How the 'Haves' Manage the 'Have-Nots': Latin America and the Debt Crisis. In *Debt and Democracy in Latin America*. B. Stallings and R. Kaufman, eds. Boulder, CO: Westview Press.

Rogoff, K. 1985. The Optimal Degree of Commitment to an Intermediate Target. *Quarterly Journal of Economics* 100: 1169–90.

Rogoff, K., and Siebert, A. 1988. Equilibrium Political Business Cycles. *Review of Economic Studies* 55: 1–16.

Rogoff, K. 1990. Equilibrium Political Budget Cycles. *American Economic Review*, 80, 21–36.

Rogoff, K. 1993. Third World Debt. In *Fortune Encyclopedia of Economics*. D. Henderson, ed. New York: Time Warner: 751–54.

Romer, C., and Romer., D. 1998. Monetary Policy and the Well-Being of the Poor. NBER Working Paper 6793. Washington, D.C.: *National Bureau of Economic Research*.

Rosendorff, B. P., and Vreeland, J. R. 2006. Democracy and Data Dissemination: The Effect of Political Regime on Transparency. *Working Paper*.

Rose-Ackerman, S. 1999. *Corruption and Government: Causes, Consequences, and Reform*. Cambridge: Cambridge University Press.

Rose-Ackerman, S., and Bowen, J. 2003. Partisan Politics and Executive Accountability: Argentina in Comparative Perspective. *Superior Court Economic Review* 10: 157–210.

Rosenbluth, F., and Schaap, R. 2003. The Domestic Politics of Banking Regulation. *International Organization* 57: 307–36.

Rudra, N. 2002. Globalization and the Decline of the Welfare State in Less Developed Countries. *International Organization* 56, no. 2: 411–445.

Rudra, N. 2008. *Globalization and the Race to the Bottom in Developing Countries: Who Really Gets Hurt?* New York: Cambridge University Press.

Ruggie, J. G. 1982. International Regimes, Transactions, and Change: Embedded Liberalism in the Postwar Economic Order. *International Organization* 36: 379–415.

Sachs, J. 1989a. Social Conflict and Populist Policies in Latin America. NBER Working Paper, 2987. Washington, D.C.: *National Bureau of Economic Research*.

Sachs, J. 1989b. Will the Banks Block Debt Relief? *New York Times*. 21 March.

Sachs, J., and Larrain, F. 1993. *Macroeconomics in the Global Economy*. Prentice, N.J.: Prentice Hall Inc.

Samuelson, P. A. 1948. *Economics*. New York: McGraw-Hill Book Company, Inc.

Samuelson, P. A., and Nordhaus, W. D. 1995. *Economics*. 15th ed. New York: McGraw-Hill Book Company, Inc.

Santiso, J. 2006. *Latin America's Political Economy of the Possible*. Cambridge: The MIT Press.

Scartascini, C., Spiller, P., Stein, E. H., and Tommasi, M. 2008. *Policymaking in Latin America. How Politics Shapes Policies*. Washington, D.C.: IDB and DRCLAS, Harvard University.

Schamis, H., and Way, C. 2003. Political Cycles and Exchange Rate Stabilization. *World Politics* 56, no. 1: 43–78.

Scheve, K. 2004. Public Inflation Aversion and the Political Economy of Macroeconomic Policymaking. *International Organization*, 58, 1–34.

Schneider, B. R. 2004. *Business Politics and the State in 20th Century Latin America*. New York: Cambridge University Press.

Schneider, B. R. 2010. Business Politics in Latin America. In *The Oxford Handbook of Business and Government*. David Coen, Wyn Grant, and Graham Wilson, eds. New York: Oxford University Press.

Schuknecht, L. 1996. Political Business Cycles and Fiscal Policies in Developing Countries. *Kyklos* 49: 155–70.

Schukneht, L. 2000. Fiscal Policy and Public Expenditure in Developing Countries. *Public Choice* 102: 115–30.

Schuldt, J. 1994. *Elecciones y Politica Economica en el Ecuador: 1983–1994*. Quito, Ecuador, Instituto Latinoamericano de Investigaciones Sociales (ILDES).

Schultz, K. 1995. The Politics of Political Business Cycles. *British Journal of Political Science*, 25, 79–99.

Segura-Ubiergo. 2007. *The Political Economy of the Welfare State in Latin America: Globalization, Democracy, and Development*. New York: Cambridge University Press.

Segura-Ubiergo, A., Simone, A., Gupta, S., and Cui, Q. 2010. New Evidence on Fiscal Adjustment and Growth in Transition Economies. *Comparative Economic Studies* 52: 18–37.

Sell, S. 2003. *Private Power, Public Law: The Globalization of Intellectual Property Rights*. Cambridge: Cambridge University Press.

Shi, M., and Svensson, J. 2003. Political Budget Cycles: A Review of Recent Developments. *Nordic Journal of Political Economy* 29, no. 1: 67–76.

Shi, M., and Svensson, J. 2006. Political Budget Cycles: Do They Differ Across Countries and Why? *Journal of Public Economics* 90: 1367–89.

Shifter, M. 2006. In Search of Hugo Chavez. *Foreign Affairs.* May/June.

Shiller, R. 1997. Why Do People Dislike Inflation? In *Reducing Inflation: Motivation and Strategy.* C. Romer and D. Romer, eds. National Bureau of Economic Research, Studies in the Business Cycles.

Sigelman, L. 1999. Publication Bias Reconsidered. *Political Analysis.* 8: 201–10.

Silva, E. 1996. From Dictatorship to Democracy: The Business-State Nexus in Chile's Economic Transformation, 1975–1994. *Comparative Politics* 28, no. 3: 299–320.

Silva, P. 2001. Toward Technocratic Mass Politics in Chile? The 1999–2000 Elections and the Lavín Phenomenon. *European Review of Latin American and Caribbean Studies.* 70: 357–358.

Singer, D. 2007. *Regulation Capital: Setting Standards for the International Financial System.* Ithaca, NY: Cornell University Press.

Simmons, B. 1996. Rulers of the Game: Central Bank Independence During the Interwar Years. *International Organization* 50, no. 3: 407–433.

Simmons, B. 2000. International Law and State Behavior: Commitment and Compliance in International Monetary Affairs. *American Political Science Review* 94, no. 4: 819–35.

Simmons, B., and Elkins, Z. 2004. The Globalization of Liberalization: Policy Diffusion in the International Economy. *American Political Science Review* 98, no. 1: 171–89.

Simmons, B., Dobbin, F., and Garrett, G. 2008. *The Global Diffusion of Markets and Democracy.* Cambridge: Cambridge University Press.

Sniderman, P. M., and Theriault, S. M. 2004. The Dynamics of Political Argument and The Logic of Issue Framing. In *Studies in Public Opinion: Attitudes, Nonattitudes, Measurement Error, and Change.* W. E. Saris and P. M. Sniderman, eds. Princeton, N.J.: Princeton University Press.

Spilimbergo, A. 1999. Copper and the Chilean Economy, 1960–98. *IMF Working Paper* Washington, D.C.: International Monetary Fund.

Stallings, B. 1987. *Banker to the Third World: US Portfolio Investment in Latin America, 1900–1986.* Berkeley: University of California Press.

Stallings, B., and Studart, R. 2006. *Finance for Development: Latin American in Comparative Perspective.* Washington, D.C.: Brookings Institution.

Stasavage, D. 2003. Transparency, Democratic Accountability, and the Economic Consequences of Monetary Institutions. *American Journal of Political Science* 47, no. 3, 389–402.

Stiglitz, J. 2002. *Globalization and Its Discontents.* New York: W.W. Norton & Company, Inc.

Stein, E., Talvi, E., and Grisanti, A. 1999. Institutional Arrangements and Fiscal Performance: The Latin American Experience. In *Fiscal Institutions and Fiscal Performance.* J. Porteba and J. von Hagen, eds. Chicago, I.L.: The University of Chicago Press.

Stokes, S. 1997. Democratic Accountability and Policy Change: Economic Policy in Fujimori's Peru. *Comparative Politics* 29, no. 2: 209–26.

Stokes, S. C., 2001a. *Mandates and Democracy.* Cambridge: Cambridge University Press.

Stokes, S. C., ed. 2001b. *Public Support for Market Reforms in New Democracies.* New York: Cambridge University Press.

Stokes, S. C., 2005. Peverse Accountability: A Formal Model of Machine Politics with Evidence from Argentina. *American Political Science Review* 99, no. 3: 315–25.

Stokes, S. C., 2009. Globalization and the Left in Latin America. Working Paper. *Yale University Program on Democracy*.

Strange, S. 1996. *The Retreat of the State: The Diffusion of Power in the World Economy*. New York: Cambridge University Press.

Swank, D. 2002. *Diminished Democracy: Globalization, Political Institutions and the Welfare State in Advanced Market Economies*. Cambridge: Cambridge University Press.

Teichman, J. 2001. *The Politics of Freeing Markets in Latin America: Chile, Argentina, and Mexico*. Chapel Hill: University of North Carolina.

Teitelbaum, M. 2011. *Mobilizing Restraint: Democracy and Industrial Conflict in Post-Reform South Asia*. Ithaca, NY: Cornell University Press.

Thacker, S. 1999. The High Politics of IMF Lending. *World Politics* 52: 38–75.

Thacker, S. 2000. *Big Business, the State, and Free Trade: Constructing Coalitions in Mexico*. Cambridge: Cambridge University Press.

Tietmeyer, H. 2001. Fifty Years of the Deutsche Mark-a Currency and its Consequences. In *50 Years of the Deutsche Mark*. J. Holscher, ed. New York: Ltd.

Tomz, M. 2001. Democratic Default: Domestic Audiences and Compliance with International Agreements. *2002 Annual Meeting of the Political Science Association*. Boston, August 29–September 1.

Tomz, M. 2007. *Reputation and International Cooperation: Sovereign Debt Across Three Centuries*. Princeton, N.J.: Princeton University Press.

Tucker, J. A. 2006. *Regional Economic Voting: Russia, Poland, Hungary, Slovakia, and the Czech Republic, 1990–1999*. Cambridge: Cambridge University Press.

Tufte, E. 1978. *Political Control of the Economy*. Princeton, N.J.: Princeton University Press.

UNDP (United Nations Development Programme. 2005. *Democracy in Latin America: Towards a Citizen's Democracy*. Bogota, Colombia: Panamericana Formas e Impresos S.A.

Vaaler, P., Schrage, B., and Block, S. 2006. Elections, Opportunism, Partisanship and Sovereign Ratings in Developing Countries. *Review of Development Economics* 10, no. 1: 154–70.

Valenzuela, A. 1978. *The Breakdown of Democratic Regimes: Chile*. Baltimore, M.D.: The Johns Hopkins University Press.

Váquez, I. 1996. The Brady Plan and Market-Based Solutions to Debt Crisis. *The Cato Journal* 16, no. 2: 233–43.

Velasco, A. 1994. The State and Economic Policy: Chile 1952–92. In *The Chilean Economy. Policy Lessons and Challenges*. B. Bosworth, R. Dornbusch, and R. Labán, eds. Washington, D.C.: Brookings Institution.

Vera, L. 2001. El Balance es Neoliberal! *Venezuela Analytica*. 23 July 2001.

Vicuña Izquierdo, L. 2000. *Politica Economica del Ecuador: Dos Décadeas Perdidas (Los Años 80–90)*. Ecuador, Escuela Superior Politécnica del Litoral.

von Hagen, J. 1992. Budgeting Procedures and Fiscal Performance in the European Community. *Commission of the European Communities*. Economic Paper: 96.

von Hagen, J. 1995. Budget Processes and the Commitment to Fiscal Discipline. *European Economic Review* 39: 771–79.

Vreeland, J. 2003. *The IMF and Economic Development.* New York: Cambridge University Press.

Webb, S. B. 1989. *Hyperinflation and Stabilization in the Weimer Republic.* New York: Oxford University Press.

Weber, E. U., Böckenholt, U., Hilton, D. J., and Wallace, B. 1993. Determinants of Diagnostic Hypothesis Generation: Effects of Information, Base Rates, and Experience. *Journal of Experimental Psychology: Learning, Memory, and Cognition* 19, no. 5: 1151–64.

Weber, E., Shafir, S., and Blais, A. 2004. Predicting Risk Sensitivity in Humans and Lower Animals: Risk as Variance or Coefficient of Variation. *Psychological Review* 111, no. 2: 430–45.

Weisner, E. 2008. *The Political Economy of Macroeconomic Policy Reform in Latin America: The Distributional and Institutional Context.* Northampton: Edward Elgar Publishing, Inc.

Weyland, K. 1998. Swallowing the Bitter Pill: Sources of Popular Support for Neoliberal Reform in Latin America. *Comparative Political Studies* 31, no. 5: 539–68.

Weyland, K. 2002. *The Politics of Market Reform in Fragile Democracies: Argentina, Brazil, Peru, and Venezuela.* Princeton, N.J.: Princeton University Press.

Weyland, K. 2007. *Bounded Rationality and Policy Diffusion: Social Sector Reform in Latin America.* Princeton, N.J.: Princeton University Press.

Weyland, K. 2009. The Rise of Latin America's Two Lefts: Insights from Rentier State Theory. *Comparative Politics* 41, no. 2: 145–64.

Weyland, K., Madrid, R., and Hunter, W. 2010. *Leftist Governments in Latin America: Successes and Shortcomings.* New York: Cambridge University Press.

Whitehead, L. 1989. Latin American Debt: An International Bargaining Perspective. *Review of International Studies* 15, no. 3: 231–49.

Wibbels, E., and Arce, M. 2003. Globalization, Taxation, and Burden-Shifting in Latin America. *International Organization* 57: 111–36.

Wibbels, E. 2006. Dependency Revisted: International Markets, Business Cycles, and Social Spending in the Developing World. *International Organization* 60: 433–68.

Wibbels, E., and Ahlquist, J. 2011. Development, Trade, and Social Insurance. *International Studies Quarterly* 55: 125–49.

Woods, N. 1995. Rethinking International Relations. *The Round Table: Commonwealth Journal of International Affairs.*

Woods, N. 2006. *The Globalizers: The IMF, the World Bank, and Their Borrowers.* New York: Cornell University Press.

Zucco, C. 2008. The President's 'New' Constituency: Lula and the Pragmatic Vote in Brazil's 2006 Presidential Elections. *Journal of Latin American Studies* 40, no. 1: 229–49.

Index

Acción Democrática (AD), 144, 150, 151n83, 180
Alarcón, Fabían, 177–9, 178n35, 179nn36–9
Alckmin, Geraldo, 246
Alencar, José, 275
Alesina, Alberto, 13n43, 73n4, 79n21, 82n32, 97n58, 135n21, 286n31
Alessandri, Jorge, 141n39, 205n64
Alfonsín, Raúl, 53, 191, 191n13, 209, 226–9, 227n149, 228n152, 229n157, 228nn154–5, 229n159, 230n164, 230n166, 263
Alianza por el Trabajo, la Justicia y la Educación, 238
Allende, Salvadore, 24, 51, 141n39, 142, 143
   Chile economic policy under, 24, 51, 142, 143, 191
Allende's economic policies
   in H_3 comparative case study evidence, 201–11
   neoliberal policy diffusion and, 208–11
   overview, 201–3, 202nn50–4
   post-crisis thinking, 205–8
   pre-crisis thinking, 203–5
Alt, James, 73n4, 74n8
Ames, Barry, 16n57, 25nn1–2, 74n7, 86n44, 278n6
Arce, Luis Alberto, 13
Arellano-Bond first-differenced GMM estimator, 89, 94
Argentina
   budget surplus (2007), 2–3

Latin American left and, 1–2, 5
Argentina debt
   crisis and default (2001–2002), 2, 43, 44, 263–4, 263n32, 264n34
   restructuring (2003) through IMF agreement, 263, 263n31
Argentina economic policy, 43n44, 57, 282
   under Alfonsín, 53, 191, 191n13, 209, 226–9, 227n149, 228n152, 229n157, 228nn154–5, 229n159, 230n164, 230n166, 263
   analysis and interviews about, 3n7
   Austral Plan, 227–8, 228n152, 228n154, 229
   bank lending in, 265, 265n41
   bond financing, 234–5, 258
   Brady bond restructurings in, 258
   central bank in, 266, 266nn45–6
   convertibility, 190, 232, 232n173, 233, 236, 238, 237n191, 239, 241, 244, 255, 255n6, 256–7
   under Duhalde, 263–6, 263n33
   economic ministry professionalization under democracy, 231, 230n168
   fiscal policy stance in presidential elections (2002–2007), 4f
   under Kirchner, Cristina, 2, 3–4, 3n9, 44, 44nn46–7, 135, 288
   under Kirchner, Néstor, 2–3, 6, 19, 44, 44n46, 230–1, 231n170, 283, 287–8

315

Argentina economic policy (*cont.*)
  under Menem, 24, 26, 64, 64n120, 190,
    232–41, 232n173, 232nn175–6,
    233nn177–8, 234nn179–80, 235n182,
    236n189, 237n193, 239n203, 239n205,
    240n209, 241n214, 240nn211–12, 251,
    255–62, 255nn7–8, 256n10, 256n12,
    257n16, 258nn19–20, 259n23, 283
  privatization, 233–4, 233n178
  spending (1990s), 237f
  superpoderes law and, 3, 19, 283
  Tequila crisis and, 255, 257, 259–61
  Venezuela economic policy compared to,
    1–6, 5n12, 57
Argentina elections
  fiscal policy stance (2002–2007), 4f
  1995, 255–62
  2003, 263–6, 266f
Argentina elections (1999), 238n194, 239n203
  in H_3 comparative case study evidence,
    233–41
  privatization earnings and, 233
Argentina elections, politics, credit crunch and
    anti-inflation bias
  in H_4 comparative case study evidence,
    255–66
  IMF conditionality and, 262–3
  1995 elections, 255–62
  overview, 255
  2003 elections, 263–6
Argentina hyperinflation, 2, 3–4, 49,
    49nn57–8
Argentina hyperinflation and politics
  in H_3 comparative case study evidence,
    226–32
  overview, 225–6
  post-crisis thinking, 231–3
  pre-crisis thinking, 227–31
Argentina inflation, 2, 3–4, 64, 191n12. *See
    also* Argentina elections (1999); *specific
    Argentina inflation topics*
  inflation-unemployment trade-off
    (1991–1995), 256–7
Argentina trade policy, 3
Arrate, Jorge, 208, 210
austerity, 26. *See also specific austerity topics*
  in developed countries implications, 288–90
  electoral economic strategies during, 282–4
  euro-zone crisis and, 288–9
  Latin America left and, 50, 50n63, 96
  left-wing policies for, 77, 96
  as policy of risk-aversion, 246n234

political supporters targeting during, 282–4
  right-wing policies for, 59–60, 77, 96
austerity politics. *See also* globalization and
    austerity politics
  of developed countries, 19–20, 290
  partisan politics and, 76–7, 286
  rise of, 12–15, 12nn41–2, 14n47, 14n51
Austral Plan, 227–8, 228n152
automatic stabilizers, 5n12
Aylwin, Patricio, 205n66, 208
  Chile economic policy under, 192, 205–7,
    212–16, 215n98, 215nn101–2

Bachelet, Michelle, 223, 224
Baker, Andy, 50n63, 63, 63n115, 179n38
Baker, James A., 166
Baker Plan, 166, 167, 167n12
Baldrich, Jorge, 261–2, 262n28
Ballén, Sixto Durán, 176–7, 177nn33–4
bank, central. *See* central bank
bank lending, 31, 132n12. *See also* lending
    and creditor-debtor relations structure
  in Argentina economic policy, 265, 265n41
  creditor relations under commercial central,
    39, 40f
  to Ecuador, 175, 175n29
  indebted countries and global bonds instead
    of, 279–80
  U.S., 166–7, 167n15, 167nn11–12
bank lending to Latin America, 167
  bond issuance supplanting of, 37, 38f, 168,
    267f
  1970s and 1980s, 165, 165n5
  1982–1987, 165–6, 165n7
Barro-Gordon loss-function, 71, 71n140
Bartels, Larry, 13n43, 60n99, 77, 77n13,
    97n59, 124n4, 286n31
Bates, Robert, 7n17, 188n1, 280n13
Bayesian updating, 14n49
Bernhard, William, 17n61, 33n25, 45n52
Bitar, Sergio, 51, 51n66, 204, 207, 224
Blair, Tony, 12
Blejer, Mario, 264, 264n37
Boeninger, Edgardo, 65, 65n127, 138–9, 208
Boix, Carles, 7n17, 280n13
Bolivia economic policy, 191
bonds
  indebted countries, bank lending and global,
    279–80
  Latin America and bank lending supplanted
    by, 37, 38f, 168, 267f
bond finance politics

elections and decentralized finance, 45–9, 45n50

lending and creditor-debtor relations structure, 38–44, 165–70

overview, 9–12, 30–1, 36–7, 38f

bond financing

in Argentina economic policy, 234–5, 258

in Brazil economic policy, 267–8, 267n48

creditors relations under decentralized, 42

in Ecuador economic policy, 174–9

international, 31

in Venezuela economic policy, 179–86

bond markets

capital market volatility and foreign, 284

decentralized global, 168–9, 169n21

exposure and budget balances in Latin America, 75, 76f

government dependence on, 16–17

Latin America economic policy and dependency on, 250–1

borrowers, sovereign. *See* sovereign borrowers

Brady, Nicholas J., 167n17

Brady (variable), 93

Brady bond restructurings, 11, 19, 39, 80n23, 90, 93–4, 94n55, 127

in Argentina economic policy, 258

Brady Plan, 167–9, 167n17, 168nn18–19

brady$_{it}$ (variable), 93, 94

Brazil

financial market turbulence, 268–70, 270f, 271f

political austerity, Cardoso's candidacy and incomes in, 48, 48n56

sovereign credit rating downgrade, 274n70

sovereign spread spike before 1998 election, 269, 270f

Brazil economic policy, 63–4, 70

bond financing in, 267–8, 267n48

under Cardoso, 12, 24, 26, 48, 48n55, 53, 56–7, 60, 60n101, 66, 124, 189, 190, 193, 242, 244–6, 244n227, 248, 248n245, 251, 267–76, 268nn49–50, 269n53, 270n55–6, 272n63, 273nn66–7, 274n71, 275n77, 286–7

central bank in, 231t, 242, 244, 244n224, 271–3

central bank independence and, 271–2

central bank professionalization under democracy, 231t, 242

under Collor, 242, 244nn221–2

Cruzado Plan, 243, 243n18

East Asia crisis and, 24, 60, 251, 267–8

under Itamar Franco, 53, 193, 244

under Lula, 57, 61, 61n107, 66, 124, 245–8, 248n240, 247nn235–37, 248n245, 267, 275–6, 282, 286–7

Real Plan, 48, 48n55, 60n101, 190, 193, 234n179, 244–6, 245n226, 269, 273

under Sarney, 242–3

Brazil election (1998) and sovereign spread spike, 269, 270f

Brazil elections, markets, politics and leftists

central bank independence and, 271–2

in H_4 comparative case study evidence, 267–76

1998 elections, 268–71

overview, 267–8

2002 elections, 272–6

Brazil elections and macroeconomic consensus

in H_3 comparative case study evidence, 242–8

1994 elections, 244–5

overview, 242–3

2006 elections, 246–8

Brazil's social democratic party (PSDB), 60, 268, 273

Broz, J. Lawrence, 33n25, 84n37

budget

Argentina surplus (2007), 2–3

balances in Latin America and bond market exposure, 75, 76f

Chile economic policy and deficit (1970), 140, 141f

composition and electoral spending patterns, 89

political budget cycle, 73–4, 74n5, 80

Bush, George W., 28, 72, 277

business cycle, 72. *See also* political business cycle

cacerolazos (popular protests), 18

Caldera, Rafael, 23, 127, 146, 181–6, 182n51, 183n54, 184n58, 184n61, 194

capital

market volatility and foreign bond markets, 284

political exit threat from exit of, 284–6

Caracazo protests and looting, 150, 194,
    194n26
Cardoso, Fernando Henrique, 246n231, 247,
    271n59
  Brazil economic policy under, 12, 24, 26,
    48, 48n55, 53, 56–7, 60, 60n101, 66,
    124, 189, 190, 193, 242, 244–6,
    244n227, 248, 248n245, 251, 267–76,
    268nn49–50, 269n53, 270n55–6,
    272n63, 273nn66–7, 274n71, 275n77,
    286–7
  political austerity, Brazilian incomes and
    candidacy of, 48, 48n56
Carrión, Leonardo, 159
Carville, James, 11
cash. *See also* inflation-scarred, cash-strapped
    politician case
  conditional transfers, 18, 18n72
Castro, Cipriano, 163
Cavallo, Domingo, 190, 190n11, 232,
    240n208, 255, 256, 260–1
CBC. *See* Central Bank of Chile
central bank
  in Argentina economic policy, 264, 266,
    266nn45–6
  in Brazil economic policy, 231t, 242, 244,
    244n224, 271–3, 275
  creditor relations under lending by
    commercial, 39, 40f
  funds and inflation, 133, 133n15
central bank independence, 133, 132n14,
    134–6, 186n67. *See also* Venezuela
    central bank independence and PBC
  Brazil economic policy and, 242,
    271–2
  Chile and, 138, 140–2, 141n41
  inflation rates and, 84n37, 135, 136
  Latin America economic policy and,
    132n14, 271
Central Bank Independence (variable), 84,
    84n41
Central Bank of Chile (CBC), 137–42,
    138nn29–30, 141n40–1, 170, 206, 222
central bank professionalization
  in Brazil under democracy, 231t, 242
  Chile economic policy and, 211
  in Latin America, 191, 193
Chávez Frías, Hugo Rafael, 143, 150, 152n89,
    181, 182, 182n51, 183, 194
  Venezuela economic policy under, 2, 5, 6,
    12, 26, 26n6, 127, 135, 151–7, 151n84,
    152n86, 154nn93–5, 154n98, 155n100,

    156n102, 156n104, 156n105, 162, 251,
    283, 284, 287
Chicago Boys, 143, 212, 212n91
Chile
  institutional development of, 253
  strikes (1964–1970), 139, 140f
Chile central bank
  Central Bank of Chile, 138–42,
    138nn29–30, 141nn42–3, 170, 206, 222
  independence, 140–2, 141n41
  professionalization, 211
Chile copper, 137–8, 137n25, 224,
    224nn138–9
  prices, 213, 213nn93–4, 214f
Chile economic policy, 15, 18, 18n71, 43, 58,
    70, 193, 214n96, 253. *See also* Allende's
    economic policies
  under Allende, 24, 51, 142, 143, 191
  under Aylwin, 192, 205–7, 212–16,
    215n98, 215nn101–2
  budget deficit (1970), 140, 141f
  Central Bank of Chile in, 138–42,
    138nn29–30, 141nn40–1, 170, 206,
    222
  central bank professionalization and,
    211
  under Concertación, 56, 56n89, 65
  diffusion, 199
  East Asia crisis and, 216
  economic ministry professionalization under
    democracy, 211–12
  under Frei, 23, 35, 135, 137–41, 204,
    216–21, 216n107, 218n113, 219n114,
    219nn116–19, 220nn120–2, 221n128,
    224n135, 225n141, 225nn143–4, 282
  globalization and, 222
  under Lagos, 15, 65–6, 124, 191, 210,
    221–5, 221n129, 287
Chile elections (post-Pinochet)
  in H_3 comparative case study evidence,
    211–25
  1993 elections, 212–16
  1999 elections, 216–21
  overview, 211–12
  2005 elections, 221–5, 234f
Chile elections (1970) and spending bonanza
  central bank independence and, 141–2,
    141n41
  economic crisis, 142–3
  in H_1 comparative case study evidence,
    137–43
  overview, 137–40

Chile inflation, 225n143. *See also* Allende's
  economic policies
  falling (1990s), 212, 213f, 216,
  217f
Chile socialists, 201, 204n59, 208–11,
  210nn84–5. *See also* Socialist Party
  (Chile)
Christian Democratic Party (Chile), 56n89,
  204, 205, 208, 209, 210, 216n105, 217,
  217n109. *See also* el Partido Demócrata
  Cristiano de Chile
CIEPLAN. *See* Corporación de Estudios Para
  Latinoamérica
Citibank, 37
Clark, Jack, 37
Clark, William, 33n25, 74n5, 84n37
clientelism, 70, 103, 147, 151, 151n84, 155,
  241, 257, 261, 270, 283
Clinton, Bill, 12, 12n42
collective action, 9–10, 38–44, 164–9
collective action clauses, 19, 19n75
Collor de Mello, Fernando, 243n220
  Brazil economic policy under, 242, 243,
  243nn222–3
  popularity, 243
commodity booms, 12, 46–7, 143–51, 155–8,
  159
Commodity Price Index (variable), 83
Concertación, 56, 56n89, 65, 205–9, 211n89,
  212, 214, 216–18, 218n111, 220–4,
  223n133
Concertación de Partidos por el NO, 201n48,
  205, 205n65
Concertación de Partidos por la Democracia,
  201n48, 205
conditional cash transfers, 18, 18n72
conditionality, 9–12, 12n41, 23, 37, 39–40,
  40n34, 41–3, 125, 127, 158–60, 163–75,
  181–6, 194, 209, 219, 235, 252, 262–5,
  279, 281
convergence-divergence debate, 7–8, 7n22
convertibility (Argentina), 190, 232, 232n173,
  233, 236, 238, 237n191, 239, 241, 244,
  255, 255n6, 256–7
COPEI. *See* el Partido Social Cristiano de
  Venezuela
COPOM. *See* Monetary Policy Committee
Corporación de Estudios Para Latinoamérica
  (CIEPLAN), 56, 56n90, 143, 211n89
Corrales, Javier, 150n81, 151n84, 156n102,
  156n105, 235n185, 240nn211–12,
  283n25

counterfactual analysis, 142, 142n44, 143n47
credit ratings, 45, 169, 184, 235, 247, 274n70,
  289. *See also* sovereign risk premium
creditors. *See also* lending and creditor-debtor
  relations structure
  relations under commercial central bank
    lending, 39, 40f
  relations under decentralized bond
    financing, 42
  sovereign borrowers and centralized, 39–40
  sovereign borrowers and decentralized,
    40–2
Cruzado Plan (Brazil), 243, 243n18
cultural memes, 199–200
currency
  devaluation or devaluation, 269n54
  U.S. global reserve, 289, 290

Dahl, Robert, 78, 78n16
Darwin, Charles, 199
Dawkins, Richard, 198
De la Rúa, Fernando, 238–9, 238n199,
  263n33
debt. *See also specific debt topics*
  developed countries economic policy and,
    289
  elections impact on economy and
    decentralized, 81, 80n23
  safe thresholds for emerging market
    countries, 93n54
  U.S. economic policy and, 289–90
debtors. *See* lending and creditor-debtor
  relations structure
decentralized debt, in elections impact on
  economy, 80–1, 80n23
decentralized finance. *See* elections and
  decentralized finance
decentralized global bond market, 168–9,
  169n21
delegative democracy, 136, 136n23
Delgado, Ricardo, 265, 265n40
democracy
  Chile economic ministry professionalization
    under, 212–13
  classification criteria for, 79n17
  delegative, 136, 136n23
  in elections impact on economy, 78–81
  liberal, 74, 74n6
  market's compatibility with, 280–2
democracy age (factor), 89
  new democracy, 89n49
  old democracy, 89n49

democracy and growth quality implications
  overview, 280–2
  political exit threat from capital's exit,
    284–6
  political supporters targeting during
    austerity, 282–4
Depfa bank, 250
developed countries
  austerity politics of, 19–20, 290
  debt and economic policy of, 289
  extensions of, 19–20
  global financial crisis (2008) and, 288–9
  implications of austerity in, 288–90
  political business cycles in, 28–30
developing countries
  election-year economic manipulation
    variations, 74–6
  globalization, 1
  Latin America, 6n15
  partisan politics in, 286
  political business cycles in, 28–30, 74
  psychology of economic policies of, 14n47
Diamond, Larry, 74n6
diffusion, 198. *See also* policy diffusion
diplomacy. *See* gunboat and trading-floor
  diplomacy
discretionary spending, 2, 5, 19, 26, 70–1,
  103, 157, 174, 231, 249, 283
Domestic Financial Depth (variable), 83,
  83n35
Domestic Investment (variable), 83–4
Domestic Output Gap (variable), 83
Dornbusch, Rudiger, 15n55, 25n2, 54nn76–7,
  58nn96–7, 79n20, 80n22, 163n1, 188n1
Drazen, Allan, 16n57, 25n1, 30n17, 73n4,
  74n5, 74nn7–8, 83n33, 86n44, 89n49,
  102n70, 134n16, 188n2, 271n60, 278n6
Duhalde, Eduardo, 238, 241, 257n16, 283
  Argentina economic policy under, 263–6,
    263n33
Dunning, Thad, 47, 47n54, 143n49–144n49,
  144n53

Early Term (variable), 97
East Asia crisis (1997–1998)
  Brazil economic policy response to, 24, 60,
    251, 267–8
  Chile economic policy and, 216
Easterly, William, 17n66, 56n88, 62,
  62nn109–10, 173n26, 189n3
economics
  contemporary, 191–2, 191n17

decisions in hard times, 50–3
  lessons resilience, 55–9, 56n88
economic ministry professionalization
  in Argentina under democracy, 231,
    230n168
  in Brazil under democracy, 242–3
  in Chile under democracy, 212–13
  Latin America, 191–3
economic policy. *See also specific economic
    policy topics*
  alternatives to expansion after inflation
    crisis, 278–9
  developed countries debt and, 289
  financial means and, 21
  human agency in choices about, 192n18
  implications of partisan politics and,
    286–8
  institutional constraints on macroeconomic,
    134–6
  lags in outcomes, 33, 33n25
  political business cycle and interventionist,
    25–6, 27
  political motivations and, 21
  speed compared to caution in crafting, 277
economic regressions. *See also* regression
    models, for elections and economy
  in elections impact on economy, 83–5
economic risk-aversion and inflation control
    politics. *See also* risk aversion
  economic decisions in hard times, 50–3,
    53n73
  inflation aversion and elections, 59–68
  overview, 49–50
  technocratic communities and inflation
    saliency, 53–9
economic voters, 67, 67n134
Ecuador
  bank lending to, 175, 175n29
  IMF lending to, 175
Ecuador economic policy, 158–60, 158n109,
    159n115
  under Alarcón, 177–9, 178n35,
    179nn37–40
  under Ballén, 176–7, 177nn33–4
  under Febres-Cordero, 160, 161
  under Hurtado, 160–1, 160nn124–5,
    161n124, 161n128
Ecuador elections (1980s) and economic
    populism
  in H_1 comparative case study evidence,
    158–61
  1984 elections, 160

1988 elections, 160–1
overview, 158–60
Ecuador elections (1990s) and market
  securitization
  in H_2 comparative case study evidence,
    174–9
  1996 elections, 176–7, 176n30
  1998 elections, 177–9
  overview, 174–6
Edwards, Sebastian, 11n37, 15n55, 25n2,
  40n34, 41n40, 54n76, 54n77, 58nn96–7,
  74n7, 86n44, 138n30, 169n22, 173n27,
  188n1
Eisenhower, Dwight D., 123
election$_{it}$ (variable)
  overview, 79, 79n21
  post-election$_{it}$, 80
  pre-election$_{it}$, 80
elections. *See also specific elections topics*
  competitive, 123
  economic impact of inflation crisis and, 99t
  inflation and, 55, 55n81
  marginal impact on growth rates, 87
  U.S., 123–4
elections and decentralized finance
  high growth, high inflation electoral cycle
    hypothesis, 46–7
  market-induced austerity cycle hypothesis,
    47–9
  overview, 45–6, 45n50
elections and economic policy
  Argentina's 1995 elections, 255–62
  Argentina's 1999 elections, 232–41
  Argentina's 2003 elections, 262–7
  Argentina's 2007 elections, 2–3, 19, 230–1,
    283
  Brazil's 1994 and 2006 elections, 241–8
  Brazil's 1998 and 2002 elections, 267–76
  Chile's 1970 elections, 137–42
  Chile's 1993 elections, 212–16
  Chile's 1999 elections, 216–21
  Chile's 2005 elections, 221–5
  Ecuador's 1984 and 1988 elections, 158–61
  Ecuador's 1996 and 1998 elections, 174–9
  Venezuela's 1968–1988 elections, 145–7,
    179–81
  Venezuela's 1978 elections, 146–8
  Venezuela's 1983 elections, 148
  Venezuela's 1988 elections, 149–51
  Venezuela's 1998 elections, 181–6
  Venezuela's 2006 elections, 151–8
elections and economy, economic indicators

overview and summary, 90–2, 92nn51–2,
  95
robustness, 92–5, 92n53
elections and economy, fiscal indicators
  budget composition and electoral spending
    patterns, 89
  overview, 86–8
  robustness, 88–9, 89n48
elections impact on economy, control variables
  economic regressions, 83–5
  fiscal policy regressions, 83, 83n33
elections impact on economy, independent
  variables
  decentralized debt, 80–1, 80n23
  democracy, 78–81
  inflation crisis legacy, 81
  partisanship, 82, 82nn30–2
election-year economic manipulation
  austerity politics and partisan politics,
    76–7
  developing country variations, credit and
    crises, 74–6
  overview, 73–4, 73n1
election-year fiscal stimulus (variable),
  128
election-year monetary stimulus (variable), 128
electoral boom-bust cycle
  electoral opportunism classic case, 131–6
  in H_1 comparative case study evidence,
    136–61
  Latin America case study design, 125–31
  overview and summary, 123–5, 161–2
electoral economic strategies
  administrative controls, 283
  during austerity, 282–4
  discretionary spending, 283
  line-item expenditures, 283
  macroeconomic competence signaling, 35–6
  market indebtedness and political plans,
    34–5
  overview, 33–4
  in political austerity theory, 32–6
  politically-timed boom planning, 33–4
  public works projects in, 282
  spendthrift or miser, 32–6
  stimulus as, 278n4
electoral opportunism classic case
  institutional constraints on macroeconomic
    policy, 134–6
  overview, 131, 134t
  traditional political business cycle
    hypothesis, 131–4

electoral spending patterns. *See also* electoral
  economic strategies
  budget composition and, 89
End Term (variable), 97
end-term fiscal stimulus (variable), 128
end-term monetary stimulus (variable), 128
ESM. *See* European Stability Mechanism
European Commission, 19
European economic policy, 19–20
  hyperinflation and, 51, 52
European Stability Mechanism (ESM), 19
euro-zone crisis, 288–9
exchange rate regime (factor), 89
  fixed to *floating*, 89n50
Executive Constraints (variable), 84, 84n38,
  88, 88n46

Febres-Cordero, Léon, 160, 161
Fernández, Roque, 236–7, 236n187, 239–40,
  240n208, 259–60, 259n21
finance. *See also specific finance topics*
  inequities of global system of, 285–6
  stimulus through alternative, 284
financial crisis (2008). *See* global financial
  crisis (2008)
financial means
  economic policy and, 21
  in political austerity theory, 30–1
Finnemore, Martha, 163n1, 198n37, 198n40,
  209n78, 262n30
Fiscal Balance (variable), 84
fiscal monetization, 135, 135n21
fiscal policy, 2n3, 21, 21n79
  lags, 80n22
  regressions in elections impact on economy,
    83, 83n33
fiscal policy stance in presidential elections
  Argentina, 233–41, 237f, 240f, 255–62,
    260f, 263–6, 266f
  Argentina and Venezuela, 4f
  Brazil, 244–8, 268–71, 272–6
  Chile, 138–40, 141f, 212–25, 217f, 225f
  Ecuador, 160–1, 176–9
  Latin American countries, 6f, 128–9, 129f,
    130f
  Venezuela, 145–51, 146f, 147f, 151–8,
    157f, 181–6
fiscal responsibility laws, 134–5, 134n18
fiscal space, 12n39, 31, 31n20, 34, 46, 85,
  132, 133, 137, 155, 158, 160, 170, 175,
  182, 186, 196, 233, 251, 252,
  280

Foxley, Alejandro Tomás, 192, 192n19, 193,
  193n23, 206, 207, 207n74, 211, 212,
  215, 216, 216n103, 224
Franco, Gustavo, 56–7
Franco, Itamar, 53, 193, 244
Franzese, Robert, 73n4
Frei Montalva, Eduardo, 23, 135, 137–41,
  204–5
Frei Ruiz-Tagle, Eduardo, 35, 216–21,
  216n107, 218n113, 219n114,
  219nn116–19, 220nn120–2, 221n128,
  224n135, 225n141, 225nn143–4,
  282
Frieden, Jeffrey, 148n68, 165n4, 269n54,
  280n13
Friedman, Milton, 28, 28n14, 173

García, Alan, 181
  Peru economic policy under, 57, 58, 61,
    61n107, 191, 191n14, 287
Garrett, Geoffrey, 7n21, 198n38, 280n13
General Motors (G.M.), 167, 167n13
generalized methods of moments (GMM),
  78
Germany economic policy, 52
  under Merkel, 32, 287, 287n36
Giordani, Jorge, 57, 64
global financial crisis (2008)
  developed countries and, 288–9
  Latin America economic policy and, 284–5,
    286
  U.S. municipalities and, 250
global financial system inequities, 285–6
Global Growth (variable), 83
globalization
  Chile economic policy and, 222
  debate, 281
  developing countries, 1
globalization and austerity politics
  bond finance politics, 36–49
  economic risk-aversion and inflation control
    politics, 49–68
  inflation-unemployment trade-off, 27–30
  overview and summary, 25–7, 68–71
  political austerity theory, 30–6
  summary and conclusions, 68–71
globalization and economic policy
  austerity politics rise, 12–15, 12nn41–2,
    14n47, 14n51
  convergence-divergence debate, 7–8,
    7n22
  Latin American cases, 10–11, 10n35, 11n37

market as prison, 11–12, 12n40
market enforcement mechanism, 8–10,
    9nn33–4
overview, 6–7
G.M. *See* General Motors
GMM. *See* generalized methods of moments
Gomes, Ciro, 273, 273n69, 275
González-Fraga, Javier, 42
government dependence, on bond markets,
    16–17
Greece economic policy, 19, 19n74, 42
De Gregorio, Jóse, 141, 141n40, 170, 170n23
group theory, 38
growth. *See also specific growth topics*
    elections marginal impact on rates of,
    87
    left-wing policies for, 60, 77
    quality implications and democracy, 280–6
Growth (variable), 84
Guerra, José, 146n56
Guidotti, Pablo, 235–36, 236n186, 238, 261
gunboat and trading-floor diplomacy
    in H_2 comparative case study evidence,
    174–86
    market-constrained politician case, 164–74
    overview and summary, 163–4, 186–7,
    186n66

H1. See high growth, high inflation electoral
    cycle hypothesis
H_1. *See* traditional political business cycle
    hypothesis
H_1 case study
    election cases overview, 136, 137f
    overview, 172
H_1 comparative case study evidence
    Chile 1970 elections and spending bonanza,
    137–43
    Ecuador 1980s elections and economic
    populism, 158–61
    overview, 136–7
    Venezuela central bank independence and
    PBC, 150–8
    Venezuela petro-PBC, 143–51
H_2. *See* market-induced austerity cycle
    hypothesis
H_2. *See* market-induced political austerity
    cycle hypothesis
H_2 case study
    election cases overview, 174
    overview, 172
H_2 comparative case study evidence

Ecuador 1990s elections and market
    securitization, 174–9
overview, 174
Venezuela 1990s economy without oil,
    179–86
H_3. *See* inflation-averse political austerity cycle
    hypothesis
H_3 case study
    election cases overview, 200
    overview, 197t, 254t
H_3 comparative case study evidence
    Allende's economic policy, 201–11
    Argentina 1999 elections, 233–41
    Argentina hyperinflation and politics,
    226–32
    Brazil elections and macroeconomic
    consensus, 242–8
    Chile post-Pinochet elections, 211–25
    overview, 200–1
H_4. *See* low growth, low inflation austerity
    cycle hypothesis; political austerity cycle
    hypothesis
H_4 case study
    election cases overview, 254
    overview, 197t, 254t
H_4 comparative case study evidence
    Argentina elections, politics, credit crunch
    and anti-inflation bias, 255–66
    Brazil elections, markets, politics and
    leftists, 267–76
    overview and summary, 254, 276
Haggard, Stephan, 11n37, 18n69, 18n71,
    40n34
Hall, Peter, 7nn18–19, 198nn35–6, 209n82,
    279n7
Hallerberg, Mark, 135n22
Hausman, Ricardo, 279–80
Hayek, Friedrich August von, 199, 199n41
Hemingway, Ernest, 190, 191
Herrera Campins, Luis, 148, 147n64, 148n66
heterodox programs, 54, 55, 58, 190, 190n7,
    192, 199, 226, 228n152, 228, 228n155,
    229, 243, 243n218, 288
H_{h3}. *See* inflation-averse austerity cycle
    hypothesis
Hibbs, Douglas, 13n43, 286n31
high growth, high inflation electoral cycle
    hypothesis (*H1*), 46–7
highest past inflation$_{it}$ (variable), 81n26
histogram analysis, 128
Huber, Evelyne, 18n69
Humala, Ollanta, 57, 66

Hurtado, Osvaldo, 160–1, 160n119, 160nn122–3, 161n124, 161n128
hyperinflation, 54, 54n78, 55–9, 199–201. *See also* Argentina hyperinflation
    European economic policy and, 51, 52
    Latin American, 14, 49, 49nn57–8, 50, 51, 52, 62, 64, 70, 124, 127, 143, 190, 191, 193–4, 209, 225–30, 232, 236, 238, 242–4, 248, 251, 255–6, 264, 267–8, 272, 279, 287
    life under, 49, 49nn57–8

IMF. *See* International Monetary Fund
IMF (variable), 84, 84n39, 88, 88n47
IMF conditionality
    Argentina elections, politics, credit crunch, anti-inflation bias, and, 262–3
    market-constrained politician case and, 173–4, 173n25
indebtedness
    global bonds instead of bank lending for country, 279–80
    political plans and market, 34–5
inflation, 32n23. *See also specific inflation topics*
    central bank funds and, 133, 133n15
    control and heterodox programs, 190, 190n7
    elections and, 55, 55n81
    rates and central bank independence, 84n37
    rising, 54, 54n79
    tax, 61–2, 70, 81, 133, 133n15, 189, 275, 279
    U.S., 14, 14n52
    Venezuela economic policy and, 4, 4n10, 5, 57, 64, 64nn121–2, 128, 180, 193–4
Inflation (variable), 84, 84n42
inflation aversion. *See also* Latin America inflation politics
    decision making with high, 56
    decision making with low, 58
inflation aversion and elections
    business community, 65–6
    inflation-averse austerity cycle hypothesis, 67
    low growth, low inflation austerity cycle hypothesis, 68
    low-inflation constituency, 60–1, 60n103, 61n106
    middle income and poor voters, 61–4
    overview, 59–60
inflation crisis, 50, 50n59, 58, 58n95

economic impact of elections and, 99t
economic impact of partisanship and, 100t
economic ministry professionalization and Latin America, 191–3
legacy in elections impact on economy, 81–2
policy alternatives to economic expansions after, 278–9
threshold, 200–1
inflation-averse austerity cycle hypothesis ($H3$), 33t, 35, 197t
    inflation-averse politician case and, 195–7, 196n33
    overview, 67
inflation-averse political austerity cycle hypothesis (H_3), 196t, 200f, 252t, 257, 269. *See also specific H_3 case study topics*
    overview, 21, 22, 67, 86, 126
inflation-averse politician case
    inflation-averse austerity cycle hypothesis and, 195–7, 196n33
    Latin America inflation politics and, 190–200
    neoliberal policy diffusion and, 198–200
    overview, 190–5
inflation_crisis_{it} (variable), 81
inflation-scarred, cash-strapped politician case
    overview, 251–3
    political austerity cycle and, 251–4
    political austerity cycle hypothesis and, 253–4
inflation-unemployment trade-off. *See also* Phillips curve trade-off
    in Argentina (1991-1995), 256–7
    overview, 27–8
    political business cycles in developed *vs.* developing countries and, 28–30
institutions
    Chile development of, 253
    constraints on macroeconomic policy, 134–6
International Monetary Fund (IMF), 40, 40n34, 164, 166–7, 170. *See also specific IMF topics*
    Argentina debt restructuring (2003) through, 263, 263n31
    lending to Argentina, 228, 228n155, 235, 237–8
    lending to Brazil, 274–5, 274n71
    lending to Ecuador, 160–1, 175, 178–9
    lending to Venezuela, 181–4, 194
    U.S. and, 159
It's a Wonderful Life, 36

Jenkins, P. F., 198
jobs, and left-wing policies, 60, 77

Katzenstein, Peter, 7nn20–1
Kaufman, Robert, 15n55, 18nn69, 25n2,
    54n77, 69n136, 132n13,
    188n1
Kennedy, John F., 72, 123
Keohane, Robert, 21n77, 23n81, 31n22,
    127n9, 280n13
Keynes, John Maynard, 199, 199n42
Keynesianism, 27–8, 28n11, 29, 30, 32, 71,
    191–2, 198–9
    new, 56, 56n85, 191n17
Kindleberger, Charles, 284
Kirchner, Cristina Fernández de,
    283
    Argentina economic policy under, 2, 3–4,
        3n9, 44, 44nn46–7, 135, 288
Kirchner, Néstor, 264, 265, 265n43
    Argentina economic policy under, 2–3, 6,
        19, 44, 44n46, 230–1, 231n170, 283,
        287–8
Kravchuk, Leonid, 59
De Krivoy, Ruth, 4, 194, 194n28

Lagos Escobar, Ricardo Froilán, 209n81,
    217–18, 217n110, 218n111
    Chile economic policy under, 15, 65–6,
        124, 191, 210, 221–5, 221n129,
        287
    popularity, 223, 223n134
Latin America. *See also* bank lending to Latin
    America
    bond market exposure and budget balances,
        75, 76f
    developing countries, 6n15
    partisan politics future, 287–8
Latin America case study design. *See also*
    specific case study topics
    economic policy choices first glance,
        128–31, 128n9
    overview, 70, 125–8
Latin America central bank
    credit, 196n32
    independence, 132n14, 271
Latin America economic policy, 42
    bond market dependency and, 250–1
    central bank independence and, 132n14,
        271
    central bank professionalization, 191,
        193

choices (1990–2009) overview, 128–31,
    128n9
diffusion, 199, 200
economic center in, 279
economic ministry professionalization,
    191–3
fiscal policy stance in presidential elections
    (2002–2007), 6f
global financial crisis (2008) and, 284–5,
    286
globalization and, 10–11, 10n35, 11n37,
    20–4
inflation and future of, 287–8
market instability insurance in, 285–6
overview of study of, 20–4, 22n80
partisan politics and, 286–8
political austerity theory and, 278
state-owned enterprises in, 282, 282n16
success of, 290
Latin America elections. *See also* elections;
    Latin America presidential elections
    electoral policy decisions justifications, 79,
        79n19
    Latin America inflation and, 91f
    legislative, 79
Latin America inflation, 14–15, 14n52,
    49, 49nn57–8, 58, 59f, 60–6, 68,
    70
    crisis and economic ministry
        professionalization, 191–3
    hyperinflation, 14, 49, 49nn57–8, 51, 52,
        62, 287
    Latin America economic policy future
        regarding, 287–8
    Latin America elections and, 80f
Latin America inflation politics
    in H_3 comparative case study evidence,
        200–48
    inflation-averse politician case, 190–200
    overview and summary, 188–90, 248–9
Latin America left. *See also* Brazil elections,
    markets, politics and leftists
    Argentina, Venezuela and, 1–2, 5
    austerity toleration by, 50, 50n63, 96
    rise of, 1n1
Latin America political austerity cycle. *See also*
    political austerity cycle
    political business cycle and, 278
Latin America political business cycle, 24, 74.
    See also political business cycle
    political austerity cycle instead of, 278
    theory on variation in, 21

Latin America political economy of elections.
See political economy of elections
Latin America presidential elections. *See also*
elections
contested (1961–2009), 79
immediate re-election, 79, 79n18
Latin America presidents. *See also specific
Latin American presidents*
in delegative democracies, 136, 136n23
Lauría, Carmelo, 34, 34n27, 146, 149, 150,
180
Lavagna, Roberto, 2, 18, 230, 265, 266
Leblang, David, 17n61, 45nn51–2
left-wing. *See also* Latin America left
austerity policies of, 77, 96
growth and jobs policies of, 60, 77
lending. *See also* bank lending
Argentina and the IMF, 228, 228n155, 235,
237–8
Brazil and the IMF, 274–5, 274n71
Ecuador and IMF, 160–1, 175, 178–9
Venezuela and the IMF, 181–4, 194
lending and creditor-debtor relations structure,
163–4, 165–70
centralized creditors and sovereign
borrowers, 39–40
decentralized creditors and sovereign
borrowers, 40–2, 41n35
market conditionality strength, 43–4,
43n44
market disciplining mechanism trigger, 42–3
overview, 9–12, 38
Levitsky, Steve, 1n1, 13n44, 50n62, 76n10,
237n194–238n195
Lewis-Beck, Michael, 26n8, 67n134
liberal democracies, 74, 74n6
Liberty Front Party (PFL), 270
line-item expenditures, 3, 18–19, 27, 89,
102–3, 102n70, 173, 177, 179, 187, 195,
221, 239–40, 248, 253, 255, 258, 262,
282–3
low growth, low inflation austerity cycle
hypothesis (H4), 68
low-inflation
constituency, 60–1, 60n103, 61n106
right-wing policies for, 59–60, 77, 96
Lula du Silva, 48, 243n220, 246n231, 270,
271, 271n59, 273–4, 273n69, 275n74
Brazil economic policy under, 57, 61,
61n107, 66, 124, 245–8, 248n240,
247nn235–7, 248n245, 267, 275–6, 282,
286–7

Lusinchi, Jaime, 34, 34nn27–38, 149–50,
150n76, 181, 182

Machinea, José Luis, 226, 226n146, 229,
229n161, 231, 232, 236
macroeconomic competence signaling, 35–6
macroeconomic consensus, 29, 32, 52–3,
55–9, 60–6, 142–3, 189–95
Argentina, 225–33
Brazil, 242–3
Chile, 203–11
macroeconomic policy, institutional
constraints, 134–6
macroeconomic populism, 5, 15, 25, 54,
54n76, 57–9, 188
Mainwaring, Scott, 74n6, 193n22, 275n75
Mantega, Guido, 273
Marcel, Mario, 209, 209n81, 221, 224n139
Marfan, Manuel, 206, 209, 220
markets. *See also* Brazil elections, markets,
politics and leftists
Brazil financial market turbulence, 270,
271f
conditionality strength, 43–4, 43n44
democracy's compatibility with, 280–2
disciplining mechanism trigger, 42–3
enforcement mechanism, 8–10, 9nn33–4
foreign bond markets and volatility of
capital, 284
indebtedness and political plans, 34–5
Latin America economic policy against
instability in, 285–6
as prison, 11–12, 12n40
society and, 17–20
market-constrained politician case
IMF conditionality and, 173–4, 173n25
market-induced austerity cycle hypothesis
and, 170–2
overview, 164–70
market-induced austerity cycle hypothesis
(H2), 33t, 35, 172t
market-constrained politician case and,
170–2
overview, 47–9
market-induced political austerity cycle
hypothesis (H2), 131, 132t, 170–1. *See
also specific H2 case study topics*
overview, 21–2, 49, 85, 126
Mayhew, David, 26n7
Maza-Zavala, Domingo, 136, 156, 156n103
McNamara, Kathleen, 8n26, 9n33, 192n18,
279n8, 281n15

memes, 198
  cultural, 199–200
Menem, Carlos Saúl, 190n11, 238n194,
  239n208, 255n5, 265n43
  Argentina economic policy under, 24, 26,
  64, 64n120, 190, 232–41, 232n173,
  232nn175–6, 233nn177–8,
  234nn179–80, 234n182, 236n189,
  237n193, 239n203, 239n205, 240n209,
  240nn211–12, 241n214, 251, 255–62,
  255nn7–8, 256n10, 256n12, 257n16,
  258nn19–20, 259n23, 283
Mercadante, Alóizio, 273
Merkel, Angela, 32, 287, 287n36
Milan, Pedro, 242, 273
Milner, Helen, 7n17, 31n22, 280n13
misiones programs, 152, 152n86, 155–7,
  156n104, 156n105, 284
Monetarism, 27–8, 28n11, 29, 30, 30n18, 32,
  56, 56n86, 58n93, 173, 191–2, 191n17,
  198–9
monetary policy, 21, 21n79, 28n11, 33n25,
  79, 84n42, 95
  central bank independence and, 132n14,
  134–6, 186n67, 200
  IMF conditionality and, 40
Monetary Policy Committee (COPOM), 273,
  273n64
monetary policy stance in presidential elections
  Argentina, 258, 260, 266
  Brazil, 48, 48n55, 244, 244n224, 247,
  248n240, 269, 273, 273n64, 275, 275n77
  Chile, 138, 138nn29–30, 140–1, 140n43,
  215, 215n101, 216, 220, 220nn121–2,
  225
  Ecuador, 177
  Germany, 52
  Latin America countries, 128–9, 130f,
  130f
  United States, 34, 277
  Venezuela, 5, 154, 155, 157–8, 184–5
Mosley, Layna, 8n23, 16n59, 17n61, 31n22,
  41, 41n36, 41n38, 41n40, 45, 45n49,
  45nn51–2, 70n138, 100n66, 281n15
Murillo, Maria Victoria, 13n44, 50n60,
  50n62, 60n104, 76n10, 286n32

neoclassical synthesis, 28n11, 191n17
neoliberal consensus, 50, 60, 286
neoliberal policy diffusion
  Allende's economic policies and, 208–11
  inflation-averse politician case and, 198–200

New York Metropolitan Transit Authority,
  250
Nixon, Richard M., 33–4, 73, 73n1, 123–4,
  277, 278, 278n5
non-interventionist economic policy, 25
  political business cycle and, 25, 26–7
Non-tax revenues (variable), 83
Nordhaus, William, 15n55, 25n2, 28n12, 72,
  73n2, 188n1

Obama, Barack, 14, 28, 290
O'Donnell, Guillermo, 74n6, 136, 136n23,
  229n165
Olson, Mancur, 38, 38n32, 41n35, 164,
  164n2
orthodox stabilization programs, 13, 54, 55,
  60n103, 66, 160, 161, 173, 182, 183,
  184, 186, 190–5, 198, 199–200, 242,
  244–5
Ottone, Ernesto, 222
output gap, 15n56, 17n62, 29, 29n15, 32n23,
  221n128, 226n144, 241n214, 278n4

PAC. *See* political austerity cycle
Pact of Punto Fijo, 144, 143n49–144n49
Palôcci, Antonio, 247, 275
Papandreou, George, 19
el Partido Demócrata Cristiano de Chile
  (PDC), 23, 139, 201, 201n48, 204, 205.
  See also Christian Democratic Party
  (Chile)
Partido do Movimento Democrátio Brasileiro
  (PMDB), 243, 243n219
Partido dos Trabalhadores (PT), 245, 245n228
Partido Justicialista (PJ), 230n166. *See also*
  Peronists
el Partido Por la Democracia (PPD), 204,
  204n59, 205, 217n109
el Partido Social Cristiano de Venezuela
  (COPEI), 144, 151n83
el Partido Socialista de Chile (PS), 201,
  201n48, 203, 205, 211, 217n109. *See
  also* Socialist Party (Chile)
partisan political business cycles, 76–7
partisan politics
  austerity politics and, 76–7, 286
  in developing countries, 286
  implications of economic policy and,
  286–8
  Latin America economic policy and,
  286–8
  Latin America future of, 287–8

partisanship
  economic impact of inflation crisis and,
    100t
  in elections impact on economy, 82–3,
    82nn30–2
partisanship and economy, economic
    indicators
  overview and summary, 98–9, 98nn61–3,
    99n64, 101
  robustness, 99–101, 101n69
partisanship and economy, fiscal indicators
  overview, 95–7, 97n57
  robustness, 97–8, 97n60
partisanship$_{it}$ (variable), 82
Pauly, Louis, 7n17, 280n13
PBC. *See* political business cycle
PDC. *See* el Partido Demócrata Cristiano de
    Chile
Pérez, Carlos Andrés, 150n76, 155n100,
    180n42, 182, 182n50
  Venezuela economic policy under, 147–8,
    147nn60–2, 150, 150n79, 180n41,
    194
Peronists, 82, 191, 227, 228n154, 229,
    230n163, 230n166, 238
Peru economic policy
  under García, 57, 58, 61, 61n107, 191,
    191n14, 287
  under Humala, 66
Petkoff, Teodora, 23, 23n82, 185
PFL. *See* Liberty Front Party
Phillips curve trade-off, 28, 28n10, 28n14, 29,
    29f, 30nn18–19, 31, 98
Pinochet, Augusto, 142, 143, 201n48, 205,
    206n67, 210
  Chile economic policy under, 207, 207n71
PJ. *See* Partido Justicialista
PMDB. *See* Partido do Movimento
    Democrátio Brasileiro
policy diffusion. *See also* neoliberal policy
    diffusion
  Chile, 199
  Latin America, 199, 200
  overview, 198–9, 198n39
policy lags, 33, 33n25, 35, 79–80, 80n22, 85,
    94–5
political austerity, Cardoso's candidacy,
    Brazilian incomes and, 48, 48n56
political austerity cycle (PAC), 80. *See also*
    specific political austerity cycle topics
  during Argentina elections (2003), 266f
  foundations, 278–80

H_4 comparative case study evidence, 254–76
  inflation-scarred, cash-strapped politician
    case and, 251–4
  overview and summary, 250–1, 276, 278–80
  from political business cycles to, 15–20,
    16n58, 17n65, 17nn62–3
political austerity cycle hypothesis (H_4), 196t,
    252t, 253f. *See also specific H_4 case study
    topics*
  inflation-scarred, cash-strapped politician
    case and, 253–4
  overview, 21, 22, 68, 86, 126
political austerity cycle theory. *See* political
    austerity theory
political austerity theory, 74
  electoral economic strategies in, 32–6
  financial means in, 30–1
  Latin America economic policy and, 278
  overview, 8–9, 13, 26, 30–1, 30n19, 69, 73,
    278–80
  political business cycle and, 73
  political motivations in, 30, 31–2
political budget cycle, 73–4, 74n5, 80
political business cycle (PBC), 79. *See also*
    political economy of elections; *specific
    political business cycle topics*
  costs of, 278
  in developed *vs.* developing countries, 28–30
  evidence for, 73–4, 73n1
  across globe, 277–8
  interventionist economic policy and, 25–6,
    27
  non-interventionist economic policy and,
    25, 26–7
  opportunistic and rational, 28–9
  overview, 25–6, 72
  partisan, 76–7
  political austerity cycle and, 15–20, 16n58,
    17n65, 17nn62–3
  political austerity theory and, 73
  rational expectations, 73–4, 73n3
  in U.S., 277
political business cycle theory, 29–30, 73, 75,
    78, 80
political economic strategies. *See* electoral
    economic strategies
political economy of elections. *See also*
    political business cycle
  macro to micro policy tools, 102–3, 102n70
  manipulation evidence, 73–7
  overview, 72–3
  regression models, 103–5

statistical models, concepts and measures, 77–86
statistical tests on elections and economy, 86–95
statistical tests on partisanship and economy, 95–101
political motivations
  economic policy and, 21
  in political austerity theory, 30, 31–2
political parties. *See also* left-wing; partisanship
  austerity and low-inflation policies of right-wing, 59–60, 77, 96
  codes for orientation of, 82, 82n30
political supporters targeting, and austerity, 282–4
Population (variable), 83
post-election$_{it}$ (variable), 80
PPD. *See* el Partido Por la Democracia
Prat-Gay, Alfonso, 44, 264–5, 264n36, 264n38, 266, 266n46
pre-election$_{it}$ (variable), 80
presidential elections. *See* elections; Latin America presidential elections
primary fiscal balances, 2n3, 84
privatization
  in Argentina economic policy, 233–4, 233n178
  in Brazil economic policy, 268, 268n50
  in Chile economic policy, 219–21, 219n116
  earnings and Argentina 1999 elections, 233
  in Venezuela economic policy, 184, 184n58, 194–5
Przeworski, Adam, 17n67, 78, 78n16, 79, 79n17, 127, 173n26, 280n14
PS. *See* el Partido Socialista de Chile
PSDB. *See* Brazil's social democratic party
psychology literature on risky choices, 14–15, 32, 50–3, 189–90
PT. *See* Partido dos Trabalhadores
public works projects, 282
Punto Fijo
  Pact of, 144, 143n49–144n49
  system, 145n54, 150, 151n83
Punto Fijo elections, 146f
  Venezuela petro-PBC and, 145–7

Radical party. *See* Unión Cívica Radical
Real Plan (Brazil), 48, 48n55, 60n101, 190, 193, 234n179, 244–6, 245n226, 269, 273

real wages, 15, 48, 48f, 54, 58, 61–2, 133n15, 184, 189, 227n149, 232, 257, 273
redistribution, 25, 137, 139, 152, 194–5, 199, 202–5, 204n62, 211, 214, 223, 226, 258, 265, 275–6
regression models, for elections and economy
  basic, 103
  interactive, 104–5
  overview, 103
Reinhart, Carmen, 17n60, 41nn37–8, 41n40, 69n135, 70n138, 89n50, 93n54, 100n66, 169n22, 279n9, 285n30
Remmer, Karen, 16n58, 17n63, 54n80, 55n81
resource curse, 46–7
right-wing low-inflation policies, and austerity, 59–60, 77, 96
risk-aversion. *See also* economic risk-aversion and inflation control politics
  austerity as policy of, 246n233
  economic policy, 14–15, 14n51, 49–53, 53n73, 55–9, 190–5
  elections, 59–68
  political rewards of, 54–5
Roberts, Kenneth, 1n1, 13nn44–5, 50n62, 60n100, 60n103, 76n9, 82n28, 286n32
robustness
  in elections and economy, 88–9, 88n48, 92–5, 92n53
  in partisanship and economy, 97–8, 97n60, 99–101, 101n69
Rodrik, Dani, 7nn16–17, 280n13
Rogoff, Kenneth, 30n17, 70nn137–8, 73n3, 89n50, 93n54, 100n65–6, 134n19, 168n19, 188n2
Rose-Ackerman, Susan, 282n17
Rudra, Nita, 8n29, 281n15
Russia economic policy, under Yeltsin, 12, 26, 26nn5–6

Sachs, Jeffrey, 15n55, 25n2, 54n77, 54n79, 81n27, 168n19, 188n1, 200n43
Samaras, Antonis, 19
Samuelson, Paul, 72
Sarney, José, 242–3, 242n216
Scheve, Kenneth, 27n9, 71, 140
Seidman, L. William, 166
Serra, José, 273, 273n69, 275n74
Simmons, Beth, 198nn37–9, 209n78
Simpson, Alan, 289
Socialist Party (Chile), 24, 56n89, 208–11, 217. *See also* Chile socialists; el Partido Socialista de Chile

society, and markets, 17–20
Sourrouille, Juan, 227, 228, 229
sovereign borrowers
  centralized creditors and, 39–40
  decentralized creditors and, 40–2, 41n35
sovereign risk premium, 41, 45, 178f, 185f,
    234, 235f, 239, 247, 247n236, 259–60,
    260f, 269–71, 270f, 271f, 274, 274f, 284
spending
  Argentina (1990s), 237f
  Chile 1970 elections and, 137–43
  discretionary, 283
  electoral spending patterns and budget
    composition, 89
  social spending in Argentina, 226–7, 257,
    257n16, 262
  social spending in Chile, 202, 202n51, 206,
    214–15, 224
  social spending in Venezuela, 155, 154n98,
    156n105, 183
  social spending overview, 18, 18n71–2, 20,
    282
Stasavage, David, 84n37
state-owned enterprises, 282, 282n16
statistical models for elections impact on
    economy
  control variables, 83–5
  hypotheses and expected effects, 84–6
  independent variables, 78–83
  overview, 77–8, 78n15
statistical tests on elections and economy
  economic indicators, 89–95, 92nn51–2
  fiscal indicators, 86–9
statistical tests on partisanship and economy
  economic indicators, 98–101
  fiscal indicators, 95–8
Stephens, John, 18n69
Stiglitz, Joseph, 155n112, 173n24, 262n30
stimulus
  election-year fiscal stimulus (variable), 128
  election-year monetary stimulus (variable),
    128
  as electoral economic strategy, 278n4
  end-term fiscal stimulus (variable), 128
  end-term monetary stimulus (variable), 128
Stokes, Susan, 13n44, 50nn60–1, 55n81,
    60nn103–4, 64nn119–20, 76n10, 82n31,
    148n66, 158n111, 161n125, 182n51,
    195n30, 206n68, 207n71, 207n73,
    255n8, 256n13, 256nn9–10, 257n18,
    283n22, 286n32
structural balance, 5n12

structuralists, 58, 58n93
sudden stops, 11, 16–17, 41, 68–9, 125, 169,
    176, 250, 254, 259, 267, 279, 285–6
superpoderes law, 3, 19, 283
Swank, Duane, 8n28, 281n15

Tarre, Gustavo, 180, 183, 186
technocratic communities and inflation
    saliency. *See also* macroeconomic
    consensus
  economic lessons resilience, 27, 32, 49–53,
    55–9, 56n88, 60–1, 189–95, 286–7
  ministry professionalization, 56–7, 190–5,
    192f, 211–12, 212f, 230–3, 230f, 231f,
    242–3
  overview, 53–4
  risk-aversion's political rewards, 54–5
Teichman, Judith, 65n125
Tequila crisis, 255, 257, 259–61
Terms of Trade (variable), 83
Thacker, Strom, 65n125
Thayer, Ernest Lawrence, 123
Tietmeyer, Hanz, 52
Tomic, Radomiro, 140, 141n39, 204, 204n62,
    205, 205n64
Tomz, Michael, 8n24, 50n63, 163n1,
    238n197, 239n200, 281n15
Total External Public Debt (variable), 88
Trade (variable), 83
traditional political business cycle hypothesis
    (H_1), 33t, 34, 131t, 133f, 171t. *See also*
    specific H_1 case study topics
  in electoral opportunism classic case,
    131–4
  overview, 21, 47, 85, 126
Tufte, Edward, 15n55, 25n2, 34n26, 72,
    73nn1–2, 75, 123nn1–2, 124n3, 131,
    133, 188n1

UCR. *See* Unión Civica Radical
Ugarte, Luis Carranza, 57
Ukraine economic policy, 59
unemployment. *See* inflation-unemployment
    trade-off
Unidad Popular (UP), 58, 142, 203–4
Unión Civica Radical (UCR), 191, 228, 238
United States (U.S.). *See also* U.S. economic
    policy
  bank lending, 166–7, 167n15, 167nn11–12
  Brady Plan, 167–9, 168n18, 168nn18–19
  credit crisis (2008), 250
  elections, 123–4

global reserve currency, 289, 290
IMF and, 159
inflation, 14, 14n52
municipalities and global financial crisis (2008), 250
political business cycle in, 277
UP. *See* Unidad Popular
U.S. economic policy, 25, 80
debt and, 289–90
under Dwight D. Eisenhower, 123
under George W. Bush, 28
under Nixon, 33–4
under Obama, 28

Valenzuela, Arturo, 74n6, 202n49
variance inflation factors (VIF), 100, 100n67
Velásquez, Ramón José, 5, 180, 195
Venezuela, 143n48
Caracazo protests and looting, 150, 194, 194n26
Latin American left and, 1–2, 5
Venezuela 1990s economy without oil, 183n55, 184n56
in H_2 comparative case study evidence, 179–86
1998 elections, 181–6
overview, 179–81
Venezuela central bank independence and PBC
in H_1 comparative case study evidence, 150–8, 194
overview, 151
2006 elections and, 151–8, 157n106
Venezuela economic policy, 148nn168–9
Argentina economic policy compared to, 1–6, 5n12, 57
under Caldera, 23, 127, 146, 181–6, 182n51, 183n54, 184n58, 184n61, 194
under Castro, 163
under Chávez, 2, 5, 6, 12, 26, 26n6, 127, 135, 151–7, 151n84, 152n86, 154nn93–5, 154n98, 156n102, 156n102, 156n105, 157n107, 162, 251, 283, 284, 287
fiscal policy stance in presidential elections (2002-2007), 4f
under Herrera Campins, 148, 148n66
inflation and, 4, 4n10, 5, 57, 64, 64nn121–2, 128, 180, 193–4

under Lusinchi, 34, 34nn27–38, 149–50, 181, 182
under Pérez, 147–8, 147nn60–2, 150, 150n79, 180n41, 194
under Velásquez, 5, 180
Venezuela oil. *See also* Venezuela 1990s economy without oil
revenues, 144, 144n51, 145f, 146, 147f, 146n59, 148–57, 149nn74–5
Venezuela petro-PBC
in H_1 comparative case study evidence, 143–51
1978 elections and, 147–8
1983 elections and, 148–9, 148n71
1988 elections and, 149–51, 149nn74–5
2006 elections and, 151–8, 157f, 157n106
overview, 143–5
Punto Fijo elections (1968-1988) and, 145–7
Vergara, Carlos, 222
Vial, Joaquín, 35, 218, 218n113, 219, 220
Videla, Jorge Rafael, 227n148
VIF. *See* variance inflation factors
voters. *See also* elections
economic, 67, 67n134
middle income and poor, 61–4
Vreeland, James, 12n41, 40n33, 84n39, 89n46, 173nn25–6

Walesa, Lech, 12
Walker, Ignacio, 143, 143n46
welfare state, 18, 18n71
Weyland, K., 1n1, 14n47, 14n51, 50n59, 50n61, 52–3, 53n73, 60nn103–4, 64n117, 76n10, 198n39, 209n78, 237nn191–2, 244nn221, 244n225, 246n234, 256n11, 257n17, 268n50, 270n58
Whitefish Bay High School, 250
Wibbels, Erik, 8nn30–1, 18n70, 31n22, 41n40, 60n100, 76n9, 82n28, 281n15
Woods, Ngaire, 9n33, 158n110, 173n24, 192n18, 262n30, 279n8

Yeltsin, Boris, 12, 26, 26nn5–6, 278, 278n5

Zaldívar, Andres, 138, 218, 218n111
Zuazo, Siles, 191

Other Books in the Series (continued from page iii)

Carles Boix, *Democracy and Redistribution*

Carles Boix, *Political Parties, Growth, and Equality: Conservative and Social Democratic Economic Strategies in the World Economy*

Catherine Boone, *Merchant Capital and the Roots of State Power in Senegal, 1930–1985*

Catherine Boone, *Political Topographies of the African State: Territorial Authority and Institutional Change*

Michael Bratton, Robert Mattes, and E. Gyimah-Boadi, *Public Opinion, Democracy, and Market Reform in Africa*

Michael Bratton and Nicolas van de Walle, *Democratic Experiments in Africa: Regime Transitions in Comparative Perspective*

Valerie Bunce, *Leaving Socialism and Leaving the State: The End of Yugoslavia, the Soviet Union, and Czechoslovakia*

Daniele Caramani, *The Nationalization of Politics: The Formation of National Electorates and Party Systems in Europe*

John M. Carey, *Legislative Voting and Accountability*

Kanchan Chandra, *Why Ethnic Parties Succeed: Patronage and Ethnic Headcounts in India*

Eric C. C. Chang, Mark Andreas Kayser, Drew A. Linzer, and Ronald Rogowski, *Electoral Systems and the Balance of Consumer-Producer Power*

José Antonio Cheibub, *Presidentialism, Parliamentarism, and Democracy*

Ruth Berins Collier, *Paths toward Democracy: The Working Class and Elites in Western Europe and South America*

Pepper D. Culpepper, *Quiet Politics and Business Power: Corporate Control in Europe and Japan*

Rafaela M. Dancygier, *Immigration and Conflict in Europe*

Christian Davenport, *State Repression and the Domestic Democratic Peace*

Donatella della Porta, *Social Movements, Political Violence, and the State*

Alberto Diaz-Cayeros, *Federalism, Fiscal Authority, and Centralization in Latin America*

Thad Dunning, *Crude Democracy: Natural Resource Wealth and Political Regimes*

Gerald Easter, *Reconstructing the State: Personal Networks and Elite Identity*

Margarita Estevez-Abe, *Welfare and Capitalism in Postwar Japan: Party, Bureaucracy, and Business*

Henry Farrell, *The Political Economy of Trust: Institutions, Interests, and Inter-Firm Cooperation in Italy and Germany*

Karen E. Ferree, *Framing the Race in South Africa: The Political Origins of Racial Census Elections*

M. Steven Fish, *Democracy Derailed in Russia: The Failure of Open Politics*

Robert F. Franzese, *Macroeconomic Policies of Developed Democracies*

Roberto Franzosi, *The Puzzle of Strikes: Class and State Strategies in Postwar Italy*

Timothy Frye, *Building States and Markets After Communism: The Perils of Polarized Democracy*

Geoffrey Garrett, *Partisan Politics in the Global Economy*

Scott Gehlbach, *Representation through Taxation: Revenue, Politics, and Development in Postcommunist States*

Jane R. Gingrich, *Making Markets in the Welfare State: The Politics of Varying Market Reforms*

Miriam Golden, *Heroic Defeats: The Politics of Job Loss*

Jeff Goodwin, *No Other Way Out: States and Revolutionary Movements*

Merilee Serrill Grindle, *Changing the State*

Anna Grzymala-Busse, *Rebuilding Leviathan: Party Competition and State Exploitation in Post-Communist Democracies*

Anna Grzymala-Busse, *Redeeming the Communist Past: The Regeneration of Communist Parties in East Central Europe*

Frances Hagopian, *Traditional Politics and Regime Change in Brazil*

Henry E. Hale, *The Foundations of Ethnic Politics: Separatism of States and Nations in Eurasia and the World*

Mark Hallerberg, Rolf Ranier Strauch, and Jürgen von Hagen, *Fiscal Governance in Europe*

Stephen E. Hanson, *Post-Imperial Democracies: Ideology and Party Formation in Third Republic France, Weimar Germany, and Post-Soviet Russia*

Silja Häusermann, *The Politics of Welfare State Reform in Continental Europe: Modernization in Hard Times*

Gretchen Helmke, *Courts Under Constraints: Judges, Generals, and Presidents in Argentina*

Yoshiko Herrera, *Imagined Economies: The Sources of Russian Regionalism*

J. Rogers Hollingsworth and Robert Boyer, eds., *Contemporary Capitalism: The Embeddedness of Institutions*

John D. Huber and Charles R. Shipan, *Deliberate Discretion? The Institutional Foundations of Bureaucratic Autonomy*

Ellen Immergut, *Health Politics: Interests and Institutions in Western Europe*

Torben Iversen, *Capitalism, Democracy, and Welfare*

Torben Iversen, *Contested Economic Institutions*

Lauren M. MacLean, *Informal Institutions and Citizenship in Rural Africa: Risk and Reciprocity in Ghana and Côte d'Ivoire*

Beatriz Magaloni, *Voting for Autocracy: Hegemonic Party Survival and Its Demise in Mexico*

James Mahoney, *Colonialism and Postcolonial Development: Spanish America in Comparative Perspective*

James Mahoney and Dietrich Rueschemeyer, eds., *Historical Analysis and the Social Sciences*

Scott Mainwaring and Matthew Soberg Shugart, eds., *Presidentialism and Democracy in Latin America*

Isabela Mares, *The Politics of Social Risk: Business and Welfare State Development*

Isabela Mares, *Taxation, Wage Bargaining, and Unemployment*

Cathie Jo Martin and Duane Swank, *The Political Construction of Business Interests: Coordination, Growth, and Equality*

Anthony W. Marx, *Making Race, Making Nations: A Comparison of South Africa, the United States, and Brazil*

Doug McAdam, John McCarthy, and Mayer Zald, eds., *Comparative Perspectives on Social Movements*

Bonnie M. Meguid, *Party Competition between Unequals: Strategies and Electoral Fortunes in Western Europe*

Joel S. Migdal, *State in Society: Studying How States and Societies Constitute One Another*

Joel S. Migdal, Atul Kohli, and Vivienne Shue, eds., *State Power and Social Forces: Domination and Transformation in the Third World*

Scott Morgenstern and Benito Nacif, eds., *Legislative Politics in Latin America*

Layna Mosley, *Global Capital and National Governments*

Layna Mosley, *Labor Rights and Multinational Production*

Wolfgang C. Müller and Kaare Strøm, *Policy, Office, or Votes?*

Maria Victoria Murillo, *Labor Unions, Partisan Coalitions, and Market Reforms in Latin America*

Maria Victoria Murillo, *Political Competition, Partisanship, and Policy Making in Latin American Public Utilities*

Monika Nalepa, *Skeletons in the Closet: Transitional Justice in Post-Communist Europe*

Ton Notermans, *Money, Markets, and the State: Social Democratic Economic Policies since 1918*

Eleonora Pasotti, *Political Branding in Cities: The Decline of Machine Politics in Bogotá, Naples, and Chicago*

Aníbal Pérez-Liñán, *Presidential Impeachment and the New Political Instability in Latin America*

Roger D. Petersen, *Understanding Ethnic Violence: Fear, Hatred, and Resentment in Twentieth-Century Eastern Europe*

Roger D. Petersen, *Western Intervention in the Balkans: The Strategic Use of Emotion in Conflict*

Simona Piattoni, ed., *Clientelism, Interests, and Democratic Representation*

Paul Pierson, *Dismantling the Welfare State? Reagan, Thatcher, and the Politics of Retrenchment*

Marino Regini, *Uncertain Boundaries: The Social and Political Construction of European Economies*

Marc Howard Ross, *Cultural Contestation in Ethnic Conflict*

Lyle Scruggs, *Sustaining Abundance: Environmental Performance in Industrial Democracies*

Jefferey M. Sellers, *Governing from Below: Urban Regions and the Global Economy*

Yossi Shain and Juan Linz, eds., *Interim Governments and Democratic Transitions*

Beverly Silver, *Forces of Labor: Workers' Movements and Globalization since 1870*

Theda Skocpol, *Social Revolutions in the Modern World*

Dan Slater, *Ordering Power: Contentious Politics and Authoritarian Leviathans in Southeast Asia*

Regina Smyth, *Candidate Strategies and Electoral Competition in the Russian Federation: Democracy Without Foundation*

Richard Snyder, *Politics after Neoliberalism: Reregulation in Mexico*

David Stark and László Bruszt, *Postsocialist Pathways: Transforming Politics and Property in East Central Europe*

Sven Steinmo, *The Evolution of Modern States: Sweden, Japan, and the United States*

Sven Steinmo, Kathleen Thelen, and Frank Longstreth, eds., *Structuring Politics: Historical Institutionalism in Comparative Analysis*

Susan C. Stokes, *Mandates and Democracy: Neoliberalism by Surprise in Latin America*

Susan C. Stokes, ed., *Public Support for Market Reforms in New Democracies*

Duane Swank, *Global Capital, Political Institutions, and Policy Change in Developed Welfare States*

Sidney Tarrow, *Power in Movement: Social Movements and Contentious Politics, Revised and Updated Third Edition*